Mathematics for Economics and Finance: Methods and Modeling

Mathematics for Economics and Finance: Methods and Modeling

Editor: Hope Bradley

New York

Published by NY Research Press
118-35 Queens Blvd., Suite 400,
Forest Hills, NY 11375, USA
www.nyresearchpress.com

Mathematics for Economics and Finance: Methods and Modeling
Edited by Hope Bradley

International Standard Book Number: 978-1-64725-458-2 (Hardback)

Cataloging-in-Publication Data

Mathematics for economics and finance : methods and modeling / edited by Hope Bradley.
    p. cm.
Includes bibliographical references and index.
ISBN 978-1-64725-458-2
1. Economics, Mathematical. 2. Finance--Mathematical models. 3. Econometrics.
4. Business mathematics. I. Bradley, Hope.
HB135 .M38 2023
330.015 1--dc23

Contents

Preface

The main aim of this book is to educate learners and enhance their research focus by presenting diverse topics covering this vast field. This is an advanced book which compiles significant studies by distinguished experts in the area of analysis. This book addresses successive solutions to the challenges arising in the area of application, along with it; the book provides scope for future developments.

Financial mathematics refers to the application of mathematical methods and models to financial concerns. It uses techniques from statistics, economic theory, probability, and stochastic processes. The application of mathematics to the financial sector is based on several financial or economic hypotheses. It employs abstract mathematical methods in order to build mathematical models of the functioning of financial mechanisms. Mathematics is also used in economics for building economic models that utilize mathematical methods and principles for analyzing economic problems. In economics, mathematics is used to conduct quantitative experiments and develop models for forecasting future economic growth. Mathematical economics is based on modern data methods, computing models, and other advanced mathematical applications. This book unravels the recent studies in the field of mathematical finance and mathematical economics. Most of the topics introduced herein cover new methods and modeling techniques used in mathematical finance and mathematical economics. The book will serve as a valuable source of reference for graduate and postgraduate students.

It was a great honour to edit this book, though there were challenges, as it involved a lot of communication and networking between me and the editorial team. However, the end result was this all-inclusive book covering diverse themes in the field.

Finally, it is important to acknowledge the efforts of the contributors for their excellent chapters, through which a wide variety of issues have been addressed. I would also like to thank my colleagues for their valuable feedback during the making of this book.

Editor

Non-Linear Macroeconomic Models of Growth with Memory

Vasily E. Tarasov [1,2] (iD)

[1] Skobeltsyn Institute of Nuclear Physics, Lomonosov Moscow State University, Moscow 119991, Russia; tarasov@theory.sinp.msu.ru

[2] Faculty of Information Technologies and Applied Mathematics, Moscow Aviation Institute (National Research University), Moscow 125993, Russia

Abstract: In this article, two well-known standard models with continuous time, which are proposed by two Nobel laureates in economics, Robert M. Solow and Robert E. Lucas, are generalized. The continuous time standard models of economic growth do not account for memory effects. Mathematically, this is due to the fact that these models describe equations with derivatives of integer orders. These derivatives are determined by the properties of the function in an infinitely small neighborhood of the considered time. In this article, we proposed two non-linear models of economic growth with memory, for which equations are derived and solutions of these equations are obtained. In the differential equations of these models, instead of the derivative of integer order, fractional derivatives of non-integer order are used, which allow describing long memory with power-law fading. Exact solutions for these non-linear fractional differential equations are obtained. The purpose of this article is to study the influence of memory effects on the rate of economic growth using the proposed simple models with memory as examples. As the methods of this study, exact solutions of fractional differential equations of the proposed models are used. We prove that the effects of memory can significantly (several times) change the growth rate, when other parameters of the model are unchanged.

Keywords: fractional differential equation; growth model; fading memory; fractional derivative; solow model

PACS: 45.10.Hj; 89.65.Gh

MSC: 26A33; 34A08

1. Introduction

The Solow model is a dynamic single-sector model of economic growth (see Solow articles [1,2] and books [3–5]). In this model, the economy is considered without structural subdivisions, i.e., as a one-sector model. It is assumed that the economy produces only universal products, which can be consumed both in the non-production and production consumptions, i.e., can be consumed, $C(t)$, or invested, $I(t)$, (see [4] p. 25). Exports and imports are not taken into account. This model describes the capital accumulation, labor or population growth, and increases in productivity, which is commonly called the technological progress. The Solow model can be used to estimate the separate effects on economic growth of capital, labor, and technological change.

The Solow model is a generalization of the Harrod–Domar model, which includes a productivity growth as new effect. This relatively simple growth model was independently proposed by Robert M. Solow in 1956 [1,2]. In 1987 Solow was awarded the Nobel Memorial Prize in Economic

Sciences for his contributions to the theory of economic growth [6]. Mathematically, the Solow model is actually represented by the non-linear ordinary differential equation, which describes the evolution of the per capita stock of capital.

In the standard Solow model, the memory effects and memory fading are neglected. From a mathematical point of view, the neglect of memory effects in standard models with continuous time is due to the fact that only equations with derivatives of integer orders are used to describe the economic process. These derivatives are determined by the properties of the function in an infinitely small neighborhood of the considered time. Therefore, standard models of economic growth do not account for memory effects. However, it is obviously strange to assume amnesia in all economic agents. Economic agents can take into account previous changes in economic processes over a certain period of time, and this can influence their decision-making. Therefore, it is important to take memory effects into account when constructing economic models.

The presence of memory in the economic process means that the behavior of the process depends not only on the variables and parameters of this process at the present time, but also on the history of changes in these variables and parameters on a finite time interval [7]. The concept of memory is very important for an adequate description of real economic processes (for example, see [8–20]). For the first time, the importance of long-range time dependence in economic data was recognized by Clive W.J. Granger in his article [9] in 1966 (see also [8,10,11,14]). Granger showed that a number of spectral densities, which are estimated from economic time series, have a similar form. We can state that the phenomenon of long memory in modern economics was discovered by Granger. Then, to describe economic processes with memory Granger and Joyeux [11] in 1980 proposed the fractional ARIMA models, which are also called ARFIMA(p, d, q). The fractional ARIMA(p, d, q) models are generalization of ARIMA(p, d, q) model from a positive integer order d to non-integer (positive and negative) orders d [14,15]. To generalize ARIMA models, Granger and Joyeux [11] proposed the so-called fractional differencing and integrating for discrete time case (see books [14–19] and reviews [20–24]). Note that Granger received the Nobel Memorial Prize in Economic Sciences in 2003 "for methods of analyzing economic time series with common trends (cointegration)" [13]. The fractional difference operators of Granger and Joyeux were proposed and then began to be used in economics up to the present time without any connection with the fractional calculus and the well-known fractional differences of non-integer orders. In fact, these fractional differencing and integrating are the well-known Grunwald-Letnikov fractional differences, which were suggested in 1867 and 1868 in works [25,26]. Then, the Grunwald-Letnikov fractional differences are actively used in the fractional calculus [27–32] and began to apply in physics and other sciences. We should also note that in the continuous limit the Grunwald-Letnikov fractional differences of positive orders can give the Grunwald-Letnikov, Marchaud, and Liouville fractional derivatives [27].

The approach to describing economic processes with memory, based on discrete operators of Granger and Joyeux, is the most widespread among economists [21–24]. We should note that this approach is really based on the Grunwald-Letnikov fractional differences and it is restricted by only one type of fractional finite differences. Unfortunately, this approach is used without an explicit connection with the modern mathematics and the development of fractional calculus in the last two hundred years. It should be emphasized that the Granger-Joyeux approach to economics with memory is restricted by models with discrete time and application of the Grunwald-Letnikov fractional differences. Obviously, the restriction of mathematical tools to only to the discrete Grunwald-Letnikov operators significantly reduces the possibilities to describe processes with memory and non-locality in time.

In recent years, various linear economic models with fading memory have been investigated. In the framework of such models, the presence of various nontrivial effects was proved due to taking into account fading memory with the remaining other parameters of the models unchanged. For example, the following models have been proposed: The Harrod-Domar model with memory [7,33–35], the Evans model with memory [33,36], and the dynamic Leontief (intersectoral) model with memory [33,37,38].

A more detailed overview of economic models with memory is presented in work [39] (see also book [40] pp. 5–32 and references therein).

However, non-linear economic models with fading memory and exact solutions of fractional differential equations of such models have not been investigated. This article proposes two non-linear models of economic growth with memory. The suggested models are generalizations of two well-known models, which are proposed by two Nobel laureates in economics, Robert M. Solow and Robert E. Lucas in works [1,41], respectively.

The first proposed model is a generalization of the model of long-run growth, which is considered Robert M. Solow in paper "A contribution to the theory of economic growth" [1]. In the standard model, the capital depreciation is neglected. In the proposed generalization, we take into account the power-law memory. Moreover, we assume the power-law form of the dynamics of the labor and knowledge. The exact analytical solution of the non-linear fractional differential equation, which describes the proposed model, is suggested.

The second proposed model is the standard growth model for closed economy without capital depreciation, which is considered by Robert E. Lucas in paper "Making a Miracle" [41], (see also [42–45]). In the generalized model, we take into account the memory with power-law fading [46]. The suggested model with memory is described by the non-linear fractional differential equation. The explicit expression of analytical solution of this non-linear equation is obtained.

The aim of the work is not to search for memory effects in economics, but to provide mathematical proof of the possibility of the existence of (at least) acceleration in growth rates, when the parameter of memory fading changes, while other parameters of the process remain unchanged.

The main hypothesis used in this article is the assumption of the power-law character of memory fading, which is described by a single fading parameter. The assumption allows us to use fractional calculus and the fractional differential equations [27–32], where the non-integer order of the derivatives and integrals is described by this fading parameter.

We should note that the power-law form of memory fading is distinguished by the fact that this form can be considered as a first approximation for wide class of memory functions. In paper [47], using the generalized Taylor series in the Trujillo-Rivero-Bonilla form, we proved that the memory function for a wide class of functions can be represented through the sum of one or several power-law memory functions. As a result, the integr-differential equations of economic models with general memory functions approximately can be written [47] through the Riemann-Liouville fractional integrals and the Caputo fractional derivatives of non-integer orders [29–32,48].

In this article, simple non-linear economic models with memory are investigated by using the obtained exact solutions of the fractional differential equations of the proposed models. The main aim of this article is to study the possible influence of memory effects on the rate of economic growth using the proposed simple models. As the methods of this study, we use exact solutions of equations, which describe economic growth with power-law memory. Expressions of the warranted rates of growth with memory are suggested and compared with the warranted rates of standard models. We prove that the effects of memory can significantly (several times) change the growth rate, when other parameters of the model are unchanged.

Note that non-linear growth models with continuous time, which take into account memory effects, have not previously been proposed in the modern literature. The exact solutions of the equations of these models and expressions for growth rates which take into account the influence of memory effects have not been proposed before this article.

The article is organized as follows. In Section 2, an economic model with memory is proposed, which is a generalization of the well-known Solow model, considered by Robert M. Solow in paper "A contribution to the theory of economic growth" [1]. In Section 3, we proposed an economic model with memory, which is a generalization of the well-known Solow model, considered by Robert E. Lucas in paper "Making a Miracle" [41]. In each section, the standard models of economic growth without memory are first considered, then the equations of the generalized models with memory are derived, solutions of these equations are obtained, expressions of the warranted rate of growth with memory are derived, and then compared with the growth rate without memory. In the last paragraphs of Sections 2 and 3, three principles are formulated that make it possible to qualitatively describe the changes arising in the behavior of the economic process, when taking into account the effects of power memory. Finally, brief conclusions of the article are drawn.

2. Solow Model of Long-Run Growth with Memory

In this section, we consider a generalization of the model of long-run growth, which is considered in Solow's paper "A contribution to the theory of economic growth" [1]. In this model, the capital depreciation is neglected. In the proposed generalization, we take into account the power-law memory. Moreover, we assume the power-law form of the dynamics of the labor and knowledge. The exact analytical solution of the non-linear fractional differential equation, which describes the proposed model, is suggested.

2.1. Long-Run Growth without Memory

Let us describe the standard economic model of growth, which is considered in Solow's paper [1] pp. 66–67. The Solow model uses four variables: Output $Y(t)$, capital $K(t)$, labor $L(t)$, and knowledge $A(t)$. At any time, the economy has some amounts of capital, labor, and knowledge, which are combined to produce output. The production function is considered in the following form:

$$Y(t) = F(K(t), A(t)L(t)).$$
(1)

The Solow model uses assumptions about how the stocks of labor $L(t)$, knowledge $A(t)$, and capital $K(t)$ change over time. The initial levels of capital, labor, and knowledge are taken as given, and are assumed to be strictly positive. In the standard model, the labor and knowledge growth are described [3] p. 13, by the following equations:

$$L^{(1)}(t) = \rho\, L(t),$$
(2)

$$A^{(1)}(t) = g\, A(t),$$
(3)

where ρ and g are exogenous parameters and $f^{(1)}(t)$ denotes a first derivative with respect to time. The solutions of Equations (2) and (3) can be represented in the following form:

$$L(t) = L(t_0) \exp\{\rho\,(t - t_0)\}, \quad A(t) = A(t_0) \exp\{g(t - t_0)\}.$$
(4)

Let us consider a power-law generalization of Equations (2) and (3) in the following form:

$$L^{(1)}(t) = \rho\, L^q(t),$$
(5)

$$A^{(1)}(t) = g\, A^p(t),$$
(6)

where q and p are exogenous parameters. For $q = 1$ and $p = 1$, Equations (5) and (6) give the standard Equations (2) and (3).

Let us obtain solutions of Equations (5) and (6) for the case $q \neq 1$ and $p \neq 1$.

Equation (5) can be written as:

$$L^{-q}(t)L^{(1)}(t) = \rho.$$
(7)

Using the standard chain rule, we get:

$$\frac{d}{dt}\left(L^{1-q}(t)\right) = \rho\,(1 - q).$$
(8)

The solution of Equation (8) has the following form:

$$L^{1-q}(t) = \rho\,(1-q)\,t + c, \tag{9}$$

where $c = L^{1-q}(0)$. For simplicity, we will assume that $L(0) = 0$. Then, $c = 0$ and Equation (9) is given as:

$$L(t) = (\rho\,(1-q)\,t)^{1/(1-q)}, \tag{10}$$

where $t > 0$ and $\rho\,(1-q) > 0$. For $t = t_0 > 0$, Equation (10) has the following form:

$$L(t_0) = (\rho\,(1-q)\,t_0)^{1/(1-q)}. \tag{11}$$

Using expression (11), we can represent solution (10) by the following expression:

$$L(t) = L(t_0)\left(\frac{t}{t_0}\right)^{1/(1-q)}. \tag{12}$$

Analogously, we get:

$$A(t) = (g\,(1-p)\,t)^{1/(1-p)}, \tag{13}$$

where we assume that $A(0) = 0$. Then, we represent solution (13) in the following form:

$$A(t) = A(t_0)\left(\frac{t}{t_0}\right)^{1/(1-p)}. \tag{14}$$

Output $Y(t)$ is divided between the consumption $C(t)$ and investment $I(t)$. In the standard model, the fraction $s \in [0,\,1]$ of the output devoted to investment is exogenous and constant such that:

$$I(t) = s\,Y(t). \tag{15}$$

Equation (15) describes the economic multiplier without memory and lag.

It is known that depreciation (and disposal of fixed assets) can be described as a truncated exponential distribution of the time lag (up to a numerical factor), which can be represented as a differential equation of the first order ([49] p. 20, [50] p. 86, [51] pp. 252–253 (see also [52] pp. 25–27)).

In a general case, the depreciation can be described by the following equation:

$$K(t) = \int_0^t D(t-\tau)I(\tau)d\tau, \tag{16}$$

where $D(t-\tau)$ is the kernel of the integral operator that describes the depreciation. The kernel $D(t-\tau)$ characterizes the share of fixed assets put into the operation at the time and continuing to operate at time $t > \tau$.

In economics, depreciation is usually described by the kernel in the following exponential form:

$$D(t-\tau) = e^{-\delta\,(t-\tau)}. \tag{17}$$

Therefore, the standard form of depreciation and the exponential distributed lag up to a numerical factor can be considered as a truncated mathematical expectation value with an exponential distributed delay time in the following form:

$$K(t) = \int_0^t e^{-\delta\,(t-\tau)}I(\tau)d\tau \tag{18}$$

Equation (18) can be represented in the form of the ordinary differential equation of the first order. Let us consider the derivative of the first order for Equation (18). Then, we get:

$$\frac{dK(t)}{dt} = \frac{d}{dt}\left(e^{-\delta t}\int_0^t e^{\delta \tau}I(\tau)d\tau\right) =$$
$$\frac{d}{dt}\left(e^{-\delta t}\right)\int_0^t e^{\delta \tau}I(\tau)d\tau + e^{-\delta t}\frac{d}{dt}\left(\int_0^t e^{\delta \tau}I(\tau)d\tau\right) = \tag{19}$$
$$-\delta\, e^{-\delta t}\int_0^t e^{\delta \tau}I(\tau)d\tau + e^{-\delta t}e^{\delta t}I(t) = -\delta\, K(t) + I(t).$$

As a result, Equation (18) gives:

$$\frac{dK(t)}{dt} = -\delta\, K(t) + I(t). \tag{20}$$

Substituting expression (20) into Equation (21), that is, taking into account that the capital depreciates at a rate of $\delta \in [0,\ 1]$, we obtain for the standard model the following differential equation:

$$K^{(1)}(t) = s\, Y(t) - \delta\, K(t). \tag{21}$$

Let us consider the model without capital depreciation, i.e., $\delta = 0$. Then, Equation (21) takes the following form:

$$K^{(1)}(t) = s\, Y(t). \tag{22}$$

The substitution of (1) into Equation (22) gives:

$$K^{(1)}(t) = s\, F(K(t), A(t)L(t)), \tag{23}$$

where $L(t)$ and $A(t)$ are described by Equations (12) and (14). The substitution of (12) and (14) into Equation (23) gives:

$$K^{(1)}(t) = s\, F\!\left(K(t), A(t_0)L(t_0)(t/t_0)^{1/(1-p)+1/(1-q)}\right), \tag{24}$$

where $q \neq 1$ and $p \neq 1$.

The solution of Equation (24), which describes a model without memory, will be obtained as a special case of the generalized model, when the memory fading parameter is equal to one which means the absence of memory [7,33].

2.2. Long-Run Growth with Power-Law Memory

We should note that Equation (22) cannot take into account the memory, since the derivative $K^{(1)}(t)$ is determined by the behavior of $Y(\tau)$ only at the same time instant $\tau = t$, and does not take into account the history of changes of $Y(\tau)$ in the past, when $\tau \in (0, t)$.

To take into account the changes of $Y(\tau)$ in the past, instead of Equation (15), we can consider the equation of the multiplier with memory in the following form:

$$I(t) = \int_0^t s(t - \tau)Y(\tau)d\tau, \tag{25}$$

where the function $s(t - \tau)$ allows us to take into account the changes of output $Y(\tau)$ in the past $\tau \in (0, t)$. The function $s(t - \tau)$ is interpreted as a memory function. In order to have standard dimensions of economic quantities, the time variable t is considered as a dimensionless parameter, i.e., we change the variable $t_{old} \to t_{new} = t_{old}/t_c$, where t_c is a characteristic time of processes.

The sequential action of the memory effects, which are described by Equation (25) and the depreciation, which is described by Equation (17) can be represented in the following form:

$$K(t) = \int_0^t M(t-\tau)\, Y(\tau)d\tau, \tag{26}$$

where we use the associativity of the Laplace convolution $*$ and the kernel:

$$M(t) = (D * s)(t) = \int_0^t D(t-\tau)\, s(\tau)d\tau. \tag{27}$$

This representation allows us to interpret Equation (26) as an equation describing some generalized form of memory and/or depreciation.

If the integral operator in (26) is a fractional integral operator, then for such an operator a left inverse operator, which is a fractional derivative must exist [48]. We should emphasize that the main property of any generalized (fractional) derivative is to be a left-inverse operator to the corresponding generalized (fractional) integral operator. This requirement is important for a self-consistent mathematical theory of the fractional operators to have a general fractional calculus of these operators.

For example, if the integral operator in (26) is the Riemann-Liouville fractional integral $I^\alpha_{RL,0+}$ of the order $\alpha > 0$, then Equation (26) can be rewritten in the following form:

$$K(t) = s\left(I^\alpha_{RL,0+}Y\right)(t). \tag{28}$$

Considering the action of the Caputo fractional derivative $D^\alpha_{C,0+}$ and taking into account that this derivative is the left inverse to the integral operator $I^\alpha_{RL,0+}$, we obtain the following equation:

$$\left(D^\alpha_{C,0+}K\right)(t) = sY(t). \tag{29}$$

The parameter $\alpha > 0$ is the order of the fractional derivative or integral. This parameter is interpreted as a memory fading parameter. For integer values of α, these fractional operators take the form of standard integrals and derivatives of integer orders (for example, $\left(D^1_{C,0+}K\right)(t) = K^{(1)}(t)$).

The path described briefly opens up broad prospects for accounting for sequential and simultaneous actions of two and three effects, namely, fading memory, depreciation, and distributed lag.

To simplify the description, this article will consider a more simple way of describing the effect of power memory based on exact analytical expressions for solutions. The substitution of expression (25) into Equation (21) with $\delta = 0$ gives:

$$K^{(1)}(t) = \int_0^t s(t,\tau)Y(\tau)d\tau. \tag{30}$$

Let us consider the power-law memory. In this case, the memory function can be described by the following equation:

$$s(t,\tau) = \frac{s}{\Gamma(\mu)}(t-\tau)^{\mu-1} \tag{31}$$

where s is the savings parameter, and $\Gamma(\alpha)$ is the gamma function. For function (31), Equation (30) can be written in the following form:

$$K^{(1)}(t) = s\left(I^\mu_{RL;0+}Y\right)(t) \tag{32}$$

where $I^\mu_{RL;0+}$ is the Riemann-Liouville fractional integral [29] of the order $\mu > 0$. Note that Equation (32) with the Riemann-Liouville fractional integral can be considered [33,47] as an approximation of Equation (30) with generalized memory functions $s(t,\tau)$.

Using the property that the Caputo fractional derivative is the left inverse operator for the Riemann-Liouville fractional integral (see Lemma 2.21 of [29] p. 95), the action of the Caputo derivative on Equation (32) gives:

$$\left(D_{C;0+}^{\mu+1}K\right)(t) = s\,Y(t),$$

(33)

where $D_{C;0+}^{\mu}$ is the Caputo fractional derivative [29] of the order $\mu > 0$.

As a result, to take into account the power-law memory, we can use the following equation:

$$\left(D_{C;0+}^{\alpha}K\right)(t) = s\,Y(t),$$

(34)

where $D_{C;0+}^{\alpha}$ is the Caputo fractional derivative of the order $\alpha = \mu + 1 > 1$ with $\mu > 0$, i.e., $\alpha > 1$. In the general case, we can consider Equation (34) for the order $\alpha > 0$ including $\alpha \in (0,1)$.

Note that Equation (34) coincides with Equation (29), which is based on the approach described at the beginning of this subsection.

Let us consider the specific example of a production function. We will use the Cobb-Douglas function. In this case, Equation (1) takes the following form:

$$Y(t) = K^a(t)(A(t)L(t))^b,$$

(35)

where we can consider $b = 1 - a$. This production function is easy to analyze, and it appears to be a good first approximation to actual production functions. Therefore, the Cobb-Douglas function is useful for modeling.

The substitution of expression (35) into Equation (34) gives:

$$\left(D_{C;0+}^{\alpha}K\right)(t) = s\,(A(t)L(t))^b K^a(t).$$

(36)

Then, substituting expressions (12) and (14) into Equation (36), we obtain the following equation:

$$\left(D_{C;0+}^{\alpha}K\right)(t) = \lambda(t_0)\,t^{\beta}K^a(t),$$

(37)

where

$$\lambda(t_0) = sA^b(t_0)L^b(t_0)t_0^{-\beta},$$

(38)

$$\beta = \frac{b}{1-p} + \frac{b}{1-q}.$$

(39)

Equation (37) is the non-linear fractional differential equation that describes the generalization of the Solow model without capital depreciation, where we take into account the power-law fading memory.

Using equations 3.5.47 and 3.5.48 of Section 3.5.3 in [29], p. 209, Equation (37) with $\lambda(t_0) \neq 0$, $a, q, p \neq 1$, and $\alpha > 0$ has the following solution:

$$K(t) = \left(\frac{\Gamma(\alpha - \gamma(\alpha) + 1)}{\lambda(t_0)\Gamma(1 - \gamma(\alpha))}\right)^{1/(a-1)} t^{\alpha - \gamma(\alpha)},$$

(40)

where

$$\gamma(\alpha) = \frac{\beta + a\alpha}{a - 1}, \quad \alpha - \gamma(\alpha) = \frac{\alpha + \beta}{1 - a},$$

(41)

and $\lambda(t_0)$ is defined by (38), β is defined by Equation (39).

For $t = t_0$, Equation (40) has the following form:

$$K(t_0) = \left(\frac{\Gamma(\alpha - \gamma(\alpha) + 1)}{\lambda(t_0)\Gamma(1 - \gamma(\alpha))}\right)^{1/(a-1)} t_0^{\alpha - \gamma(\alpha)}.$$

(42)

Using Equation (42), solution (40) can be written as:

$$K(t) = K(t_0)\left(\frac{t}{t_0}\right)^{\alpha-\gamma(\alpha)}. \tag{43}$$

The Caputo fractional derivative of the power-law function is given (see Example 3.1 of book [30] p. 49) by the following equation:

$$\left(D_{C;t_0+}^{\alpha}\tau^{\delta}\right)(t) = \frac{\Gamma(\delta+1)}{\Gamma(\delta-\alpha+1)}\, t^{\delta-\alpha}, \tag{44}$$

if $\delta > n-1$ and

$$\left(D_{C;t_0+}^{\alpha}\tau^{\delta}\right)(t) = 0, \tag{45}$$

if $\delta = 0, 1, \ldots n-1$. In all the remaining cases ($\delta < n-1$ such that $\delta \neq 0, 1, \ldots, n-1$), the integral in the definition of the Caputo fractional derivative is improper and divergent.

Remark 1. *Using Equation (44), it is directly verified that expression (40) is the explicit solution of Equation (37) if $\delta = \alpha - \gamma(\alpha) > n-1$, where $n-1 = [\alpha]$ for non-integer values of $\alpha > 0$. As a result, the condition $\alpha - \gamma(\alpha) > n-1$ (or $(\alpha+\beta)/(a-1) > n-1$) with $t > 0$ should be satisfied for parameters of Equation (40) with the Caputo derivative instead of $\alpha - \gamma(\alpha) \geq 0$ that is used in [29].*

Remark 2. *Note that in equations 3.5.48 and 3.5.49 of [29] p. 209, there are typos: The signs of the parameters $\gamma(\alpha)$ and α in the gamma functions must be opposite. In Equation (40), these signs are correct.*

Taking into account these Remarks and Propositions 3.8 and 3.9 of [29] pp. 209–210, we can formulate the following conditions for the existence of solution (40) for Equation (37).

Statement 1. *Non-linear fractional differential Equation (37) with $\alpha \in (n-1, n)$, $n \in \mathbb{N}$, has the solution, which is given by Equations (40) and (41), if the following conditions are satisfied:*

$$\begin{cases} a \in (0,1), \\ \beta > -\alpha - (n-1)(a-1), \end{cases} \quad or \quad \begin{cases} a > 1, \\ \beta < -\alpha - (n-1)(a-1). \end{cases} \tag{46}$$

Here, we take into account that $\delta = \alpha - \gamma(\alpha) > n-1$ instead of $\delta = \alpha - \gamma(\alpha) > 0$ which is used in Propositions 3.8 and 3.9 of [29].

Conditions (46) for the parameters, under which solution (40) exists, are important for applications in economic models.

2.3. Rate of Growth with Power-Law Memory

For solution (40), the rate of growth with power-law memory at time $t > 0$ is approximately equal to:

$$R(\alpha) = \frac{\alpha - \gamma(\alpha)}{t} = \frac{\alpha+\beta}{(1-a)\,t}, \tag{47}$$

where $a \neq 1$. For case $\alpha = 1$, which corresponds to the absence of memory, Equation (47) can be written in the following form:

$$R(1) = \frac{1 - \gamma(1)}{t} = \frac{1+\beta}{(1-a)\,t}. \tag{48}$$

Let us consider the case when we have growth with memory, i.e., the increasing function $K(t)$ for non-integer values of α. In this case, the growth rate with memory, $R(\alpha)$ should be positive for non-integer values of $\alpha \in (n-1, \alpha)$, $n \in \mathbb{N}$, i.e., we have the following inequality:

$$R(\alpha) > 0. \tag{49}$$

Solutions (40) and (41) exist only if the following conditions are satisfied:

$$\alpha - \gamma(\alpha) = \frac{\alpha + \beta}{1 - a} > n - 1, \ \gamma(\alpha) < 1. \tag{50}$$

Obviously, using Equations (47) and (50), we get that condition (49) has the following form:

$$R(\alpha) = \frac{\alpha - \gamma(\alpha)}{t} = \frac{\alpha + \beta}{(1 - a)\, t} > 0, \tag{51}$$

which will be satisfied for any solutions for $t > 0$. Mathematically, this statement follows from the fact that if $\alpha - \gamma(\alpha) > n - 1$ with $n \in \mathbb{N}$, then $\alpha - \gamma(\alpha) > 0$.

As a result, we can formulate the following principle.

Principle 1. *Principle of Inevitability of Growth with Memory: For economic models with memory, which are described by Equations (5), (6), and (36) with $a \ne 1$, $q \ne 1$, and $p \ne 1$, the rate of growth with power-law memory (47) is positive.*

$$R(\alpha) = \frac{\alpha + \beta}{(1 - a)\, t} = \frac{\alpha(1 - p)(1 - q) + \beta(2 - p - q)}{(1 - a)\,(1 - p)\,(1 - q)\, t} > 0 \tag{52}$$

for non-integer values of α. As a result, the inclusion of power-law memory effects leads to the inevitability of capital growth $K(t)$.

In addition, we have the lower boundary of the growth rates for processes with memory, which is described by the following statement.

Statement 2. *The rate of growth with power-law memory for processes, which are described by Equation (37), has the lower boundary that is defined by the inequality:*

$$R(\alpha) > \frac{n - 1}{t}, \tag{53}$$

where $n = [\alpha] + 1$ for non-integer values of α.

This statement is based on the fact that the solution exists only if the following condition holds:

$$\alpha - \gamma(\alpha) = \frac{\alpha + \beta}{(1 - a)} > n - 1. \tag{54}$$

Using definition (47) of the rate of growth with memory, we get (53).

Remark 3. *Solutions, in which the decline (recession) is realized, do not exist within the framework of the suggested model with memory. In this model, the processes with memory cannot have negative values of the rate of growth with a power-law memory. Note that for processes without memory, which are described by Equation (47) with $\alpha = 1$, the negative growth rates ($R(1) < 0$) can be realized.*

Let us consider the condition under which the growth rate with memory, $R(\alpha)$, is greater than the growth rate without memory, $R(1)$. This condition is represented by the inequality:

$$R(\alpha) > R(1). \tag{55}$$

Using expressions (47) and (48), inequality (55) gives:

$$R(\alpha) - R(1) = \frac{\alpha - 1}{(1 - a)\, t} > 0, \tag{56}$$

where we assume that $a \in (0, 1)$.

Taking into account conditions (46) for the existence of solution (40) and that $n = 1$ for $\alpha \in (0, 1)$, we can formulate the following statement.

Statement 3. *The rate $R(\alpha)$ of growth with memory for the capital $K(t)$ is greater than the rate $R(1)$ of growth without memory $R(\alpha) > R(1)$, if the following conditions are satisfied:*

$$
\begin{cases}
\alpha \in (0, 1), \\
a > 1, \\
\beta < -\alpha,
\end{cases}
\quad or \quad
\begin{cases}
\alpha \in (n-1, n), \ n \in \mathbb{N}, \ n \neq 1, \\
a \in (0, 1), \\
\beta > -\alpha + (n-1)(1-a).
\end{cases}
\tag{57}
$$

Let us consider the question of how much growth with memory can be greater than growth without memory. To describe this, we give the ratio of growth rates $R(\alpha)$ and $R(1)$. This ratio has the following form:

$$
\frac{R(\alpha)}{R(1)} = \frac{\alpha + \beta}{1 + \beta},
\tag{58}
$$

where we assume that $R(1) > 0$, conditions (57) are satisfied, and β is given by (39). Note that $\alpha \in (0, 1)$, in inequality $R(\alpha) > R(1)$ is also satisfied since $a > 1$ and $\alpha + \beta < 1 + \beta < 0$.

2.4. Dynamics of Capital Per Unit of Effective Labor

The amount of capital per unit of effective labor [3] p. 10, is defined by the following equation:

$$
k(t) = \frac{K(t)}{A(t)L(t)}.
\tag{59}
$$

The solution of capital in form (43) and expressions (12) and (14) allow us to describe the amount of capital per unit of effective labor (59) by the following equation:

$$
k(t) = \frac{K(t_0)}{A(t_0)L(t_0)} \left(\frac{t}{t_0} \right)^{\alpha - \gamma(\alpha) - 1/(1-q) - 1/(1-p)}.
\tag{60}
$$

Remark 4. *Note that the memory model described by the equation with a fractional derivative cannot be reduced to changing the parameterization of the standard model. This is due to the qualitatively different properties of the derivative of non-integer orders. For example, such standard properties of the first-order derivative, as the product rule and the chain rule, do not hold for fractional derivatives. For example, the expression $k(t)$, which is given by solutions of equations for $k(t)$, cannot coincide (for processes with memory) with the expression of $k(t) = K(t)/A(t)L(t)$, which is given by solutions of equations for $K(t)$, and $L(t)$, $A(t)$. For standard models, both expressions are the same. We can state that the variable per capita (per unit of effective labor) constructed from the solutions of original variables is not a solution of the equation for the variable per capita (per unit of effective labor). Let us give a brief explanation of this statement (for a detailed description, see article [46]. Let us assume that we have the solution $L_{sol}(t)$ and $A_{sol}(t)$ of differential equations for $L(t)$ and $A(t)$, respectively. We can consider two variables $K(t)$ and $k(t)$ and two equations $K^{(1)}(t) = F(t, K(t))$ and $k^{(1)}(t) = f(t, k(t))$. In the standard model, solutions $K_{sol}(t)$ and $k_{sol}(t)$ of these equations can be derived by the formula $K_{sol}(t) = k_{sol}(t)A_{sol}(t)L_{sol}(t)$. The fractional differential equations for the variables $K(t)$ and $k(t)$ cannot be related by such formulas, if the memory effect is taken into account.*

For the capital per unit of effective labor $k(t)$, the rate of growth with power-law memory at $t > t_0$ is approximately equal to:

$$
r(\alpha) = \frac{\alpha - \gamma(\alpha)}{t} - \frac{1}{t} \left(\frac{1}{1-q} + \frac{1}{1-p} \right),
\tag{61}
$$

where $q \neq 1, p \neq 1, a \neq 1$, and β is defined by Equation (38). Expression (61) can be represented in the following form:

$$r(\alpha) = \frac{\alpha + \beta}{(1-a)\,t} - \frac{\beta}{b\,t} = \frac{b(\alpha + \beta) - \beta(1-a)}{(1-a)\,b\,t}. \tag{62}$$

For $\alpha = 1$, which describes the case of absence memory, expression (62) takes the following form:

$$r(1) = \frac{b(1+\beta) - \beta(1-a)}{(1-a)\,b\,t}. \tag{63}$$

Expression (63) describes the rate of growth without memory for $a \neq 1$.

Let us consider the condition under which the growth rate with memory, $r(\alpha)$, is greater than the growth rate without memory, $r(1)$. This condition is represented by the following inequality:

$$r(\alpha) > r(1). \tag{64}$$

Using Equations (62) and (63), inequality (64) takes the following form:

$$r(\alpha) - r(1) = \frac{\alpha - 1}{(1-a)\,t} > 0. \tag{65}$$

Inequality (65) coincides with inequality (56). Therefore, Statement 3 and the system of inequalities (57) also should be satisfied for dynamics of the capital per unit of effective labor.

For the capital per unit of effective labor $k(t)$, the rate $r(\alpha)$ of growth with memory is greater than the rate $r(1)$ of growth without memory $r(\alpha) > r(1)$ if conditions (57) are satisfied.

Let us consider the question of how much growth with memory can be greater than growth without memory. Using Equations (62) and (63), the ratio of $r(\alpha)$ and $r(1)$ is expressed by the following equation:

$$\frac{r(\alpha)}{r(1)} = \frac{\alpha b + \beta(a + b - 1)}{b + \beta(a + b - 1)}, \tag{66}$$

where we assume that $r(1) > 0$, and the parameter β is defined by Equation (38).

For $b = 1 - a$ with $a \in (0,1)$, we have the linearly homogeneous production functions Cobb-Douglas. In this case, the rate of growth with power-law memory (62) takes the following form:

$$r(\alpha) = \frac{\alpha}{(1-a)\,t}. \tag{67}$$

Using that $\alpha \in (n-1, n)$, we get:

$$r(\alpha) > \frac{n-1}{(1-a)\,t} \tag{68}$$

for non-integer values of α. In this case, the ratio of $r(\alpha)$ and $r(1)$ is expressed by the following equation:

$$\frac{r(\alpha)}{r(1)} = \alpha. \tag{69}$$

Using that $\alpha \in (n-1, n)$, we obtain the following inequality:

$$\frac{r(\alpha)}{r(1)} > n - 1 \tag{70}$$

for non-integer values of α.

Example 1. *Using expression (69), we see that the rate of growth with memory can be several times (in $\alpha > 1$ time) higher than the standard rate of growth without memory. For example, if $\alpha = 3.2$, then the rate of growth* *with memory is 220% more (is 3.2 times more) than the standard rate of growth without memory, when other initial parameters of the models (with memory and without memory) are the same.*

As a result, we find that the growth rate with memory is greater than the growth rate without memory by α times. This allows us to formulate the following principle, where we assume that conditions (57) are satisfied.

Principle 2. *Principle of Changing Growth Rates by Memory: In the case $b = 1 - a$ with $a \in (0, 1)$ and conditions (57) are satisfied, the rate of growth with a power-law memory for capital per unit effective labor can be greater than the rate of growth without memory $(r(\alpha) > r(1))$ in α times, if the parameter of memory fading α is more than one $(\alpha > 1)$. The growth rate with memory is less than the growth rate without memory, i.e., $r(\alpha) < r(1)$, if the parameter α is less than one $(0 < \alpha < 1)$.*

As a result, we can conclude that the fading memory can significantly (several times) change the growth rate, when other parameters of the model are unchanged. Therefore, we should not neglect the memory in economic models.

As a prospect for further studies of non-linear economic growth models with memory, it is possible to emphasize the need to take into account both simultaneous and sequential actions of the effects of memory and depreciation.

3. Solow–Lucas Model of Closed Economy with Memory

In this section, we consider a generalization of the standard growth model for closed economy without capital depreciation, which is considered by Robert E. Lucas in paper "Making a Miracle" [41]. In the generalized model, we take into account the memory with power-law fading. The suggested model with memory is described by the non-linear fractional differential equation. The explicit expression of analytical solution of this non-linear equation is obtained.

3.1. Solow–Lucas Model for Closed Economy without Memory

Let us consider the Solow model for closed economy that is described by Robert E. Lucas in [41] pp. 253–254 (see also Section 3.2 in [42] pp. 73–75). We will call this economic model the Solow–Lucas model. Note that Robert E. Lucas Jr received the Nobel Memorial Prize in Economic Sciences in 1995 "for having developed and applied the hypothesis of rational expectations, and thereby having transformed macroeconomic analysis and deepened our understanding of economic policy" [43,44].

Let us consider an economy that uses physical capital $k(t)$ and the human capital $h(t)$ to produce a single good $y(t)$, the dynamics of which is described by the following equation:

$$y(t) = Ak^a(t)[uh(t)]^{1-a}. \tag{71}$$

Here, the human capital input is multiplied by u, where u is the fraction of time that people spend on producing goods.

The growth of human capital $h(t)$ depends on the amount of time spent on production, adjusted for quality (see Equation (13) in [45]) in the following form:

$$\frac{dh(t)}{dt} = \delta (1 - u)h(t). \tag{72}$$

The solution of Equation (72) can be written as:

$$h(t) = h(0) \exp\{\delta (1 - u)t\}, \tag{73}$$

where $h(0)$ is the human capital at time $t = 0$.

The growth of physical capital depends on the savings rate s, such that we have the following equation:

$$\frac{dk(t)}{dt} = sy(t) \tag{74}$$

which is interpreted as an economic accelerator without memory and lag. The substitution of expressions (71) and (73) into Equation (74) gives:

$$\frac{dk(t)}{dt} = sAu^{1-a}h^{1-a}(0)\exp\{\delta\,(1-a)(1-u)\,t\}k^a(t). \tag{75}$$

In this model, it is assumed that variables s and u are considered as given constants. The model, which is described by Equations (71)–(75), will turn out to be a Solow model rewritten for a closed economy [41,42].

In this model, the rate of technological changes (the average Solow balance) is described by the following expression:

$$\lambda_0 = \delta\,(1-a)(1-u), \tag{76}$$

and the initial technology level is equal to $Ah^{1-a}(0)$.

The long run growth rate of both capital and production per worker is $\delta\,(1-u)$. The growth rate of human capital, and the ratio of physical and human capital converge to constant values. In the long run, the level of income is proportional to the economy's initial stock of human capital.

Remark 5. *Note that in the Solow–Lucas model, the average values of $k(t)$, $h(t)$, and $y(t)$ are taken as original variables to build a model, in contrast to the Solow model that use $K(t)$, $L(t)$, $Y(t)$ as original variables. In standard models, the use of these two types of variables is equivalent. Unlike standard models, in models with memory the use of different types of variables leads to different models that are not equivalent in the general case [46]. This non-equivalence is associated with the violation of the standard form of the product rule for the fractional derivative of non-integer orders. As a consequence, we have a violation of the standard relationship of the rates of change of absolute (volume) and relative (specific) indicators.*

3.2. Solow–Lucas Model for Closed Economy with Memory

In the proposed generalization of the standard Solow-Lucas model, we will use the generalizations of Equations (71), (72), and (74).

(1) We assume that the economy, which uses physical capital $k(t)$ and the human capital $h(t)$ to produce a single good $y(t)$, is described by the following equation:

$$y(t) = Ak^a(t)[uh(t)]^b, \tag{77}$$

where u is the fraction of time people spend producing goods. If $b = 1 - a$, then Equation (77) gives Equation (71).

(2) The growth of human capital is assumed to be the power law in the following form:

$$\frac{dh(t)}{dt} = \delta\,(1-u)h^\theta(t). \tag{78}$$

If $\theta = 1$, then Equation (78) gives Equation (72) of the standard model.

(3) Equation (74) does not take into account the memory effects, since the derivative $dk(t)/dt$ is determined by the behavior of $y(\tau)$ only at the same time of instant $\tau = t$, and does not take into

account the history of changes of $y(\tau)$ in the past, when $\tau \in (0,t)$. To take into account the changes of $y(\tau)$ in the past, we can use the following equation:

$$\frac{dk(t)}{dt} = \int_0^t s(t,\tau)y(\tau)d\tau, \tag{79}$$

where function $s(t,\tau)$ allows us to take into account that the growth of physical capital $k(t)$ depends on the changes of $y(\tau)$ in the past at $\tau \in (0,t)$. Function $s(t,\tau)$ can be interpreted as a memory function. In order to have standard dimensions of economic quantities, the time variable t is considered as a dimensionless parameter, i.e., we changed the variable $t_{old} \to t_{new} = t_{old}/t_c$, where t_c is a characteristic time of economic process.

An important property of memory is described by the principle of memory fading, which states that the increasing of the time interval leads to a decrease in the corresponding contribution [7,33]. Let us consider the power-law form of the memory fading. In this case, the memory function can be described by the following equation:

$$s(t,\tau) = \frac{s}{\Gamma(\mu)}(t-\tau)^{\mu-1}, \tag{80}$$

where s is the savings rate and $\Gamma(\alpha)$ is the gamma function. For function (80), Equation (79) can be written in the following form:

$$\frac{dk(t)}{dt} = s\left(I_{RL;0+}^{\mu}y\right)(t), \tag{81}$$

where $I_{RL;0+}^{\mu}$ is the Riemann-Liouville fractional integral of the order $\mu > 0$, [29] pp. 69–70.

We should note that (81) with the Riemann-Liouville fractional integral can be considered as an approximation of the equations with generalized memory functions (79). In paper [47], using the generalized Taylor series in the Trujillo-Rivero-Bonilla form for the memory function, we proved that Equation (79) for a wide class of memory functions can be represented through the Riemann-Liouville fractional integrals (and the Caputo fractional derivatives) of non-integer orders.

The action of the Caputo derivative on Equation (81) gives:

$$\left(D_{C;0+}^{\mu}k^{(1)}\right)(t) = s\left(D_{C;0+}^{\mu}I_{RL;0+}^{\mu}y\right)(t), \tag{82}$$

where $D_{C;0+}^{\mu}$ is the Caputo fractional derivative of the order $\mu > 0$, [29] pp. 90–99.

In Equation (82), we can use the property that the Caputo fractional derivative is the left inverse operator for the Riemann-Liouville fractional integral (see the equation of Lemma 2.21 in [29] p. 95), in the following form:

$$\left(D_{C;0+}^{\mu}I_{RL;0+}^{\mu}y\right)(t) = y(t) \tag{83}$$

for $y(t) \in L_\infty(0,t)$ or $y(t) \in C[0,t]$, and the property of the Caputo fractional derivative:

$$\left(D_{C;0+}^{\mu}k^{(1)}\right)(t) = \left(D_{C;0+}^{\mu+1}k\right)(t). \tag{84}$$

Using expressions (83) and (84), Equation (82) can be written as:

$$\left(D_{C;0+}^{\alpha}k\right)(t) = sy(t), \tag{85}$$

with $\alpha = \mu + 1$. If $\alpha = 1$, then Equation (85) takes the form of (74).

The substitution of (77) into (85) gives the equation which describes the dynamics with memory for physical capital $k(t)$ in the following form:

$$\left(D_{C;0+}^{\alpha}k\right)(t) = sAk^a(t)[uh(t)]^b, \tag{86}$$

where the behavior of $h(t)$ is given by Equation (78). Equation (86) describes the proposed generalization of the Solow–Lucas model for a closed economy with power-law memory.

For $\alpha = 1$, Equation (86) describes the Solow–Lucas model without memory, where $b \neq 1 - a$ and $\theta \neq 1$.

3.3. Growth Rates of Closed Economy with Memory

Let us obtain the solution of the non-linear fractional differential Equation (78) which describes the Solow–Lucas model of closed economy with power-law memory.

We first solve Equation (78) with $\theta \neq 1$ for the human capital. Equation (78) can be written as:

$$\frac{d}{dt}\left(h^{1-\theta}(t)\right) = \delta\,(1-u)(1-\theta), \tag{87}$$

Therefore, the solution of Equation (87) with $\theta \neq 1$ has the following form:

$$h^{1-\theta}(t) = \delta\,(1-u)(1-\theta)t + c, \tag{88}$$

where we can use $c = h^{1-\theta}(0)$.

For simplicity, we will assume that $h(0) = 0$ and $h(t_0) = 1$. Then, we get $c = 0$ and solution (88) can be written in the following form:

$$h(t) = (\delta\,(1-u)(1-\theta))^{1/(1-\theta)}t^{1/(1-\theta)}. \tag{89}$$

Equation (89) with $t = t_0 > 0$ has the following form:

$$h(t_0) = (\delta\,(1-u)(1-\theta))^{1/(1-\theta)}t_0^{1/(1-\theta)}, \tag{90}$$

where $\delta\,(1-u)(1-\theta) > 0$. Assuming that $h(t_0) = 1$, we get:

$$t_0 = \frac{1}{\delta(1-u)(1-\theta)}, \tag{91}$$

and solution (89) can be represented by the following equation:

$$h(t) = h(t_0)\left(\frac{t}{t_0}\right)^{1/(1-\theta)}. \tag{92}$$

The substitution of (92) into (86) gives:

$$\left(D_{C;0+}^{\alpha}k\right)(t) = sA[uh(t_0)]^b\left(\frac{t}{t_0}\right)^{b/(1-\theta)}k^a(t), \tag{93}$$

where $\alpha = \mu + 1$ with $\mu > 0$. Equation (93) can be written in the following form:

$$\left(D_{C;0+}^{\alpha}k\right)(t) = \lambda\,t^{b/(1-\theta)}\,k^a(t), \tag{94}$$

where $\theta \neq 1$ and the constant λ is defined as:

$$\lambda = sA[uh(t_0)]^b t_0^{-b/(1-\theta)}. \tag{95}$$

Using equations 3.5.47 and 3.5.48 of Section 3.5.3 in [29] p. 209, the following equation:

$$\left(D_{C;0+}^{\alpha}k\right)(t) = \lambda t^{\beta}k^a(t), \tag{96}$$

with $\lambda \neq 0, a \neq 1, \alpha = \mu + 1 > 1$, and

$$\beta = \frac{b}{1 - \theta},$$ (97)

has the following solution:

$$k(t) = \left(\frac{\Gamma(\alpha - \gamma(\alpha) + 1)}{\lambda \Gamma(1 - \gamma(\alpha))} \right)^{1/(a-1)} t^{\alpha - \gamma(\alpha)},$$ (98)

where λ is defined by Equation (95), and

$$\gamma(\alpha) = \frac{\beta + a\alpha}{a - 1}, \quad \alpha - \gamma(\alpha) = \frac{\beta + \alpha}{1 - a}.$$ (99)

The condition for the existence of a solution can be written as:

$$\alpha - \gamma(\alpha) > n - 1, \quad \gamma(\alpha) < 1.$$ (100)

As a result, the rate of growth with power-law memory $(\alpha \neq 1)$ at time $t > 0$ is approximately equal to:

$$R(\alpha) = \frac{\alpha - \gamma(\alpha)}{t} = \frac{\beta + \alpha}{(1 - a) t} = \frac{\alpha + b - \alpha\theta}{(1 - a)(1 - \theta) t}$$ (101)

for $t > t_0 > 0$ and $\theta \neq 1, a \neq 1$, where we use (97).

For $\alpha = 1$, expression (101) takes the following form:

$$R(1) = \frac{\beta + 1}{1 - a} = \frac{1 + b - \theta}{(1 - a)(1 - \theta) t}.$$ (102)

Expression (102) describes the rate of growth without memory for the case $\theta \neq 1, a \neq 1$.

Using that solution (98) exists if conditions (100) are satisfied, i.e., $\alpha - \gamma(\alpha) > n - 1$, we get:

$$R(\alpha) > \frac{n - 1}{t}$$ (103)

for non-integer values of $\alpha \in (n - 1, n)$ and $t > 0$.

As a result, we get that $R(\alpha) > 0$ for non-integer values of α. Therefore, the rate of growth with power-law memory is positive for $t > 0$ and non-integer values of α.

We should note that the generalized model, which is described by Equation (79) assumes that $\alpha = \mu + 1$, where $\mu > 0$. Therefore, we may not consider the case with $0 < \alpha < 1$.

Let us consider the condition, under which the rate of growth with memory, $R(\alpha)$, is greater than the rate of growth without memory, $R(1)$, that is:

$$R(\alpha) > R(1).$$ (104)

Using expressions (101) and (102), inequality (104) gives:

$$R(\alpha) - R(1) = \frac{\alpha - 1}{(1 - a)t} = \frac{\mu}{(1 - a)t} > 0,$$ (105)

where we assume that $a \in (0, 1)$.

Using Equation (105), we can state that for $a \in (0, 1)$, we have $R(\alpha) > R(1)$ for all $t > 0$. As a result, we can formulate the following principle.

Principle 3. *Principle of Changing Growth Rates by Memory: If a solution of Equation (96) for the physical capital $k(t)$ exists and $a < 1$, then the rate of growth with power-law memory, $R(\alpha)$, is greater than the rate of growth without memory, $R(1)$, i.e., $R(\alpha) > R(1)$.*

Using conditions (57) for the existence of solution (98), and that $\alpha = \mu + 1$ with $\mu > 0$, $m = n - 1$, we can formulate the following statement.

Statement 4. *The rate $R(\alpha)$ of growth with memory for the physical capital $k(t)$ is greater than the rate $R(1)$ of growth without memory $(R(\alpha) > R(1))$, if the following conditions are satisfied:*

$$\begin{cases} \mu \in (m-1, m) \ m \in \mathbb{N} \\ a \in (0,1) \\ \beta > -\mu - 1 + m(1-a) \end{cases} . \tag{106}$$

The ratio of $R(\alpha)$ and $R(1)$, which are given by expressions (101) and (102), is expressed by the following equation:

$$\frac{R(\alpha)}{R(1)} = \frac{\alpha(1-\theta) + b}{1 - \theta + b} = \frac{1 - \theta + b + \mu(1-\theta)}{1 - \theta + b}. \tag{107}$$

For the special case $0 < 1 - \theta = b < 1$, Equation (107) gives:

$$\frac{R(\alpha)}{R(1)} = \frac{\alpha + 1}{2} = 1 + \frac{\mu}{2}, \tag{108}$$

where we use $\alpha = \mu + 1$.

Example 2. *Using expression (108), we see that the rate of growth with memory can be several times (in $\mu > 0$ time) higher than the standard rate of growth without memory. For example, if $\alpha = 3.2$ and $1 - \theta = b \in (0,1)$, then the rate of growth with memory is 110% more (is 2.1 times more) than the standard rate of growth without memory, when other initial parameters of the models (with memory and without memory) are the same.*

In this case, we see that the effects of memory can increase the growth rate by more than two times in comparison with the standard Solow–Lucas model without memory.

As a result, we can conclude that the memory effects can significantly (several times) change the growth rate, when other parameters of the model are unchanged, and we should not neglect the memory in economic models.

4. Conclusions

This article proposes generalizations of two well-known standard models with continuous time, which are described by Nobel laureates in economics, Robert M. Solow and Robert E. Lucas. In the suggested generalizations of the standard models, the memory with power-law fading is taken into account. As a mathematical tool for accounting for fading memory, the article uses integral derivatives of non-integer order. Note that the violation of the standard product (Leibniz) rule for fractional derivatives of non-integer orders leads to the non-equivalence of models that are equivalent in the absence of memory [46]. For the suggested model with memory, we derive non-linear fractional differential equations and its explicit analytical solutions. We prove that the rate of growth with power-law memory can be greater than the rate of growth without memory. For non-linear growth models with power-law memory, the growth rates can be changed by memory effects.

In this article, we proposed the following three principles, which can be used to describe the changes arising in the economic dynamics, when taking into account the power-law memory:

(I)   The Principle of Inevitability of Growth with Memory states that in the first proposed model, which are described by Equations (5),(6) and (36), with $a \neq 1$, $q \neq 1$, and $p \neq 1$, the rate of growth with power-law memory (47) is positive (52) for non-integer values of α. As a result, the inclusion of power-law memory effects leads to the inevitability of capital growth $K(t)$.

(II)   The Principle of Changing Growth Rates by Memory states that in the first proposed model, the rate of growth with power-law memory for capital per unit of effective labor can be greater than the rate of growth without memory in α times, if the parameter of memory fading α is more than one ($\alpha > 1$).

(III)   The Principle of Changing Growth Rates by Memory states that in the second proposed model, the rate of growth with power-law memory is greater than the rate of growth without memory, if a solution of Equation (96) for the physical capital $k(t)$ exists and $a < 1$.

Therefore, we should emphasize that the memory effects can significantly (several times) change the growth rate, when other parameters of the model are unchanged, and we should not neglect the memory in economic models. For example, if $\alpha = 3.2$, then the rate of growth with memory is 220% more (3.2 times more) and 110% more (2.1 times more) for first and second proposed models, respectively than the standard rate of growth without memory.

Let us note here a possible direction for further mathematical research on non-linear models of economic growth with memory. An interesting and important part of future research is to account for both simultaneous and sequential actions of memory effects and depreciation. Standard economic models often use the exponential kernel of the integral operator to describe depreciation. In Equation (17), kernel $D(t - \tau) = e^{-\delta\,(t-\tau)}$ describes the standard (exponentially distributed) depreciation (up to a numerical factor) in form (18). The following types of integral operator kernels can be used to account for memory and depreciation effects in economic growth models:

(a)   In Equation (17), kernel $D(t - \tau) = (t - \tau)^{\alpha-1}/\Gamma(\alpha)$ describes the interconnection of variables with power-law memory. In this case, integral operator (17) is called the Riemann-Liouville fractional integral. Economic models of this type were considered, for example, in works [7,33–36,38].

(b)   We can use kernel $D(t - \tau) = e^{-\delta\,(t-\tau)}(t - \tau)^{\alpha-1}/\Gamma(\alpha)$, which describes the gamma distributed lag by Equation (17). The economic model with this type of distributed lag was considered in work [53]. Note that kernels of exponential amortization and power-law memory are special cases of this kernel for the case $\delta = 0$ and $\alpha = 1$, respectively.

(c)   To describe the sequential action of two such effects as fading memory and continuously distributed delay (or continuously distributed amortization), it is necessary to use integral fractional operators with distributed lag, proposed in works [54] and then applying them in linear economic models [55–58].

(d)   Kernel $D(t - \tau) = (t - \tau)^{\alpha-1}E_{\rho,\alpha}^{\gamma}[\omega(t - \tau)^{\rho}]$ describes the connection of variables with power-law memory and depreciation in special cases. Here, $E_{\rho,\alpha}^{\gamma}[\omega(t - \tau)^{\rho}]$ is the three-parameter Mittag-Leffler function [59,60], which is also called the Prabhakar function [61–63]. Integral operator (17) with this kernel is called the Prabhakar fractional integral [61–63]. The economic model with this type was considered in works [64,65], where a new economic model through learning-by-doing with memory was proposed. For the first time, the fractional derivative of Riemann-Liouville type, which has the Prabhakar function in the kernel, was proposed by Anatoly A. Kilbas, Megumi Saigo, and Ram K. Saxena in work [61] in 2004. This operator can be known as the Kilbas-Saigo-Saxena (KSS) fractional derivative. Note that the KSS operators are left-inverse for the Prabhakar fractional integrals [61]. Then, the fractional derivatives and integrals began to be studied in various papers (for example, see [62–64] and references therein). An application of these operators in economics with memory is proposed in papers [64,65]. We should emphasize that the main property of any generalized (fractional) derivative is to be a left-inverse operator to the corresponding generalized (fractional) integral operator. This requirement is important for a self-consistent mathematical theory of the fractional operators to have a general fractional calculus of these operators.

References

1. Solow, R.M. A contribution to the theory of economic growth. *Q. J. Econ.* **1956**, *70*, 65–94. Available online: http://piketty.pse.ens.fr/files/Solow1956.pdf (accessed on 12 October 2020). [CrossRef]
2. Solow, R.M. Neoclassical growth theory. In *Handbook of Macroeconomics*; Elsevier Science B.V.: Amsterdam, The Netherlands, 1999; Volume 1, pp. 637–667. [CrossRef]
3. Romer, D. *Advanced Macroeconomics*, 3rd ed.; McGraw-Hill Companies: Boston, MA, USA, 2006; 678p, ISBN 978-0-07-287730-8.
4. Barro, R.J.; Sala-i-Martin, X.I. *Economic Growth*, 2nd ed.; The MIT Press: Cambridge, MA, USA; London, UK, 2003; p. 654. ISBN 978-0262025539.
5. Volgina, O.A.; Golodnaya, N.Y.; Odiyako, N.N.; Shuman, G.I. *Mathematical Modeling of Economic Processes and Systems*, 3rd ed.; Knorus: Moscow, Russia, 2016; p. 196. ISBN 978-5-406-04805-4.
6. NobelPrize.org. The Sveriges Riksbank Prize in Economic Sciences in Memory of Alfred Nobel 1987. Press Release. Nobel Media AB 2019. Available online: https://www.nobelprize.org/prizes/economic-sciences/1987/press-release/ (accessed on 12 October 2020).
7. Tarasova, V.V.; Tarasov, V.E. Concept of dynamic memory in economics. *Commun. Nonlinear Sci. Numer. Simul.* **2018**, *55*, 127–145. [CrossRef]
8. Granger, C.W.J. *The Typical Spectral Shape of an Economic Variable*; Technical Report; Department of Statistics, Stanford University: Stanford, CA, USA, 1964; Volume 11, pp. 1–21. Available online: https://statistics.stanford.edu/research/typical-spectral-shape-economic-variable (accessed on 12 October 2020).
9. Granger, C.W.J. The typical spectral shape of an economic variable. *Econometrica* **1966**, *34*, 150–161. [CrossRef]
10. Granger, C.W.J. Essays in Econometrics: Collected Papers of Clive W.J. Granger. In *Spectral Analysis, Seasonality, Nonlinearity, Methodology, and Forecasting*; Ghysels, E., Swanson, N.R., Watson, M.W., Eds.; Cambridge University Press: Cambridge, UK; New York, NY, USA, 2001; Volume I, p. 523.
11. Granger, C.W.J.; Joyeux, R. An introduction to long memory time series models and fractional differencing. *J. Time Ser. Anal.* **1980**, *1*, 15–39. [CrossRef]
12. Granger, C.W.J. Essays in Econometrics Collected Papers of Clive W.J. Granger. In *Causality, Integration and Cointegration, and Long Memory*; Ghysels, E., Swanson, N.R., Watson, M.W., Eds.; Cambridge University Press: Cambridge, UK, 2001; Volume II, p. 398. ISBN 978-0-521-79207-3.
13. NobelPrize.org. The Sveriges Riksbank Prize in Economic Sciences in Memory of Alfred Nobel 2003. Press Release. Nobel Media AB 2019. Available online: https://www.nobelprize.org/prizes/economic-sciences/2003/summary/ (accessed on 12 October 2020).
14. Beran, J. *Statistics for Long-Memory Processes*; Capman and Hall: New York, NY, USA, 1994; 315p, ISBN 0-412-04901-5.
15. Beran, J.; Feng, Y.; Ghosh, S.; Kulik, R. *Long-Memory Processes: Probabilistic Properties and Statistical Methods*; Springer: Berlin/Heidelberg, Germany; New York, NY, USA, 2013; 884p, ISBN 978-3-642-35511-0. [CrossRef]
16. Palma, W. *Long-Memory Time Series: Theory and Methods*; Wiley-InterScience: Hoboken, NJ, USA, 2007; 304p, ISBN 978-0-470-11402-5. [CrossRef]
17. Robinson, P.M. *Time Series with Long Memory*; Series: Advanced Texts in Econometrics; Oxford University Press: Oxford, UK, 2003; 392p, ISBN 978-0199257300.
18. Teyssiere, G.; Kirman, A.P. *Long Memory in Economics*; Springer: Berlin/Heidelberg, Germany, 2007; 389p. [CrossRef]
19. Tschernig, R. *Wechselkurse, Unsicherheit und Long Memory*; Physica-Verlag: Heidelberg, Germany, 1994; 232p, ISBN 978-3-7908-0753-0. [CrossRef]
20. Granger, C.W.J. Current perspectives on long memory processes. *Acad. Econ. Pap.* **2000**, *28*, 1–16. [CrossRef]
21. Baillie, R.N. Long memory processes and fractional integration in econometrics. *J. Econom.* **1996**, *73*, 5–59. [CrossRef]
22. Parke, W.R. What is fractional integration? *Rev. Econ. Stat.* **1999**, *81*, 632–638. [CrossRef]
23. Banerjee, A.; Urga, G. Modelling structural breaks, long memory and stock market volatility: An overview. *J. Econom.* **2005**, *129*, 1–34. [CrossRef]
24. Gil-Alana, L.A.; Hualde, J. Fractional Integration and Cointegration: An Overview and an Empirical Application. In *Palgrave Handbook of Econometrics. Volume 2: Applied Econometrics*; Mills, T.C., Patterson, K., Eds.; Springer: Berlin, Germany, 2009; pp. 434–469. [CrossRef]

25. Grunwald, A.K. About "limited" derivations their application. *J. Appl. Math. Phys.* **1867**, *12*, 441–480.

26. Letnikov, A.V. Theory of Differentiation with Arbitrary Pointer. *Mat. Sb.* **1868**, *3*, 1–68. Available online: http://mi.mathnet.ru/eng/msb8039 (accessed on 12 October 2020).

27. Samko, S.G.; Kilbas, A.A.; Marichev, O.I. *Fractional Integrals and Derivatives Theory and Applications*; Gordon and Breach: New York, NY, USA, 1993; 1006p, ISBN 9782881248641.

28. Podlubny, I. *Fractional Differential Equations*; Academic Press: San Diego, CA, USA, 1998; p. 340.

29. Kilbas, A.A.; Srivastava, H.M.; Trujillo, J.J. *Theory and Applications of Fractional Differential Equations*; Elsevier: Amsterdam, The Netherlands, 2006; 540p.

30. Diethelm, K. *The Analysis of Fractional Differential Equations: An Application-Oriented Exposition Using Differential Operators of Caputo Type*; Springer: Berlin, Germany, 2010; 247p. [CrossRef]

31. Kochubei, A.; Luchko, Y. Handbook of Fractional Calculus with Application. Volume 1. Basic Theory. Walter de Gruyter GmbH: Berlin, Germany; Boston, MA, USA, 2019; 481p, ISBN 978-3-11-057081-6. [CrossRef]

32. Kochubei, A.; Luchko, Y. *Handbook of Fractional Calculus with Applications. Volume 2. Fractional Differential Equations*; Walter de Gruyter GmbH: Berlin, Germany; Boston, MA, USA, 2019; 519p, ISBN 978-3-11-057082-3. [CrossRef]

33. Tarasov, V.E.; Tarasova, V.V. *Economic Dynamics with Memory: Fractional Calculus Approach*; Walter de Gruyter GmbH: Boston, MA, USA, 2021; 678p, ISBN 978-3-11-062460-1.

34. Tarasova, V.V.; Tarasov, V.E. Macroeconomic models with dynamic memory: Fractional calculus approach. *Appl. Math. Comput.* **2018**, *338*, 466–486. [CrossRef]

35. Tarasov, V.E. Economic models with power-law memory. In *Handbook of Fractional Calculus with Applications: Volume 8. Applications in Engineering, Life and Social Sciences, Part B*; Baleanu, D., Lopes, A.M., Machado, J.A.T., Eds.; De Gruyter: Berlin, Germany; Boston, MA, USA, 2019; Chapter 1; pp. 1–32. ISBN 978-3-11-057092. [CrossRef]

36. Tarasov, V.E. Fractional econophysics: Market price dynamics with memory effects. *Phys. A Stat. Mech. Appl.* **2020**, *557*, 124865. [CrossRef]

37. Tarasova, V.V.; Tarasov, V.E. Dynamic intersectoral models with memory that generalize Leontief model. *J. Econ. Entrep.* **2017**, *2*, 913–924. Available online: https://elibrary.ru/item.asp?id=28791089 (accessed on 12 October 2020).

38. Tarasova, V.V.; Tarasov, V.E. Dynamic intersectoral models with power-law memory. *Commun. Nonlinear Sci. Numer. Simul.* **2018**, *54*, 100–117. [CrossRef]

39. Tarasov, V.E. On history of mathematical economics: Application of fractional calculus. *Mathematics* **2019**, *7*, 509. [CrossRef]

40. Tarasov, V.E. *Mathematical Economics: Application of Fractional Calculus*; MDPI: Basel, Switzerland; Beijing, China, 2020; 278p, ISBN1 978-3-03936-118-2. ISBN2 978-3-03936-119-9. [CrossRef]

41. Lucas, R.E. Making a Miracle. *Econometrica* **1993**, *61*, 251–272. Available online: http://www.dklevine.com/archive/refs42101.pdf (accessed on 12 October 2020). [CrossRef]

42. Lucas, R.E. *Lectures on Economic Growth*; Harvard University Press: Cambridge, UK; London, UK, 2002; 204p, ISBN 0-674-00627-5.

43. NobelPrize.org. The Sveriges Riksbank Prize in Economic Sciences in Memory of Alfred Nobel 1995. Nobel Media AB 2019. Available online: https://www.nobelprize.org/prizes/economic-sciences/1995/summary/ (accessed on 12 October 2020).

44. The Royal Swedish Academy of Sciences. The Scientific Contributions of Robert E. Lucas, Jr. 1995. Available online: https://www.nobelprize.org/prizes/economic-sciences/1995/advanced-information/ (accessed on 12 October 2020).

45. Lucas, R.E. On the mechanics of economic development. *J. Monet. Econ.* **1988**, *22*, 3–42. [CrossRef]

46. Tarasov, V.E. Rules for fractional-dynamic generalizations: Difficulties of constructing fractional dynamic models. *Mathematics* **2019**, *7*, 554. [CrossRef]

47. Tarasov, V.E. Generalized memory: Fractional calculus approach. *Fractal Fract.* **2018**, *2*, 23. [CrossRef]

48. Hilfer, R.; Luchko, Y. Desiderata for fractional derivatives and integrals. *Mathematics* **2019**, *7*, 149. [CrossRef]

49. Moiseev, N.N. *Simplest Mathematical Models of Economic Forecasting*; Znanie: Moscow, Russia, 1975; 64p, Available online: https://booksee.org/book/505314 (accessed on 12 October 2020).

50. Ivanilov, Y.P.; Lotov, A.V. *Mathematical Models in Economics*; Nauka: Moscow, Russia, 1979; 304p, Available online: http://www.library.fa.ru/files/Ivanilov.pdf (accessed on 12 October 2020).

51. Lotov, A.V. *Introduction to Economic and Mathematical Modeling*; Nauka: Moscow, Russia, 1984; 392p.

52. Allen, R.G.D. *Mathematical Economics*, 2nd ed.; Macmillan: London, UK, 1963; 812p, ISBN 978-1-349-81547-0. [CrossRef]

53. Tarasov, V.E.; Tarasova, V.V. Logistic equation with continuously distributed lag and application in economics. *Nonlinear Dyn.* **2019**, *97*, 1313–1328. [CrossRef]

54. Tarasov, V.E.; Tarasova, S.S. Fractional and integer derivatives with continuously distributed lag. *Commun. Nonlinear Sci. Numer. Simul.* **2019**, *70*, 125–169. [CrossRef]

55. Tarasov, V.E.; Tarasova, V.V. Harrod-Domar growth model with memory and distributed lag. *Axioms* **2019**, *8*, 9. [CrossRef]

56. Tarasov, V.E.; Tarasova, V.V. Phillips model with exponentially distributed lag and power-law memory. *Comput. Appl. Math.* **2019**, *38*, 13. [CrossRef]

57. Tarasov, V.E.; Tarasova, V.V. Dynamic Keynesian model of economic growth with memory and lag. *Mathematics* **2019**, *7*, 178. [CrossRef]

58. Tarasov, V.E.; Tarasova, V.V. Dynamic Keynesian model of economic growth with memory and lag. In *Advanced Mathematical Methods Theory and Applications*; Mainardi, F., Giusti, A., Eds.; MDPI: Basel, Switzerland; Beijing, China; Wuhan, China; Barcelona, Spain; Belgrade, Serbia, 2020; 198p, pp. 116–132. ISBN 978-3-03928-247-0. [CrossRef]

59. Gorenflo, R.; Kilbas, A.A.; Mainardi, F.; Rogosin, S.V. *Mittag-Leffler Functions, Related Topics and Applications*; Springer: Berlin, Germany, 2014; p. 443. [CrossRef]

60. Prabhakar, T.R. A Singular Integral Equation with a Generalized Mittag-Leffler Function in the Kernel. *Yokohama Math. J.* **1971**, *19*, 7–15. Available online: https://irdb.nii.ac.jp/00822/0001826467 (accessed on 12 October 2020).

61. Kilbas, A.A.; Saigo, M.; Saxena, R.K. Generalized Mittag-Leffler function and generalized fractional calculus operators. *Integral Transform. Spec. Funct.* **2004**, *15*, 31–49. [CrossRef]

62. Giusti, A.; Colombaro, I.; Garra, R.; Garrappa, R.; Polito, F.; Popolizio, M.; Mainardi, F. A practical guide to Prabhakar fractional calculus. *Fract. Calc. Appl. Anal.* **2020**, *23*, 9–54. [CrossRef]

63. Giusti, A. General fractional calculus and Prabhakar's theory. *Commun. Nonlinear Sci. Numer. Simul.* **2020**, *83*, 105114. [CrossRef]

64. Tarasov, V.E.; Tarasova, S.S. Fractional derivatives and integrals: What are they needed for? *Mathematics* **2020**, *8*, 164. [CrossRef]

65. Tarasov, V.E. Fractional nonlinear dynamics of learning with memory. *Nonlinear Dyn.* **2020**, *100*, 1231–1242. [CrossRef]

Risk Management for Bonds with Embedded Options

Antonio Díaz [1] and **Marta Tolentino** [2,*]

[1] Department of Economics and Finance, University of Castilla-La Mancha, 02071 Albacete, Spain;
    antonio.diaz@uclm.es
[2] Department of Economics and Finance, University of Castilla-La Mancha, 13003 Ciudad Real, Spain
*   Correspondence: marta.tolentino@uclm.es

Abstract: This paper examines the behavior of the interest rate risk management measures for bonds with embedded options and studies factors it depends on. The contingent option exercise implies that both the pricing and the risk management of bonds requires modelling future interest rates. We use the Ho and Lee (HL) and Black, Derman, and Toy (BDT) consistent interest rate models. In addition, specific interest rate measures that consider the contingent cash-flow structure of these coupon-bearing bonds must be computed. In our empirical analysis, we obtained evidence that effective duration and effective convexity depend primarily on the level of the forward interest rate and volatility. In addition, the higher the interest rate change and the lower the volatility, the greater the differences in pricing of these bonds when using the HL or BDT models.

Keywords: bonds with embedded options; nonarbitrage interest rates models; effective duration; effective convexity

1. Introduction

The aim of this paper is to analyze and interpret interest rate risk management measures for option-embedded bonds under different specifications of interest rate dynamics. In addition, we studied the factors, on which they depend, based on the assumption that the choice of the consistent interest rate model used to price these securities can have a significant impact on the calculation of those measures. The cash flows from a callable (putable) bond depend on the possible exercise of the call (put) option, i.e., early redemption in favor of the issuer (bondholder). Therefore, the pricing of these bonds requires modelling of future interest rates from the actual term structure of interest rates and the actual term structure of volatility. We used two consistent term structures of interest rates models, the Ho and Lee (HL) [1] and Black, Derman, and Toy (BDT) [2] models. We estimated different measures of interest risk management and examine the main factors that determine their behavior, such as the interest rate volatility, the shape of the yield curve, and the changes in the yield curve. To illustrate the process, we examined the daily price behaviors of two annual coupon corporate bonds with embedded options throughout their lifetimes. These bonds were selected, because they were actively traded in a sample period that was particularly interesting for our analysis, given the dramatic changes in both the level and the slope of the term structure of interest rates.

Managing these option-embedded bonds, of which the cash flow structure depends on future interest rates, requires two additional challenges over any plain vanilla bond. On the one hand, the bond's price in an interest rate model is needed to apply to the bond's price. There are two different approaches to modelling the dynamics of interest rates: equilibrium models and nonarbitrage models. Both of them start from a stochastic differential equation for a short interest rate but differ in the procedure used to implement the models. Thus, equilibrium models are based on the estimation of parameters from historical data, assuming that they are constant for a given period. On the other hand, consistent models or nonarbitrage models replicate exactly the term structure corresponding to the calibration date. The latter is preferred by the financial industry over the former. Some of the most popular models among practitioners are those proposed by HL and BDT.

On the other hand, traditional bond sensitivity measures that do not incorporate options, i.e., duration and convexity, are no longer appropriate, and instead, the effective or option-adjusted duration and convexity are used. In addition, there is the concept of option-adjusted spread (OAS), which takes into account the fact that the securities contain early redemption provisions although similar to the concept of yield spread applied to the pricing of straight bonds.

In our paper, we applied the HL and BDT models in the analyses of two coupon-bearing bonds with embedded options, a callable bond and a putable bond. Both were actively traded in the Spanish corporate debt market during a broad sample period 1993–2003 and were chosen for its dramatic changes in both the level and the slope of the time structure of interest rates. This interest rate behavior makes it easier to draw conclusions from our analysis.

The main contributions of our paper are the following. Firstly, we carried out a daily analysis of the relationship between traditional interest rate risk management measures and option-adjusted measures based on the expected future evolution of interest rates at any given time, showing the attractiveness of the option to the investor. Secondly, the main factors determining the behaviors of these measures were analyzed. Finally, the implications of the choice of a model for the dynamics of interest rates and the extent of rate changes used in the calculation of effective duration (ED) and convexity were studied.

2. Bonds with Embedded Options

The two most common types of embedded options are call provisions and put provisions, so we can distinguish two main types of bonds with embedded options—callable bonds and putable bonds. A callable bond is a bond that can be redeemed by the issuer before its maturity date, and a putable bond can be sold by the bondholder before its maturity date. A callable bond allows its issuer to repurchase its debt at par value before maturity in the event that interest rates fall below the issue's coupon rate or its credit rating improves. In both cases, the issuer has the opportunity to issue a new bond at a lower coupon rate. This is a disadvantage for the investor. In the event of early redemption, the investor will be paid the price at par, far below the price of an equivalent straight bond, and will have to reinvest in another bond at a time when interest rates are lower than the coupon rate of the original issue. Hence, buying a callable bond comes down to buying an option-free or plain vanilla bond and selling a call option to the issuer of the bond. The value of a callable bond can be estimated from the price of an identical straight bond minus the value or premium of the embedded call option sold.

A putable bond allows its holder to sell the bond at a face value before maturity, in case that interest rates exceed the issue coupon rate. This gives you the opportunity to buy a new bond with a higher coupon rate. The purchase of a putable bond comes down to buying an option-free bond as well as a put option. The price of the putable bond is the price of an identical straight bond plus an embedded put option purchased. The embedded option can be exercised from a specific date on (American option) or on a specific date (European option), depending on the bond, at the strike price.

Unlike an option-free straight bond, an embedded option bond is a contingent claim, i.e., its future cash flows are uncertain, because they depend on the future value of interest rates. To price such a bond, it is necessary to use a model that explains the fact that future interest rates are uncertain. This uncertainty is described by the term structure of the volatilities of the relative changes in interest rates. The most commonly used method for pricing these bonds is the binomial interest tree model.

3. Consistent Interest Rate Models

The HL model is the first consistent term structure of an interest rates model and is presented as an alternative to equilibrium models [3,4]. It proposes a general methodology to price a wide range of interest rates contingent claims. The model is presented in the form of a binomial bond price tree with two parameters—the volatility of the short interest rate and the market price of the short rate risk. The inputs of the model are the yield curve and the short rate volatility. The main limitation is that interest rates are normally distributed, so we can get negative values.

The short-interest-rate dynamic dr in the continuous time version can be represented by Equation (1):

$$dr = \theta(t)dt + \sigma dz, \tag{1}$$

where σ is the instantaneous standard deviation of the short rate, r is a constant, $\theta(t)$ is the drift of the process, and z is a standard Wiener process.

The drift $\theta(t)$ is chosen so as to exactly fit the term structure of interest rates being currently observed in the market. It depends on the time t, on the slope of the instantaneous forward curve in 0, $f(0, t)$, and on the constant short rate volatility, σ. The drift $\theta(t)$ can be written as:

$$\theta(t) = \frac{\partial f(0,t)}{\partial t} + \sigma^2 t. \tag{2}$$

The BDT model assumes that interest rates follow a lognormal distribution. This model has the advantage over the HL model, i.e., the interest rate cannot become negative. The equivalent stochastic process corresponding to the model is described as:

$$d \ln r = \left[\theta(t) + \frac{\sigma'(t)}{\sigma(t)} \ln r\right]dt + \sigma(t)dz, \tag{3}$$

where $\theta(t)$ and $\sigma(t)$ are two independent functions of time chosen so that the model fits the term structure of spot interest rates and the term structure of spot rate volatilities.

Both models are implemented using their original discrete version through binomial trees. These trees are calibrated from the previously estimated zero-coupon yield curve and the historical term structure of interest rate volatility for each maturity. The calibration process requires the joint adjustment of several binomial trees. We followed the method proposed by [5]. The main output of the process is the short-term interest rate at each time, t, and interest state, i. State prices can be obtained from the trees. State-contingent claims are securities that pay off in some interest rate states, but not in others. Thus, each state price is the current value of \$1 received at a given interest rate state and a given time in the future. If the option has been exercised in this node, state security pays nothing.

For the sake of brevity, the calibration process is not described. By way of illustration, here are some basic ideas about the procedure in the case of the BDT model. We followed the forward process developed by [6] that proves that the level of the short rate in t can be estimated from Equation (4):

$$r(t) = U(t)exp(\sigma(t)z(t)), \tag{4}$$

where $U(t)$ is the median of the log short rate distribution in t, $\sigma(t)$ is the short rate volatility, and $z(t)$ represents a Brownian motion.

Although most practitioners make extensive use of a simplification of the BDT model assuming constant interest rate volatility, we used the original version. The term structure of the volatility was calibrated from Equation (5):

$$\sigma(i) \sqrt{\Delta t} = \frac{1}{2} ln \frac{r_U(i)}{r_D(i)}, \tag{5}$$

where Δt is the width of each of the time steps, into which the bond's term to maturity is divided, $\sigma(i)$ is the interest rate volatility at the interest state i with i being each of the possible interest rate nodes for term t, $r_U(i)$ and $r_D(i)$ are the short interest rates as seen from the nodes U and D, respectively.

$P_U(i)$ and $P_D(i)$ are the corresponding discount functions, i.e., the prices of zero-coupon bonds, when interest rates rise and fall, respectively, which can be written as:

$$P_D(i) = P_U(i)^{exp(-2\sigma(i)\sqrt{\Delta t})}. \tag{6}$$

The calibration process is carried out for each of the dates [7], on which each of the two coupon-bearing bonds analyzed is traded throughout its life cycle. We used daily estimates of the zero-coupon yield curve as inputs in the calibration process, which we previously estimated via a weighted version of the Nelson and Siegel model [8] (see [9,10]). We assumed a heteroskedastic price error scheme, and a generalized least square (GLS) method was employed. The data in the previous analysis were the Spanish Treasury bill and bond prices of all actual transactions from the sample period. These daily term structures of interest rates and the historic term structures of volatilities were used to calibrate the binomial trees for the short rate with monthly time steps.

4. Interest Rate Risk Measures

The behaviors of callable and putable bonds were analyzed by taking into account their risk arising from changes in the underlying variables, such as volatility or yield curve changes. Traditional interest rate risk measures, modified duration (MD) and convexity, are not suitable for option-embedded bonds, because they do not consider the possibility of option exercise. Instead, ED is defined as a rough measure of the sensitivity of the bond's price to changes in interest rates. More specifically, it is the percentage change in the bond's price to a parallel shift in the yield curve by a certain number of basis points (Δy). Effective convexity (EC) approximates the second derivative of the bond price function with respect to the yield curve. This concept is useful, when a portfolio manager expects a potentially large shift in the term structure. The calculation of these measure requires the estimation from the current price P_0 of prices in the case of declining (P_D) and increasing (P_U) interest rates. ED can be calculated as follow:

$$ED = \frac{P_D - P_U}{2P_0(\Delta y)}. \tag{7}$$

EC was given by Equation (8):

$$EC = \frac{P_D + P_U - 2P_0}{2P_0(\Delta y)^2}. \tag{8}$$

To estimate these interest risk management measures, we followed the procedure described in [8,9]. We recalibrate the HL and BDT models after shifting the Treasury yield curve by ±25 and ±100 bp. In addition, we calculated the OAS for each date. The OAS is the constant spread, which equalizes the theoretical price of a bond at its market price when added to all the short-term interest rates on the binomial tree.

5. Sample Description and Estimation Procedure

In order to meet our objectives, we chose a sample period with strong changes in the term structure of interest rates, in which default risk hardly changed. The Spanish fixed-income market, both corporate and government, during the period 1993 to 2004 was particularly suitable. The first part of the sample was characterized by strong monetary tensions, including currency devaluations, and sharp and severe interest rate swings. The slope of the yield curve went from rising to falling. Subsequently, there were sharp reductions in levels to meet the convergence criteria to ensure entry into the single currency. The final part of the sample was characterized by a surge in interest rates in 2001. We examined the two most actively traded corporate bond issues with embedded options in the Spanish corporate fixed-income market AIAF during the period. One issue contained a call option, and the other included a put option. Both were European options. Table 1 describes the main features of the issues.

Table 1. Main features of the issues, i.e., Banco de Crédito Local (BCL) and Túnel del Cadí (TC).

Bond Characteristics	BCL	TC
Issuance date	14 December 1993	31 May 1994
Maturity date	1 July 2003	31 May 2004
Annual coupon rate (%)	8.4	9.85
Outstanding amount	€178 million	€48 million
Rating	Aa3	No rated
Percentage of traded days (%)	9.5%	5.1%
Daily trading volume	€6.5 million	€1.0 million
Type of option	Call (European)	Put (European)
Option exercise price (%)	100	100
Option exercise date	1 July 1998	31 May 2000
# Observations up to exercise date	106	101
# Observations	106	128

As mentioned, we calibrated the HL and BDT models to the Spanish Treasury yield curve. Estimates of the term structure of interest rates were made from the daily trading of Spanish Treasury debt securities using the Nelson and Siegel duration-weighted model.

To calculate sensitivity measures for bonds with embedded options, we applied the following steps [11,12]. First, we calculated the theoretical price of the bonds from the HL and BDT yield curve models. Second, we obtained the OAS for all days, of which issues were traded during the period 1993–2004. Third, we shifted the on-the-run yield curve up and down by ±25 and ±100 bp and constructed new binomial interest rate trees. Fourth, we added a constant OAS to each node of the new interest rates trees. Fifth, we used the adjusted trees to determine the value of bonds, from which we calculated ED using Equation (7) and EC using Equation (8).

In addition, we computed for the entire sample period of the MD and convexity assuming two possibilities. In the first case, the option was not exercised, so we had the MD- and convexity-to-maturity. In the second one, we supposed that the option was exercised, so we had the MD- and convexity-to-call/put. We compared these new measures with ED and EC.

6. Results

Figure 1 shows graphically the estimates of ED calculated from each of the two consistent models, HL and BDT. In the calculation of ED, we used a parallel variation of ±100 bp along the entire yield curve. The top line shows the MD-to-maturity, i.e., assuming an option-free bond. The lower line represents the MD to the date of the option exercise and was calculated assuming that the option was exercised for certain (MD-to-call or MD-to-put). On dates, when the bond was not traded and there was no market price, we obtained a theoretical price, based on which the MD was estimated. We assumed that the bond's yield-to-maturity (YTM) was the spot interest rate provided by the yield curve for the term to maturity (top line) or to the exercise date (bottom line) on that date plus the average OAS of the issue over its life (55 bp for the Banco de Crédito Local (BCL) and 126 bp for the Túnel del Cadí (TC)). This YTM made it possible to obtain the theoretical price of the bond for each date and the MD for each interest rate model.

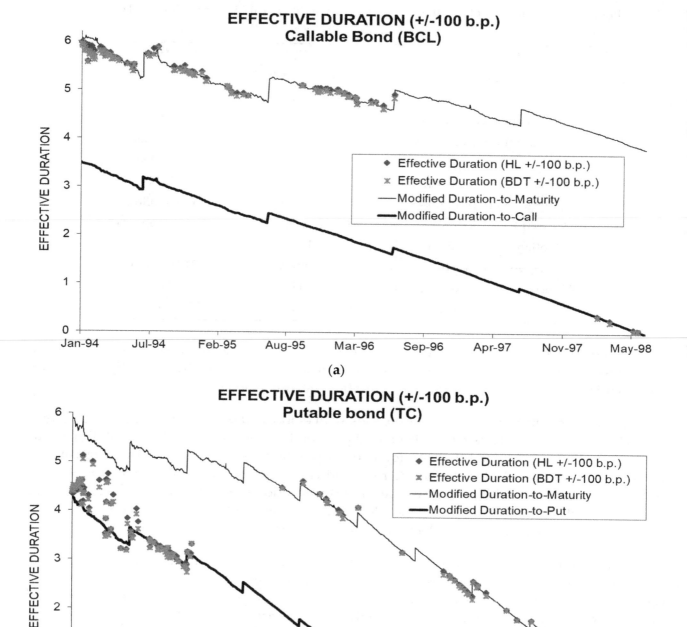

Figure 1. Evolution of the effective duration (ED) estimated from the Ho and Lee (HL) model and the Black, Derman, and Toy (BDT) model. Upper and lower black lines are the modified duration (MD)-to-maturity and the MD-to-option. Both lines limit the possible values of the ED according to the expectation of exercising the option. (**a**) shows the results for the Callable bond (BCL) and (**b**) for the Putable bond (TC).

The price of bonds with embedded options depends on investors' expectations about the possible future exercise of the option. If future interest rates that are deducted from the current yield curve, i.e., forward rates, indicate that they will remain above the bond's coupon rate, the possibility of call exercise will be remote and the price of the callable bond will be slightly lower than a similar nonoption bond. In contrast, the price of a putable bond should be well above that of a similar straight bond. Expectations of future interest rate behavior are key in pricing these bonds. This is how we proposed the variable, option attractiveness (OA), for the bondholder. It was calculated from Equation (9):

$$\text{Option attractiveness} = \text{Forward}\,(t, T) + \text{OAS} - \text{Coupon rate}, \tag{9}$$

where Forward (t, T) is the prediction, assuming the expectative theory is true, of future interest rates for the period between the strike date t and the maturity date T. Hence, for callable bonds, the option is attractive when the OA gets negative values, while for putable bonds the option is attractive when the OA is positive.

Figure 2 shows the time evolution of the OA from the point of view of the bondholder. It can be seen that the OA of the callable issue, BCL, was positive for a large part of the sample, which indicated a few possibilities of exercise that were corroborated by an ED, which was very close to the MD-to-maturity (top line in Panel (a) of Figure 1). As of mid-1996, the OA became negative, at which point the exercise of the call became probable. At the dates, when the bond was traded in 1998, the market took the call exercise for granted. In that period, the ED practically coincided with the MD-to-call (bottom line in Panel (a) of Figure 1). The behavior of the putable bond, TC, was completely different (Panel (b) of Figure 2). From the beginning of the sample, the evolution of interest rates pointed to a probable exercise of the put option, as they were above the coupon rate. The ED in that period was between the two MD limits, i.e., the MD-to-maturity (upper line) and the MD-to-put (lower line). However, as a result of persistent rate falls, from the third quarter of 1996, interest rates were well below the coupon rate and the ED was virtually the same as the MD-to-maturity, so that the early repayment clause was worthless. The put option expired without being exercised, and the bond was redeemed at maturity. In view of the above results, the OA measure and the ED's position with regard to the MD thresholds clearly showed the possibilities to exercise the options embedded in the bonds.

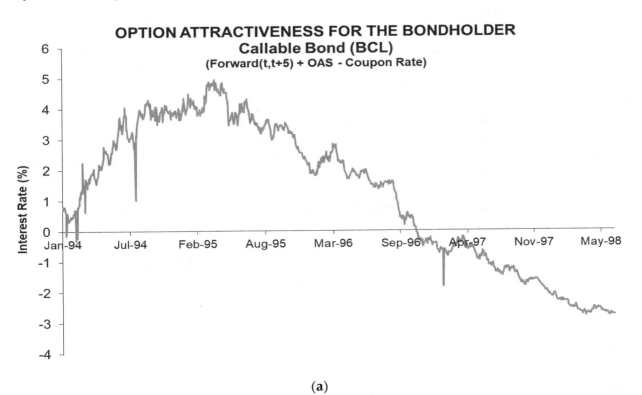

(a)

Figure 2. *Cont.*

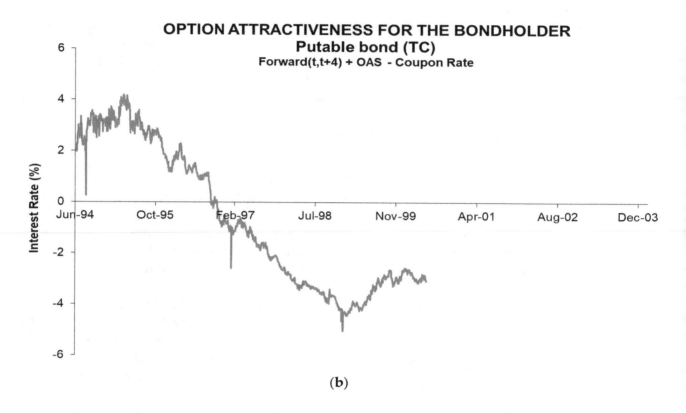

Figure 2. Evolution of the option attractiveness for the bondholder. (**a**) shows the results for the Callable bond (BCL) and (**b**) for the Putable bond (TC).

We represent the EC in Figure 3, and we can see a similar pattern for the results. As in the ED analysis, we estimated two thresholds, between which the EC had to be situated, the convexity until maturity and the convexity until the date of the exercise of the option. However, the phenomenon known as "price compression" made it possible for the EC to occasionally be outside these thresholds. Figure 3a,b shows that in the first few days of trading there was great instability in estimates as a result of the extreme movements in the level and slope of the yield curve. The call option put a ceiling on the price of callable bonds, and the put option put a floor on putable bonds. This ceiling/floor pushed the EC outside the thresholds of convexity calculated for an option-free bond. Another aspect to be highlighted in this analysis was the large differences observed in the estimated EC according to the interest rate model used in its estimation. Logically, these differences had significant implications for risk management of these issues.

Table 2 shows some statistics of the differences in risk management measures calculated using the HL model or from the BDT model. For the callable bond, the HL model provided values of the ED around 0.04 years (about two weeks in terms of working days) higher than those of the BDT model. This difference in ED by using these two models was very similar, regardless of whether it was calculated from variations of ±25 or ±100 bp. The median differences in terms of EC were around 0.24, but the high standard deviations by using the HL and BDT models (i.e., 3.90 and 3.40, respectively) and the high mean values (i.e., 1.49 and 1.67, respectively) indicated that the differences between the two models were significant. In any case, the HL model provided estimates of ED and EC that were always higher than those of the BDT model. For the callable bond, the differences in ED and EC were significantly lower than for the callable bond, and sometimes the EC of the BDT model was slightly higher than that of the HL model. The high volatility of EC estimates was noteworthy.

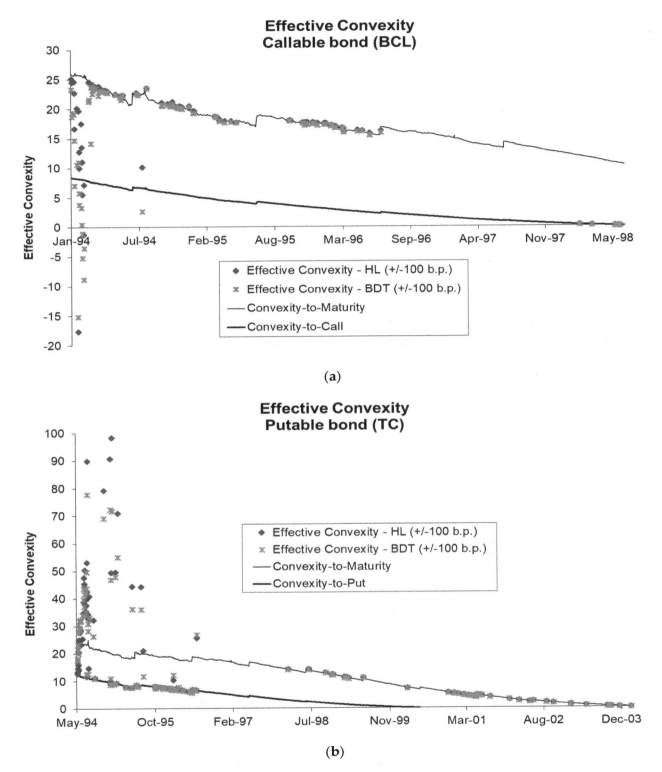

Figure 3. Evolution of the effective convexity (EC) estimated from the HL model and the BDT model. Upper and lower black lines are the convexity-to-maturity and the convexity-to-option. Both lines limit the possible values of the EC according to the expectation of exercising the option. (**a**) shows the results for the Callable bond (BCL) and (**b**) for the Putable bond (TC).

Table 2. Differences between the HL and BDT models in terms of ED, EC, and option price. These differences were calculated as the value of the variable obtained using the HL model minus the value of the variable obtained using the BDT model.

Type of Bond	Differences in ED (the Value Obtained by the HL Model—the Value Obtained by the BDT Model) for a ±25 bp Change in the Yield Curve	Differences in ED (the Value Obtained by the HL Model—the Value Obtained by the BDT Model) for a ±100 bp Change in the Yield Curve	Differences in EC (the Value Obtained by the HL Model) for a ±25 bp Change in the Yield Curve	Differences in EC (the Value Obtained by the HL Model—the Value Obtained by the BDT Model) for a ±100 bp Change in the Yield Curve	Differences in Option Price (the Value Obtained by the HL Model—the Value Obtained by the BDT Model)
Callable bond					
- Average	0.0388	0.0490	1.4863	1.6681	−0.1288
- Median	0.0373	0.0433	0.2307	0.2423	−0.1227
SD	0.0258	0.0362	3.8977	3.3989	0.1274
Putable bond					
- Average	0.0062	0.0268	−0.8147	0.6357	−0.0649
- Median	0.0215	0.0284	0.0906	0.1368	−0.0535
SD	0.0736	0.0511	20.0785	5.0451	0.0463

These results gave rise to different values of the price of the implicit options for both models. In the last column of Table 2, it can be seen how, in median, the BDT model provided prices 12 bp higher than those of the HL model for the call and 5 bp for the put. The price of the option by the BDT model was never below that provided by the HL model.

Finally, the determinants of the differences in the estimation of risk management measures caused by the use of two alternative interest rate models, HL and BDT, when applied to option-embedded bonds were further analyzed. We regressed these differences between models on a number of the proposed determinants related to the shape and time behavior of the term structure of interest rates. Table 3 shows the results.

Table 3. Determinants of the differences between the HL and BDT models in terms of ED and EC obtained for the parallel shift of the yield curve of ±100 bp.

Model	Callable Bond: Difference in ED (the Value Obtained by the HL Model—the Value Obtained by the BDT Model)		Putable Bond: Difference in ED (the Value Obtained by the HL—the Value Obtained by the BDT Model)		Callable Bond: Difference in EC (the Value Obtained by the HL Model—the Value Obtained by the BDT Model)		Putable Bond: Difference in EC (the Value Obtained by the HL Model—the Value Obtained by the BDT Model)	
Intercept	−0.40	(−2.77) ***	0.14	(3.06) ***	−1.50	(−0.73)	8.46	(2.76) ***
Level	3.23	(2.34) **	1.67	(2.55) **	−411.91	(−2.08) **	−444.54	(−1.82) *
Slope	5.44	(1.24)	−0.28	(−0.12)	3028.7	(1.92) *	5130.7	(2.32) **
Curvature	−27.60	(−1.00)	22.72	(1.52)	−0.16	(−0.82)	0.92	(0.98)
Forward	−0.03	(−2.24) **	−0.02	(−1.06)	40.91	(0.74)	−282.17	(−2.97) ***
Volatility	−2.10	(−3.25) ***	−4.78	(−5.23) ***	0.25	(2.48) **	−0.18	(−0.70)
MD	0.05	(4.38) ***	−0.03	(−2.19) **				
Adj. R²	0.3289		0.4536		0.4737		0.2474	
# Observ	106		101		101		101	

This table reports the results of the regressions of the differences between the estimates of ED and EC obtained by the HL and BDT models. Level is the one-month interest rate. Slope is the difference between the one-year interest rate and the three-month rate. Curvature is the difference between the two-year rate and the average of the one- and three-year rates. Forward is the forward interest rate from the exercise date to the maturity date. Volatility is the SD of the interest rate for the remaining term to maturity on each date. MD is the MD-to-maturity. The data set includes actual transactions on these bonds while they are outstanding. The t statistics are based on the Newey–West's estimates of the covariance matrix and are represented in parentheses. *, **, and *** represent significance at the levels of 10%, 5%, and 1%, respectively.

Differences in ED were directly related to the level of interest rates and inversely related to volatility. Thus, the greatest differences between models were observed with high interest rates and calm markets. The choice of one model or another to calculate sensitivity measures for option bonds was particularly relevant in stable interest rate scenarios. The higher the forward, i.e., the interest rate, at which the issuer of the callable bond must be financed if the option is exercised, the lower the chances of exercising the call option and the smaller the differences between the models. In the case of the EC differences, the slope and curvature coefficients were significant in several scenarios, with the slope reducing the differences and the curvature widening them. Again, volatility reduced differences between models, although it was only significant in the case of the putable bond.

7. Discussion

In this paper, we applied two alternative interest rate dynamics models to the pricing of bonds with embedded options and to the estimation of specific interest risk management measures for these bonds with contingent cash flows. The calibration of the models and their use to obtain the ED and EC in real cases throughout the life cycles of these bonds allowed us to perform analyses of their behaviors and explanatory factors.

We obtained evidence that the differences between the measures proposed for option-embedded bonds, ED and EC, and the traditional measures applied for option-free bonds were generated and depended on the probability of exercising the call or put options at each moment. When the option was in the money, the values of ED and EC were less than the duration- and convexity-to-maturity and approximated the duration- and convexity-to-call/put.

The option price mainly depended on the interest rates volatility and the future rates, so we can see that, when Forward (t, T) increased, the call premium decreased and the put premium increased. This happened, because when interest rates were higher than the coupon rate, the put was in the money (the bondholder would sell the bond and acquire another one with higher coupon rate), while the issuer of a bond with a call option would not refinance if the interest rates were above the coupon rate. Interest rate volatility was directly related to the premium of both types of options.

When comparing the interest rate models, the HL and BDT models, we can see that the HL model generated higher values than the BDT model for ED and EC and smaller values than the BDT model for the options. Thus, for the HL model, the DE estimates were the closest to the MD to maturity, because HL option values were the smallest. On the other hand, the differences between models were slightly smaller, when ED and EC were estimated from the shifts of the term structure of interest rates with an amount of ±25 bp. However, the results were much more stable and consistent, when the risk measures were estimated from the shifts of the yield curve of ±100 bp. We can see that the interest rate volatility is the key factor in determining these differences between models. Thus, the higher the volatility of interest rates, the closer the results we obtained with both models. This happened, because the volatility we introduced as an input in the HL Model is the short rate volatility, which is constant for all terms while the BDT model includes the entire term structure of volatilities as an input. Therefore, the choice of the interest rate model for estimating ED and EC and for calculating option prices on bonds with embedded options is especially relevant in stable scenarios of interest rates.

Author Contributions: Conceptualization, A.D. and M.T.; methodology, A.D. and M.T.; software, A.D. and M.T.; validation, A.D. and M.T.; formal analysis, A.D. and M.T.; investigation, A.D. and M.T.; writing of the original draft preparation, A.D. and M.T.; writing of review and editing, A.D. and M.T.; supervision, A.D.; project administration, A.D. All authors have read and agreed to the published version of the manuscript.

Acknowledgments: We gratefully acknowledge guest editors of the Special Issue, comments, and suggestion of the reviewers, the collaboration of the assistant editor, Caitlynn Tong, and the support of Faculty of Law & Social Science, University of Castilla-La Mancha, Spain.

References

1. Ho, T.S.Y.; Lee, S.-B. Term structure movements and pricing interest rate contingent claims. *J. Financ.* **1986**, *41*, 1011–1029. [CrossRef]
2. Black, F.; Derman, E.; Toy, W. A one-factor model of interest rates and its application to Treasury bond options. *Financ. Anal. J.* **1990**, *46*, 33–39. [CrossRef]
3. Vasicek, O.A. An Equilibrium Characterisation of the Term Structure. *J. Financ. Econ.* **1977**, *5*, 177–188. [CrossRef]
4. Cox, J.; Ingersoll, J.; Ross, S. A theory of the term structure of interest rates. *Econometrica* **1985**, *53*, 385–407. [CrossRef]
5. Clelow, L.; Strickland, C. Term Structure Consistent Models. In *Implementing Derivatives Models*; John Wiley and Sons: Chichester, UK, 1998; p. 209.
6. Jamshidian, F. Forward induction and construction of Yield Curve Diffusion Models. *J. Fixed Income* **1991**, *1*, 62–74. [CrossRef]

7.   Skinner, F. Interest Rate Modelling: The Term Structure Consistent Approach. In *Pricing and Hedging Interest and Credit Risk Sensitive Instruments*; Elsevier Science: Burlington, VT, USA, 2005; pp. 110–112.

8.   Nelson, C.; Siegel, A. Parsimonious modelling of yield curves. *J. Bus.* **1987**, *60*, 473–489. [CrossRef]

9.   Díaz, A.; Jareño, F.; Navarro, E. Term structure of volatilities and yield curve estimation methodology. *Quant. Financ.* **2011**, *11*, 573–586. [CrossRef]

10.   Annaert, J.; Claes, A.G.; De Ceuster, M.J.; Zhang, H. Estimating the long rate and its volatility. *Econ. Lett.* **2015**, *129*, 100–102. [CrossRef]

11.   Fabozzi, F.J. Using the Lattice Model to Value Bonds with Embedded Options, Floaters, Options, and Caps/Floors. In *Interest Rate, Term Structure and Valuation Modeling*; John Wiley and Sons: Hoboken, NJ, USA, 2002; pp. 357–378.

12.   Martellini, L.; Priaulet, P.; Priaulet, S. Bond Pricing and Yields. In *Fixed-Income Securities: Valuation, Risk Management and Portfolio Strategies*; John Wiley and Sons: Chichester, UK, 2003; pp. 41–60.

3

An Integral Equation Approach to the Irreversible Investment Problem with a Finite Horizon

Junkee Jeon [1] and Geonwoo Kim [2,*]

[1] Department of Applied Mathematics & Institute of Natural Science, Kyung Hee University, Seoul 01811, Korea; junkeejeon@khu.ac.kr
[2] School of Liberal Arts, Seoul National University of Science and Technology, Seoul 01811, Korea
* Correspondence: geonwoo@seoultech.ac.kr

Abstract: This paper studies an irreversible investment problem under a finite horizon. The firm expands its production capacity in irreversible investments by purchasing capital to increase productivity. This problem is a singular stochastic control problem and its associated Hamilton–Jacobi–Bellman equation is derived. By using a Mellin transform, we obtain the integral equation satisfied by the free boundary of this investment problem. Furthermore, we solve the integral equation numerically using the recursive integration method and present the graph for the free boundary.

Keywords: investment problem; free boundary; Mellin transform; integral equation

1. Introduction

In economics, optimal investment problems have received much attention over the last few decades. In particular, optimal investment problems under uncertainty have been widely studied with the mathematical approaches. Abel and Eberly [1] provided an explicit analytic function for optimal investment under the uncertainty of a firm with costly reversibility. To formulate the investment problem, a constant-return-to-scale Cobb–Douglas production function facing an isoelastic demand curve was considered over infinite time. Eberly and Mieghem [2] showed an optimal investment strategy in a non-stationary case with uncertainty, a concave profit function and a horizon of arbitrary length. Bertola [3] studied an irreversible investment problem under uncertainty with an infinite horizon. In [3], the problem was solved under Cobb–Douglas technology and constant elasticity demand. Dangl [4] investigated an irreversible investment problem when a firm decides on optimal investment timing and optimal capacity choice at the same time under the condition of uncertainty demand. In this paper, we deal with an irreversible investment problem under uncertainty. More specifically, the main contribution of this paper is an efficient derivation of the integral equation for an irreversible investment problem using Mellin transforms.

We consider an optimal irreversible investment problem under uncertainty with a finite horizon. Specifically, we employ the partial differential equation (PDE) approach to solve the problem and derive the integral equation for the free boundary of the investment problem using Mellin transforms. The important advantage of Mellin transforms is that they convert the given PDE into the simple ordinary differential equation (ODE). This leads to closed-form or analytic solutions of the PDEs. Thus, Mellin transforms have been used widely as a relevant tool to handle the PDE in the financial area. In recent years, the diverse options have been studied with Mellin transforms by many researchers (cf. [5–9]). In particular, pricing formulas for vulnerable options under the structural model have been derived using the double Mellin transforms (cf. [10–15]). We also adopt a Mellin transform approach to derive the integral equation for irreversible optimal investment with a finite horizon. The properties of double Mellin transforms are used appropriately to obtain the integral equation for the optimal investment with a finite horizon. This approach induces the integral equation more efficiently.

The remainder of this paper is organized as follows. Section 2 presents a brief literature review on optimal investment problems. In Section 3, we formulate the model for the irreversible investment problem with the production function. In Section 4, we deal with the free boundary problem for the irreversible optimal investment. Concretely, the integral equation for the free boundary (the investment threshold) to maximize firm value is derived by using Mellin transforms. We give the concluding remarks in Section 5.

2. Literature Review

Optimal investment problems have been developed by many researchers. Chiarolla and Haussmann [16] studied an irreversible investment problem in a stochastic, continuous time model over a finite time and obtained the free boundary for optimal stopping problem from a nonlinear integral. Ewald and Wang [17] dealt with an irreversible investment problem under the Cox–Ingersoll–Ross (CIR) model. They showed various advantages of the CIR model. Riedel and Su [18] studied a sequential irreversible investment problem under uncertainty and provided a general approach for irreversible investment problems. Chiarolla, Ferrari and Riedel [19] dealt with a stochastic irreversible investment problem in a market with N firms. Chiarolla and Ferrari [20] and Ferrari [21] also found a new integral equation for the free boundaries of irreversible investment problems on finite and infinite time horizons, respectively. In addition, Ferrari and Salminen [22] studied a general irreversible investment problem under Lévy uncertainty as a two-dimensional, degenerate, singular stochastic control problem. De Angelis, Federico and Ferrari [23] investigated a Markovian model for optimal irreversible investment when a firm aims at minimizing total expected costs of production. More recently, Christensen and Salminen [24] proposed the Riesz representation approach for the efficient study of multidimensional investment problems. Federico, Rosestolato and Tacconi [25] dealt with a model of irreversible investment choices. They characterized an optimal stochastic impulse control problem with an infinite time horizon using techniques of viscosity. Jeon and Kim [26] considered an investment problem with partial reversibility. They derived the coupled integral equations for the optimal investment and solved the equations numerically.

3. The Model

In this paper, we assume that a firm chooses a dynamic capacity expansion plan over a finite horizon $T > 0$. The firm decides on irreversible investments to expand its production capacity to achieve better productivity and its instantaneous profit is given by a constant elasticity function $\Pi(X, K)$ of

$$\Pi(X_t, K_t) = X_t K_t^\gamma, \quad 0 < \gamma < 1, \tag{1}$$

where $(X_s)_{s=t}^T$ is the per-unit profit margin of the output and $(K_s)_{s=t}^T$ is the firm's capital stock process. We model the firm's output function as Q given by

$$Q_t = K_t^\gamma L_t^{1-\gamma} = K_t^\gamma,$$

where we consider the case in which the labor L is constant over time ($L \equiv 1$).

The dynamics of the per-unit profit margin $(X_s)_{s=t}^T$ are governed by geometric Brownian motion

$$dX_s = \mu X_s ds + \sigma X_s dW_s, \quad X_s > 0, \tag{2}$$

where μ and σ are positive constants; $(W_t)_{t=0}^T$ is some standard Brownian motion on a complete probability space $(\Omega, \mathcal{F}, \mathbb{P})$ equipped with a filtration $(\mathcal{F}_t)_{t \geq 0}$ satisfying the usual conditions.

Within the present model, the firm's capital stock process $\{K_s\}$ evolves according to

$$dK_s = dL_s - \delta K_s ds, \tag{3}$$

where $\delta \geq 0$ is a depreciation rate of the firm's capital stock and (L_s) represents the cumulative purchase of capital until time $s \in [t, T]$, which is right-continuous with the left limit, nonnegative and non-decreasing for $\mathcal{F}$-adapted stochastic process with $L_{t-} = 0$.

An irreversible investment policy $(L_s)_{s=t}^{T}$ is called admissible if

$$\mathbb{E}\left[\int_t^T e^{-\beta(s-t)}(X_s ds + dL_s)\right] < +\infty. \tag{4}$$

We denote by $\mathcal{A}_t(x, k)$ with $X_t = x\ K_t = k$ the class of all admissible policies.

The firm's objective is to maximize the following expected utility by choosing the irreversible investment plan $(L_s)_{s=t}^{T}$:

$$V(t, x, k) = \sup_{L \in \mathcal{A}_t} \mathbb{E}\left[\int_t^T e^{-\beta(s-t)}(\Pi(X_s, K_s)ds - pdL_s) \mid X_t = x,\ K_t = k\right], \tag{5}$$

on region $\mathcal{R} = \{(t, x, k) \mid 0 \leq t \leq T,\ 0 < x, k < +\infty\}$, where $\beta > 0$ is a discount factor.

4. Free Boundary Problem

Following Fleming and Soner [27], the associated Hamilton–Jacobi–Bellman (HJB) equation of (5) is given by

$$\min\{-\partial_t V - \mathcal{L}V - \Pi,\ p - \partial_k V\} = 0,\quad V(T, x, k) = 0, \tag{6}$$

with

$$\mathcal{L} = \frac{\sigma^2}{2}x^2\partial_{xx} + \mu x \partial_x - \delta k \partial_k - \beta.$$

From the HJB Equation (6), we can define the investment region and the no-investment region as follows.

$$\begin{aligned}
\mathbf{IR} &= \{(t, x, k) \mid \partial_k V(t, x, k) = p\},\quad \text{(the investment region)}, \\
\mathbf{NR} &= \{(t, x, k) \mid \partial_k V(t, x, k) < p\},\quad \text{(the no-investment region)}.
\end{aligned} \tag{7}$$

Then, the boundary that separates $\mathbf{IR}$ from $\mathbf{NR}$ is referred to as the free boundary, or optimal investment threshold, and is given by

$$B(t, k) = \sup\{x \in \mathbb{R}_+ \mid (t, x, k) \in \mathbf{NR}\}. \tag{8}$$

The investment region and the no-investment region correspond to $x \geq B(t, k)$ and $x < B(t, k)$, respectively. In terms of the free boundary $B(t, k)$, the investment region $\mathbf{IR}$ can be written as

$$\mathbf{IR} = \{(t, x, k) \mid x \geq B(t, k)\}.$$

Moreover, at the free boundary $x = B(t, k)$, the following smooth-pasting condition is established:

$$\partial_k V(t, B(t, k), k) = p \quad \text{and} \quad \partial_{xk} V(t, B(t, k), k) = 0. \tag{9}$$

As in [28], we consider the following substitution

$$z = \frac{x^m}{k}, \quad u(t,z) = V(t,x,k)/k,$$

where $m = 1/(1-\gamma)$.

Under above substitution, the HJB Equation (6) can be reduced to one-dimensional HJB equation

$$\min\{ -\partial_t u - \mathcal{L}^\star u - \Pi^\star, \ p - (u - z\partial_z u)\} = 0, \quad u(T,z) = 0, \tag{10}$$

where

$$\hat{\mu} = \mu m + m(m-1)\sigma^2/2,$$
$$\mathcal{L}^\star = \frac{\sigma^2 m^2}{2} z^2 \partial_{zz} + (\hat{\mu} + \delta)z\partial_z - (\beta + \delta) \quad \text{and} \quad \Pi^\star(z) = z^{1-\gamma}. \tag{11}$$

In terms of the value function $u(t,z)$, the investment region $\widetilde{\mathbf{IR}}$ and the no-investment region $\widetilde{\mathbf{NR}}$ are defined by

$$\begin{aligned}\widetilde{\mathbf{IR}} &= \{(t,z) \mid u(t,z) - \partial_z u(t,z) = p\} \\ &= \{(t,z) \mid 0 \leq t < T, \ z \geq B^\star(t)\},\end{aligned}$$

and

$$\begin{aligned}\widetilde{\mathbf{NR}} &= \{(t,z) \mid u(t,z) - \partial_z u(t,z) < p\} \\ &= \{(t,z) \mid 0 \leq t < T, \ z < B^\star(t)\},\end{aligned}$$

respectively.

Here, the free boundary $B^\star(t)$ is given by

$$B^\star(t) = \frac{B(t,k)^m}{k}.$$

Let us define the function $H(t,z)$ as

$$H(t,z) \equiv u(t,z) - z\partial_z u(t,z).$$

In investment region $\widetilde{\mathbf{IR}}$,

$$H(t,z) = p.$$

In no-investment region $\widetilde{\mathbf{NR}}$, since

$$\partial_t u + \mathcal{L}^\star u + z^{1-\gamma} = 0,$$

It is easy to check that

$$\partial_t H + \mathcal{L}^\star H + \gamma z^{1-\gamma} = 0.$$

Thus, $H(t,z)$ satisfies the following non-homogeneous PDE.

$$\begin{aligned}&\partial_t H + \mathcal{L}^\star H + \gamma z^{1-\gamma}\mathbf{1}_{\{z < B^\star(t)\}} + p(\beta + \delta)\mathbf{1}_{\{z \geq B^\star(t)\}} = 0, \\ &H(T,z) = 0.\end{aligned} \tag{12}$$

with the smooth-pasting condition $H(t, B^\star(t)) = p$.

Proposition 1. *The value function $H(t,z)$ can be expressed by*

$$
H(t,z) = p(\beta + \delta) \int_t^T e^{-M_1(\eta - t)} \mathcal{N}\left(\frac{\log \frac{z}{B^\star(\eta)} + (\hat{\mu} + \delta - \frac{1}{2}\sigma^2 m^2)(\eta - t)}{\sigma m \sqrt{\eta - t}}\right) d\eta
$$

$$
+ \gamma z^{1-\gamma} \int_t^T e^{-M_2(\eta - t)} \mathcal{N}\left(-\frac{\log \frac{z}{B^\star(\eta)} + (\beta + \delta - \gamma\sigma^2 m^2 + \frac{1}{2}\sigma^2 m^2)(\eta - t)}{\sigma m \sqrt{\eta - t}}\right) d\eta,
$$

(13)

and the free boundary $B^\star(t)$ satisfies the following integral equation:

$$
p = p(\beta + \delta) \int_t^T e^{-M_1(\eta - t)} \mathcal{N}\left(\frac{\log \frac{B^\star(t)}{B^\star(\eta)} + (\hat{\mu} + \delta - \frac{1}{2}\sigma^2 m^2)(\eta - t)}{\sigma m \sqrt{\eta - t}}\right) d\eta
$$

$$
+ \gamma(B^\star(t))^{1-\gamma} \int_t^T e^{-M_2(\eta - t)} \mathcal{N}\left(-\frac{\log \frac{B^\star(t)}{B^\star(\eta)} + (\beta + \delta - \gamma\sigma^2 m^2 + \frac{1}{2}\sigma^2 m^2)(\eta - t)}{\sigma m \sqrt{\eta - t}}\right) d\eta,
$$

(14)

where $\mathcal{N}(\cdot)$ is standard normal cumulative distribution function and the constants M_1 and M_2 are defined by

$$
M_1 = \beta + \delta, \; M_2 = \beta + \delta - (1 - \gamma)(\hat{\mu} + \delta - \frac{1}{2}\sigma^2 m^2) - \frac{1}{2}(1-\gamma)^2\sigma^2 m^2.
$$

Proof. Let us define
$$
f(t,z) = \gamma z^{1-\gamma} \mathbf{1}_{\{z < B^\star(t)\}} + p(\beta + \delta)\mathbf{1}_{\{z \geq B^\star(t)\}}.
$$

Then, from the PDE (12), we have
$$
\partial_t H + \mathcal{L}^\star H = -f(t,z),
$$
$$
H(T,z) = 0.
$$

(15)

Let us consider the Mellin transform $\hat{H}(t,w)$ of $H(t,z)$; then
$$
\hat{H}(t,w) = \int_0^\infty H(t,z)z^{w-1}dz.
$$

By the inverse Mellin transform,
$$
H(t,z) = \frac{1}{2\pi i}\int_{c-i\infty}^{c+i\infty} \hat{H}(t,w)z^{-w}dw.
$$

(16)

From (16) and (15), the PDE (15) can be represented by
$$
\frac{d\hat{H}}{dt} + \frac{\sigma^2 m^2}{2}\mathcal{Q}(w)\hat{H} = \hat{f}(t,w),
$$
$$
\mathcal{Q}(w) = w^2 + (1 - k_2)w - k_1, \; \text{and} \; k_1 = \frac{2(\beta + \delta)}{\sigma^2 m^2}, \; k_2 = \frac{2(\hat{\mu} + \delta)}{\sigma^2 m^2},
$$

(17)

where the terminal condition is $\hat{H}(T,z) = 0$ and $\hat{f}(t,w)$ is the Mellin transform of $f(t,z)$.
Then, we can obtain the solution for the non-homogeneous ODE (17) as

$$
\hat{H}(t,w) = \int_t^T e^{\frac{\sigma^2 m^2}{2}\mathcal{Q}(w)(\eta - t)}\hat{f}(\eta, w)d\eta.
$$

(18)

Hence, from (16),

$$H(t,z) = \frac{1}{2\pi i} \int_{c-i\infty}^{c+i\infty} \int_t^T e^{\frac{\sigma^2 m^2}{2} \mathcal{Q}(w)(\eta-t)} \hat{f}(\eta,w) z^{-w} \, d\eta \, dw. \tag{19}$$

Meanwhile, if we define

$$\mathcal{G}(t,z) := \frac{1}{2\pi i} \int_{c-i\infty}^{c+\infty} e^{\frac{\sigma^2 m^2}{2} \mathcal{Q}(w)t} z^{-w} \, dw, \tag{20}$$

then from Lemma 1 in [6], $\mathcal{G}(t,z)$ leads to

$$\mathcal{G}(t,z) = e^{-\frac{\sigma^2 m^2}{2}\{\left(\frac{1-k_2}{2}\right)^2 + k_1\}t} \frac{z^{\frac{1-k_1}{2}}}{\sigma m \sqrt{2\pi t}} e^{-\frac{1}{2}(\log z/(\sigma m \sqrt{t}))^2}. \tag{21}$$

Since $e^{\frac{\sigma^2 m^2}{2} \mathcal{Q}(w)(\eta-t)}$ and $\hat{f}(\eta,w)$ are the Mellin transforms of $\mathcal{G}(\eta-t,z)$ and $f(\eta,z)$, by the Mellin convolution property in [6], $H(t,z)$ yields

$$\begin{aligned}
H(t,z) &= \int_t^T \int_0^\infty f(\eta,u) \mathcal{G}(\eta-t,\frac{z}{u}) \frac{du}{u} \, d\eta \\
&= \int_t^T \int_{B^\star(\eta)}^\infty p(\beta+\delta) \mathcal{G}(\eta-t,\frac{z}{u}) \frac{du}{u} \, d\eta + \gamma \int_t^T \int_0^{B^\star(\eta)} u^{1-\gamma} \mathcal{G}(\eta-t,\frac{z}{u}) \frac{du}{u} \, d\eta.
\end{aligned} \tag{22}$$

By Appendix A, we can obtain

$$\begin{aligned}
H(t,z) = {} &p(\beta+\delta) \int_t^T e^{-M_1(\eta-t)} \mathcal{N}\left(\frac{\log \frac{z}{B^\star(\eta)} + (\hat{\mu} + \delta - \frac{1}{2}\sigma^2 m^2)(\eta-t)}{\sigma m \sqrt{\eta-t}} \right) d\eta \\
&+ \gamma z^{1-\gamma} \int_t^T e^{-M_2(\eta-t)} \mathcal{N}\left(-\frac{\log \frac{z}{B^\star(\eta)} + (\beta + \delta - \gamma\sigma^2 m^2 + \frac{1}{2}\sigma^2 m^2)(\eta-t)}{\sigma m \sqrt{\eta-t}} \right) d\eta.
\end{aligned} \tag{23}$$

By smooth-pasting condition, we have

$$\begin{aligned}
p = {} &p(\beta+\delta) \int_t^T e^{-M_1(\eta-t)} \mathcal{N}\left(\frac{\log \frac{B^\star(t)}{B^\star(\eta)} + (\hat{\mu} + \delta - \frac{1}{2}\sigma^2 m^2)(\eta-t)}{\sigma m \sqrt{\eta-t}} \right) d\eta \\
&+ \gamma(B^\star(t))^{1-\gamma} \int_t^T e^{-M_2(\eta-t)} \mathcal{N}\left(-\frac{\log \frac{B^\star(t)}{B^\star(\eta)} + (\beta + \delta - \gamma\sigma^2 m^2 + \frac{1}{2}\sigma^2 m^2)(\eta-t)}{\sigma m \sqrt{\eta-t}} \right) d\eta.
\end{aligned} \tag{24}$$

$\square$

Proposition 2. *When time to maturity $T-t$ goes to zero, the free boundary $B^\star(t)$ goes to infinity; i.e.,*

$$\lim_{t\to T-} B^\star(t) = +\infty.$$

Proof. In Proposition 1, $B^\star(t)$ can be represented by

$$\gamma(B^\star(t))^{1-\gamma} = \frac{p - p(\beta+\delta) \int_t^T e^{-M_1(\eta-t)} \mathcal{N}\left(\frac{\log \frac{B^\star(t)}{B^\star(\eta)} + (\hat{\mu} + \delta - \frac{1}{2}\sigma^2)(\eta-t)}{\sigma m \sqrt{\eta-t}} \right) d\eta}{\int_t^T e^{-M_2(\eta-t)} \mathcal{N}\left(-\frac{\log \frac{B^\star(t)}{B^\star(\eta)} + (\beta + \delta - \gamma\sigma^2 m^2 + \frac{1}{2}\sigma^2 m^2)(\eta-t)}{\sigma m \sqrt{\eta-t}} \right) d\eta}. \tag{25}$$

Letting $t \to T-$, we obtain that $B^{\star}(t) \to +\infty$. $\quad\square$

By using recursive integration method proposed by [29], we solve numerically the integral Equations (14) for free boundary $B^{\star}(t)$ and the value function $H(t,z)$, respectively.

From the substitution

$$z = \frac{x^m}{k}, \quad u(t,z) = V(t,x,k)/k,$$

we can obtain the following theorem.

Theorem 1. *The investment that maximizes value of firm is characterized by the investment threshold* $B(t,k)$ *satisfying*

$$
\begin{aligned}
p =& p(\beta + \delta) \int_t^T e^{-M_1(\eta - t)} \mathcal{N} \left(\frac{\log\left(\frac{B(t,k)}{B(\eta,k)}\right)^m + (\hat{\mu} + \delta - \frac{1}{2}\sigma^2 m^2)(\eta - t)}{\sigma m \sqrt{\eta - t}} \right) d\eta \\
&+ \frac{B(t,k)}{K^m} \int_t^T e^{-M_2(\eta - t)} \mathcal{N} \left(-\frac{\log\left(\frac{B(t,k)}{B(\eta,k)}\right)^m + (\beta + \delta - \gamma\sigma^2 m^2 + \frac{1}{2}\sigma^2 m^2)(\eta - t)}{\sigma m \sqrt{\eta - t}} \right) d\eta.
\end{aligned}
\tag{26}
$$

Moreover, the marginal valuation of capital, $\partial_k V(t,x,k)$, *is given by*

$$
\begin{aligned}
\partial_k V(t,x,k) =& p(\beta + \delta)k \int_t^T e^{-M_1(\eta - t)} \mathcal{N} \left(\frac{\log\left(\frac{x}{B(\eta,k)}\right)^m + (\hat{\mu} + \delta - \frac{1}{2}\sigma^2 m^2)(\eta - t)}{\sigma m \sqrt{\eta - t}} \right) d\eta \\
&+ xk^{\gamma} \int_t^T e^{-M_2(\eta - t)} \mathcal{N} \left(-\frac{\log\left(\frac{x}{B(\eta,k)}\right)^m + (\beta + \delta - \gamma\sigma^2 m^2 + \frac{1}{2}\sigma^2 m^2)(\eta - t)}{\sigma m \sqrt{\eta - t}} \right) d\eta,
\end{aligned}
\tag{27}
$$

The two regions **IR** and **NR** are rewritten as

$$
\begin{aligned}
\mathbf{IR} &= \{(t,x,k) \mid x^m/k \geq B^{\star}(t)\}, \quad \text{(the investment region)}, \\
\mathbf{NR} &= \{(t,x,k) \mid 0 < x^m/k < B^{\star}(t)\}, \quad \text{(the no-investment region)}.
\end{aligned}
\tag{28}
$$

By the Skorohod lemma (For more details, see [30]), the optimal processes K^* and L^* can be characterized as follows:

Corollary 1. *Given any initial state variable* $X_t = x \geq 0$ *and free boundary* $B^{\star}$, *there exists a unique adapted process* K^*, *a non-decreasing process* L^*, *right-continuous,* $L^*_{t-} = 0$, *satisfying the Skorohod problem* $\mathcal{S}(x,k,B^{\star}(t))$:

$$
\begin{aligned}
dX_s &= \mu X_s ds + \sigma X_s dW_s, \quad X_t = x > 0, \; s \in (t,T), \\
dK_s^* &= dL_s^* - \delta K_s^* ds, \quad K_t^* = k > 0, \; s \in (t,T), \\
\int_t^T & \mathbf{1}_{\{(X_s, K_s^*) \in \mathbf{NR}\}} dL_s^* = 0.
\end{aligned}
\tag{29}
$$

Moreover, if $(X_s, K_s^*) \in \mathbf{NR}$, *then* L^* *is continuous. When* $(X_s, K_s^*) \in \mathbf{IR}$, $L_0^* = x^m/B^{\star}(t) - k$.

Corollary 1 means that if the initial (x,k) lies in **IR**, it jumps immediately to the non-investment region NI by increasing the process L^*. Moreover, the optimal firm's capital stock K^* is a regulator such that $(X_s^*, K_s^*) \in \mathbf{NR}$ for any $s \in (t,T)$ by adjusting the cumulative purchase process L^*. As shown in Figure 1, the level of firm's capital stock process K^* stays constant ($\delta = 0$) while the process X^m/K^*

lies inside **NR**. On the other hand, the cumulative purchase L^* jump up if and only if the process X^m/K^* hits the free boundary B^*.

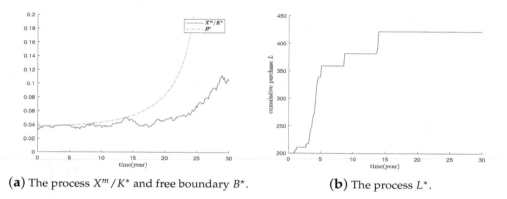

(**a**) The process X^m/K^* and free boundary B^*.   (**b**) The process L^*.

Figure 1. Simulation of the processes X^m/K^* and L^*. The base parameters are as follows: $x = 40$, $k = 200$, $T = 30$, $\mu = 0.1$, $\beta = 0.08$, $\delta = 0$, $\sigma = 0.2$, $\gamma = 0.5$ and $p = 1$.

5. Concluding Remarks

In this paper, we studied an irreversible optimal investment problem with the finite horizon. To model the optimal invest problem, there have been many approaches—a stochastic control problem, dynamic programming techniques, the Bank–El Karoui representation theorem, etc. Among them, we consider the HJB equation as a singular stochastic control problem. In fact, in the mathematical economic literature, the singular stochastic control problems have been often used the irreversible optimal investment problem under an uncertain environment (See [16,18,21,23]). We dealt with a free boundary problem arising from the irreversible investment problem using the HJB equation.

We derived the integral equation for optimal irreversible investment with a finite horizon by the PDE approach. The dynamic capacity production of the firm was assumed to follow a geometric Brownian motion (GBM) process, and the Cobb–Douglas production function was used for the operating profit of the firm. To obtain the integral equation from the PDE for optimal investment, we used the Mellin transforms. The integral equation derived from the PDE was solved by using the recursive integration method. In other words, we solved numerically the integral equation for optimal irreversible investment. We also provided the graph to illustrate the movements of free boundaries for optimal investment with respect to time to maturity.

Author Contributions: Conceptualization, G.K.; formal analysis, J.J.; methodology, J.J.; visualization, J.J.; writing–original draft, G.K. All authors have read and agreed to the published version of the manuscript.

Appendix A. Supplement of Proposition 1

From (21), we have

$$\int_0^b u^{-\alpha}\mathcal{G}\left(t,\frac{z}{u}\right)\frac{1}{u}du = z^{-\alpha}e^{-\frac{1}{2}\{k_1-(1-k_2)\alpha-\alpha^2\}\sigma^2 m^2 t}\mathcal{N}\left(\frac{-\log\frac{z}{b}+\left(\frac{1-k_2}{2}+\alpha\right)\sigma^2 m^2 t}{\sigma m\sqrt{t}}\right),$$

$$\int_b^\infty u^{-\alpha}\mathcal{G}\left(t,\frac{z}{u}\right)\frac{1}{u}du = z^{-\alpha}e^{-\frac{1}{2}\{k_1-(1-k_2)\alpha-\alpha^2\}\sigma^2 m^2 t}\mathcal{N}\left(\frac{\log\frac{z}{b}-\left(\frac{1-k_2}{2}+\alpha\right)\sigma^2 m^2 t}{\sigma m\sqrt{t}}\right),$$

where α is any real number, $\mathcal{G}(t,y)$ is the kernel function and $\mathcal{N}(\cdot)$ is a cumulative distribution function of standard normal distribution.

Proof. If we use the transformation $w = \log(z/u)$, we have

$$\int_0^b u^{-\alpha} \mathcal{G}\left(t, \frac{z}{u}\right) \frac{1}{u} du$$

$$= \int_0^b u^{-\alpha} e^{-\frac{1}{2}\left\{\left(\frac{1-k_2}{2}\right)^2 + k_1\right\}\sigma^2 m^2 t} \cdot \frac{\left(\frac{z}{u}\right)^{\frac{1-k_2}{2}}}{\sigma m \sqrt{2\pi t}} e^{-\frac{1}{2}\left(\frac{\log(z/u)}{\sigma\sqrt{t}}\right)^2} \frac{1}{u} du$$

$$= -z^{-\alpha} e^{-\frac{1}{2}\left\{\left(\frac{1-k_2}{2}\right)^2 + k_1\right\}\sigma^2 m^2 t} \int_\infty^{\log\frac{z}{b}} e^{\alpha w} \frac{e^{\left(\frac{1-k_2}{2}\right)w}}{\sigma m \sqrt{2\pi t}} e^{-\frac{1}{2}\frac{w^2}{\sigma^2 m^2 t}} dw$$

$$= -z^{-\alpha} e^{-\frac{1}{2}\left\{\left(\frac{1-k_2}{2}\right)^2 + k_1 - \left(\frac{1-k_2}{2}+\alpha\right)^2\right\}\sigma^2 m^2 t} \int_\infty^{\log\frac{z}{b}} \frac{1}{\sigma m \sqrt{2\pi t}} \exp\left\{-\frac{1}{2}\left(\frac{w - \sigma^2 m^2 t\left(\frac{1-k_2}{2}+\alpha\right)}{\sigma m \sqrt{t}}\right)^2\right\} dw$$

$$= z^{-\alpha} e^{-\frac{1}{2}\left\{k_1 - (1-k_2)\alpha - \alpha^2\right\}\sigma^2 m^2 t} \mathcal{N}\left(\frac{-\log\frac{z}{b} + \sigma^2 m^2 t\left(\frac{1-k_2}{2}+\alpha\right)}{\sigma\sqrt{t}}\right),$$

In a similar way, we obtain

$$\int_b^\infty u^{-\alpha} \mathcal{G}\left(t, \frac{z}{u}\right) \frac{1}{u} du = z^{-\alpha} e^{-\frac{1}{2}\left\{k_1 - (1-k_2)\alpha - \alpha^2\right\}\sigma^2 m^2 t} \mathcal{N}\left(\frac{\log\frac{z}{b} - \left(\frac{1-k_2}{2}+\alpha\right)\sigma^2 m^2 t}{\sigma m \sqrt{t}}\right).$$

$\square$

References

1. Abel, A.B.; Eberly, J.C. Optimal investment with costly reversibility. *Rev. Econom. Stud.* **1996**, *63*, 581–593. [CrossRef]
2. Eberly, J.C.; Mieghem, J. A. V. Multi-factor Dynamic Investment under Uncertainty. *J. Econ. Theory* **1997**, *75*, 345–387. [CrossRef]
3. Bertola, G. Irreversible investment. *Res. Econ.* **1998**, *52*, 3–37. [CrossRef]
4. Dangl, T. Investment and capacity choice under uncertain demand. *Eur. J. Oper. Res.* **1999**, *117*, 415–428. [CrossRef]
5. Frontczak, R.; Schöbel, R. On modified Mellin transforms, Gauss-Laguerre quadrature, and the valuation of American call options. *J. Comput. Appl. Math.* **2010**, *234*, 1559–1571. [CrossRef]
6. Yoon, J.H. Mellin transform method for European option pricing with Hull-White stochastic interest rate. *J. Appl. Math.* **2017**, *2017*, 759562. [CrossRef]
7. Jeon, J.; Han, H.; Kim, H.U.; Kang, M. An integral equation representation approach for Russian options with finite time horizon. *Commun. Nonlinear Sci.* **2016**, *36*, 496–516. [CrossRef]
8. Jeon, J.; Yoon, J.H. Pricing external-chained barrier options with exponential barriers. *Bull. Korean Math. Soc.* **2016**, *53*, 1497–1530. [CrossRef]
9. Jeon, J.; Han, H.; Kang, M. Valuing American floating strike lookback option and Neumann problem for inhomogeneous Black-scholes equation. *J. Comput. Appl. Math.* **2017**, *313*, 218–234. [CrossRef]
10. Yoon, J.H.; Kim, J-H. The pricing of vulnerable options with double Mellin transforms. *J. Math. Anal. Appl.* **2015**, *422*, 838–857. [CrossRef]
11. Jeon, J.; Yoon, J.H.; Kang, M. Valuing vulnerable geometric Asian options. *Comput. Math. Appl.* **2016**, *71*, 676–691. [CrossRef]
12. Kim, G.; Koo, E. Closed-form pricing formula for exchange option with credit risk. *Chaos Soliton Fract.* **2016**, *91*, 221–227. [CrossRef]

13. Jeon, J.; Yoon, J.H.; Kang, M. Pricing vulnerable path-dependent options using integral transforms. *J. Comput. Appl. Math.* **2017**, *313*, 259–272. [CrossRef]

14. Jeon, J.; Kim, G. Pricing of vulnerable options with early counterparty credit risk. *N. Am. J. Econ. Financ.* **2019**, *47*, 645–656. [CrossRef]

15. Jeon, J.; Choi, S.Y.; Yoon, J.H. Analytic valuation of European continuous-installment barrier options. *J. Comput. Appl. Math.* **2020**, *363*, 392–412. [CrossRef]

16. Chiarolla, M.B.; Haussmann, U.G. On a Stochastic, Irreversible Investment Problem. *SIAM J. Control Optim.* **2009**, *48*, 438–462. [CrossRef]

17. Ewald, C.-O.; Wang, W.-K. Irreversible investment with Cox-Ingersoll-Ross type mean reversion. *Math. Soc. Sci.* **2010**, *59*, 314–318. [CrossRef]

18. Riedel, F.; Su, X. On irreversible investment. *Financ. Stoch.* **2011**, *15*, 607–633. [CrossRef]

19. Chiarolla, M.; Ferrari, G.; Riedel, F. Generalized Kuhn–Tucker conditions for n-firm stochastic irreversible investment under limited resources. *SIAM J. Control Optim.* **2013**, *51*, 3863–3885. [CrossRef]

20. Chiarolla, M.; Ferrari, G. Identifying the free boundary of a stochastic, irreversible investment problem via the BankEl Karoui representation theorem. *SIAM J. Control Optim.* **2014**, *52*, 1048–1070. [CrossRef]

21. Ferrari, G. On an integral equation for the free-boundary of stochastic, irreversible investment problems. *Ann. Appl. Probab.* **2015**, *25*, 150–176. [CrossRef]

22. Ferrari, G.; Salminen, P. Irreversible investment under Lévy uncertainty: An equation for the optimal boundary. *Adv. Appl. Probab.* **2016**, *48*, 298–314. [CrossRef]

23. Angelis, T. D.; Federico, S.; Ferrari, G. Optimal Boundary Surface for Irreversible Investment with Stochastic Costs. *Math. Oper. Res.* **2017**, *42*, 1135–1161. [CrossRef]

24. Christensen, S.; Salminen, P. Multidimensional investment problem. *Math. Financ. Econ.* **2018**, *12*, 75–95. [CrossRef]

25. Federico, S.; Rosestolato, M.; Tacconi, E. Irreversible investment with fixed adjustment costs: A stochastic impulse control approach. *Math. Financ. Econ.* **2019**, *13*, 579–616. [CrossRef]

26. Jeon, J.; Kim, G. An integral equation approach for optimal investment policies with partial reversibility. *Chaos Soliton Fract.* **2019**, *125*, 73–78. [CrossRef]

27. Fleming, W.H.; Soner, H.M. *Controlled Markov Processes and Viscosity Solutions*; Springer: New York, NY, USA, 2006.

28. Guo X.; Miao, J.; Morellec, E. Irreversible investment with regime shifts. *J. Econ. Theory* **2005**, *122*, 37–59. [CrossRef]

29. Huang, J.; Subrahmanyam, M.; Yu, G. Pricing and hedging American options: A recursive integration method. *Rev. Financ. Stud.* **1996**, *9*, 277–300. [CrossRef]

30. Lions, P.L.; Snitaman, A.S. Stochastic differential equations with reflecting boundary conditions. *Commun. Pure Appl. Math.* **1984**, *37*, 511–537. [CrossRef]

4

Equilibria and Stability of One Class of Positive Dynamic Systems with Entropy Operator: Application to Investment Dynamics Modeling

Yuri S. Popkov [1,2,3]

[1] Federal Research Center "Computer Science and Control" of Russian Academy of Sciences, 119333 Moscow, Russia; popkov@isa.ru

[2] Institute of Control Sciences of Russian Academy of Sciences, 117997 Moscow, Russia

[3] Department of Software Engineering, ORT Braude College, 216100 Karmiel, Israel

Abstract: Dynamical systems with entropy operator (DSEO) form a special class of dynamical systems whose nonlinear properties are described by the perturbed mathematical programming problem with entropy objective functions. A subclass of DSEO is the system with positive state coordinates (PDSEO), which are used as mathematical models of the spatiotemporal evolution of demographic and economic processes, dynamic image restoration procedures in computer tomography and machine learning. A mathematical model of the PDSEO with a connectivity parameter characterizing the influence of the entropy operator on the dynamic properties of the system is constructed. PDSEO can have positive stationary states of various classes depending on the number of positive components in the state vector. Classes with p positive components of the state vector ($p \leq n$, where n is the order of the system) are considered. The framework of formal power series and the method of successive approximations for the formation of existence conditions of stationary states are developed. The conditions of existence are obtained in the form of relations between the parameters of the system. We used the method of differential Bellman inequalities to study the stability of classes of stationary states in a limited region of phase space. The parametric conditions of instability of the zero stationary state and p positive stationary states depending on the connectivity parameter are obtained. The framework of formal power series and the method of successive approximations for the formation of existence conditions and classification of stationary states are developed. The stability conditions "in large" stationary states are obtained, based on the method of differential Bellman inequalities. The developed methods of existence, classification and stability are illustrated by the analysis of the dynamic properties of the economic model with stochastic investment exchange. Positive stationary states characterize the profitability of economic subsystems. The conditions of profitability and their stability for all subsystems in the system and their various groups are obtained.

Keywords: equilibrium; stability; entropy; entropy operator; investment exchange; profitable states; connective index; differential inequalities; formal series

1. Introduction

Dynamic systems with an entropy operator are widely used for mathematical modeling of real processes. Apparently, research in this field was pioneered by A.J. Wilson [1], who suggested a thermodynamic approach to the mathematical modeling of transport and regional systems based on the hypothesis about the random nature of exchange processes and the existence of a stationary state that maximizes entropy. This approach turned out to be very fruitful, as is indicated by a large number of publications in which it was applied and further developed for modeling of macro systems [2], entropy restoration of tomographic images [3–5], demoeconomic modeling [6], machine learning [7] and others.

Of particular interest are dynamic processes with positive states. For their study, a fundamental principle of statistical thermodynamics—the principle of local equilibria—was developed. In accordance with this principle, a dynamic system is assumed to have "fast" and "slow" processes. A "fast" process is considered a sequence of locally stationary states that correspond to a "slow" process. There are many examples of such processes, but the main difficulties are connected with mathematical modeling of a "fast" process, i.e., with the description of a sequence of locally stationary states. The first idea introduced in [8] was to describe a "fast" process in terms of the local maximum of entropy that depends on the state of a corresponding "slow" process. This approach turned out to be very fruitful as well, and it was successfully applied in many problems, such as population dynamics modeling [9], the spatiotemporal development of settlements [10–12] and the dynamic entropy-based procedures of image restoration [13].

The integration of dynamic models of a "slow" process with entropy maximization models describing the locally stationary states of a "fast" process actually formed a new class of dynamic systems with the entropy operator (DSEO) [14]. Generally, the entropy operator in these systems was described by a perturbed mathematical programming problem with entropy objective functions that characterized the mapping of the state space of a "slow" process into the state space of a "fast" process. In most applications of positive dynamic systems with the entropy operator (PDSEO), the models of entropy operators of simpler form were used; namely, the ones described by perturbed problems of constrained entropy maximization. For this class of entropy operators, the conditions of existence, continuity, differentiation, and boundedness were obtained [15]. The Lipschitz constant is an important characteristic of an entropy operator that determines the dynamic properties of PDSEO. In [16,17], a linear majorant method was proposed and some estimates of the Lipschitz constant for the Fermi entropy operator were derived.

This paper is dedicated to the study of positive dynamic systems with the Boltzmann-type entropy operator and constraints on "fast" variables. The properties of a system are analyzed depending on the degree of influence of the entropy operator on them, which is characterized by the connectivity index. A method for calculating stationary positive states is developed and all such states are classified. Parametric conditions for the existence of positive stationary states and their stability in large are established. The proposed methods are used to study stationary states and their stability in an economic system that exchanges investments.

2. Positive Dynamic System with Entropy Operator

Positive dynamic systems are characterized by the state vector with nonnegative components. A subclass of such systems consists of positive dynamic systems with an entropy operator (PDSEO). The structural diagram of a PDSEO can be seen in Figure 1.

It includes three feedback loops with autonomous integrators as follows. One of them is the feedback loop by the state vector $\mathbf{y} \in R_+^n$ with the multiplying block $\mathbb{M}$; the other contains a nonlinear vector function $\mathbf{L}(\mathbf{y})$ with components $L_1(y_1), \ldots, L_n(y_n)$; the third feedback loop incorporates an entropy operator $\mathcal{H}[\mathbf{y}] = X_*(\mathbf{y})$, where X_* is a nonnegative matrix of dimensions $(n \times n)$. The block $\mathbb{S}$ calculates the so-called **s**-*decrement* of the matrix X_*, i.e., the difference between its column and row sums. The degree of influence of the entropy operator on the dynamic properties of the system is characterized by the *connectivity index* μ.

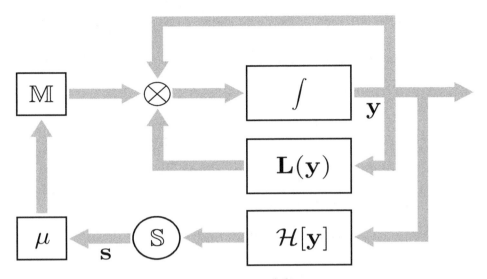

Figure 1. Functional diagram.

The PDSEO under study is described by Equation [11]

$$\dot{\mathbf{y}} = \mathbf{y} \otimes [\mathbf{L}(\mathbf{y}) + \mu \mathbf{s}(\mathbf{y})], \qquad \mathbf{L}(\mathbf{y}) = \{L_i(y_i) \,|\, i = \overline{1,n}\}$$
$$\mathbf{s}(\mathbf{y}) = \left(X_*^{\mathsf{T}}(\mathbf{y}) - X_*(\mathbf{y})\right)\mathbf{e}, \qquad \mathbf{e} = \{1,\dots,1\} \in R^n$$
$$\mathcal{H}[\mathbf{y}] = X_*(\mathbf{y}) = \arg\max\{H(X) \,|\, 0 \le X \le C(\mathbf{y})\} \tag{1}$$
$$H(X) = -\operatorname{tr}(X\, X_{ln}),$$

with the following notations: $\operatorname{tr}(\bullet)$ as the trace of a matrix $\bullet$; X_{ln} as a matrix of dimensions $(n \times n)$ with elements $\ln\frac{x_{ij}}{\tilde{v}_{ij}}$; $\tilde{v}_{ij} \in [0,1]$ and $\sum_{j=1}^{n} \tilde{v}_{ij} = 1$, $i = \overline{1,n}$, as parameters; finally, $C(\mathbf{y})$ as a matrix of dimensions $(n \times n)$ with elements $c_{ij}(\mathbf{y})$.

Let us write system (1) in a more convenient form. Consider an entropy operator $\mathcal{H}(\mathbf{y})$ described by a perturbed mathematical programming problem: maximize the Boltzmann information entropy [2] on the nonnegative polyhedron $0 \le X \le C(\mathbf{y})$. This problem can be simplified, i.e., reduced to an unconstrained maximization problem by passing to the entropy function

$$\tilde{H}(X) = -\operatorname{tr}\left\{(X\, X_{ln}) + [(C(\mathbf{y}) - X)(C(\mathbf{y}) - X)_{ln}]\right\}. \tag{2}$$

The entropy function (2) structurally resembles the Fermi informational entropy [2]. As is easily observed, this function is defined on the above polyhedron, meaning that its absolute maximum belongs to the latter:

$$X_*(\mathbf{y}) = \arg\max \tilde{H}(X). \tag{3}$$

In accordance with (2), the elements of the matrix $X_*(\mathbf{y})$ have the form

$$x_{ij}^*(\mathbf{y}) = v_{ij}c_{ij}(\mathbf{y}), \qquad v_{ij} = \frac{\tilde{v}_{ij}}{1 + \tilde{v}_{ij}}. \tag{4}$$

The vector of the **s**-decrement of the matrix X_* consists of the components

$$s_i(\mathbf{y}) = \sum_{j=1}^{n} \left(v_{ji}c_{ji}(\mathbf{y}) - v_{ij}c_{ij}(\mathbf{y})\right), \quad i = \overline{1,n}. \tag{5}$$

Consider the case in which the functions $c_{ij}(\mathbf{y})$ linearly depend on y_i:

$$c_{ij}(\mathbf{y}) = \alpha_{ij} + \beta_{ij}y_i, \qquad (i,j) = \overline{1,n}, \tag{6}$$

where α_{ij} and β_{ij} are constant coefficients. In this case, the components of the vector $\mathbf{s}$ have the form

$$s_i(\mathbf{y}) = A_i - B_i y_i + \sum_{j=1}^{n} \nu_{ji}\beta_{ji}y_j, \qquad i = \overline{1,n}, \tag{7}$$

where

$$A_i = \sum_{j=1}^{n}(\nu_{ji}\alpha_{ji} - \nu_{ij}\alpha_{ij}), \quad B_i = \sum_{j=1}^{n}\nu_{ij}\beta_{ij}. \tag{8}$$

Substituting these relations into Equation (1), we derive the PDSEO equation

$$\dot{\mathbf{y}} = \mathbf{y} \otimes \left(\mu\mathbf{A} + \tilde{\mathbf{L}}(\mathbf{y},\mu) + \mu B^{\mathsf{T}}\mathbf{y}\right), \tag{9}$$

where the vector function $\mathbf{L}(\tilde{\mathbf{y}})$ consists of the components

$$\tilde{L}_i(\mathbf{y},\mu) = -\mu B_i y_i + L_i(\mathbf{y}), \qquad i = \overline{1,n}, \tag{10}$$

while the elements of the matrix B are $\nu_{ij}\beta_{ij}$.

Consider the PDSEO with

$$L_i(\mathbf{y}) = l_i^0 + l_i y_i, \qquad i = \overline{1,n}. \tag{11}$$

Then Equation (9) takes the form

$$\dot{\mathbf{y}} = \mathbf{y} \otimes (D(\mu)\mathbf{y} + \mathbf{g}(\mu)), \qquad \mathbf{y}(0) \geq \mathbf{0}, \tag{12}$$

where the elements of the matrix $D(\mu)$ are given by

$$d_{ij}(\mu) = \begin{cases} l_i - \mu B_i & \text{for } i = j, \\ \mu\nu_{ji}\beta_{ji} & \text{for } i \neq j, \end{cases} \tag{13}$$

while the vector $\mathbf{g}(\mu)$ consists of the components

$$g_i(\mu) = l_i^0 + \mu A_i. \tag{14}$$

Equations (12) with nonnegative initial conditions have a nonnegative solution, thereby representing an adequate model of the PDSEO.

3. Classification of Stationary States and Existence Conditions

An important problem connected with the study of PDSEOs is the existence of stationary states (equilibria) and their classification. The existence of stationary states depends on the degree of influence of the entropy operator on the dynamic properties of a system, i.e., on the connectivity index μ. The stationary states of a PDSEO can be divided into three classes as follows.

The first class contains the unique trivial state $\mathbb{N} = \{\mathbf{y}^* = \mathbf{0}\}$. From Equation (12) it follows that this state always exists, regardless of the connectivity index.

The second class consists of the states with positive components of the state vector. Such a state will be called n-positive and denoted by $\mathbb{P}^n(\mu) = \{\mathbf{y}^*(\mu) > \mathbf{0}\}$.

Finally, the third class includes the states with $i_1, \ldots, i_p$ positive components of the state vector. Such states will be called $(i_1, \ldots, i_p)$-positive and denoted by $\mathbb{P}^{i_1,\ldots,i_p}(\mu) = \{y_{i_1}^*(\mu) > 0, \ldots, y_{i_p}^*(\mu) > 0; y_{k_1}^*(\mu) = 0, \ldots, y_{k_{(n-p)}}^*(\mu) = 0\}$, where the numbers $i_1, \ldots, i_p$ and $k_1, \ldots, k_{n-p}$ are different non-coinciding integers from the range $[1, n]$.

3.1. n-Positive States $\mathbb{P}^n(\mu)$

Consider system (11)–(13) with a fixed value of the connectivity index μ. The matrix $D(\mu)$ is assumed to be nondegenerate, i.e., $\det D(\mu) \neq 0$. Then the existence of a state $\mathbb{P}^n(\mu)$ of this system is determined by the existence of a positive solution to the linear equation

$$D(\mu)\mathbf{y} = -\mathbf{g}(\mu), \quad \mathbf{y}(0) > \mathbf{0}. \tag{15}$$

In this case,

$$\mathbf{y}^*(\mu) = -D^{-1}(\mu)\mathbf{g}(\mu) \geq \mathbf{0}, \qquad \mu \in [0,1]. \tag{16}$$

In particular, if $\mu = 0$, then

$$y_i^*(0) = -\frac{l_i^0}{l_i} > 0, \qquad i = 1,\ldots,n. \tag{17}$$

Hence, for $\mathbf{y}^*(0)$ to be positive the parameters l_i^0 and l^i must have different signs:

$$l_i^0 \geq 0 \,\&\, l_i \leq 0, \text{ or } l_i^0 \leq 0 \,\&\, l_i \geq 0, \qquad i = \overline{1,n}. \tag{18}$$

Consider the case in which $\mu(0,1]$. Reverting to Equation (15), we write it in the form

$$(D_1 + \mu D_2 + \mu D_3)\,\mathbf{y} = -\mathbf{g}^{(0)} - \mu\mathbf{g}^{(1)}, \tag{19}$$

where:

— the vectors $\mathbf{g}^{(0)}$ and $\mathbf{g}^{(1)}$ consist of the components l_i^0 and A_i, respectively;
— the matrices D_1–D_3 are given by

$$D_1 = \text{diag}\,[l_i \,|\, i = \overline{1,n}], \qquad D_2 = \text{diag}\,[B_i \,|\, i = \overline{1,n}]; \tag{20}$$

$$D_3(\mu) = \begin{pmatrix} 0 & B_{21} & \cdots & B_{n1} \\ B_{12} & 0 & \cdots & B_{n2} \\ \cdots & \cdots & \cdots & \cdots \\ B_{1n} & B_{2n} & \cdots & 0 \end{pmatrix}. \tag{21}$$

Clearly, the matrix D_3 is degenerate, i.e., $\det D_3 = 0$. We will construct the solution to Equation (19) as the formal series [18]

$$\mathbf{y}^*(\mu) = \mathbf{y}^{(0)} + \mu\mathbf{y}^{(1)} + \mu^2\mathbf{y}^{(2)} + \cdots. \tag{22}$$

In this equality, the initial approximation $\mathbf{y}^{(0)}$ satisfies the equation

$$D_1\mathbf{y}^{(0)} = -\mathbf{g}^{(0)}, \qquad \mathbf{y}^{(0)} = \mathbf{y}^*(0); \tag{23}$$

the first approximation $\mathbf{y}^{(1)}(\mu)$, the equation

$$D_2\mathbf{y}^{(1)} = -\mathbf{g}^{(1)}, \qquad \mathbf{y}^{(1)} = \left\{ -\frac{A_1}{B_1}, \ldots, -\frac{A_n}{B_n} \right\}. \tag{24}$$

Thus, in the first approximation the solution to (15) consists of the components

$$y_i^*(\mu) \cong -\frac{l_i^0}{l_i} - \mu\frac{A_i}{B_i}, \qquad i = \overline{1,n}. \tag{25}$$

Direct analysis of the signs of all terms in these formulas allows us to establish the following result.

Theorem 1. *Suppose that*

$$\left\{ (l_i^0 \geq 0) \,\&\, (l_i \leq 0) \,\|\, (l_i^0 \leq 0) \,\&\, (l_i \geq 0) \right\} \,\&$$
$$\left\{ (A_i \geq 0) \,\&\, (B_i \leq 0), \,\|\, (A_i \leq 0) \,\&\, (B_i \geq 0) \right\} \quad (26)$$
$$i = \overline{1, n}.$$

Then system (15) has the approximate $\mathbb{P}^n(\mu)$*-state (25).*

3.2. $(i_1, \ldots, i_p)$-Positive States $\mathbb{P}^{i_1, \ldots, i_p}(\mu)$

For identifying positive components in a state $\mathbb{P}^{i_1, \ldots, i_p}(\mu)$, we consider condition (26) with an appropriate modification. More specifically, we construct the matrix $D^{i_1, \ldots, i_p}(\mu)$ by removing the rows and columns with numbers $k_1, \ldots, k_{(n-p)}$ from the matrix $D(\mu)$. We perform the same procedure for the vector $\mathbf{g}(\mu)$ and denote the resulting truncated vector by $\mathbf{g}^{i_1, \ldots, i_p}(\mu)$. The existence conditions of a $\mathbb{R}^{i_1, \ldots, i_p}(\mu)$-state are also provided by Theorem 1, which should be formulated for the components of the state vector with numbers $i_1, \ldots, i_p$.

4. Stability of Stationary States

Now, we get back to the nonlinear Equation (12), for which there exists a stationary state $\mathbf{y}^*(\mu)$ from one of the above classes. For analyzing its stability, we introduce the deviation

$$\mathbf{x}(t) = \mathbf{y}(t) - \mathbf{y}^*(\mu) \quad (27)$$

and study the latter's behavior as $t \to \infty$.

4.1. Stability of Trivial State

For this stationary state, the deviation is $\mathbf{x}(t) = \mathbf{y}(t)$, and the equation takes the form

$$\frac{d\mathbf{x}(t)}{dt} = [G(\mu)\mathbf{x}(t) + \mathbf{x}(t) \otimes D(\mu)]\mathbf{x}(t), \quad (28)$$

where

$$G(\mu) = \text{diag}\left[g_i(\mu), i = \overline{1, n} \right]. \quad (29)$$

We construct the transition matrix [19]

$$W_\tau^t(\mu) = \exp(G(\mu)(t - \tau)). \quad (30)$$

Since the matrix $G(\mu)$ is diagonal with constant elements, the transition matrix is bounded by norm:

$$\| \exp(G(\mu)(t - \tau)) \| \leq \exp(g_{max}(\mu)(t - \tau)), \quad (31)$$

where $\| \bullet \| = (\sum_i (\bullet)_i^2)^{1/2}$ and

$$g_{max}(\mu) = \max_i g_i(\mu) = \max_i \left(l_i^0 + \mu A_i \right). \quad (32)$$

Consider the integral equation that is equivalent to (28):

$$\mathbf{x}(t) = W_0^t(\mu)\mathbf{x}(0) + \int_0^t W_\tau^t(\mu) \left(\mathbf{x}(\tau) \otimes D(\mu)\mathbf{x}(\tau) \right) d\tau. \quad (33)$$

In view of (31), we may write [20]

$$\|\mathbf{x}(t)\| = u(t) \le v(t), \tag{34}$$

where

$$v(t) = \exp(g_{max}(\mu)t)u(0) + \int_0^t \exp(g_{max}(\mu)(t - \tau)\rho(\mu)u^2(\tau))d\tau \tag{35}$$

and here we use designation $\|D(\mu)\| = \rho(\mu)$.

Differentiating this equality, we easily establish that the nonnegative variable $v(t)$ is the solution to the nonlinear differential equation

$$\dot{v}(t) = g_{max}(\mu)v(t) + \rho(\mu)v^2(t), \qquad v(0) = \|\mathbf{x}(0)\| > 0. \tag{36}$$

The convergence $\lim_{t \to \infty} v(t) = 0$ holds if the right-hand side of this equation is negative:

$$v(t) \in [0, -g_{max}(\mu)/\rho(\mu)]. \tag{37}$$

Because $v(t)$ is a nonnegative variable, $g_{max}(\mu) < 0$. Since $g_{max}(\mu)$ is the maximum component of the vector $\mathbf{g}(\mu)$, all its components must satisfy the condition

$$g_i(\mu) = l_i^0 + \mu A_i < 0, \qquad i = 1, \ldots, n. \tag{38}$$

Hence, the connectivity index is

$$\mu < -\frac{l_i^0}{A_i}, \qquad i = \overline{1, n}. \tag{39}$$

Theorem 2. *Suppose that for all $i \in [1, n]$ the values l_i^0 and A_i are simultaneously positive or simultaneously negative. Then there does not exist a value $\mu \in [0, 1]$ that would satisfy at least one of the inequalities of system (39), and hence the trivial state $\mathbb{N}$ is unstable.*

Corollary 1. *If for all $i \in [1, n]$ the values l_i^0 and A_i have different signs, then for the connectivity indices $0 < \mu < \frac{l_i^0}{A_i}$ the trivial state is stable.*

4.2. Stability of Stationary States $\mathbb{P}^n(\mu)$

The differential equation in the deviation $\mathbf{x}(t)$ from a stationary state of the class $\mathbb{P}^n(\mu)$ has the form

$$\frac{d\mathbf{x}(t)}{dt} = R(\mu, \mathbf{y}^*)\mathbf{x}(t) + (\mathbf{x}(t) + \mathbf{y}^*) \otimes [D(\mu)\mathbf{x}(t)], \tag{40}$$

where the elements of the matrix $D(\mu)$ are given by (13) and

$$R(\mu, \mathbf{y}^*) = \text{diag}[g_i(\mu) + w_i(\mu, \mathbf{y}^*)], \qquad w_i(\mathbf{y}^*) = \sum_{j=1}^n d_{ij}(\mu)y_j^*. \tag{41}$$

First of all, consider the case in which the connectivity index is $\mu = 0$. In accordance with (13), (14), (17) and (18), we obtain

$$R(0, \mathbf{y}^*) = 0, \qquad D(0) = \text{diag}[l_i \mid i = \overline{1, n}]. \tag{42}$$

As a result, Equation (40) is transformed into

$$\frac{dx_i(t)}{dt} = l_i^0 x_i(t) + l_i x_i^2(t), \qquad i = \overline{1, n}. \tag{43}$$

Theorem 3. *Suppose for all $i = \overline{1,n}$ the variables l_i^0 and l_i have different signs. Then the state $\mathbb{P}^n(0)$ is asymptotically stable in the domain of initial deviations $\mathcal{X} = \otimes_{i=1}^n [0, -\frac{l_i^0}{l_i}]$.*

The proof is straightforward: under the above hypotheses, the right-hand sides of Equation (43) take negative values in the domain $\mathcal{X}$.

Consider the case in which $\mu \neq 0$. We revert to Equation (40) for $0 < \mu \le 1$ and adopt the approximate formula (22) for the stationary state $\mathbb{P}^n$.

Let the matrix $R(\mu, \mathbf{y}^*)$ in Equation (40) be Hurwitz stable, i.e.,

$$\lambda_{max} = \max_{i \in [1,n]} g_i(\mu) + w_i(\mu, \mathbf{y}^*) = g^*(\mu) + w^*(\mu, \mathbf{y}^*) < 0, \tag{44}$$

and also let the matrix $D(\mu)$ have a finite norm $\rho(\mu)$.

We introduce the transition matrix

$$W_\tau^t(\mu, \mathbf{y}^*) = \exp(R(\mu, \mathbf{y}^*)(t - \tau)). \tag{45}$$

Like before, the transition matrix is bounded by norm:

$$\|W_\tau^t(\mu, \mathbf{y}^*)\| \le \exp(-\lambda_{max}(t - \tau)). \tag{46}$$

Using the transition matrix (45), we pass to the integral equation that is equivalent to the differential Equation (40):

$$\mathbf{x}(t) = W_0^t(\mu, \mathbf{y}^*)\mathbf{x}(0) + \int_0^t W_\tau^t(\mu, \mathbf{y}^*)\mathbf{x}(\tau) \otimes D(\mu)\mathbf{x}(\tau)d\tau. \tag{47}$$

The following bound is valid [20]:

$$\|\mathbf{x}(t)\| = u(t) \le v(t), \quad v(t) = \exp(\lambda_{max}t)u(0) + \int_0^t \exp(\lambda_{max}(t - \tau))\rho(\mu)u^2(\tau)d\tau. \tag{48}$$

Please note that the variables $u(t)$ and $v(t)$ are nonnegative. Differentiating the expression of $v(t)$ yields

$$\frac{dv(t)}{dt} = \lambda_{max}\exp(\lambda_{max}t)u(0) + \rho(\mu)u^2(t) + (\lambda)_{max}\int_0^t \exp(\lambda_{max}(t - \tau))\rho(\mu)u^2(\tau)d\tau. \tag{49}$$

A direct comparison of (48) and (49) indicates that $v(t)$ is the solution to the differential equation

$$\frac{dv(t)}{dt} = \lambda_{max}v(t) + \rho(\mu)v^2(t). \tag{50}$$

Due to (48), we have the differential inequality

$$\frac{dv(t)}{dt} \le \lambda_{max}v(t) + \rho(\mu)v^2(t). \tag{51}$$

In accordance with the theorem on differential inequalities [20], $u(t) \le \tilde{v}(t)$, where $\tilde{v}(t)$ satisfies the differential equation

$$\frac{d\tilde{v}(t)}{dt} = \lambda_{max}\tilde{v}(t) + \rho(\mu)\tilde{v}^2(t), \tilde{v}(0) = u(0) = \|x(0)\| > 0. \tag{52}$$

The right-hand side of this equation is negative if $\tilde{v}(0) \in [\rho(\mu)/\lambda_{max}, 0]$ ($\lambda_{max} < 0$). For any initial deviations from this range, $v(t) \to 0$ as $t \to \infty$.

Actually, we have established the following fact:

Theorem 4. *Suppose that the matrix $R(\mu, \mathbf{y}^*)$ in Equation (40) is Hurwitz stable and $\lambda_{max} < 0$ is its maximum negative eigenvalue. Then the state $\mathbb{P}^n$ is asymptotically stable in the domain of initial deviations*

$$\|\mathbf{x}(t)\| = u \in Dom(\mathbb{R}, \mu) = [0, -\rho(\mu)/\lambda_{max}]. \tag{53}$$

4.3. Stability of Stationary States $\mathbb{P}^{i_1,...,i_p}(\mu)$

Theorem 4 also applies to the states from the class $\mathbb{P}^{i_1,...,i_p}(\mu)$, with the only difference that the vector $\mathbf{y}^* = \{y_{i_1}^*, \ldots, y_{i_p}^*\}$ and the matrices R and D are compiled from the rows of the original matrices with numbers $i_1, \ldots, i_p$.

5. Equilibria and Stability in Investment Dynamics Models

5.1. Model of Economic System with Investment Exchange

Consider an economic system composed of three subsystems $i = \overline{1,3}$ exchanging investments. The state of each subsystem is characterized by its investment-conditioned yield $Y_i(t)$ (output in value units) and total investments $I_i(t)$ (the sum of investments per unit time). The investment relations between the subsystems are an important economic indicator of their interaction, which is described by the connectivity index $\mu \in [0, 1]$.

The investment balance of the economic system has the form

$$I_i(t) = N_i(t) + \mu[W_i(t) - E_i(t)], \quad i = \overline{1,3}, \tag{54}$$

with the following notations: $N_i(t)$ as the investment flow in own manufacture; $W_i(t)$ as the investment flow from other subsystems into subsystem i; finally, $E_i(t)$ as the investment flow from subsystem i into other subsystems. Denote by $x_{ij}(t)$ the investment flows from subsystem i into subsystem j. Then

$$E_i(t) = \sum_{j=1, j \neq i}^{3} x_{ij}(t), \qquad W_i(t) = \sum_{j=1, j \neq i}^{3} x_{ji}(t), i = \overline{1,3}. \tag{55}$$

Consider a random mechanism of investment flows between subsystems. Let the portions of investments be randomly and independently distributed among subsystems with some prior probabilities a_{ij}. Please note that with a prior probability $a_{ii} \neq 0$ the portions of investments stay within subsystem i. In the aggregate, all portions of investments form the investment flow $N_i(t)$.

For each subsystem, the admissible investment flow is completely exhausted. Therefore, the probabilities a_{ij} satisfy the constraint

$$\sum_{j=1}^{3} a_{ij} = 1, \qquad i = \overline{1,3}. \tag{56}$$

We assume that the portions of investments are distributed rather fast, and hence at each time instant t the dynamics of this process can be considered a sequence of locally stationary states with the entropy [2,21]

$$H(X(t)) = -\sum_{i,j=1}^{n} x_{ij}(t) \ln \frac{x_{ij}(t)}{a_{ij}} \Rightarrow \max \tag{57}$$

subject to upper constraints on an admissible investment flow $\tilde{I}_i(t)$ for each subsystem. By definition, the admissible investment flow $\tilde{I}_i(t) > 0$ depends on the yield of subsystem i. This dependence will be characterized by functions $\varphi_i(Y_i(t)) > 0$. As is well-known, initial investments are required for the operation of an economic system, which are not connected with yield. At initial stages of system operation, there may be no yield at all. Therefore, the functions $\varphi_i(Y_i(t))$ have a constant term $\alpha_i > 0$ and also a variable term $\tilde{\varphi}_i(Y_i) > 0$ that linearly depends on yield (in first approximation), i.e.,

$$\varphi_i(Y_i(t)) = \alpha_i + \beta_i Y_i(t), \quad \alpha_i > 0, \beta_i > 0; i = \overline{1,3}. \tag{58}$$

Using the functions $\varphi_i(Y_i(t))$, we write the corresponding system of constraints on the investment activity of all subsystems as

$$\sum_{j=1}^{n} x_{ij}(t) = \varphi_i(Y_i(t)), \; i = \overline{1,3}. \tag{59}$$

The entropy operator that maps the space of yields into the space of investment flow matrices is described by the perturbed constrained maximization problem of entropy (57) on set (59). In view of relations (56), the solution to this problem has the form

$$x_{ij}^*(t) = a_{ij}\varphi_i(Y_i(t)), \; (i,j) = \overline{1,3}. \tag{60}$$

Please note that the own investment flows $N_i(t)$ in (54) are given by

$$N_i(t) = a_{ii}\varphi_i(Y_i(t)), \quad i = \overline{1,3}. \tag{61}$$

The total investment flow makes up

$$I_i(t) = A_{ii}\varphi_i(Y_i) + \mu \sum_{j \neq i}^{n} a_{ji}\varphi_j(Y_j(t)), \; i = \overline{1,3}, \tag{62}$$

where

$$A_{ii} = a_{ii}(1 + \mu) - \mu. \tag{63}$$

Now, consider the phenomenology of yield dynamics, taking into account that this variable is nonnegative. A change in yield occurs under the influence of two oppositely directed processes: the depreciation of yield due to its consumption (accumulation) and the update of yield through investments. To ensure the nonnegativity of yield, for convenience its variability can be interpreted in terms of the relative rate of change $V_y(t) = \dot{Y}_i(t)/Y_i(t)$. In the first approximation, the relative rate of change $V_y(y)$ is proportional to the difference in the aging rates, due to depreciation and update, through investments. Assuming that each of the listed components of the rate of change $V_y(t)$ is in turn proportional to the yield $Y_i(t)$ with a coefficient s_i and also to the total investment flow $I_i(t)$ with a coefficient b_i, we can write the balance relation

$$V_y(t) = -s_i Y_i(t) + b_i I_i(t), \; Y_i(0) > 0, \quad i = \overline{1,3}. \tag{64}$$

Substituting the total investments expression (62) into this relation, we obtain the following system of nonlinear differential equations describing yield dynamics in the economic system composed of three interacting subsystems:

$$\frac{dY_i(t)}{dt} = Y_i(t)[-s_i Y_i(t) + A_{ii}\varphi_i(Y_i) + \mu \sum_{j \neq i}^{n} a_{ji}\varphi_j(Y_j(t))], \; Y_i(0) > 0. \quad i = \overline{1,3}. \tag{65}$$

Suppose that the total investments are linearly connected with yield (58). In this case, the above system of nonlinear differential equations takes the form

$$\frac{dY_i(t)}{dt} = Y_i(t)[\sum_{j=1}^{3} d_{ij}(\mu)Y_i(t) + c_i(\mu)], \quad Y_i(0) > 0, i = \overline{1,3}. \tag{66}$$

Here the vector c consists of the components

$$c_i(\mu) = a_{ii}\alpha_i + \mu\left(\sum_{j=1}^{n} a_{ji}\alpha_j - \alpha_i\right), \tag{67}$$

and the elements of the matrix $D(\mu)$ are given by

$$d_{ij}(\mu) = \begin{cases} \mu a_{ji}\beta_j & \text{for } j \neq i, \\ -s_i + a_{ii}\beta_i(1+\mu) - \mu\beta_i & \text{for } j = i. \end{cases} \tag{68}$$

System (66) with positive initial conditions (nonzero initial yield) has nonnegative solutions.

5.2. Model Parameters

These parameters are an illustration of the PDSEO analysis. The yields produced in each subsystem are depreciated with specific rates $s_1 = 0.07[1/year]$, $s_2 = 0.03[1/year]$ and $s_3 = 0.1[1/year]$. All yields are measured in $\$10^{10}$.

The random exchange of investments is described by the prior probability matrix

$$A = \begin{pmatrix} 0.3 & 0.6 & 0.1 \\ 0.1 & 0.6 & 0.3 \\ 0.2 & 0.1 & 0.7 \end{pmatrix} \tag{69}$$

The parameters of the functions $\varphi_i(Y_i)$ are presented in Table 1.

Table 1. Parameters of functions $\varphi_i(Y_i)$.

i	1	2	3
α	1.50	0.75	0.50
β	0.06	0.03	0.04

5.3. Analysis of Stationary States: Existence and Stability

Of economic interest are the states $\mathbb{P}^3(\mu)$ in which the yields in all subsystems are positive. In economic literature, such states are called full profitability states. The dependence of full profitability states and their stability on the connectivity index μ is illustrated in Table 2. Clearly, such states exist and are stable only for the values $\mu \in [0, 0.681]$. For $\mu > 0.681$, they do not exist. The following notations are adopted in this table: Dom as the stability domain (53); Stb as the stability indicator, $+$ for stable and $-$ for unstable; λ_{max} as the maximum eigenvalue.

Table 2. Full profitability states.

μ	0	0.1	0.2	0.4	0.6	0.681	0.682	0.8	1.0
Y_1^*	8.65	6.75	5.15	2.61	0.67	0.005	−0.003	−0.87	2.12
Y_2^*	37.5	41.03	43.21	45.26	45.66	45.58	45.57	45.29	44.56
Y_3^*	4.86	5.65	6.44	7.93	9.27	9.76	9.77	10.44	11.47
Dom	4.22	4.19	3.18	1.66	0.43	0.004	—	—	—
Stb	+	+	+	+	+	+	−	−	−
λ_{max}	−0.379	−0.391	−0.309	−0.175	−0.05	−0.0004	0.0002	0.07	0.189

The dependence of the stationary yields of different subsystems on the connectivity index $(Y_1^*(\mu), Y_2^*(\mu), Y_3^*(\mu))$ and also the stability domains $(Dom^*(\mu))$ are shown in Figure 2. Please note that these states exist for $\mu = [0, 1]$ and are stable up to $\mu^* = 0.681$.

Now, consider (i_1, i_2)-profitability states ($\mathbb{R}^{(i_1, i_2)}$). There may exist three states from this class, namely

$(2, 3)$: $Y_1^* = 0, Y_2^* > 0, Y_3^* > 0$;

$(1, 3)$: $Y_1^* > 0, Y_2^* = 0, Y_3^* > 0$;

$(1, 2)$: $Y_1^* > 0, Y_2^* > 0, Y_3^* = 0$;

The dependence of $(2, 3)$, $(1, 3)$, $(1, 2)$-profitability states on the connectivity index is illustrated in Tables 3–5.

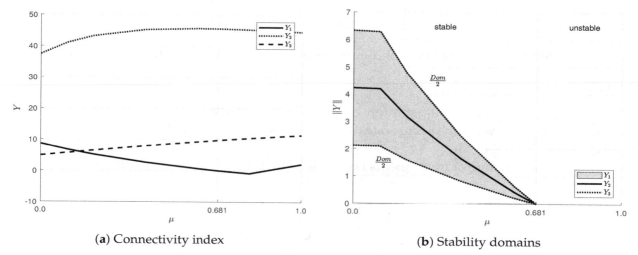

(a) Connectivity index   (b) Stability domains

Figure 2. Full profitability states.

Table 3. The (23)-profitability states.

μ	0	0.2	0.4	0.51	0.52	0.6	0.8	1.0
Y_1^*	0	0	0	0	0	0	0	0
Y_2^*	37.5	40.63	43.0	44.09	44.2	44.9	45.58	47.83
Y_3^*	4.86	6.29	7.74	8.54	8.75	9.18	9.77	11.97
Dom	−	−	−	−	0.045	0.654	1.24	3.17
Stb	−	−	−	−	+	+	+	+
λ_{max}	0.45	0.275	0.1	0.004	−0.005	−0.075	−0.147	−0.425

Table 4. The (13)-profitability states.

μ	0	0.2	0.4	0.54	0.545	0.6	0.8	1.0
Y_1^*	8.65	4.69	1.72	0.046	−0.008	−0.59	−2.44	−3.96
Y_2^*	0	0	0	0	0	0	0	0
Y_3^*	4.86	5.38	5.78	6.01	6.02	6.1	6.35	6.56
Dom	−	−	−	−	−	−	−	−
Stb	−	−	−	−	−	−	−	−
λ_{max}	0.45	0.58	0.71	0.8	0.81	0.84	0.97	1.1

Table 5. The (12)-profitability states.

μ	0	0.2	0.4	0.6	0.605	0.61	0.8	1.0
Y_1^*	8.65	4.98	2.22	0.05	0.001	−0.047	−1.72	−3.21
Y_2^*	37.5	42.77	44.17	43.8	43.78	43.76	42.61	41.01
Y_3^*	0	0	0	0	0	0	0	0
Dom	−	−	−	−	−	−	−	−
Stb	−	−	−	−	−	−	−	−
λ_{max}	0.35	0.395	0.44	0.485	0.486	0.487	0.53	0.575

From these tables it follows that the (23)-profitability states exist for all values of the connectivity indices, but they are stable only for $\mu \geq 0.515$; the (13)-profitability states exist for $\mu \leq 0.54$, but are unstable; the (12)-profitability states exist for $\mu \leq 0.605$.

The last class of states consists of $1, 2, 3$-profitability states.

The dependence of (1)-profitability states on the connectivity index is illustrated in Table 6.

Table 6. The (1)-profitability states.

μ	0	0.2	0.4	0.514	0.52	0.6	0.8	1.0
Y_1^*	8.65	4.55	1.45	0.003	-0.068	-0.97	-2.92	-4.52
Y_2^*	0	0	0	0	0	0	0	0
Y_3^*	0	0	0	0	0	0	0	0
Dom	$-$	$-$	$-$	$-$	$-$	$-$	$-$	$-$
Stb	$-$	$-$	$-$	$-$	$-$	$-$	$-$	$-$
λ_{max}	0.45	0.58	0.71	0.784	0.788	0.84	0.97	1.1

From Table 6 it can be observed that the 1-profitability states exist for the connectivity index $\mu \in [0, 0.514]$, but sufficient stability conditions for them are not satisfied.

The dependence of (2)-profitability states on the connectivity index is illustrated in Table 7.

Table 7. The (2)-profitability states.

μ	0	0.2	0.4	0.6	0.8	1.0
Y_1^*	0	0	0	0	0	0
Y_2^*	37.5	40.28	42.26	43.75	44.91	45.83
Y_3^*	0	0	0	0	0	0
Dom	$-$	$-$	$-$	$-$	$-$	$-$
Stb	$-$	$-$	$-$	$-$	$-$	$-$
λ_{max}	0.45	0.395	0.44	0.485	0.53	0.57

From Table 7 it can be observed that the 2-profitability states exist for all values of the connectivity index $\mu \in [0, 1]$, but sufficient stability conditions for them are not satisfied.

The dependence of (3)-profitability states on the connectivity index is illustrated in Table 8.

Table 8. The (3)-profitability states.

μ	0	0.2	0.4	0.6	0.8	1.0
Y_1^*	0	0	0	0	0	0
Y_2^*	0	0	0	0	0	0
Y_3^*	4.86	5.31	5.73	6.12	6.49	6.84
Dom	$-$	$-$	$-$	$-$	$-$	$-$
Stb	$-$	$-$	$-$	$-$	$-$	$-$
λ_{max}	0.45	0.58	0.71	0.84	0.97	1.1

From Table 8 it can be observed that the 3-profitability states exist for all values of the connectivity index $\mu \in [0, 1]$, but sufficient stability conditions for them are not satisfied.

Thus, the complete range of the connectivity index can be divided into the following subintervals:

- $[0, 0.515)$, on which all types of stationary states exist, but only full profitability states are stable;
- $[0.515, 0.542)$, on which all types of stationary states exist, except for the (1)-profitability ones; full and (23)-profitability states are stable;
- $[0.542, 0.607)$, on which all types of stationary states exist, except for the (1)- and (13)-profitability ones; full and (23)-profitability states are stable;
- $[0.607, 0.681)$, on which full-, (23)-, (2)- and (3)-profitability states exist; full and (23)-profitability states are stable.

6. Discussion and Future Work

The proposed method for the analysis of stationary states is based on an approximate solution of the stationary equations, which is constructed using a formal power series with respect to the connectivity parameter μ. The first order approximation is used. It would be useful to study higher-order approximations, which would clarify the obtained conditions for the existence of positive stationary states.

The PDESO mathematical model contains the simplest Boltzmann entropy operator whose mathematical model taking into account the interval constraints on the variables transforms into the Fermi information entropy maximization problem.

However, in many applied problems in the above areas, mathematical models of PDSEO arise with equalities and inequalities conditions, which have more diverse dynamic properties, namely periodic, non-periodic modes and chaotic attractors.

7. Conclusions

A mathematical model of a positive dynamical system with an entropy operator was formed, focused on studying the influence of the entropy operator on the dynamic properties of the system. A classification of positive stationary states is given and the conditions for their existence are obtained. A theorem on the instability of the zero stationary state is proved. Using the method of differential Bellman inequalities, stability conditions "in large" of positive stationary states are obtained. For the model of the economic system of stochastic investment exchange, the concept of positive profitability conditions is introduced and the conditions for their existence and stability are obtained.

The results obtained can serve as the basis for the study of PDSEO with other classes of entropy operators, for example, the Fermi-entropy operator.

References

1. Wilson, A.G. *Entropy in Urban and Regional Modelling*; Pion Ltd: London, UK, 1970.
2. Popkov, Y.S. *Teoriya Makrosistem. Ravnovesnye Modeli*; (Theory of Macrosystems. Equilibrium Models); URSS: Moscow, Russia, 1999.
3. Herman, G.T. *Image Reconstruction from Projections: The Fundamentals of Computerized Tomography*; Academic Press: New York, NY, USA, 1980.
4. Censor, Y.; Segmon, J. On Block-Iterative Entropy Optimization. *J. Inf. Optim. Sci.* **1987**, *8*, 275–291.
5. Burne, C.L. Block-iterative Method for Image Reconstruction from Projections. *IEEE Trans. Img. Proc.* **1996**, *5*, 792–794. [CrossRef] [PubMed]
6. Popkov, Y.S. *Mathematical Demoeconomy: Integrating Demographic and Economic Approaches*; De Gruiter GmbH: Berlin, Germany, 2014.
7. Popkov, Y.S.; Popkov, A.Y.; Dubnov, Y.A. *Randomizirovannoe Mashinnoe Obuchenie*; (Randomized Machine Learning); LENAND: Moscow, Russia, 2019.
8. Popkov, Y.S.; Ryazantsev, A.N. *Spatio-Functional Models of Demographic Processes*; UN Fund for Population Activity: New York, NY, USA, 1980; Preprint.
9. Popkov, Y.S.; Shvetsov, V.I. A Principle of Local Equilibrium in the Regional Dynamic Models. *Math. Model.* **1990**, *2*, 40–50.
10. Wilson, A.G. *Catastrophe Theory and Bifurcations. Application to Urban and Regional Systems*; Croom Helm: London, UK, 1981.
11. Popkov, Y.S.; Shvetsov, V.I.; Weidlich, W. Settlement Formation Models with Entropy Operator. *Ann. Reg. Sci.* **1998**, *32*, 267–294. [CrossRef]
12. Fan, Y.; Guo, R.; He, Z.; Li, M.; He, B.; Yang, H.; Wen, N. Spatio-temporal Pattern of Urban System Network in the Huaihe River Basin Based on Entropy Theory. *Entropy* **2019**, *2*, 20–32. [CrossRef]

13. Popkov, Y.S.; Rublev, M.V. Dynamic Procedures of Image Reconstruction from Projections (Computer Tomography). *Autom. Remote Control* **2006**, *67*, 233–241. [CrossRef]

14. Popkov, Y.S. Theory of Dynamic Entropy-operator Systems and Its Applications. *Autom. Remote Control* **2006**, *67*, 900–926. [CrossRef]

15. Popkov, A.Y.; Popkov, Y.S.; van Wissen, L. Positive Dynamic Systems with Entropy Operator: Application to Labour Market Modelling. *EJOR* **2005**, *164*, 811–828. [CrossRef]

16. Popkov, Y.S. Upper Bound Design for Lipschitz Constant of the $F(v, q)$-Entropy Operator. *Mathematics* **2018**, *6*, 1–9. [CrossRef]

17. Popkov, Y.S. Method of Linear Majorant in the Theory of Monotonic Entropy Operators. *Dokl. Math.* **2018**, *97*, 277–278. [CrossRef]

18. Krasnosel'skii, M.A., Vainikko, G.M., Zabreyko, R.P., Ruticki, Y.B., Stet'senko V.Y. *Approximate Solution of Operator Equations*; Springer Netherlands: Dordrecht, Netherlands, 1972; p. 496.

19. Tikhonov, A.N.; Vasil'eva, A.B.; Sveshnikov, A.G. *Differentsial'nye Uravneniya*; (Differential Equations); Fizmatlit: Moscow, Russia, 2005.

20. Beckenbach, E.F.; Bellman, R. *Inequalities*; Springer: Berlin/Heidelberg, Germany, 1961.

21. Puu, T. *Nonlinear Economic Dynamics*; Springer: Berlin/Heidelberg, Germany, 1997.

5

Inclusive Financial Development and Multidimensional Poverty Reduction: An Empirical Assessment from Rural China

Yanlin Yang and Chenyu Fu *

Center for Economic Development Research and Center of Population, Resource & Environmental Economics Research, School of Economics and Management, Wuhan University, Wuhan 430072, China; yyl7772@163.com
* Correspondence: 2016101050047@whu.edu.cn

Abstract: Inclusive finance is often considered to be a critical element that makes growth inclusive, as access to finance can enable the poor to lift themselves from income poverty. However, can it play such a role when the poor are in multidimensional poverty? Why does financial exclusion and poverty still exist in countries with vigorous development of inclusive finance? We build an evolutionary game model to analyze the equilibrium strategies of inclusive financial institutions and the poor in poverty reduction activities to find the answers. As there is a high incidence of poverty and serious financial exclusion in rural areas of China, we test the poverty reduction effectiveness of inclusive financial development on the poor with different labor capacity in rural China from 2010 to 2016 based on survey data of China Family Panel Studies and relevant statistics collected from 21 provinces. Our study finds there are differences in poverty alleviation effects of inclusive financial development among the poor with different labor capacities; if financial institutions target the service precisely to the working-age population in rural areas, they will achieve the dual goals of maintaining institutional sustainable development and alleviating poverty; And the development of inclusive finance in aspects of permeability, usability, and utility can significantly reduce multidimensional poverty. Therefore, to further improve the multidimensional poverty reduction performance and stimulate the endogenous motivation of the poor, it is necessary to strengthen the support for financial resources served to the working-age population, and to improve the development of rural inclusive finance in aspects of quality and affordability.

Keywords: inclusive finance; multidimensional poverty; targeted poverty reduction; evolutionary game; China

1. Introduction

To achieve the Millennium Development Goals on ending extreme poverty and hunger, the United Nations explicitly proposed to develop an inclusive financial system in 2005. The experience of Bangladesh's Grameen Bank, Bolivia's Banco Solidario, Indonesia's Bank Rakyat, rural Indonesia's Bank Kredit Desa and Latin America's Village Bank have confirmed that inclusive finance is an effective tool for achieving poverty alleviation and sustainable development [1]. In fact, poverty entails more than a lack of income and productive resources to ensure sustainable livelihoods. Its manifestations include hunger and malnutrition, limited access to education and other basic services, social discrimination and exclusion, as well as the lack of participation in insurance and decision-making. As multidimensional poverty is treated as matters of degree determined in terms of the individual's position in the distribution of some aspects of their living conditions and basic feasible capacity [2], we should use a new multidimensional method to measure poverty and analyze whether inclusive financial development can effectively alleviate multidimensional poverty, which helps countries gauge program effectiveness and guide their development strategy in a rapidly changing economic environment.

China is a developing country with a large number of rural poor. Ending poverty is also a major task for China to achieve sustainable development. Under the rural vitalization strategy, issues relating to agriculture, rural areas, and rural people are fundamental to China as they directly concern a country's stability and people's wellbeing. Therefore, the Chinese government has always adhered to the development-oriented poverty alleviation strategy and rural vitalization strategy. "Decision of the CPC Central Committee and the State Council on Winning the Fight against Poverty" was put forward, and the goal of poverty alleviation is to ensure that the rural poor will not worry about food and clothing anymore, and they will have the basic rights of compulsory education, basic medical treatment, and housing, in accordance with the policy of the United Nations on multidimensional poverty alleviation. Under the development-oriented poverty alleviation strategy, the method of poverty alleviation has shifted from "blood transfusion" to "blood creation"—poor people should depend on their own hard work to lift themselves out of poverty and get richer. However, the rural poor do not have enough money to strengthen nutrition, to improve welfare, or to develop production; worse, they are also excluded by formal financial sectors and cannot obtain the financial services they need. These factors lead to a vicious cycle [3]. In this case, inclusive finance can play a critical role in poverty alleviation, as increasing the rural poor's access to financial services at an affordable cost and with equal chance [4]. Access to a well-functioning financial system empowers the rural poor, can help them improve their livelihoods, protect them against economic shocks and provide funds for creating jobs or learning; in this way, developing inclusive finance targeted towards the poor in rural areas has become a key financial policy for China to promote inclusive economic growth.

However, inclusive finance does not alleviate poverty in the form of social assistance; it generally only addresses poverty issues with economic development prospects to maintain the sustainable development of its institutions, so its clients should have the potential for development and have the ability to repay the capital and interest [5]. Among the poor in rural areas, the group with the strongest labor capacity and development potential is the poor working-age population. They are also the key group for realizing the goal of "a people to work pull a family out of poverty". If a rural poor working-age population can improve its multidimensional poverty through access to the needed financial resources, the dual effect of promoting inclusive financial development and raising the level of human capital in rural areas can be achieved. As financial resources and labor resources are two essential factors for economic growth, it is also an important method for promoting the sustainable development of local economy [6]. Therefore, in the context of targeted poverty reduction and alleviation, can the development of inclusive finance achieve the goal of sustaining institutional sustainable development and achieving poverty alleviation? Are there any different poverty alleviation effects of inclusive financial development among the poor with different labor capacities? To better achieve poverty reduction targets, what is the developing direction of inclusive finance?

As there is a high incidence of poverty and serious financial exclusion in rural areas of China [7], we specialize in poverty alleviation effects of rural inclusive financial development under the rural vitalization strategy. Based on survey data of China Family Panel Studies (CFPS) and relevant statistics collected from 21 provinces, we measure poverty in a multidimensional method, studying the poverty reduction effects of rural inclusive financial development among the poor with different labor capacities, and analyze the difference of poverty reduction effects in different aspects of inclusive finance. Innovations are as follows: firstly, we analyzed the equilibrium strategies of inclusive financial institutions and the poor in poverty reduction activities from the perspective of the evolutionary game. Secondly, we analyzed the poverty alleviation effects of rural inclusive financial development on the rural poor with different labor capacities.

The remainder of this article is organized as follows. Section 2 reviews related literature, while Section 3 builds an evolutionary game model to analyze the action strategies of inclusive financial institutions and the poor in poverty reduction activities. Section 4 presents approaches to rural inclusive financial development measurement and multidimensional poverty measurement, and constructs the metrological model. Section 5 analyzes the empirical results, and Section 6 provides a conclusion and suggestions.

2. Literature Review

A lot of literature has studied the relationship between inclusive financial development and poverty alleviation. Some studies argue that (rural) inclusive financial development provides the poor with access to credit, savings, and other financial products and services, so that they can enjoy financial functions for poverty reduction directly. For instance, Kabeer found that microfinancial development in South Asia can and does make vital contributions to the economic productivity and social welfare of poor women and their households by financial empowerment [8]. Park and Mercado found that access to finance can enable the poor to make longer-term consumption and investment decisions, participate in productive activities, and cope with unexpected short-term shocks, which helps to alleviate poverty and income inequality [9]. Corrado and Corrado suggest that access to credit is a key instrument to access other primary services and social activities, so inclusive finance empowers the poor to exploit better economic and social opportunities and enable them to participate in productive economic activities [4]. He and Kong found that inclusive finance can increase poor farmers' income by the mechanism of releasing rural credit constraints, which helps them to improve the risk resistance ability and reduces the cost of obtaining financial services [10]. Some studies hold that (rural) inclusive financial development can further enhance the promotion of economic development and the optimization of income distribution in breadth, and indirectly achieve the results of income growth and poverty alleviation through the "trickle-down effect". Beck et al., Su and Liao, Ding, Cui and Sun, Chen and Zhang have verified this mechanism from the positive side by theoretical and empirical studies [11–15]. Leyshon and Thrift, Kempson and Whyley, Liu have verified this conclusion from the opposite side, finding that restraining financial development would increase the disparity of economic development and income distribution between regions, thus exacerbating the imbalance of regional economic development and resulting in more general social exclusion, which is not conductive to poverty alleviation [16–18]. Furthermore, some studies suggest that although inclusive finance can alleviate poverty and promote economic growth, it has different poverty reduction effects among different poor groups, the main beneficiaries being slightly poor families, and the effect of poverty reduction on extremely poor families being not significant [19]. Khaki and Sangmi found that access to finance can alleviate poverty, but funds are allocated to non-poor sections rather than absolute poor [20].Zhu and Wang showed that inclusive financial development can effectively alleviate poverty by promoting economic growth, but this effect is heterogeneous for different income groups, that is the benefit of poverty reduction and income increase of high-income rural poor is greater than that of low-income rural poor [21].

The literature above has studied the relationship between inclusive finance and poverty reduction from the point of view of different mechanisms, but ignores the premise that inclusive financial institutions are willing to provide financial products and services to the poor. Why does financial exclusion and poverty still exist in countries with vigorous development of inclusive finance? It maybe relates to the game between inclusive financial institutions and the poor. Based on the game model, some studies analyze the evolution process of cooperation between financial institutions and the poor. For example, Kong and Li deem that credit default leads to financial exclusion, and trust promotes cooperation [22]; Wang and Wang suggest that a bank's lending decision mainly depends on the possibility of farmers' repayment [23]. However, the poor need financial resources to enhance their production development ability to get out of poverty. Without considering malicious credit default, their repayment ability ultimately depends on the results of production development, which in turn depends on their labor ability. Therefore, there may be differences in poverty reduction between the working-age population and the non-working-age population.

In addition, the definition of poverty in current research is mainly limited to low income levels, and the effect of poverty alleviation is mainly judged by the income growth among all people. Moreover, the existing literature has not studied the poverty reduction effects of inclusive finance on the poor with different labor capacity, so the precision analysis of financial development for poverty alleviation is not enough. Based on this, an evolutionary game model is built to analyze the equilibrium strategies of inclusive financial institutions and the poor in poverty reduction activities, and we study the relationship between inclusive financial development and multidimensional poverty alleviation in rural areas of China.

3. An Evolutionary Game Model

As absolute poverty develops to relative poverty and social exclusion, it is more realistic to use multidimensional poverty to identify the poor. Multidimensional poverty mainly refers to the deficiency or deprivation of people's basic feasible capacity in many aspects, such as low income, ill health, inadequate education, lack of insurance, unemployment, and so on. Financial products and services help to enhance the self-development ability of the poor, so they need access to financial resources to alleviate poverty. However, the essence of inclusive finance is still finance, which is a commercial economic activity, and always refuses to provide products and services to the poor, especially the multidimensional poor, for the purposes of maintaining sustainable development. The poor have no mechanism to be lifted out of poverty. Therefore, financial institutions and the poor are stakeholders, and there is a game between them.

Suppose financial institutions and the poor are the two main players in the game of poverty reduction, and are both bounded rationality and limited information. To achieve the goal of poverty reduction, the poor need to obtain financial loans to carry out business activities. As a result, the poor have two strategies—one is to apply for loans, and the other is not to apply for loans. Although financial loans can help reduce multidimensional poverty, the poor may not be able to repay, which will affect the sustainable development of inclusive financial institutions. Therefore, financial institutions also have two strategies, accordingly—one is to provide loans and the other is not to provide loans. Suppose the probability of financial institutions providing loans is x and the probability of the poor applying for loans is y, then the probability of financial institutions not to providing loans is $1 - x$, and the probability of the poor not to applying for loans is $1 - y$. In addition, it is assumed that the loan amount is L, the interest rate is r, the investment rate of the loan is β, the transaction cost ratio of financial institutions providing loans is c_1, and the transaction cost ratio of the poor applying for loans is c_2, the success rate of developing production and management for the poor people is k. Under the condition that the poor apply for a loan, if the financial institutions provide the loan, then the return of the financial institution is $Lr - Lc_1$, the return of the poor is $k[L(\beta - r) - Lc_2] + (1 - k)(-Lc_2)$, if the financial institutions not to provide the loan, then the return of the financial institution is 0, the return of the poor is $k(-L\beta - Lc_2) + (1 - k)(-Lc_2)$. Under the condition that the poor not apply for a loan, if the financial institutions provide the loan, then the return of the financial institution is $-Lc_1$, the return of the poor is $-kL\beta$, if the financial institutions not to provide the loan, then the return of the financial institution is 0, the return of the poor is $-kL\beta$. The return matrix for financial institutions and the poor is shown in Table 1.

Table 1. The return matrix for financial institutions and the poor.

		The Poor	
		Apply	Not to Apply
Financial institutions	provide	$Lr - Lc_1, kL\beta - Lr - Lc_2$	$-Lc_1, -kL\beta$
	not to provide	$0, -kL\beta - Lc_2$	$0, -kL\beta$

As a result, the expected return on providing loans of financial institutions is $\pi_{11} = y(Lr - Lc_1) + (1-y)(-Lc_1) = yLr - Lc_1$. The expected return on not providing loans of financial institutions is $\pi_{12} = y \times 0 + (1-y) \times 0 = 0$. The average expected return of financial institutions is $\pi_1 = x\pi_{11} + (1-x)\pi_{12}$. Then the replicator dynamic model of financial institutions can be expressed as $F(x) = x(\pi_{11} - \pi_1) = x(1-x)(Lry - Lc_1)$. Make $F(x) = 0$, then $x_1 = 0$, $x_2 = 1$, $y^* = \frac{c_1}{r}$. The expected return on applying for loans of the poor is $\pi_{21} = x(kL\beta - Lr - Lc_2) + (1-x)(-kL\beta - Lc_2) = 2xkL\beta - xLr - kL\beta - Lc_2$. The expected return on not to applying for loans of the poor is $\pi_{22} = x(-kL\beta) + (1-x)(-kL\beta) = -kL\beta$. The average expected return of the poor is $\pi_2 = y\pi_{21} + (1-y)\pi_{22}$. Then the replicator dynamic model of the poor can be expressed as $F(y) = y(\pi_{21} - \pi_2) = y(1-y)[(2kL\beta - Lr)x - Lc_2]$. Make $F(y) = 0$, then $y_1 = 0$, $y_2 = 1$, $x^* = \frac{c_2}{2k\beta - r}$. Five equilibrium points of the evolutionary game can be obtained that are $(0,0), (0,1), (1,0), (1,1), (x^*, y^*)$.

However, the above five equilibrium points are local equilibrium points and not all of them are the equilibrium points of evolutionary stability strategy (ESS). Therefore, it is necessary to use a Jacobian matrix to verify the equilibrium points of ESS. Jacobian matrix can be obtained as shown in formula (1). If and only if the determinant value of the Jacobian matrix is greater than 0 and the trace value of the Jacobian matrix is less than 0, the equilibrium point of ESS can be obtained. Then the stability analysis results at each local equilibrium point are shown in Table 2.

$$J = \left\{ \begin{matrix} \frac{\partial F(x)}{\partial x} & \frac{\partial F(x)}{\partial y} \\ \frac{\partial F(y)}{\partial x} & \frac{\partial F(y)}{\partial y} \end{matrix} \right\} = \left\{ \begin{matrix} (1-2x)(Lry - Lc_1) & x(1-x)Lr \\ y(1-y)(2kL\beta - Lr) & (1-2y)[(2kL\beta - Lr)x - Lc_2] \end{matrix} \right\} \quad (1)$$

Table 2. The stability analysis results at each local equilibrium point.

Point	det(J)	Sign	tr(J)	Sign	Stability
$(0,0)$	$Lc_1 \times Lc_2$	+	$-Lc_1 - Lc_2$	-	ESS
$(0,1)$	$(Lr - Lc_1) \times Lc_2$	+	$(Lr - Lc_1) + Lc_2$	+	No
$(1,0)$	$Lc_1 \times (2kL\beta - Lr - Lc_2)$	+	$Lc_1 + (2kL\beta - Lr - Lc_2)$	+	No
$(1,1)$	$(Lc_1 - Lr) \times [-(2kL\beta - Lr - Lc_2)]$	+	$(Lc_1 - Lr) + [-(2kL\beta - Lr - Lc_2)]$	-	ESS
(x^*, y^*)	0		0		No

So $(0,0)$ and $(1,1)$ are the two equilibrium point of ESS. As obtaining loans helps poverty reduction, the equilibrium $(1,1)$ will be the optimal equilibrium point, i.e., the poor apply for loans and financial institutions provide the loan as the purpose of inclusive finance. However, the equilibrium of evolutionary game is not achieved overnight. Financial institutions and poor people will adjust the strategy of action according to their own return, and make the choice of strategy in a dynamic adjustment process. As the region consisting of points $(x^*, y^*), (0,1), (1,1)$ and $(1,0)$ will converge to $(1,1)$, and the region consisting of points $(x^*, y^*), (0,1), (0,0)$ and $(1,0)$ will converge to $(0,0)$, so if (x^*, y^*) is far from $(1,1)$, financial institutions and poor people will take the strategy $(1,1)$. For the point $(x^*, y^*) = \left(\frac{c_2}{2k\beta - r}, \frac{c_1}{r}\right)$, when k is larger, the region consisting of points $(x^*, y^*), (0,1), (1,1)$ and $(1,0)$ will converge to $(1,1)$.

In practice, the stronger the labor capacity of the poor, the higher the success rate of their production and management. Since the poor working-age population with the strongest labor capacity and development potential, therefore, compared with the poor non-working-age population, if financial institutions provide loans to poor working-age population, they will achieve the dual goals of maintaining institutional sustainable development and alleviating poverty.

4. Variables and Models

4.1. Variables Measurement

4.1.1. China'sRural Inclusive Financial Development Index (CRIFI)

To reflect the development level of rural inclusive finance in China, it is necessary to construct an index system of rural inclusive financial development. At present, scholars have mainly measured the development level of inclusive finance from some perspectives of permeability, usability, utility, quality, and affordability—see Beck et al. [11], Sarma and Pais [24], Gupte et al. [25], Wang and Guan [26], Wu and Xiao [27], Chen et al. [28], Guo and Ding [29], Li et al. [30], Luo et al. [31], Zhang [32]—but their index system did not fully covered these five aspects above, and the inclusive development level studied by most of them is for the whole country rather than rural areas. Since the core of inclusive financial development is to enable more poor people and low-income people to enjoy equal access to financial services, and China's main battleground for poverty alleviation is in rural areas, especially in remote and the most difficult rural areas. Therefore, the development scope of inclusive finance in China is focused on the rural areas with the highest degree of financial exclusion and poverty in this article. Referring to the existing literature and combining it with the reality of rural financial development and the availability of rural financial data, we select the following indicators to construct the rural inclusive financial development index, as shown in Table 3. It should be noted that although internet finance and mobile finance are the new forms of inclusive finance and they have indeed greatly promoted the development of inclusive finance, considering they are mainly used in urban areas, the poor in rural areas are still largely excluded, so our index system does not include the related indicators.

Table 3. China's rural inclusive financial development index system.

Aspect	Index	Property
Permeability	Numbers of rural financial institutions per 10,000 square kilometers in rural areas [1]	positive
	Employees of rural financial institutions per 10,000 square kilometers in rural areas	positive
	Numbers of rural financial institutions per 10,000 people in rural areas	positive
	Employees of rural financial institutions per 10,000 people in rural areas	positive
Usability	Per capita deposit of rural population	positive
	Per capita loan of rural population	positive
Utility	Balance of deposits in rural financial institutions to primary industry added value [2]	positive
	Balance of loan in rural financial institutions to primary industry added value [2]	positive
Quality	Ratio of deposit to loan in rural financial institutions	negative
	Bad loan ratio of rural financial institutions [3]	negative
Affordability	Percentage of floating range of RMB loan interest rate	negative

[1] The rural financial institutions in this article include rural commercial banks, rural cooperative banks, rural credit cooperatives, village banks, rural loan companies, rural fund mutual aid cooperatives; Land area indicator is substituted by agricultural land area. [2] Limited by provincial data, the deposit balance and loan balance in this article are substituted by the deposit balance and loan balance of rural credit cooperatives. [3] In this article, the bad loan ratio of rural financial institutions in each province is obtained by the conversion of the bad loan ratio of the commercial banks in various provinces according to the ratio of bad loan between national rural commercial banks and national commercial banks.

As Beijing, Tianjin, and Shanghai are the developed regions of China, where the incidence of poverty is almost zero, we discard their rural inclusive financial development. Furthermore, although the incidence of poverty in Chongqing and Tibet are very high, these areas have also been excluded, as their statistical data are insufficient. Finally, taking into account the availability of data and the pertinence of the research, we use "Euclidean distance method" as formula (2), similar to Sarma and Pais [24], Wang and Guan [26] and Chen et al. [28], to calculate the development level of rural inclusive finance in 26 provinces of China from 2007 to 2016. Data is derived from the China Statistical Yearbook, the China Financial Yearbook, the Regional Financial Operation Report and the wind database. Partial calculation results are shown in Table 4.

$$\text{CRIFI} = 1 - \frac{\sqrt{(w_{1t} - V_{1t})^2 + (w_{2t} - V_{2t})^2 + \cdots + (w_{mt} - V_{mt})^2}}{\sqrt{w_{1t}{}^2 + w_{2t}{}^2 + \cdots w_{mt}{}^2}} \tag{2}$$

Table 4. General situation of China's rural inclusive financial development from 2007 to 2016.

Region	Province	CRIFI	Rank	Permeability	Usability	Utility	Quality	Affordability
Eastern region	Guangdong	0.539	2	0.666	0.712	0.365	0.683	0.459
	Hebei	0.469	3	0.525	0.694	0.363	0.732	0.131
	Zhejiang	0.467	4	0.819	0.450	0.236	0.508	0.049
	Shandong	0.445	5	0.696	0.492	0.214	0.570	0.203
	Liaoning	0.364	7	0.495	0.558	0.163	0.501	0.372
	Jiangsu	0.321	9	0.761	0.102	0.044	0.647	0.268
	Fujian	0.258	14	0.308	0.391	0.133	0.639	0.216
	Hainan	0.237	16	0.291	0.446	0.086	0.749	0.663
	Average	0.388		0.570	0.480	0.200	0.629	0.295
Central region	Shanxi	0.622	1	0.508	0.837	1.000	0.450	0.303
	Henan	0.397	6	0.597	0.331	0.218	0.642	0.249
	Jiangxi	0.273	11	0.309	0.280	0.205	0.568	0.217
	Hunan	0.241	15	0.341	0.199	0.111	0.642	0.360
	Anhui	0.234	18	0.443	0.033	0.055	0.675	0.373
	Jilin	0.230	19	0.268	0.332	0.120	0.531	0.541
	Heilongjiang	0.184	22	0.170	0.382	0.121	0.483	0.371
	Hubei	0.179	24	0.278	0.091	0.042	0.701	0.652
	Average	0.295		0.364	0.311	0.234	0.586	0.383
Western region	Ningxia	0.324	8	0.226	0.534	0.388	0.610	0.260
	Shaanxi	0.320	10	0.249	0.528	0.342	0.640	0.497
	Guizhou	0.263	12	0.191	0.290	0.339	0.658	0.274
	Sichuan	0.259	13	0.253	0.341	0.223	0.468	0.275
	Yunnan	0.236	17	0.081	0.503	0.390	0.687	0.408
	Gansu	0.228	20	0.139	0.303	0.309	0.593	0.491
	Guangxi	0.222	21	0.200	0.325	0.176	0.710	0.474
	Inner Mongolia	0.181	23	0.105	0.563	0.161	0.574	0.190
	Xinjiang	0.151	25	0.044	0.448	0.176	0.573	0.747
	Qinghai	0.149	26	0.033	0.296	0.248	0.380	0.781
	Average	0.233		0.152	0.413	0.275	0.589	0.440

Data sources: Authors' calculations.

In formula (2), w_{mt} is the weight of index m in Table 1 in year t, which is determined by the coefficient of variation method as per Zhou et al. [6]. That is the ratio of the standard deviation to the average of the index in all provinces in each year. V_{mt} is the calculated value of index m in Table 1 in year t. That is, the data obtained by unifying the actual data and multiply it by the weight of index.

As shown in Table 4, there is a wide gap between regions in the development level of rural inclusive finance. The permeability, usability, and quality of rural inclusive financial development in eastern China are relatively high, but utility and affordability of inclusive financial development are relatively low. Therefore, in the eastern region it is necessary to further improve the use efficiency of the poverty alleviation funds and reduce the transaction costs of financial services. The development of inclusive finance in the central and western regions is relatively backward, so they should strengthen the development of all aspects of rural inclusive finance, in particular to further increase the coverage of financial institutions and support those in more rural poverty to have access to financial resources.

4.1.2. Multidimensional Poverty Index

At present, the research on multidimensional poverty mainly identifies the multidimensional poverty of households or farmers from the aspects of income, education, medical treatment, insurance, assets, and living standards, as per Wang and Alkire [33], Li [34], Zou and Fang [35], Alkire and Santos [36], Santos [37], Alkire and Seth [38], Zhang and Zhou [39], Guo and Zhou [40]. However, there is little research on individual multidimensional poverty, in which the index selection only includes income, health, education, and insurance dimensions, and does not emphasize the development of production or employment [41–43]. Since inclusive financial services are intended primarily for individuals rather than households, it is more effective and accurate to identify the poor from the individual level than from the family level. Furthermore, the existing literature only focuses on income, health, education, and insurance poverties, but neglects employment poverty. In fact, unemployment is also a crucial cause of individual poverty, which directly determines people's income level and social status [44]. Therefore, combined with factors affecting individual poverty, we calculate the multidimensional poverty of rural working-age population from five dimensions of income (economic capability), health (physical function), education (learning ability), insurance (risk-resisting ability) and employment (survival ability) by using the "dual cutoff method" of Alkire and Foster [45,46]. All dimensional indicators and deprivation cutoffs refer to the existing literature, the UN Millennium Development goals, Chinese poverty line, and the characteristics of survey data. There is equal weight for each indicator. Details are shown in Table 5.

Table 5. Five poverty dimensions and deprivation cutoffs.

Dimensions	Deprivation Cutoffs
Income	Income below the income poverty line 2300 RMB yuan (comparable prices based on year 2010) is regarded as "Income poverty".
Health	If body mass index (BMI) is outside the range of (18.5 kg/m^2, 30 kg/m^2)and self-rated health is unhealthy, that is regarded as "Health poverty".
Education	Failure to complete compulsory primary education (maximum length of education less than 6 years) is regarded as "Education poverty".
Insurance	Failure to enjoy any kind of endowment insurance or medical insurance is regarded as "Insurance poverty".
Employment	No job now and no formal work experience for more than six months is regarded as "Employ poverty" [1].

[1] Employment here includes do agricultural work and self-employment.

"Dual cutoff method" is also called "AF method", which uses deprivation cutoffs and poverty cutoffs to measure people's multidimensional poverty and was created by Alkire and Foster [45,46]. Assuming that the achievement level of ith individual in jth dimension is $y_{ij}(i = 1,2,\cdots n; j = 1,2,\cdots d)$, so an $(n \times d)$ data matrix Y is formed for n individuals and d dimensions. The row vector $y_{ij} = (y_{i1}, y_{i2}, \cdots y_{id})$ is the achievement level of each individual in a given dimension, and the column vector $y_{ij} = \left(y_{1j}, y_{2j}, \cdots y_{nj}\right)$ is the achievement level of each dimension for a given individual. A vector $z = (z_1, \cdots, z_d)$ of deprivation cutoffs is used to determine whether an individual is deprived. If y_{ij} falls short of the respective deprivation cutoff z_j, then this individual is said to be deprived in that dimension and considered to be poverty in that dimension; If y_{ij} is at least as great as the respective deprivation cutoff z_j, then this individual is not deprived in that dimension and not considered to be poverty in that dimension. The deprivation vector g_{ij}^0 is used to represent an individual's deprivation. If ith individual is deprived in jth dimension,

$g_{ij} = 1$; if ith individual is not deprived in jth dimension, $g_{ij} = 0$. The deprivation vector of all individuals consists of a deprivation matrix $g^0 = \left[g_{ij}^0\right]$, which is composed of 0 and 1 elements. A column vector $c_{ij} = (c_{i1}, c_{i2}, \cdots c_{id})'$ of deprivation counts reflects the breadth of each individual's deprivation, so $c_{ij} = \sum g_{ij}$. A poverty cutoff k $(0 < k \leq d)$ is used to determine whether an individual is a multidimensional poverty people. If the deprivation counts c_{ij} falls short of the poverty cutoff k, the individual is not considered to be a multidimensional poverty people. In contrast, if the deprivation counts c_{ij} is at least as great as the poverty cutoff k, the individual is considered to be in multidimensional poverty. According to deprivation counts c_{ij}, n individuals and d dimensions, the value of multidimensional poverty M can be calculated, the formula is $M = \sum_{1}^{n} c_i(k)/nd$. The headcount ratio H is the proportion of multidimensional poverty people, if there are q multidimensional poverty peoples among n individuals, the headcount ratio H is calculated by q/n. The intensity A is the average deprivation share among the multidimensional poverty people, and it can be calculated by $\sum_{1}^{n} c_i(k)/qd$. The relationship between M, H and A is $M = H \times A$.

In this article, data of identifying multidimensional poverty population comes from the database of CFPS, which has been surveyed since 2010 for full sample data and each investigation lasts two years. To ensure the continuity and comparability of the samples, we select the survey data from 2010, 2012, 2014 and 2016, and only selects 21 provinces from 30 provinces that have been involved in the survey and rural inclusive financial development index have been calculated. Among the 30 provinces surveyed by CFPS, Inner Mongolia and Hainan Province were only included in the survey in 2014, and the valid samples were only 10 and 5, respectively. Qinghai were only included in the survey in 2012, and the valid samples were only 1. Ningxia and Xinjiang were included in the survey in 2012 and 2014, but their valid samples were only 6 and 19, respectively; Beijing, Tianjin, Shanghai, and Chongqing are dismissible for not calculating the rural inclusive financial development index. Thus, the nine provinces mentioned above are all excluded.

In summary, the 21 provinces and regions are Hebei Province, Shanxi Province, Liaoning Province, Jilin Province, Heilongjiang Province, Jiangsu Province, Zhejiang Province, Anhui Province, Fujian Province, Jiangxi Province, Shandong Province, Henan Province, Hubei Province, Hunan Province, Guangdong Province, Guangxi Zhuang Autonomous region, Sichuan Province, Guizhou Province, Yunnan Province, Shaanxi Province, and Gansu Province. To ensure the validity of the sample, missing values and the abnormal values are deleted directly, and 20,094 valid samples are retained to calculate the multidimensional poverty of the rural population. Among them, there are 10,987 valid samples in 2010, 4582 valid samples in 2012, 3865 valid samples in 2014, and 660 valid samples in 2016.

Partial calculation results are shown in Table 6. As shown in Table 6, the multidimensional poverty situation of rural population has improved as a whole, but the task of targeted poverty reduction and alleviation has not yet been completed; some rural populations still have problems of low income, ill health, inadequate education, lack of insurance, and unemployment. Health poverty and education poverty are the main poverty problems faced by them. It is necessary to continue to intensify efforts of poverty alleviation.

Table 6. Multidimensional poverty of rural population from 2010 to 2016.

Dimensions	Year	Poverty Status			Dimension Contribution Rate				
		M	H	A	Income	Health	Education	Insurance	Employ
One dimension	2010	0.212	0.626	0.336	0.251	0.208	0.311	0.109	0.121
	2012	0.126	0.452	0.274	0.178	0.370	0.354	0.021	0.077
	2014	0.175	0.516	0.334	0.241	0.275	0.244	0.069	0.171
	2016	0.174	0.593	0.292	0.085	0.243	0.298	0.209	0.165
	Avg	0.172	0.547	0.309	0.189	0.274	0.302	0.102	0.133
Two dimensions	2010	0.147	0.302	0.483	0.264	0.210	0.299	0.099	0.127
	2012	0.064	0.142	0.447	0.207	0.341	0.336	0.019	0.096
	2014	0.118	0.234	0.498	0.274	0.247	0.239	0.051	0.189
	2016	0.099	0.218	0.463	0.104	0.217	0.290	0.189	0.201
	Avg	0.107	0.224	0.473	0.212	0.254	0.291	0.090	0.153
Three dimensions	2010	0.069	0.106	0.644	0.265	0.225	0.275	0.092	0.143
	2012	0.020	0.034	0.603	0.258	0.329	0.305	0.027	0.081
	2014	0.061	0.090	0.667	0.273	0.253	0.232	0.027	0.215
	2016	0.032	0.049	0.640	0.123	0.241	0.235	0.212	0.189
	Avg	0.045	0.070	0.639	0.230	0.262	0.262	0.089	0.157
Four dimensions	2010	0.019	0.023	0.808	0.232	0.220	0.236	0.128	0.185
	2012	0.000	0.000	0.800	0.000	0.250	0.250	0.250	0.250
	2014	0.026	0.033	0.800	0.250	0.250	0.250	0.000	0.250
	2016	0.008	0.010	0.800	0.125	0.194	0.250	0.194	0.236
	Avg	0.013	0.017	0.802	0.152	0.229	0.246	0.143	0.230
Five dimensions	2010	0.001	0.001	0.000	0.200	0.200	0.200	0.200	0.200
	2012	0.000	0.000	0.000	0.000	0.000	0.000	0.000	0.000
	2014	0.000	0.000	0.000	0.000	0.000	0.000	0.000	0.000
	2016	0.000	0.000	0.000	0.000	0.000	0.000	0.000	0.000
	Avg	0.000	0.000	0.000	0.050	0.050	0.050	0.050	0.050

Data sources: Authors' calculations.

4.2. Model Selection and Variable Description

To test whether rural inclusive financial development can effectively reduce the multidimensional poverty of the rural population, this article constructs a benchmark regression model (3). In model (3), samples are divided into two groups: the working-age population and the non-working-age population.

$$MP_{it} = \alpha_1 + \beta_1 CRIFI_{it} + \theta_1 X_{it} + \varepsilon_{it} \tag{3}$$

MP_{it} is the multidimensional poverty situation of the rural population, which describes whether the people are in multidimensional poverty on one of the five dimensions of income, health, education, insurance, and employment. If the rural population is in multidimensional poverty, MP_{it} takes 1, and if not, MP_{it} takes 0. In addition, $CRIFI_{it}$ means Chinese rural inclusive financial development index, X_{it} is control variables, including personal characteristics variables such as gender, age, the square of age, household register, marital status, and family characteristics variables such as family size, family burden ratio, etc. ε_{it} is the random error. Since the explained variables in the benchmark regression model (3) are virtual variables, the panel Logit model is used for estimating. The main variable description is shown in Table 7.

Table 7. Variable description.

Variable	Description	N	Mean	St dev	Min	Max
MP_{it}	Poverty = 1 non-poverty = 0	20,094	0.559	0.497	0	1
CRIFI	continuous variable	20,094	0.356	0.130	0.136	0.653
crifi1	permeability	20,094	0.414	0.220	0.069	0.896
crifi2	usability	20,094	0.480	0.251	0	1
crifi3	utility	20,094	0.280	0.208	0	1
crifi4	quality	20,094	0.625	0.151	0.023	0.893
crifi5	affordability	20,094	0.311	0.191	0	1
gender	men = 1; women = 0	20,094	0.606	0.489	0	1
age	continuous variable	20,094	43.027	15.257	16	99
age2		20,094	2084.056	1403.238	256	9801
marriage	married = 0; others = 1 (Others include unmarried, cohabitation, divorce, widowhood.)	20,094	0.189	0.391	0	1
registration	rural household = 1; non-rural household = 0	20,094	0.915	0.279	0	1
family size		20,094	4.560	1.893	1	26
burden ratio		20,094	1.778	2.748	0.003	100
district	Eastern = 1; Central = 2; West = 3	20,094	1.992	0.839	1	3

5. Empirical Results

5.1. Benchmark Regression Results

According to the benchmark regression model (3), the influence coefficient and marginal effect of rural inclusive finance development on multidimensional poverty alleviation of rural population is shown in Table 8; columns (1), (3) are the influence coefficient, and columns (2), (4) are the marginal effect. From the empirical results, the p-value corresponding to all Wald statistics was 0.000, so model (3) passed the test as a whole. Then, it can be seen that the influence coefficient and marginal effect of rural inclusive finance on the multidimensional poverty of rural working-age population are significantly negative, but the influence coefficient and marginal effect of rural inclusive finance on the multidimensional poverty of rural non-working-age population are not significant. It suggests that in the case of other factors remaining unchanged, the development of rural inclusive finance will reduce the probability of rural working-age population falling into multidimensional poverty by 43.8%, but there is no significant impact of rural inclusive financial development on the poverty situation of rural non-working-age population. Therefore, compared with the poor non-working-age population, if financial institutions provide loans to poor working-age population, they will achieve the dual goals of maintaining institutional sustainable development and alleviating poverty. However, non-working-age population is less able to work, so the effect of inclusive finance on their poverty alleviation is not significant, which also proves the reason for there still existing financial exclusion to a small number of poor people.

In addition, from the empirical results we can also find that the influence coefficient and marginal effect of gender and the multidimensional poverty of rural population is significantly negative, which is shown by men being less likely to fall into multidimensional poverty than women in the case of other factors remaining unchanged. The relationship between age and the multidimensional poverty of the rural population is an "inverted U-shaped". The coefficient and marginal effect of marital status and the multidimensional poverty of rural population are significantly positive, indicating that the population in the marital status of unmarried, cohabiting, divorced, and widowed has a higher probability of falling into multidimensional poverty than those in the married state. The coefficient and marginal effect of household register and the multidimensional poverty of rural population is significantly positive, indicating that the population with a rural household register is more likely to fall into multidimensional poverty than those with a non-rural household register. Furthermore, the coefficient and marginal effect of family size and the multidimensional poverty of rural population is also negative. There is also a negative correlation between family burden ratio and multidimensional poverty of rural population. It shows that the rural population with lower family burden is more likely to get rid of poverty through hard work, and the rural population with higher family burden is more likely to fall into multidimensional poverty.

Table 8. Impact of rural inclusive financial development on multidimensional poverty.

Variables	Benchmark Regression				Robustness Test			
	(1)	(2)	(3)	(4)	(5)	(6)	(7)	(8)
	Working-Age		Non-Working Age		Working-Age		Non-Working Age	
CRIFI	−2.035 ***	−0.438 ***	−2.966	−0.318	−1.604 ***	−0.345 ***	−3.525	−0.378
	(0.632)	(0.136)	(2.405)	(0.258)	(0.528)	(0.113)	(2.251)	(0.241)
gender	−1.024 ***	−0.220 ***	−1.892 ***	−0.203 ***	−1.024 ***	−0.220 ***	−1.894 ***	−0.203 ***
	(0.036)	(0.007)	(0.198)	(0.020)	(0.036)	(0.007)	(0.198)	(0.020)
age	−0.104 ***	−0.022 ***	−0.948 **	−0.102 **	−0.104 ***	−0.022 ***	−0.956 **	−0.102 **
	(0.012)	(0.003)	(0.400)	(0.043)	(0.012)	(0.003)	(0.401)	(0.043)
age2	0.002 ***	0.000 ***	0.008 ***	0.001 ***	0.002 ***	0.000 ***	0.008 ***	0.001 ***
	(0.000)	(0.000)	(0.003)	(0.000)	(0.000)	(0.000)	(0.003)	(0.000)
marriage	0.219 ***	0.047 ***	0.637 ***	0.068 ***	0.219 ***	0.047 ***	0.638 ***	0.068 ***
	(0.058)	(0.012)	(0.220)	(0.023)	(0.058)	(0.012)	(0.220)	(0.023)
registration	0.485 ***	0.104 ***	0.488 ***	0.052 ***	0.483 ***	0.104 ***	0.490 ***	0.052 ***
	(0.071)	(0.015)	(0.168)	(0.018)	(0.071)	(0.015)	(0.168)	(0.018)
family size	−0.017	−0.004	−0.035	−0.004	−0.017	−0.004	−0.035	−0.004
	(0.011)	(0.002)	(0.030)	(0.003)	(0.010)	(0.002)	(0.030)	(0.003)
burden ratio	−0.032 ***	−0.007 ***	−0.015	−0.002	−0.032 ***	−0.007 ***	−0.015	−0.002
	(0.011)	(0.002)	(0.022)	(0.002)	(0.011)	(0.002)	(0.022)	(0.002)
year	Y	Y	Y	Y	Y	Y	Y	Y
province	Y	Y	Y	Y	Y	Y	Y	Y
Intercept	2.412 ***	-	33.153 **	-	2.268 ***	-	33.842 **	-
	(0.391)	-	(13.671)	-	(0.369)	-	(13.696)	-
N	15,590	15,590	2603	2603	15,590	15,590	2603	2603
Quasi R2	0.106	0.106	0.177	0.177	0.106	0.106	0.178	0.178
Wald test	1928.38	-	255.34	-	1927.28	-	256.41	-
p-value	0.000	-	0.000	-	0.000	-	0.000	-

Note: The values in parentheses are standard deviations; *, **, *** indicate the level of significance of 10%, 5%, and 1%, respectively. Data is calculated by authors using Stata13.

5.2. Robustness Test

Based on Sarma and Pais [24], Sarma [47] improved the calculation method of the inclusive financial development index. In contrast to the calculation method of the normalized inverse Euclidian distance between the achievement point and the ideal point in the past, Sarma [47] uses a simple average of the normalized Euclidian distance between the achievement point and the worst point and the normalized inverse Euclidian distance between the achievement point and the ideal point as formula (4). Therefore, we use this new method to recalculate the CRIFI, and apply the modified index to the benchmark model (3). The results are unchanged as shown in Table 8.

$$\text{CRIFI} = \tfrac{1}{2}\left[\frac{\sqrt{(V_{1t})^2+(V_{2t})^2+\cdots+(V_{mt})^2}}{\sqrt{w_{1t}^2+w_{2t}^2+\cdots w_{mt}^2}} + \left(1 - \frac{\sqrt{(w_{1t}-V_{1t})^2+(w_{2t}-V_{2t})^2+\cdots+(w_{mt}-V_{mt})^2}}{\sqrt{w_{1t}^2+w_{2t}^2+\cdots w_{mt}^2}}\right)\right] \tag{4}$$

From the results of the robustness test we can also find that the influence coefficient and marginal effect of rural inclusive finance on the multidimensional poverty of rural working-age population are significantly negative, but the influence coefficient and marginal effect of rural inclusive finance on the multidimensional poverty of rural non-working-age population are not significant. It suggests our conclusion is robust.

5.3. Endogenous Test

As finance is an important method of development-oriented poverty alleviation, the Chinese government has issued several documents to support the financial sector in strengthening poverty alleviation, especially in areas with deep poverty, so multidimensional poverty of rural population may also affect the development of inclusive finance. Furthermore, there may be some endogenous problems in model setting, such as missing variables, which make the estimation result biased. Therefore, we select an index that lags two years behind the rural inclusive financial development as the instrumental variable, and use the Ivprobit model for a two-step method. The regression result is shown in Table 9. The result of Wald endogenous test shows that the model is endogenetic and the instrumental variable is highly correlated with the endogenous variable. However, the endogenous influence can be eliminated by Ivprobit model regression, and the regression result is consistent with the benchmark model.

Table 9. Endogenous test.

Variables	Working-Age		Non-Working Age	
	First Step	Second Step	First Step	Second Step
IFI		−2.423 ***		−0.697
		(0.618)		(1.943)
IFI2(instrumental variable)	0.610 ***		0.647 ***	
	(0.005)		(0.011)	
X_{it}	Y	Y	Y	Y
year	Y	Y	Y	Y
province	Y	Y	Y	Y
N	15,590	15,590	2603	2603
Wald test	6.24	6.24	0.45	0.45
P	0.013	0.013	0.5003	0.5003

Note: The values in parentheses are standard deviations; *** indicate the level of significance of 1%, respectively. Data is calculated by authors using Stata13.

5.4. Further analysis

The result of benchmark regression has proved that inclusive financial development can effectively alleviate the multidimensional poverty of the working-age population. In addition, to study which aspects of inclusive finance are more effective for poverty reduction of the working-age population, we study the poverty reduction effectiveness of permeability, usability, utility, quality, and affordability of inclusive finance based on model (3). The test result is shown in Table 10. We can see that the development of inclusive finance in aspects of permeability, usability, and utility can significantly reduce multidimensional poverty, but the development of inclusive finance in aspects of quality and affordability has no significant effect on the alleviation of multidimensional poverty. As the development of "permeability" is manifested in the expansion of the network coverage of financial institutions and the further sinking of financial services, which can extend the financial markets to more remote and poorer areas. The development of "usability" is manifested in the increased demand and participation of rural inclusive finance among rural poor people, so that more of them can have access to financial services without the restriction of mortgage conditions. The development of "utility" is manifested in the expansion of agricultural credit scale and the enhancement of the capacity to promote agricultural production and rural economic development, which is conducive to letting the poverty alleviation funds exert the maximum benefits, and truly achieve poverty alleviation and deliver genuine outcomes. Therefore, the development of rural inclusive finance can alleviate the multidimensional poverty of rural working-age population by improving the availability of financial products and services. However, the role of improving the quality of inclusive financial services and reducing the cost of services for poverty reduction has not yet been played, and the development of these two aspects should be further improved in the future.

Table 10. Impact of each aspect of rural inclusive financial development on multidimensional poverty.

	(1)	(2)	(3)	(4)	(5)
ifi1	−1.569 *				
	(0.801)				
ifi2		−0.392 **			
		(0.170)			
ifi3			−0.970 **		
			(0.378)		
ifi4				−0.079	
				(0.159)	
ifi5					0.178
					(0.130)
X_{it}	Y	Y	Y	Y	Y
year	Y	Y	Y	Y	Y
province	Y	Y	Y	Y	Y
_cons	2.324 ***	1.750 ***	1.761 ***	1.538 ***	1.453 ***
	(0.505)	(0.284)	(0.281)	(0.287)	(0.257)
N	15,590	15,590	15,590	15,590	15,590
r2_p	0.106	0.106	0.106	0.106	0.106

Note: The values in parentheses are standard deviations; *, **, *** indicate the level of significance of 10%, 5%, and 1%, respectively. Data is calculated by authors using Stata13.

6. Conclusions and Suggestion

Based on the evolutionary game model and empirical analysis, there are different poverty alleviation effects of inclusive financial development among the poor with different labor capacities. The development of China's rural inclusive finance can significantly alleviate the multidimensional poverty of rural working-age population, but this effect is not significant to the non-working-age population. Therefore, compared with the poor non-working-age population, if financial institutions provide loans to poor working-age population, they will achieve the dual goals of maintaining institutional sustainable development and alleviating poverty. In addition, the study also found that gender, age, marital status, household registration, family size and family burden ratio had significant effects on improving the multidimensional poverty of the rural population, and women are more likely to fall into multidimensional poverty than men, adults who are not married are more likely to fall into multidimensional poverty than those who are married, and the population with a rural household registration is more likely to fall into multidimensional poverty than those with a non-rural household registration, and the population with heavy family burden is more likely to fall into multidimensional poverty. Furthermore, the development of inclusive finance in aspects of permeability, usability, and utility can significantly reduce multidimensional poverty, but the development of inclusive finance in aspects of quality and affordability has not played its role on poverty alleviation.

Therefore, this article argues that in the game of poverty reduction, the stronger the labor capacity of the poor, the easier it is for the financial institutions and the poor to reach the equilibrium strategy of providing loans and applying for loans. So improving the financial availability of the working-age population is an effective way to fully realize the strategic goal of poverty alleviation in China. Furthermore, it even provides a new idea for poverty alleviation in the world. To further promote the development of rural inclusive finance, and guide rural inclusive finance to help target poverty alleviation, this paper puts forward the following policy suggestions. First, inclusive finance in poverty areas such as rural areas need to be developed, especially in remote and destitute rural areas. Second, rural areas, especially in the central and western regions, should speed up the development of the permeability, usability, and utility of inclusive finance. The quality and affordability of inclusive finance should be improved, especially in the east regions. Therefore, the eastern region should constantly innovate financial products and services, accelerate the development of internet finance and mobile finance, appropriately reduce transaction costs of financial services based on improving the quality of financial services, and effectively enable the poor to enjoy the benefits of inclusive financial development. The central and western regions should accelerate rural financial reforms, fully encourage and guide the policy-oriented financial institutions, commercial financial institutions, internet financial and mobile finance institutions to establish multi-level, wide-coverage, and sustainable rural inclusive financial systems in rural areas. Third, it is necessary to guide rural inclusive finance to give priority to serving the poor working-age population with the strongest ability to work and develop in rural areas, and constantly stimulate their endogenous motivation to lift themselves out of poverty through hard work, and improve their capacity for study and production. It is necessary to continuously improve the effectiveness and sustainability of alleviation effects of rural inclusive financial development on the multidimensional poverty of the rural working-age population.

Author Contributions: Writing—review & editing, Y.Y.; Writing—original draft, C.F.

References

1. Morduch, J. The microfinance promise. *J. Econ. Lit.* **1999**, *37*, 1569–1614. [CrossRef]
2. Ciani, M.; Gagliardi, F.; Riccarelli, S.; Betti, G. Fuzzy measures of multidimensional poverty in the Mediterranean Area: A focus on financial dimension. *Sustainability* **2019**, *11*, 143. [CrossRef]
3. Bihari, S.C. Financial inclusion for Indian scense. *SCMS J. Indian Manag.* **2011**, *8*, 7–18.
4. Corrado, G.; Corrado, L. Inclusive finance for inclusive growth and development. *Curr. Opin. Environ. Sustain.* **2017**, *24*, 19–23. [CrossRef]
5. He, D.; Miao, W. Financial exclusion, financial inclusion and inclusive financial institution in China. *J. Financ. Trade Econ.* **2015**, *3*, 5–16.
6. Zhou, G.; Gong, K.; Luo, S.; Xu, G. Inclusive finance, human capital and regional economic growth in China. *Sustainability* **2018**, *10*, 1194. [CrossRef]
7. Laborde, D.; Martin, W. Implications of the global growth slowdown for rural poverty. *Agric. Econ.* **2018**, *49*, 325–338. [CrossRef]
8. Kabeer, N. Is microfinance a 'magic bullet' for women's empowerment? Analysis of findings from South Asia. *Econ. Political Wkly.* **2005**, *10*, 4709–4718.
9. Park, C.Y.; Mercado, R. *Financial Inclusion, Poverty, and Income Inequality in Developing Asia*; Asian Development Bank Economics Working Paper Series; Asian Development Bank: Manila, Philippines, 2015.
10. He, X.; Kong, R. Mechanism analysis and empirical test of inclusive financial system alleviating rural poverty. *J. Northwest A&F Univ.* **2017**, *3*, 76–83.
11. Beck, T.; Demirgüç-Kunt, A.; Levine, R. Finance, inequality and the poor. *J. Econ. Growth* **2007**, *12*, 27–49. [CrossRef]
12. Su, J.; Liao, J. Empirical analysis of financial development, income distribution and poverty: Based on dynamic panel data. *J. Financ. Econ.* **2009**, *12*, 10–16.
13. Ding, Z.; Tan, L.; Zhao, J. The effect of rural financial development on poverty reduction. *Issues Agric. Econ.* **2011**, *11*, 72–77.
14. Cui, Y.; Sun, G. Is financial development the cause of poverty alleviation? Evidence from China. *J. Financ. Res.* **2012**, *11*, 116–127.
15. Chen, Y.; Zhang, D. County financial development and multidimensional poverty alleviation: Empirical research based on 51 poor counties in Hunan province. *Theory Pract. Financ. Econ.* **2018**, *39*, 109–114.
16. Leyshon, A.; Thrift, N. Geographies of Financial Exclusion: Financial Abandonment in Britain and the United States. *Trans. Inst. Br. Geogr.* **1995**, *20*, 312–341. [CrossRef]
17. Kempson, H.; Whyley, C. *Kept Out or Opted Out? Understanding and Combating Financial Exclusion*; The Policy Press: Bristol, UK, 1999.
18. Liu, C.; Tian, L.; Chen, B.; Dai, K. Rural financial exclusion and urban-rural income gap—An empirical study based on Chinese provincial-level panel data model. *J. Econ. Theory Bus. Manag.* **2013**, *10*, 17–27.
19. Kondo, T.; Orbeta, A.; Dingcong, C.; Infantado, C. Impact of microfinance on rural households in the Philippines. *IDS Bull.* **2008**, *39*, 51–70. [CrossRef]
20. Khaki, A.R.; Sangmi, M.D. Does access to finance alleviate poverty? A case study of SGSY beneficiaries in Kashmir Valley. *Int. J. Soc. Econ.* **2017**, *44*, 1032–1045. [CrossRef]

21. Zhu, Y.; Wang, W. How does inclusive finance achieve precise poverty alleviation? *J. Financ. Econ.* **2017**, *10*, 43–54.
22. Kong, R.; Li, X. A Study on the credit game relationship between poor farmer and rural credit cooperatives based on trust: Shaanxi province as an example. *J. Chongqing Univ.* **2010**, *16*, 1–7.
23. Wang, H.; Wang, J. Farmer's credit behavior evolution based on evolutionary game model in financial linkage mode. *J. Cap. Univ. Econ. Bus.* **2019**, *29*, 42–49.
24. Sarma, M.; Pais, J. Financial inclusion and development. *J. Int. Dev.* **2011**, *23*, 613–628. [CrossRef]
25. Gupte, R.; Venkataramani, B.; Gupta, D. Computation of financial inclusion index for India. *Procedia-Soc. Behav. Sci.* **2012**, *37*, 133–149. [CrossRef]
26. Wang, X.; Guan, J. The income distribution effect and measure of rural financial inclusion in China. *China Soft Sci. Mag.* **2014**, *8*, 150–161.
27. Wu, X.; Xiao, X. Study on the financial inclusion index in a global perspective. *J. South China Financ.* **2014**, *6*, 15–20.
28. Chen, Y.; Sun, Q.; Xu, W. Dynamic and spatial convergent of distribution of Chian's inclusive finance development. *J. Financ. Econ.* **2015**, *6*, 72–81.
29. Guo, T.; Ding, X. International comparative study of inclusive finance—Based on the perspective of banking services. *Stud. Int. Financ.* **2015**, *2*, 55–64.
30. Li, T.; Xu, X.; Sun, S. Inclusive finance and economic growth. *J. Financ. Res.* **2016**, *4*, 1–16.
31. Luo, S.; Chen, X.; Yao, Y. Research on poverty reduction effect of inclusive financial development in China. *J. Contemp. Econ. Res.* **2016**, *12*, 84–93.
32. Zhang, H.; Luo, J.; Hao, Y. An analysis of the rural inclusive finance and its determinants: An empirical analysis based on data collected from 107 rural credit cooperatives in Shannxi province. *J. China Rural Econ.* **2017**, *1*, 2–15.
33. Wang, X.; Alkire, S. Multidimensional poverty measurement in China: Estimates and policy implications. *J. Chin. Rural Econ.* **2009**, *12*, 4–10.
34. Li, J. Measurement of multi-dimensional poverty among farmers: A case study of 30 key counties in S province for poverty alleviation and development. *J. Financ. Trade Econ.* **2010**, *10*, 63–68.
35. Zou, W.; Fang, Y. A study on the dynamic multidimensional measurement of China's poverty. *Chin. J. Popul. Sci.* **2011**, *6*, 49–59.
36. Alkire, S.; Santos, M.E. Measuring acute poverty in the developing world: Robustness and scope of the multidimensional poverty index. *World Dev.* **2014**, *59*, 251–274. [CrossRef]
37. Santos, M.E. *Measuring Multidimensional Poverty in Latin America: Previous Experience and the Way Forward*; OPHI Working Paper66; University of Oxford: Oxford, UK, 2014.
38. Alkire, S.; Seth, S. Multidimensional poverty reduction in India between 1999 and 2006: Where and how? *World Dev.* **2015**, *72*, 93–108. [CrossRef]
39. Zhang, Q.; Zhou, Q. Poverty measurement: Multidimensional approaches and an empirical application in China. *China Soft Sci. Mag.* **2015**, *7*, 29–41.
40. Guo, X.; Zhou, Q. Chronic multidimensional poverty, inequality and cause of poverty. *Econ. Res. J.* **2016**, *6*, 143–156.
41. Chen, L. Measurement and decomposition of multidimensional poverty in China during the transformation period. *J. Econ. Rev.* **2008**, *5*, 5–10.
42. Wang, C.; Ye, Q. Evolution on the multi-dimensional poverty of Chinese rural migrant workers. *Econ. Res. J.* **2014**, *12*, 159–174.
43. Gao, S.; Bi, J. Dynamic multidimensional poverty in rural China: Persistence and transition. *J. China Popul. Resour. Environ.* **2016**, *2*, 76–83.
44. Bhalla, S. Inclusive growth? Focus on employment. *Soc. Sci.* **2007**, *35*, 24–43.
45. Alkire, S.; Foster, J. Counting and multidimensional poverty measurement. *J. Public Econ.* **2011**, *95*, 476–487. [CrossRef]
46. Alkire, S.; Foster, J. Understandings and misunderstandings of multidimensional poverty measurement. *J. Econ. Inequal.* **2011**, *9*, 289–314. [CrossRef]
47. Sarma, M. Measuring Financial Inclusion. *Econ. Bull.* **2015**, *35*, 604–611.

6

Variance and Dimension Reduction Monte Carlo Method for Pricing European Multi-Asset Options with Stochastic Volatilities

Yijuan Liang [1,2,*] and Xiuchuan Xu [2]

[1] Agricultural Education and Development Research Center, Southwest University, Chongqing 400715, China
[2] School of Economics and Management, Southwest University, Chonging 400715, China; xiuchuan@swu.edu.cn
*   Correspondence: yijuanliang@swu.edu.cn

Abstract: Pricing multi-asset options has always been one of the key problems in financial engineering because of their high dimensionality and the low convergence rates of pricing algorithms. This paper studies a method to accelerate Monte Carlo (MC) simulations for pricing multi-asset options with stochastic volatilities. First, a conditional Monte Carlo (CMC) pricing formula is constructed to reduce the dimension and variance of the MC simulation. Then, an efficient martingale control variate (CV), based on the martingale representation theorem, is designed by selecting volatility parameters in the approximated option price for further variance reduction. Numerical tests illustrated the sensitivity of the CMC method to correlation coefficients and the effectiveness and robustness of our martingale CV method. The idea in this paper is also applicable for the valuation of other derivatives with stochastic volatility.

Keywords: conditional Monte Carlo; variance reduction; multi-asset options; stochastic volatility; martingale control variate

MSC: 65C05; 62P05; 97M30

---

1. Introduction

In the last 40 years, financial derivatives have become increasingly important in finance. They are actively traded on many exchanges throughout the world, and are entered into by financial institutions, fund managers, and corporate treasurers in the over-the-counter market. They are especially important for market anticipants because they can be used to transfer a wide range of risks in the economy from one entity to another. Efficient use of financial derivatives can certainly promote financial and social sustainability. For instance, there are many different types of energy and agricultural commodity derivatives that are designed and used to contest weather and market risks, and to protect the benefit and reduce the potential loss of anticipants. Another example is that the real options approach is very popular in valuing the real estate sustainable investment. Conversely, inappropriate use of derivatives may cause great, even global, disasters, for example, the credit crisis that started in 2007. As pointed out by Hull [1], "we have now reached the stage where those who work in finance, and many who work outside finance, need to understand how derivatives work, how they are used, and how they are priced."

The accurate and fast pricing of financial derivatives is one of the most important things in financial engineering since many of the problems in economics and finance eventually turn into the pricing of financial derivatives. For example, Kim et al. [2] decided the optimal investment timing using rainbow options valuation for economic sustainability appraisement. Yoo et al. [3] determined an optimum combination of financial models including options to achieve a sustainable profit for overseas investment projects. The pioneering work of Black and Scholes [4] and Merton [5] lay the foundations for option pricing models. It is well known that the stochastic volatility model can be used to generalize the constant volatility assumption in the Black–Scholes model to capture the character of empirical observations from financial markets, such as the observed volatility smile and the leptokurtic features of the asset return distribution [6,7]. Stochastic volatility models describe volatility behavior with another stochastic differential equation. There are many studies on stochastic volatility models, such as those of Hull and White [8], Scott [9], Stein and Stein [10], Ball and Roma [11], Heston [12], Schöbel and Zhu [13], and Hagan et al. [14]. In addition to these one-factor stochastic volatility models, Fouque et al. [15–18] proposed a multi-factor mean-reverting stochastic volatility model. A comprehensive treatment of stochastic volatility models can be found in Reference [19].

Multi-asset options refer to a wide variety of contingent claims whose payoff depends on the overall performance of more than one underlying asset. Usually, they can be grouped into three categories: rainbow options, basket options, and quanto options. The prices of rainbow options rely on price changes of underlying assets, such as exchange options, outperformance options, spread options, chooser options, max-call options, and their variations. Basket options prices are always determined by the average price of underlying assets, while the value of a quanto option depends on the performance of domestic and foreign underlying assets. Jiang [20] introduced the concepts and constructed the pricing models of multi-asset options in detail, where the volatilities were constant. The pricing problem of multi-asset options pricing is essentially equivalent to a high dimensional integral. It is challenging to compute such a high dimensional integral, especially when the number of underlying assets is large, or stochastic volatilities are considered in the model.

There are mainly three pricing methods for multi-asset options: the analytic approximation method, the fast Fourier transformation (FFT) method, and the MC simulation method. The analytic approximation method typically constructs an approximate pricing model for the original problem that results in a closed form solution, and this method is always elegantly designed to the original problem. Several studies focus on this approach, for instance, those by Turnbull and Wakeman [21], Curran [22], Milevsky and Posner [23], Ju [24], Zhou and Wang [25], Alexander and Venkatramanan [26], Datey et al. [27], Brigo et al. [28], Borovkova et al. [29], Deelstra et al. [30,31], and Li et al. [32]. The main disadvantage of the analytic approximation method is that the size of the error is unknown and there is no way to systematically reduce it. The FFT method, which was prosed by Carr and Madan [33], has successfully been used in option pricing problems with a low dimension because of its high efficiency (see Carr and Wu [34], Heston [12], Grzelak et al. [35–37], and He and Zhu [38]). However, the FFT method depends on the availability of a characteristic function (usually in an affine framework), which is not always promised in a general stochastic volatility model. It is also difficult to apply the FFT method to high dimensional problems due to their dimensionality. Thus, for higher dimensional options, the most practical method seems to be MC simulations. Kim et al. [2] and Yoo et al. [3] also used MC simulations to price the embedded option prices in valuation real investment projects since the high dimension of problem. MC uses the sample mean as an estimator for the expectation of a random variable. Its speed of convergence is not influenced by the dimension of the problem. In addition, it allows for a simple error bound, given by the central limit theorem.

The major drawback of an MC simulation is that its convergence rate is quite slow, that is, $O(m^{-1/2})$, where m is the number of samples in MC simulation. As a result, often the main challenge in developing an efficient MC method is to find an effective variance reduction technique. There are a lot of studies about how to improve the efficiency of an MC simulation, and we refer the reader to Glasserman [39] and relevant references therein for a detailed discussion on various variance reduction techniques. Kemna and Vorst [40] presented one of the classical works on accelerating MC simulations. They used the geometric average option as a CV to price the arithmetic average option, which proved to be very successful. For a European multi-asset option pricing problem, Barraquand [41] proposed a "quadratic resampling" method by matching the moments of the underlying assets to reduce the variance of the MC simulation. Pellizari [42] designed a CV method called mean Monte Carlo to gain variance reduction of an MC simulation. The key of their success was that a Black–Scholes formula could be obtained when all underlying assets except for one were replaced by their mean. Borogovac and Vakili [43] proposed a "database Monte Carlo" CV method that avoids computing the expectation of CV, but the database, constructed in advance, requires huge calculations. Dingeç and Hörmann [44] exploited the property that the geometric average price was larger than the arithmetic average price to construct a CV by conditioning the payoff on the assumption that the geometric average of all prices was larger than the strike price. The expectation of their CV was computed by numerical methods, and their numerical tests for Asian options and basket options showed a great accelerating effect on the MC simulations. Liang et al. [45] designed a CV for European multi-asset options based on principal component analysis. Sun and Xu [46] used the CMC method with the importance sampling technique to accelerate MC simulations for basket options. There are some other approaches to speed up MC simulations, such as the quasi-Monte Carlo method [39,47–52], and parallelized implementations of MC simulations on CPUs/GPUs [53–58].

However, there is little research on variance reduction of MC simulations in pricing multi-asset options with stochastic volatilities. Du et al. [59] proposed a variance reduction method in multi-asset options under stochastic volatility models by matching the moments of the volatilities. Although their method shows great variance reduction of MC simulations, there are some restrictions to it. (1) All underlying assets are assumed to be driven by one stochastic volatility factor, which is not reasonable in practice. A more reasonable model is to assume that each underlying asset is driven by its own stochastic volatility factor (see Antonelli et al. [60], Shiraya and Takahashi [61], and Park et al. [62]). (2) Their moment matching technique greatly depends on the Hull–White stochastic volatility model, and is not applicable to general stochastic volatility models. (3) They only conducted numerical tests for options with two assets, which is not general enough for most multi-asset options.

In this paper, we aim to develop an efficient dimension and variance reduction method for MC simulations in pricing European multi-asset options with general stochastic volatilities. In our pricing framework, the underlying asset is assumed to be driven by its own stochastic volatility process, and full correlations between factors are allowed. The stochastic volatility model, which could be the Hull–White [8] or Heston [12] models, is quite general, such that our pricing model has a wide range of applicability. Our dimension and variance reduction method is built on the idea developed by Liang and Xu [63], who designed a CMC simulation with martingale CV to price single-asset European options with stochastic volatility. Our main contributions are: (1) A CMC pricing framework is deduced for European multi-asset options with general stochastic volatility models, which results in dimension and variance reduction. (2) A martingale CV based on a martingale representation theorem is combined with the CMC to obtain further variance reduction of the MC simulations. (3) The algorithm was tested on typical multi-asset options, such as exchange options, basket options (which can be more than two assets), and quanto options, showing the broad applicability and high efficiency of our method.

The paper is organized as follows. In Section 2, we introduce the pricing model of multi-asset options with stochastic volatilities. In Section 3, we deduce the CMC pricing framework, prove the martingale presentation theorem, and construct the martingale CV in detail. We present numerical tests and their results in Section 4, to evaluate the efficiency of our proposed method. Finally, we conclude the paper in Section 5.

2. Pricing Model

In this section, we give the pricing model of multi-asset options with stochastic volatilities. Specifically, in a risk-neutral world, let $S_i(t)$ be the price of the ith underlying asset ($i = 1, 2, \cdots, n$) at time t, which we assume obeys the following stochastic differential equations:

$$\frac{dS_i(t)}{S_i(t)} = (r - \delta_i)dt + f_i(Y_i(t))dW_i(t), \tag{1}$$

$$dY_i(t) = \mu_i(t, Y_i(t))dt + g_i(t, Y_i(t))dZ_i(t), \tag{2}$$

where r is the constant risk-free interest rate and δ_i is the continuous dividend rate. Y_i is the stochastic variance, and the functions $f_i(y), \mu_i(t, y)$, and $g_i(t, y)$ determine the specific volatility model, which can be quite general. $dW_i(t)$, and $dZ_i(t)$ are standard Brownian noise terms, and the covariance between them is captured as follows:

$$\text{cov}(dW_i(t), dW_j(t)) = \rho_{ij}dt, \quad i \neq j, \tag{3}$$

$$\text{cov}(dW_i(t), dZ_i(t)) = \rho_i dt, \quad i = 1, 2, \cdots, n, \tag{4}$$

$$\text{cov}(dW_i(t), dZ_j(t)) = 0, \quad i \neq j, \tag{5}$$

$$\text{cov}(dZ_i(t), dZ_j(t)) = 0, \quad i \neq j. \tag{6}$$

where the correlation coefficients ρ_{ij}, ρ_i are constant.

Equation (3) indicates that the underlying assets are correlated. Equations (4) and (5) indicate that any underlying asset is driven by only one stochastic variance factor and is not directly affected by the other stochastic variance factors. Equation (6) indicates that the random stochastic variance factors are mutually independent, but this assumption could be relaxed allowing for correlated random processes. Several popular stochastic volatility models are collected in Table 1.

Table 1. Models of stochastic volatility.

Reference	ρ_i	$f_i(y)$	$\mu_i(t, y)$	$g_i(t, y)$
Hull–White [8]	0	$\sqrt{y}$	μy	σy
Scott [9]	0	e^y	$a(\theta - y)$	σ
Stein–Stein [10]	0	$\|y\|$	$a(\theta - y)$	σ
Ball–Roma [11]	0	$\sqrt{y}$	$a(\theta - y)$	$\sigma\sqrt{y}(2a\theta > \sigma^2)$
Heston [12]	$\neq 0$	$\sqrt{y}$	$a(\theta - y)$	$\sigma\sqrt{y}(2a\theta > \sigma^2)$
Hagan et al. [14]	$\neq 0$	y	0	σy

Notes: μ is the drift of Hull–White stochastic volatility model. σ is the volatility of stochastic volatility. a is the rate of mean reversion and θ is the long-term mean of stochastic volatility. All parameters μ, a, θ, σ here are constants. The functions $\mu_i(t, y), g_i(t, y)$ here have no explicit dependence of time t.

In the following, we introduce our notations for convenience. The underlying asset vector is $S(t) = (S_1(t), \cdots, S_n(t))'$, and the stochastic variance vector is $Y(t) = (Y_1(t), \cdots, Y_n(t))'$, where $'$ represents the transpose of a vector or matrix. Additionally, the correlation matrix is given by $\Gamma = (\rho_{ij})$.

Suppose the payoff function of the European multi-asset option at maturity T is given by:

$$h(S_1(T), S_2(T), \cdots, S_n(T)) =: h(S(T)). \tag{7}$$

Denote $V(t, s, y)$ as the value of a European multi-asset option with stochastic volatilities at time t; then, by the no-arbitrage pricing principle we obtain:

$$V(t, s, y) = E\left[e^{-r(T-t)}h(S(T)) \mid S(t) = s, Y(t) = y\right], \tag{8}$$

where $E[\cdot]$ is the expectation in a risk-neutral world. Given the initial asset price $S(0)$ and initial variance $Y(0)$, the European option price at the initial time is actually:

$$V(0, S(0), Y(0)) = E[e^{-rT}h(S(T))]. \tag{9}$$

MC simulation can be used to compute the option price based on Equation (9) (please see Glasserman [39]). Suppose the number of samples in MC simulation is m. Firstly, for the jth sample, we need to simulate the processes of the Brownian motions $W_i^{(j)}(t)$ and $Z_i^{(j)}(t), i = 1, 2, \cdots, n$ to get the processes of $Y^{(j)}(t)$ and $S^{(j)}(t)$ and the discounted payoff $V^{(j)} = e^{-rT} h(S^{(j)}(T)), j = 1, 2, \cdots, m$. Then, we average the samples of discounted payoff and use the sample mean $\overline{V} = \frac{1}{m} \sum_{j=1}^{m} V^{(j)}$ as an estimation of the option price. The law of large numbers guarantees the convergence of MC simulation. The central limit theorem guarantees that the standard error—the standard deviation of sample mean $\overline{V}$—from MC simulation has a form of $Std = \frac{\text{var}(V^{(j)})}{\sqrt{m}}$. The standard error can be used to measure how far the sample mean is likely to be from the option price or to make confidence intervals of the option price, for instance, a 95% confidence interval $\overline{V} \pm 1.96 Std$. It also indicates that the MC simulation has a convergence rate as $O(m^{-1/2})$, which is rather low. Thus, in the next section, using a similar idea as in Liang and Xu [63], we propose our efficient CMC simulation framework with martingale CV for this option pricing problem.

If the stochastic volatility $f_i(Y_i(t))$ in Equation (1) is replaced by a constant volatility σ_i, we can obtain the dynamic process of an underlying asset with constant volatility as follows:

$$\frac{dS_i(t)}{S_i(t)} = (r - \delta_i)dt + \sigma_i dW_i(t), \quad i = 1, 2, \cdots, n. \tag{10}$$

The correlations between $dW_i(t)$ are defined by Equation (3). Jiang [20] carefully studied the explicit expression for a European multi-asset option value with constant volatility. Denote $V^{BS}(t, S(t); \sigma, \Gamma)$ as the corresponding price at time t, where the volatility vector is $\sigma = (\sigma_1, \sigma_2, \cdots, \sigma_n)'$. However, an analytic solution exists only for some specific options [20], such as exchange options, outer performance options, spread options, two dimension chooser options, basket options with a geometric average price, and quanto options. We give the specific expression for some of these in the numerical tests.

3. Dimension and Variance Reduction

In this section, we apply the acceleration methods of Liang and Xu [63] to price European multi-asset options with stochastic volatilities. The idea is that a martingale CV can be combined with the CMC method to reduce the variance of an MC simulation.

3.1. CMC Method

CMC can be used to reduce the variance of an MC simulation. Willard [64] initially put forward the CMC simulation to price options with stochastic volatilities. His method is feasible for those options that have a closed-form solution under the constant volatility model. Drimus [65] used CMC to analyze the variance products under the log-Ornstein–Uhlenbeck (log-OU) model. Boyle et al. [66] also used the CMC approach in pricing a down-and-in call option with a discretely monitored barrier. Broadie and Kaya [67] applied the CMC to accelerate exact simulations of the stochastic volatility with affine jump diffusion processes. Yang et al. [68] employed the CMC to reduce the variance of MC simulations when calculating the prices and greeks of barrier options. Dingeç and Hörmann [44] and Sun and Xu [46] combined CMC simulations and other variance reduction techniques to price basket options.

When we consider computing the expectation $E[Y]$ of a random variable Y, the conditional expectation $E[Y|X]$ of Y on some other variable X is also an unbiased estimator of $E[Y]$. This results from the double expectation formula $E[Y] = E[E[Y|X]]$, and the variance decomposition formula [69]:

$$\text{var}(Y) = \text{var}(E[Y|X]) + E[\text{var}(Y|X)] \geq \text{var}(E[Y|X]),$$

which indicates that the variance of $E[Y|X]$ is always smaller than that of Y. The so-called CMC method uses the conditional expectation of the random variable $E[Y|X]$ instead of that of the original random variable Y, which can obviously reduce variance. The key is that we need to have a closed form of $E[Y|X]$.

Now, we intend to deduce the CMC pricing formula for the pricing problem of Equation (8). The most important thing is to obtain the conditional expectation of the discounted payoff $e^{-rT}h(S(T))$ on other random variables or stochastic information. First, a Cholesky decomposition of Brownian noise $dW_i(t)$ is conducted according to Equation (4):

$$dW_i(t) = \rho_i dZ_i(t) + \sqrt{1 - \rho_i^2} d\tilde{Z}_i(t), \quad (i = 1, 2, \cdots, n), \tag{11}$$

where $dZ_i(t)$ and $d\tilde{Z}_i(t)$ are independent standard Brownian noises, which means that:

$$\text{cov}(dZ_i(t), d\tilde{Z}_i(t)) = 0, \quad (i = 1, 2, \cdots, n). \tag{12}$$

If we denote the vectors $d\mathbf{W}(t) = (dW_1(t), \cdots, dW_n(t))'$, $d\mathbf{Z}(t) = (dZ_1(t), \cdots, dZ_n(t))'$, and $d\tilde{\mathbf{Z}}(t) = (d\tilde{Z}_1(t), \cdots, d\tilde{Z}_n(t))'$, then Equation (11) can be rewritten to:

$$d\mathbf{W}(t) = diag(\boldsymbol{\rho})d\mathbf{Z}(t) + diag(\boldsymbol{q})d\tilde{\mathbf{Z}}(t). \tag{13}$$

where $\boldsymbol{\rho} = (\rho_1, \cdots, \rho_n)'$, $\boldsymbol{q} = \left(\sqrt{1 - \rho_1^2}, \cdots, \sqrt{1 - \rho_n^2}\right)'$, and $diag(\boldsymbol{v})$ is a diagonal matrix, with diagonal values from the vector $\boldsymbol{v}$. According to Equations (12) and (13), it is obvious that:

$$\text{cov}(d\mathbf{W}(t)) = diag(\boldsymbol{\rho})^2 dt + diag(\boldsymbol{q})\text{cov}(d\tilde{\mathbf{Z}}(t))diag(\boldsymbol{q}). \tag{14}$$

Notice that Equation (3) implies:
$$\text{cov}(d\mathbf{W}(t)) = \Gamma dt. \tag{15}$$

We can solve for the covariance of $d\tilde{\mathbf{Z}}(t)$ by Equations (14) and (15) as:

$$\text{cov}(d\tilde{\mathbf{Z}}(t)) = diag(\boldsymbol{q})^{-1}\left(\Gamma - diag(\boldsymbol{\rho})^2\right)diag(\mathbf{q})^{-1}dt =: \tilde{\Gamma}dt. \tag{16}$$

The entries of matrix $\tilde{\Gamma}$ are

$$\tilde{\Gamma}_{ii} = 1, \quad \tilde{\Gamma}_{ij} = \frac{\rho_{ij}}{\sqrt{1 - \rho_i^2}\sqrt{1 - \rho_j^2}} \quad (i \neq j). \tag{17}$$

To ensure the matrix $\tilde{\Gamma}$ is well-defined, the condition of correlation coefficients $|\rho_i| < 1, |\tilde{\Gamma}_{ij}| < 1$ should be satisfied.

Then, applying the Itô formula to $\ln(S_i(t))$, with the help of Equations (1) and (11), results in:

$$d\ln(S_i(t)) = \left(r - \delta_i - \tfrac{1}{2}f_i^2(Y_i(t))\right)dt + \rho_i f_i(Y_i(t))dZ_i(t) + \sqrt{1 - \rho_i^2}f_i(Y_i(t))d\tilde{Z}_i(t), \quad (i = 1, 2, \cdots, n). \tag{18}$$

Integrating both sides of the above equation from t to T results in:

$$S_i(T) = S_i(t)\xi_i(t, T)\exp\left((r - \delta_i)(T - t) - \tfrac{1 - \rho_i^2}{2}\int_t^T f_i^2(Y_i(s))ds + \sqrt{1 - \rho_i^2}\int_t^T f_i(Y_i(s))d\tilde{Z}_i(s)\right), \tag{19}$$

where

$$\xi_i(t, T) = \exp\left(-\frac{1}{2}\rho_i^2\int_t^T f_i^2(Y_i(s))ds + \rho_i\int_t^T f_i(Y_i(s))dZ_i(s)\right). \tag{20}$$

Note that $\xi_i(t, T)$ is actually an exponential martingale with expectation $E[\xi_i(t, T)] = 1$.

Let $\bar{\sigma}_i(t, T)$ denote the average volatility of underlying asset S_i on the interval $[t, T]$, which is given by:

$$\bar{\sigma}_i(t, T)^2 = \frac{1}{T - t}\int_t^T f_i^2(Y_i(s))ds. \tag{21}$$

It is observed that, given the information of stochastic processes $\{Z_1(t), Z_2(t), \cdots, Z_n(t)\}$, the quantities $\xi_i(t, T)$, and $\bar{\sigma}_i(t, T)(i = 1, 2, \cdots, n)$ are totally determined. The pricing problem of Equation (8) then becomes the expectation of random variables $\{\tilde{Z}_1(t), \tilde{Z}_2(t), \cdots, \tilde{Z}_n(t)\}$. Assume there exists a Black–Scholes formula with constant volatilities. Then, calculating expectations with $\{\tilde{Z}_1(t), \tilde{Z}_2(t), \cdots, \tilde{Z}_n(t)\}$ gives us the CMC pricing formula of a European multi-asset option with stochastic volatility, as follows:

$$V(t, \boldsymbol{S}(t), \boldsymbol{Y}(t)) = E\left[V^{\text{BS}}\left(t, \boldsymbol{S}(t) \cdot \boldsymbol{\xi}(t, T); \boldsymbol{q} \cdot \bar{\sigma}(t, T), \tilde{\Gamma}\right)\right]. \tag{22}$$

where $\cdot$ is the dot product of two vectors, $\boldsymbol{\xi}(t, T) = (\xi_1(t, T), \cdots, \xi_n(t, T))'$, and $\bar{\sigma}(t, T) = (\bar{\sigma}_1(t, T), \cdots, \bar{\sigma}_n(t, T))'$.

Compared with the MC formula in Equation (8), we now only need to simulate the n random variables $\{\boldsymbol{Z}(t)\}$ instead of the $2n$ random variables $\{\boldsymbol{W}(t), \text{ and } \boldsymbol{Z}(t)\}$. Thus, the dimension and variance are reduced by the properties of the CMC.

3.2. Martingale Control Variate (CV)

To further reduce the simulation variance of the variable $V^{\text{BS}}\left(t, \boldsymbol{S}(t) \cdot \boldsymbol{\xi}(t, T); \boldsymbol{q} \cdot \bar{\sigma}(t, T), \tilde{\Gamma}\right)$ in Equation (22), a general martingale CV is proposed to combine with the CMC simulation. Some brief introductions about the CV method are given at first (for more details and references, please refer to Glasserman [39]).

When the CV method is used to compute the expectation $E[Y]$, the CV estimator is:

$$Y(b) = Y - b(X - E[X]),$$

where X is called a CV and $E[X]$ is the closed-form expectation of X. The constant b can be selected as $b^* = \text{cov}(X, Y)/\text{var}(X)$ to minimize the variance of the CV estimator with an optimal variance reduction ratio $R^2 = \text{var}(Y)/\text{var}(Y(b^*)) = 1/(1 - \rho_{XY}^2)$. The efficiency of the CV method can be measured by the variance reduction ratio R^2 or the standard error reduction ratio R. The success of the CV depends on high correlations with the naive variable Y and the availability of its expectation $E[X]$. Thus, the CV is always elegantly designed to a specific problem. In this paper, a martingale whose expectation equals to zero is used as a CV, which avoids any extra effort needed to obtain its expectation.

To construct an efficient CV in the CMC framework, a martingale representation theorem for the stochastic volatility pricing model of Equations (1) and (2) is proved in the following theorem.

Theorem 1 (Martingale Representation Theorem). *If the underlying assets satisfy Equations (1) and (2), the European multi-asset option price at the initial time $V(0, \boldsymbol{S}(0), \boldsymbol{Y}(0))$ with payoff $h(\boldsymbol{S}(T))$ can be expressed as:*

$$e^{-rT}h(\boldsymbol{S}(T)) - V(0, \boldsymbol{S}(0), \boldsymbol{Y}(0)) = \int_0^T e^{-rt}\left(\sum_{i=1}^n S_i(t) f_i(Y_i(t))\frac{\partial V}{\partial S_i}dW_i(t) + \sum_{i=1}^n \mu_i(t, Y_i(t))\frac{\partial V}{\partial Y_i}dZ_i(t)\right), \tag{23}$$

which can be rewritten in vector form as:

$$e^{-rT}h(\boldsymbol{S}(T)) - V(0, \boldsymbol{S}(0), \boldsymbol{Y}(0)) = \int_0^T e^{-rt}\left((\boldsymbol{S}(t) \cdot \boldsymbol{f}(\boldsymbol{Y}(t)) \cdot \nabla_S V)'d\boldsymbol{W}(t) + (\boldsymbol{\mu}(t, \boldsymbol{Y}(t)) \cdot \nabla_Y V)'d\boldsymbol{Z}(t)\right), \tag{24}$$

where $\boldsymbol{f}(\boldsymbol{Y}(t)) = (f_1(Y_1(t)), \cdots, f_n(Y_n(t)))'$, $\boldsymbol{\mu}(t, \boldsymbol{Y}(t)) = (\mu_1(t, Y_1(t)), \cdots, \mu_n(t, Y_n(t)))'$, $\nabla_S V = (\frac{\partial V}{\partial S_1}, \cdots, \frac{\partial V}{\partial S_n})'$, and $\nabla_Y V = (\frac{\partial V}{\partial Y_1}, \cdots, \frac{\partial V}{\partial Y_n})'$.

Proof. Applying Itô's formula to $e^{-rt}V(t, \boldsymbol{S}(t), \boldsymbol{Y}(t))$ yields:

$$d\left(e^{-rt}V(t, \boldsymbol{S}(t), \boldsymbol{Y}(t))\right) = e^{-rt}LVdt + e^{-rt}\left(\sum_{i=1}^n S_i(t) f_i(Y_i(t))\frac{\partial V}{\partial S_i}dW_i(t) + \sum_{i=1}^n \mu_i(t, Y_i(t))\frac{\partial V}{\partial Y_i}dZ_i(t)\right),$$

where

$$LV = \frac{\partial V}{\partial t} + \frac{1}{2}\sum_{i,j=1}^{n}\rho_{ij}S_iS_jf_i(Y_i)f_j(Y_j)\frac{\partial^2 V}{\partial S_i \partial S_j} + \sum_{i=1}^{n}\rho_iS_if_i(Y_i)\mu_i(t,Y_i)\frac{\partial^2 V}{\partial S_i \partial Y_i}$$

$$+ \frac{1}{2}\sum_{i=1}^{n}g_i^2(t,Y_i)\frac{\partial^2 V}{\partial Y_i^2} + \sum_{i=1}^{n}(r-\delta_i)S_if_i(Y_i)\frac{\partial V}{\partial S_i} + \sum_{i=1}^{n}\mu_i(t,Y_i)\frac{\partial V}{\partial Y_i} - rV.$$

Furthermore, $LV = 0$ because of the Feynman–Kac formula [69], and thus:

$$d\left(e^{-rt}V(t,S(t),Y(t))\right) = e^{-rt}\left(\sum_{i=1}^{n}S_i(t)f_i(Y_i(t))\frac{\partial V}{\partial S_i}dW_i(t) + \sum_{i=1}^{n}\mu_i(t,Y_i(t))\frac{\partial V}{\partial Y_i}dZ_i(t)\right).$$

Now, by integrating both sides of the above equation on the interval $[0,T]$, and noticing that $V(T,S(T),Y(T)) = h(S(T))$, we obtain the conclusion of the martingale representation theorem. □

The martingale representation theorem gives us inspiration to construct efficient CVs. For simplicity, denote:

$$X = \int_0^T e^{-rt}\left((S(t)\cdot f(Y(t))\cdot\nabla_S V)'dW(t) + (\mu(t,Y(t))\cdot\nabla_Y V)'dZ(t)\right), \qquad (25)$$

The martingale expression in Equation (23) indicates that the variance of $e^{-rT}h(S(T))$ in the MC simulation is totally determined by the martingale X. Thus, the martingale X plays the role of a perfect CV for an MC simulation. Fouque and Han [18] actually gave a similar representation in their work, and used the martingales as a CV to price single-asset options under a specific multi-factor stochastic volatility model. This can be understood in financial terminology. The martingale CV corresponds to a continuous delta hedge strategy taken by a trader who sells the option. The integrands of the martingale would, in theory, be the perfect delta hedges. Even though perfect replication by delta hedging under stochastic volatility models is impossible, the variance of replication error is directly related to the variance induced by the martingale CV method.

For the CMC pricing framework, taking the conditional expectation of both sides of Equation (23) based on the information $\{Z(t), 0 \le t \le T\}$, results in:

$$V^{BS}\left(t,S(t)\cdot\xi(t,T);q\cdot\bar{\sigma}(t,T),\tilde{\Gamma}\right) - V(0,S_0,Y_0) = \hat{X}, \qquad (26)$$

where

$$\hat{X} = E\left[X|Z(t),0 \le t \le T\right]. \qquad (27)$$

We can determine the expression for $\hat{X}$ by first substituting the Cholesky decomposition, Equation (11), into the expression of X in Equation (25). Then, we compute the expectations about $\{\tilde{Z}_1(t),\tilde{Z}_2(t),\cdots,\tilde{Z}_n(t)\}$ as:

$$\hat{X} = \int_0^T e^{-rt}(\rho\cdot F_1(t))'dZ(t) + \int_0^T e^{-rt}F_2(t)'dZ(t), \qquad (28)$$

where

$$F_1(t) = E[S(t)\cdot f(Y(t))\cdot\nabla_S V|Z(s),0 \le s \le t], \qquad (29)$$

$$F_2(t) = E[\mu(t,Y(t))\cdot\nabla_Y V|Z(s),0 \le s \le t]. \qquad (30)$$

Equation (26) shows that the variance of $V^{BS}\left(t,S(t)\cdot\xi(t,T);q\cdot\bar{\sigma}(t,T),\tilde{\Gamma}\right)$ is totally determined by the zero martingale $\hat{X}$, since $V(0,S_0,Y_0)$ is a constant. This indicates that $\hat{X}$, theoretically, is a perfect CV for $V^{BS}\left(t,S(t)\cdot\xi(t,T);q\cdot\bar{\sigma}(t,T),\tilde{\Gamma}\right)$ in CMC simulations. It is a pity that we have no explicit expression of this perfect zero martingale, since there is no exact expression for $V(t, s, y)$. A possible solution is that we approximate the option price $V(t, s, y)$ with a Black–Scholes option price along with some carefully selected volatility parameters. In the following, we show our approach.

Given the information $\{Z(s), 0 \leq s \leq t\}$, the conditional expectation of $S(t)$ can be computed by Equation (19) as:

$$\hat{S}(t) = E[S(t)|Z(s), 0 \leq s \leq t] = e^{(r-\delta)t} S(0) \cdot \boldsymbol{\xi}(0, t). \tag{31}$$

We intend to use $V^{\text{BS}}(t, S(t); \boldsymbol{\theta}, \Gamma)$ as an approximation of $V(t, S(t), Y(t))$, where $\boldsymbol{\theta}$ is a constant vector whose values should be carefully selected. The partial derivatives can thus be approximated as:

$$\begin{aligned} \nabla_S V(t, S(t), Y(t)) &\approx \nabla_S V^{\text{BS}}(t, S(t); \boldsymbol{\theta}, \Gamma), \\ \nabla_Y V(t, S(t), Y(t)) &\approx \nabla_Y V^{\text{BS}}(t, S(t); \boldsymbol{\theta}, \Gamma) = \mathbf{0}. \end{aligned}$$

Now, given the information $\{Z(s), 0 \leq s \leq t\}$, by using the approximated derivatives and substituting $S(t)$ with $\hat{S}(t)$ in Equations (29) and (30), $F_1(t)$ can be approximately expressed as:

$$\hat{F}_1(t) = \hat{S}(t) \cdot f(Y(t)) \cdot \nabla_S V^{\text{BS}}(t, \hat{S}(t); \boldsymbol{\theta}, \Gamma). \tag{32}$$

Notice that $\nabla_Y V^{\text{BS}}(t, \hat{S}(t); \boldsymbol{\theta}, \Gamma) = \mathbf{0}$, so $\hat{F}_2(t) \approx \mathbf{0}$.

In the end, we obtain our martingale CV:

$$\tilde{X} = \int_0^T e^{-rt} (\boldsymbol{\rho} \cdot \hat{F}_1(t))' d\mathbf{Z}(t). \tag{33}$$

The value of the constant volatility vector $\boldsymbol{\theta}$ should be determined if we want to use the martingale $\tilde{X}$ as a CV. Fouque and Han [18] illustrated a method for pricing a single-asset option with multi-factor volatility. They picked the long-term mean of the volatility as the volatility parameter in their specific multi-factor model. However, they did not offer a solution for non-mean-reverting stochastic volatility models, such as the Hull–White model.

In this paper, we set parameter $\boldsymbol{\theta} = f(E[Y(t)])$. The idea is that, on the interval $[t, T]$, the stochastic variance $Y(t)$ is approximated by the expectations of their initial state $E[Y(t)]$. This results in a corresponding approximated stochastic volatility $f(E[Y(t)])$. We hope that the dynamic behavior of the approximated process with such parameters is similar to the original process.

Remark 1. *It is difficult to use the CMC pricing formula of Equation (22) if the analytic solution of a European multi-asset option price under constant volatility does not exist. However, we can still construct a martingale CV for an MC simulation in those cases.*

According to the martingale representation theorem (Theorem 1), the variance of $e^{-rT} h(S(T))$ in an MC simulation is totally determined by the zero martingale X (see Equation (23)). We can select a value $V^{\text{approx}}(t, S(t); \boldsymbol{\theta}, \Gamma)$ with a constant volatility parameter $\boldsymbol{\theta}$ as the approximation of option price $V(t, S(t), Y(t))$ under a stochastic volatility model. Following the idea in the CMC framework, we select $\boldsymbol{\theta} = f(E[Y(t)])$. Thus, the partial derivatives can be approximated as:

$$\begin{aligned} \nabla_S V(t, S(t), Y(t)) &\approx \nabla_S V^{\text{approx}}(t, S(t); \boldsymbol{\theta}, \Gamma), \\ \nabla_Y V(t, S(t), Y(t)) &\approx \nabla_Y V^{\text{approx}}(t, S(t); \boldsymbol{\theta}, \Gamma) = 0. \end{aligned}$$

Furthermore, the martingale CV is:

$$\tilde{X} = \int_0^T e^{-rt} (\boldsymbol{\rho} \cdot S(t) \cdot f(Y(t)) \cdot \nabla_S V^{\text{approx}}(t, S(t); \boldsymbol{\theta}, \Gamma))' d\mathbf{Z}(t).$$

Taking the arithmetic average basket option with stochastic volatilities as an example, we can use the geometric average basket option with constant volatilities as an approximation and then construct the *corresponding CV. It is expected that, for a more accurate approximated price $V^{approx}(t, S(t); \theta, \Gamma)$, a larger variance reduction ratio can be obtained by the corresponding martingale CV.*

4. Numerical Tests

In this section, we present some numerical tests designed for the typical multi-asset options—including the exchange options, basket options and quanto options—to emphasize the efficiency of our method.

4.1. Exchange Options

The exchange option, which was first studied by Margrabe [70], empowers its holder with the right to exercise it by comparing the difference between the prices or the rates of return of two underlying assets. Its payoff is:

$$h^{excha}(S_1(T), S_2(T)) = \max(S_2(T) - S_1(T), 0). \tag{34}$$

If the underlying assets evolute with constant volatilities σ_1 and σ_2, the exchange option has a pricing formula at time t, as shown by Margrabe [70] and Jiang [20] as follows:

$$V^{BS-excha}(t, S_1, S_2) = e^{-\delta_2(T-t)}S_2N(-d_2) - e^{-\delta_1(T-t)}S_1N(-d_1), \tag{35}$$

where

$$d_1 = \frac{\ln\frac{S_1}{S_2} + \left(\delta_2 - \delta_1 + \frac{1}{2}(\sigma_1^2 - 2\rho_{12}\sigma_1\sigma_2 + \sigma_2^2)\right)(T-t)}{\sqrt{(\sigma_1^2 - 2\rho_{12}\sigma_1\sigma_2 + \sigma_2^2)(T-t)}}, \tag{36}$$

$$d_2 = d_1 - \sqrt{(\sigma_1^2 - 2\rho_{12}\sigma_1\sigma_2 + \sigma_2^2)(T-t)}, \tag{37}$$

and $N(x) = \frac{1}{\sqrt{2\pi}}\int_{-\infty}^{x} e^{-\frac{t^2}{2}}dt$ is the cumulative distribution function of a standard normal variable. It is easy to derive the derivatives:

$$\frac{\partial}{\partial S_1}V^{BS-excha}(t, S_1, S_2) = -e^{-\delta_1(T-t)}N(-d_1),$$

$$\frac{\partial}{\partial S_2}V^{BS-excha}(t, S_1, S_2) = e^{-\delta_2(T-t)}N(-d_2).$$

We assumed the stochastic volatilities obey the Heston model, for $i = 1, 2$:

$$\frac{dS_i(t)}{S_i(t)} = (r - \delta_i)dt + \sqrt{Y_i(t)}dW_i(t),$$

$$dY_i(t) = a_i(\theta_i - Y_i(t))dt + \sigma_i\sqrt{Y_i(t)}dZ_i(t).$$

The parameters should satisfy the Feller condition [71] to guarantee the positiveness of variance, i.e., $2a_1\theta_1 > \sigma_1^2$ and $2a_2\theta_2 > \sigma_2^2$. We used a truncated Euler discrete scheme [39,72,73] with equal time intervals to simulate the Heston process in our tests.

At first, we wanted to examine the acceleration effect of a CMC simulation compared with a traditional MC simulation. We fixed the parameters $S_1(0) = S_2(0) = K = 30$, $r = 0.05$, $T = 1$, $\delta_1 = \delta_2 = 0$, $a_1 = a_2$, $\sigma_1 = \sigma_2 = 0.2$, $Y_1(0) = 0.01$, $Y_2(0) = 0.04$, $\theta_1 = 0.015$, and $\theta_2 = 0.05$. Additionally, we took the number of time steps $N = 100$, and the number of simulations $m = 100,000$ in all numerical simulations. Note that $\left|\frac{\rho_{12}}{\sqrt{1-\rho_1^2}\sqrt{1-\rho_2^2}}\right| < 1$ should be satisfied from Equation (17).

Taking $\rho_{12} = 0$ for simplicity, the numerical results with different correlation coefficients are recorded in Tables 2 and 3.

Table 2. Exchange option: Estimated prices for MC and CMC with different correlation coefficients.

$\rho_1\backslash\rho_2$	−0.75	−0.50	−0.25	0.00	0.25	0.50	0.75	
−0.75	2.8083	2.8218	2.8336	2.8436	2.8519	2.8587	2.8639	
−0.50	2.8169	2.8294	2.8402	2.8493	2.8567	2.8623	2.8663	
−0.25	2.8248	2.8362	2.8459	2.8539	2.8603	2.8649	2.8678	
0.00	2.8317	2.8420	2.8505	2.8573	2.8625	2.8661	2.8680	$\overline{V}_{\mathrm{MC}}$
0.25	2.8372	2.8462	2.8536	2.8594	2.8635	2.8660	2.8667	
0.50	2.8413	2.8492	2.8554	2.8600	2.8630	2.8644	2.8641	
0.75	2.8440	2.8508	2.8558	2.8592	2.8612	2.8615	2.8601	
−0.75	2.8153	2.8294	2.8420	2.8528	2.8616	2.8684	2.8731	
−0.50	2.8253	2.8377	2.8486	2.8578	2.8651	2.8703	2.8735	
−0.25	2.8340	2.8446	2.8539	2.8615	2.8672	2.8709	2.8725	
0.00	2.8413	2.8503	2.8579	2.8639	2.8679	2.8700	2.8700	$\overline{V}_{\mathrm{CMC}}$
0.25	2.8473	2.8546	2.8606	2.8649	2.8674	2.8678	2.8661	
0.50	2.8519	2.8576	2.8620	2.8647	2.8654	2.8641	2.8608	
0.75	2.8550	2.8592	2.8620	2.8630	2.8621	2.8591	2.8539	

Notes: ρ_1 is the correlation coefficient between the first underlying asset and its volatility; ρ_2 is the correlation coefficient between the second underlying asset and its volatility; $\overline{V}_{\mathrm{MC}}$ is the estimated price for MC simulation; and $\overline{V}_{\mathrm{CMC}}$ is the estimated price for CMC simulation.

Table 3. Exchange option: Numerical results for MC and CMC with different correlation coefficients.

$\rho_1\backslash\rho_2$	−0.75	−0.50	−0.25	0.00	0.25	0.50	0.75	
−0.75	0.0132	0.0137	0.0143	0.0148	0.0153	0.0159	0.0164	
−0.50	0.0132	0.0137	0.0142	0.0148	0.0153	0.0158	0.0164	
−0.25	0.0131	0.0137	0.0142	0.0147	0.0153	0.0158	0.0164	
0.00	0.0131	0.0136	0.0141	0.0147	0.0152	0.0158	0.0163	Std_{MC}
0.25	0.0130	0.0135	0.0141	0.0146	0.0152	0.0157	0.0163	
0.50	0.0130	0.0135	0.0140	0.0146	0.0151	0.0157	0.0163	
0.75	0.0129	0.0134	0.0140	0.0145	0.0151	0.0156	0.0162	
−0.75	0.0088	0.0065	0.0049	0.0045	0.0058	0.0084	0.0119	
−0.50	0.0081	0.0055	0.0036	0.0032	0.0049	0.0077	0.0115	
−0.25	0.0076	0.0048	0.0025	0.0020	0.0042	0.0073	0.0112	
0.00	0.0074	0.0045	0.0019	0.0011	0.0039	0.0071	0.0110	Std_{CMC}
0.25	0.0075	0.0046	0.0020	0.0012	0.0039	0.0072	0.0111	
0.50	0.0078	0.0050	0.0027	0.0021	0.0043	0.0074	0.0113	
0.75	0.0084	0.0057	0.0036	0.0031	0.0048	0.0078	0.0116	
−0.75	1.5014	2.1268	2.9394	3.2711	2.6283	1.8898	1.3762	
−0.50	1.6372	2.4911	3.9677	4.6222	3.1339	2.0450	1.4323	
−0.25	1.7336	2.8222	5.5991	7.3682	3.6300	2.1571	1.4677	
0.00	1.7692	2.9943	7.3944	13.0340	3.9300	2.2070	1.4805	$R = \frac{Std_{\mathrm{MC}}}{Std_{\mathrm{CMC}}}$
0.25	1.7385	2.9276	7.0000	11.8935	3.8805	2.1900	1.4714	
0.50	1.6551	2.6807	5.2352	7.0184	3.5503	2.1170	1.4433	
0.75	1.5402	2.3701	3.9081	4.7380	3.1223	2.0066	1.4001	

Notes: ρ_1 is the correlation coefficient between the first underlying asset and its volatility; ρ_2 is the correlation coefficient between the second underlying asset and its volatility; Std_{MC}, Std_{CMC} are the standard errors of estimated prices from the MC and CMC simulations respectively; and $R = \frac{Std_{\mathrm{MC}}}{Std_{\mathrm{CMC}}}$ is the ratio of standard errors.

Table 2 records the estimated option values calculated by the MC and CMC simulations, which are denoted as $\overline{V}_{\mathrm{MC}}$ and $\overline{V}_{\mathrm{CMC}}$, respectively. The upper part of Table 3 records the standard errors of an MC simulation, denoted as Std_{MC}. The standard errors are almost the same for various correlation coefficients, and increase slightly with correlation ρ_2 while decreasing with ρ_1. The exchange option can be seen as a call option on asset S_2 for fixed S_1; a higher correlation ρ_2 implies a larger variation in the price of asset S_2, thus resulting in a larger value of the option price and a larger simulation variance. Similar analysis can be conducted with respect to correlation ρ_1 by regrading the exchange option as a put option on asset S_1 for fixed S_2.

The middle part of Table 3 records the standard errors of a CMC simulation, denoted as Std_{CMC}. Obviously, the standard CMC errors are always smaller than MC. It is interesting that a standard CMC error rapidly declines as correlation coefficient ρ_1 or ρ_2 tends to zero. Thus, the ratio of the standard errors of a CMC simulation to an MC simulation reduces. We denote this ratio as $R = Std_{\text{MC}}/Std_{\text{CMC}}$ and present its values at the bottom of Table 3. R becomes larger when the correlation coefficient is getting closer to the original point, and decays rapidly in the opposite direction. For example, for $\rho_1 = \rho_2 = 0, 0.25, 0.5$, and 0.75, the reduction ratios of the standard error are $13.0340, 3.8805, 2.1170$, and 1.4001, respectively. This can be explained by Equation (11); the CMC simulation removes the randomness that is independent from the stochastic variances Y_1, Y_2, and its quantity is proportional to $\sqrt{1-\rho_1^2}$, or $\sqrt{1-\rho_2^2}$. In other words, a larger variance reduction ratio is promised when the absolute value of ρ_1 or ρ_2 is smaller. This property indicates that a CMC simulation is more competitive when the correlation between the underlying asset and stochastic volatility is weak.

We also investigated the computational costs of the MC and CMC methods. The computational platform for this paper was an Intel i5-6200U CPU, 2.30 GHz, 8 GB memory, and the software environment was Matlab R2018a for Windows 10. It took 50.88 s to calculate all of the data in the upper part of Table 3 and 25.85 s for the middle part, which means that the time cost of a CMC simulation is almost half that of an MC simulation. This is because the MC method needs to simulate four random variables, $\{W_1(t), W_2(t), Z_1(t)$, and $Z_2(t)\}$, while the CMC method only needs to simulate two random variables, $\{Z_1(t)$, and $Z_2(t)\}$.

Taking the variance reduction ratio into consideration, the speed up ratio of a CMC simulation to an MC simulation is defined as $\frac{Std_{\text{MC}}^2}{Std_{\text{CMC}}^2} \cdot \frac{t_{\text{MC}}}{t_{\text{CMC}}}$. Thus, when correlation $\rho_1 = \rho_2 = 0$, the speed up ratio of the CMC is $13.0340^2 \cdot \frac{50.88}{25.85} = 334.38$. Even for the case of a larger correlation $\rho_1 = \rho_2 = 0.75$, the speed up ratio of the CMC is $1.4001^2 \cdot \frac{50.88}{25.85} = 3.86$, which improves the efficiency of the MC simulation by roughly 75%. In summary, the CMC simulation enjoys the advantages of saving time and having a great variance reduction ratio, especially when the correlation coefficients are small.

We next tested the efficiency of our martingale CV method. As a contrast, we constructed another CV for the stochastic model, as suggested by Ma and Xu [74]. Consider dummy assets whose prices $\tilde{S}_i(t), (i = 1, 2, \cdots, n)$ satisfy the following stochastic differential equations:

$$\frac{d\tilde{S}_i(t)}{\tilde{S}_i(t)} = (r - \delta_i)dt + \tilde{\sigma}_i(t)dW_i(t),$$

where $\tilde{\sigma}_i(t)$ is a determined function. The covariance of $dW_i(t)$ is given by Equation (3). It can be computed by matching the first two moments of the underlying asset prices as $\tilde{\sigma}_i^2(t) = E[f_i^2(Y_i(t))]$. In the case of a Heston stochastic volatility model:

$$\tilde{\sigma}_i^2(t) = E[Y_i(t)] = \theta_i + (Y_i(0) - \theta_i)e^{-a_i t}, \quad i = 1, 2.$$

We used the payoff $h^{\text{excha}}(\tilde{S}_1(T), \tilde{S}_2(T))$ as a CV to the MC method, and we called this CV method a function CV method. The corresponding exchange option price can be computed using Equation (35) by replacing $\sigma_1^2 + \sigma_2^2 - 2\rho_{12}\sigma_1\sigma_2$ in Equations (36) and (37) with the average volatility on the interval $[0, T]$ given by:

$$\frac{1}{T}\int_0^T E[Y_1(t)] + E[Y_2(t)] - 2\rho_{12}\sqrt{E[Y_1(t)]E[Y_2(t)]}dt.$$

We changed the values of the correlation coefficients and kept the other parameters fixed as before. Remember that $\left|\frac{\rho_{12}}{\sqrt{1-\rho_1^2}\sqrt{1-\rho_2^2}}\right| < 1$. The detailed results are shown in Table 4.

Table 4. Exchange option: Numerical results for CVs with different correlation coefficients.

ρ_{12}	$\rho_1 = \rho_2$	Std_{MC}	Std_{Mar}	Std_{Fun}	R_1	R_2
-0.5	-0.6	0.0160	0.0015	0.0039	10.3761	4.1166
	-0.4	0.0163	0.0013	0.0040	12.2233	4.0626
	-0.2	0.0166	0.0012	0.0041	13.9129	4.0540
	0.0	0.0170	0.0011	0.0042	15.0719	4.0821
	0.2	0.0173	0.0013	0.0042	13.2504	4.1410
	0.4	0.0176	0.0016	0.0042	11.1433	4.2271
	0.6	0.0180	0.0019	0.0041	9.5880	4.3348
0.0	-0.75	0.0132	0.0014	0.0039	9.6978	3.4035
	-0.50	0.0137	0.0012	0.0040	11.2209	3.4318
	-0.25	0.0142	0.0010	0.0041	14.6458	3.4829
	0.00	0.0147	0.0009	0.0041	16.2942	3.5500
	0.25	0.0152	0.0011	0.0042	13.3596	3.6291
	0.50	0.0157	0.0015	0.0042	10.2764	3.7178
	0.75	0.0162	0.0017	0.0043	9.6550	3.8097
0.5	-0.6	0.0106	0.0010	0.0038	10.9374	2.8023
	-0.4	0.0110	0.0009	0.0040	12.9115	2.7755
	-0.2	0.0115	0.0006	0.0041	17.7294	2.7910
	0.0	0.0119	0.0006	0.0042	19.8106	2.8424
	0.2	0.0123	0.0008	0.0042	14.7523	2.9285
	0.4	0.0127	0.0012	0.0042	10.7868	3.0531
	0.6	0.0131	0.0012	0.0041	10.6183	3.2264

Notes: ρ_{12} is the correlation coefficient between the first underlying asset and the second underlying asset; ρ_1 is the correlation coefficient between the first underlying asset and its volatility; ρ_2 is the correlation coefficient between the second underlying asset and its volatility; Std_{MC}, Std_{Mar}, Std_{Fun} are the standard errors from the MC method, the martingale CV method and the function CV method respectively; $R_1 = Std_{MC}/Std_{Mar}$; and $R_2 = Std_{MC}/Std_{Fun}$.

In Table 4, Std_{MC}, Std_{Mar}, and Std_{Fun} are the standard errors from the MC simulation, the martingale CV method, and the function CV method, respectively. $R_1 = Std_{MC}/Std_{Mar}$ is the standard error reduction ratio of the martingale CV method compared to the MC simulation, and $R_2 = Std_{MC}/Std_{Fun}$ is the the standard error reduction ratio of the function CV method compared to the MC simulation.

It is obvious that the standard error reduction ratio of the CMC is much larger than that of the function CV method, the former falling in 9–20 while the latter being about 3 or 4. Table 4 also shows that, for a fixed $\rho_1 = \rho_2$, the standard errors of the MC simulation, martingale CV method, and function CV method decrease with the correlation value of ρ_{12}. For a fixed ρ_{12}, the standard errors of the MC simulation and function CV method increase with the value of $\rho_1 = \rho_2$ while the martingale CV method decreases with the absolute value of $\rho_1 = \rho_2$, which is mainly caused by the properties of the CMC. Thus, the standard error reduction ratio of the martingale CV method also decreases with the absolute value of $\rho_1 = \rho_2$.

The computing times for all values of the MC, the martingale CV, and the function CV methods are 22.33, 22.26, and 25.50 s, respectively. The time costs of the MC method and the martingale CV method are almost the same, while the function CV method is slightly slower. Thus, the martingale CV method proposed in our paper is superior to the function CV method, when considering the variance reduction ratio and the time cost.

Fixing the parameters $\rho_{12} = 0$, and $\rho_1 = \rho_2 = 0.5$, we next examined the effects of the volatility parameters for the stochastic volatility. In the Heston stochastic volatility model, the Feller condition should be satisfied [71]; thus, $\sigma_1 < \sqrt{2a_1\theta_1} = \sqrt{2 \cdot 2 \cdot 0.015} = 0.2449$, and $\sigma_2 < \sqrt{2a_2\theta_2} = \sqrt{2 \cdot 2 \cdot 0.05} = 0.4472$. Numerical results of these tests are shown in Table 5.

Table 5. Exchange option: Numerical results for CVs with different volatilities of the stochastic volatilities.

σ_1	σ_2	Std_{MC}	Std_{Mar}	Std_{Fun}	R_1	R_2
0.2	0.1	0.0151	0.0013	0.0030	11.7123	4.9767
	0.2	0.0157	0.0015	0.0042	10.2764	3.7178
	0.3	0.0163	0.0018	0.0057	9.0825	2.8678
	0.4	0.0169	0.0021	0.0073	8.1624	2.3279
0.05	0.2	0.0157	0.0014	0.0034	11.2239	4.5840
0.10		0.0157	0.0014	0.0036	10.9406	4.3545
0.15		0.0157	0.0015	0.0039	10.6170	4.0447
0.20		0.0157	0.0015	0.0042	10.2764	3.7178

Notes: σ_1 is the volatility of the first stochastic volatility; and σ_2 is the volatility of the second stochastic volatility.

As shown in Table 5, the standard errors of the three simulation methods all increase with increasing volatilities of stochastic volatilities. Standard error reduction ratios also decline with the volatility of the stochastic volatilities. However, our martingale CV method is much more efficient than the function CV method, especially in the case of large volatility.

4.2. Basket Options

The payoff of the basket option at maturity depends on the average price of the underlying assets. Since the basket option with arithmetic average price does not have a closed-form price, even with constant volatility, we considered the geometric average basket option whose payoff at time T is:

$$h^{\text{GeomBasket}}(S(T)) = \max \left(\prod_{i=1}^{n} S_i^{\alpha_i}(T) - K, 0 \right), \tag{38}$$

where n is the number of underlying assets, $\alpha_i \geq 0$ are the weights of each underlying asset with $\sum_{i=1}^{n} \alpha_i = 1$, and K is the strike price.

The geometric average basket option has a closed-form solution if the underlying assets have constant volatilities as $\sigma_1, \cdots, \sigma_n$. Denote:

$$\hat{\sigma}^2 = \sum_{i,j=1}^{n} \alpha_i \alpha_j \sigma_i \sigma_j \rho_{ij},$$

$$\hat{\delta} = \sum_{i=1}^{n} \alpha_i \left(\delta_i + \frac{\sigma_i^2}{2} \right) - \frac{\hat{\sigma}^2}{2}.$$

The geometric average basket option price at time t is given by Jiang [20]:

$$V^{\text{BS-GeomBasket}}(t, S) = S_1^{\alpha_1} \cdots S_n^{\alpha_n} e^{-\hat{\delta}(T-t)} N(d_1) - K e^{-r(T-t)} N(d_2), \tag{39}$$

where

$$d_1 = \frac{\ln \frac{S_1^{\alpha_1} \cdots S_n^{\alpha_n}}{K} + \left(r - \hat{\delta} + \frac{1}{2}\hat{\sigma}^2 \right) (T - t)}{\hat{\sigma}\sqrt{T - t}},$$

$$d_2 = d_1 - \hat{\sigma}\sqrt{T - t}.$$

Thus, the derivatives are:

$$\frac{\partial}{\partial S_j} V^{\text{BS-GeomBasket}}(t, S) = e^{-\hat{\delta}(T-t)} N(d_1) \alpha_j S_j^{-1} \prod_{i=1}^{n} S_i^{\alpha_i}, \quad j = 1, 2, \cdots, n.$$

For a basket option with n underlying assets, we still used the Heston stochastic volatility model and function CV method as a comparison. The expectation of the corresponding CV can be calculated using Equation (39) by substituting $\sigma_i \sigma_j$ with $\frac{1}{T} \int_0^T \sqrt{E[Y_i(t)]E[Y_j(t)]}dt$. We fixed the parameters $r = 0.05$, $T = 1$, $K = 30$, $S_i(0) = 30$, $\delta_i = 0$, $a_i = 2$, and $\sigma_i = 0.2$ $(i = 1, 2, \cdots, n)$. We allocated equal weights for the underlying assets, which means that $\alpha_i = 1/n$. For the initial value of the stochastic volatility, we took a linear interpolation between 0.1^2 and 0.3^2 for the n assets. In other words, the initial variance vector was $Y(0) = (0.1^2, 0.3^2)'$ for $n = 2$ and $Y(0) = (0.1^2, 0.15^2, 0.2^2, 0.25^2, 0.3^2)'$ for $n = 5$. We took the long-term mean of stochastic variance as $\theta_i = (\sqrt{Y_i(0)} + 0.05)^2$, which was $\theta = (0.15^2, 0.35^2)'$ for $n = 2$, for example. For the correlations between Brownian noises, we took $\rho_{ij} = \rho_0 (i \neq j)$ for simplicity. To guarantee the positive definiteness of the matrix $\Gamma = (\rho_{ij})$, the parameter ρ_0 should satisfy $-1/(n-1) < \rho_0 < 1$. In addition, $\left| \frac{\rho_{ij}}{\sqrt{1-\rho_i^2}\sqrt{1-\rho_j^2}} \right| < 1$ is needed for the proper definition of $\widetilde{\Gamma}$. Thus, we set $\rho_{ij} = \rho_0 = 0 (i \neq j)$ at first. We fixed the number of time steps to $N = 100$ and the number of simulations to $m = 100{,}000$. We tested the acceleration effects of the CVs for different correlation coefficients ρ_i. Numerical results are shown in Table 6.

Table 6. Geometric average basket option: Numerical results for CVs with different correlation coefficients.

n	ρ_i	Std_{MC}	Std_{Mar}	Std_{Fun}	R_1	R_2
2	−0.75	0.0110	0.0012	0.0021	9.2740	5.2542
	−0.50	0.0112	0.0009	0.0021	12.8705	5.2650
	−0.25	0.0115	0.0004	0.0022	27.4754	5.2935
	0.00	0.0117	0.0004	0.0022	30.5615	5.3375
	0.25	0.0120	0.0005	0.0022	23.5176	5.3968
	0.50	0.0122	0.0010	0.0022	11.9347	5.4719
	0.75	0.0124	0.0013	0.0022	9.2236	5.5629
5	−0.75	0.0068	0.0009	0.0013	7.6660	5.1178
	−0.50	0.0069	0.0006	0.0013	11.7653	5.1320
	−0.25	0.0069	0.0002	0.0013	27.9824	5.1434
	0.00	0.0070	0.0001	0.0014	110.3248	5.1544
	0.25	0.0071	0.0003	0.0014	25.1755	5.1663
	0.50	0.0071	0.0006	0.0014	11.1250	5.1785
	0.75	0.0072	0.0010	0.0014	7.4879	5.1952
10	−0.75	0.0049	0.0008	0.0010	6.3077	5.0690
	−0.50	0.0049	0.0005	0.0010	10.4984	5.0820
	−0.25	0.0049	0.0002	0.0010	26.5073	5.0928
	0.00	0.0050	1.7×10^{-5}	0.0010	291.4214	5.1023
	0.25	0.0050	0.0002	0.0010	24.2257	5.1104
	0.50	0.0050	0.0005	0.0010	10.0253	5.1192
	0.75	0.0050	0.0008	0.0010	6.1413	5.1310

Notes: n is number of underlying assets; and ρ_i is correlation coefficient between the ith underlying asset and its volatility.

Table 6 again shows that Std_{Mar}, the standard error of the martingale CV method, decreases as the correlation coefficients ρ_i tends to zero, resulting in a greater standard error reduction ratio R_1 in those cases. For example, R_1 goes from 30 to 9 when $|\rho_i|$ goes from 0 to 0.75. On the other hand, the simulation error Std_{Fun} and, thus, the corresponding reduction ratio R_2 of the function CV method are not sensitive to the correlation coefficient. The reduction ratio is around 5 in all cases. Considering the number of underlying assets, the reduction ratio of the martingale CV slightly decreases as the number of assets n becomes larger, except for the $\rho_i = 0$ cases. For example, the reduction ratios of the martingale CV method are 9.2740, 7.6660, and 6.3077 for $n = 2, 5$, and 10, respectively, and for $\rho_i = -0.75$. On the other hand, the ratios are 30.5615, 110.3248, and 291.4214 for the $\rho_i = 0$ case. As a contrast, the performance of the function CV method is more stable with different n. It is obvious that our martingale CV is much more efficient than the function CV method.

Next, we fixed $\rho_i = 0.5 (i = 1, 2, \cdots, n)$ and changed the value of σ_i, the volatility of the stochastic volatility. For convenience, we took an equal σ_i for every underlying asset. The results are recorded in Table 7.

Table 7. Geometric basket option: Numerical results for CVs with different volatilities of the stochastic volatility.

n	σ_i	Std_{MC}	Std_{Mar}	Std_{Fun}	R_1	R_2
2	0.1	0.0177	0.0013	0.0011	13.7479	15.6830
	0.2	0.0179	0.0013	0.0023	13.3158	7.9626
	0.3	0.0182	0.0014	0.0034	12.8095	5.4211
	0.4	0.0184	0.0015	0.0044	12.2580	4.1894
5	0.1	0.0093	0.0007	0.0006	12.7129	14.3708
	0.2	0.0093	0.0007	0.0013	12.4417	7.2688
	0.3	0.0094	0.0008	0.0019	12.1388	4.9147
	0.4	0.0094	0.0008	0.0025	11.8127	3.7571
10	0.1	0.0060	0.0005	0.0004	11.8384	13.8295
	0.2	0.0060	0.0005	0.0009	11.6365	6.9848
	0.3	0.0060	0.0005	0.0013	11.4192	4.7179
	0.4	0.0060	0.0005	0.0017	11.1910	3.5979

Notes: n is number of underlying assets; and σ_i is the volatility of the ith stochastic volatility.

As shown in Table 7, the standard errors of the three simulation methods increase with the volatilities of the stochastic volatility at fixed n, and decrease with the number of underlying assets for a fixed σ_i. The standard error reduction ratios of the two CV methods decrease with increasing volatility of the stochastic volatility and increasing number of assets. However, the martingale CV method is more robust for different volatilities compared to the function CV method. For example, for the case of $n = 2$, the standard error reduction ratio of the martingale CV method decreases from 13.7479 to 12.2580 when σ_i increases from 0.1 to 0.4, while that of the function CV method sharply decreases from 15.6830 to 4.1894. The results suggest that our martingale CV method is especially efficient in high volatility cases, while the function CV method has some advantages in a low volatility environment.

4.3. Quanto Options with Real Data

The quanto option is a contract written when someone invests money in foreign securities. Usually, its risk depends on the volatility of the securities' prices and the change of the foreign currency rate. Its main purpose is to provide exposure to a foreign asset without taking the corresponding exchange rate risk. We applied our method to price a quanto option. Park et al. [62] used a power series expansion method to obtain an analytic approximation value for the quanto option price under the Hull–White stochastic volatility model.

First, we give the quanto option pricing model with Hull–White stochastic volatility, as shown in Park et al. [62]. Let $S(t)$ be a stock price in foreign currency, and $F(t)$ be a foreign exchange (FX) rate, that is the amount of domestic currency value per one foreign currency value. In a risk-neutral world, they are assumed to obey the following stochastic differential equations:

$$
\begin{aligned}
dS(t)/S(t) &= (r_f - \rho_{12}\sigma_1(t)\sigma_2(t))dt + \sigma_1(t)dW_1(t), \\
dF(t)/F(t) &= (r_d - r_f)dt + \sigma_2(t)dW_2(t), \\
d\sigma_1(t)/\sigma_1(t) &= \mu_1 dt + \xi_1 dZ_1(t), \\
d\sigma_2(t)/\sigma_2(t) &= \mu_2 dt + \xi_2 dZ_2(t),
\end{aligned}
$$

where r_d is a risk-free domestic interest rate and r_f is a risk-free foreign interest rate.

The correlations among the Brownian noises are given by $\text{cov}(dW_1(t), dW_2(t)) = \rho_{12}dt$, $\text{cov}(dW_1(t), dZ_1(t)) = \rho_1 dt$, and $\text{cov}(dW_2(t), dZ_2(t)) = \rho_2 dt$. Additionally, $\sigma_1(t)$ and $\sigma_2(t)$ are the stochastic volatilities of the stock price and the FX rate, respectively. This form of the Hull–White stochastic volatility is a little different from that in Table 1 (for more details, please see Park et al. [62]). The parameters μ_1, μ_2, ξ_1, and ξ_2 are constants.

Park et al. [62] considered a specific quanto option with payoff:

$$h^{\text{Quanto}}(S(T)) = F_0 \max(S(T) - K, 0), \tag{40}$$

where F_0 is a predetermined FX rate, and K is the strike price. A more general quanto option payoff would be $\max(F_0, F(T)) \max(S(T) - K, 0)$ (see Jiang et al. [20]). When volatilities $\sigma_1(t)$ and $\sigma_2(t)$ take constant values σ_1 and σ_2, respectively, the authors gave the Black–Scholes quanto option price as:

$$V^{\text{BS-Quanto}}(t, S) = F_0 e^{-r_d(T-t)} \left(S e^{(r_f - \rho_{12}\sigma_1\sigma_2)(T-t)} N(d_1) - K N(d_2) \right), \tag{41}$$

where

$$d_1 = \frac{\ln\frac{S}{K} + \left(r_f - \rho_{12}\sigma_1\sigma_2 + \frac{1}{2}\sigma_1^2\right)(T-t)}{\sigma_1\sqrt{T-t}},$$
$$d_2 = d_1 - \sigma_1\sqrt{T-t}.$$

It is easy to obtain the derivative

$$\frac{\partial}{\partial S} V^{\text{BS-Quanto}}(t, S) = F_0 e^{(r_f - r_d - \rho_{12}\sigma_1\sigma_2)(T-t)} N(d_1).$$

The authors [62] supposed a quanto European call option of the S&P500 index with 1200 strike and a predetermined FX rate of 1100 (KRW/USD). The model parameters shown in Table 8 were observed on 13 October 2010. Furthermore, we assume that the contract multiplier of the S&P500 option is 100 and the maturity is 13 October 2011. Without loss of generality, we set the unobserved values as zeros.

Table 8. Market dataset parameters.

View Date	13 October 2010
S&P500	1169.77
FX Rate (KRW/USD)	1127
Volatility of S&P500	18.58%
Volatility of FX Rate	11.83%
Correlation between S&P500 and FX Rate	−0.2297
Correlation between S&P500 and its volatility	−0.55
Volatility of volatility of S&P500	11.72%
Volatility of volatility of FX Rate	16.8%
USD LIBOR(1Y)	0.77%
KRW Treasury Rate(1Y)	2.91%

Notes: FX stands for foreign exchange; KRW stands for South Korean Won; USD stands for US dollar; and LIBOR is London Interbank Offered Rate.

We changed the values of the correlation between the S&P500 and the FX rate and fixed all other parameters. The number of time steps was set to $N = 100$ and the number of simulations was set to $m = 100{,}000$. The numerical results for these models are recorded in Table 9.

Table 9. Quanto option: Numerical results with different correlation coefficients.

ρ_{12}	V_{Appro} (10^6)	V_{MC} (10^6)	Std_{MC} (10^6)	V_{Mar} (10^6)	Std_{Mar} (10^6)	V_{Fun} (10^6)	Std_{Fun} (10^6)	R_1	R_2
−0.6	9.1393	9.1082	0.0462	9.1223	0.0038	9.1162	0.0047	12.1373	9.7825
−0.4	8.8325	8.8187	0.0454	8.8316	0.0037	8.8258	0.0046	12.3813	9.8215
−0.2	8.5311	8.5357	0.0447	8.5473	0.0035	8.5416	0.0045	12.6122	9.8533
0.0	8.2352	8.2592	0.0439	8.2696	0.0034	8.2638	0.0044	12.8264	9.8768
0.2	7.9448	7.9890	0.0432	7.9984	0.0033	7.9924	0.0044	13.0198	9.8906
0.4	7.6599	7.7253	0.0424	7.7335	0.0032	7.7276	0.0043	13.1884	9.8948
0.6	7.3807	7.4679	0.0417	7.4750	0.0031	7.4691	0.0042	13.3285	9.8900

Notes: ρ_{12} is the correlation between S&P500 and FX Rate; and V_{Appro} is the the approximated values calculated by formula in [62].

In Table 9, ρ_{12} stands for the correlation between the S&P500 and FX rate. V_{Appro} is the approximated value obtained by the series expansion method in Park et al. [62]. V_{MC}, V_{Mar}, and V_{Fun} are the estimated values of the MC simulation, the martingale CV method, and the function CV method, respectively. Std_{MC}, Std_{Mar}, and Std_{Fun} are the standard errors of the MC simulation, the martingale CV method, and the function CV method, respectively. $R_1 = Std_{\mathrm{MC}}/Std_{\mathrm{Mar}}$ is the standard error reduction ratio of the martingale CV method compared to the MC simulation, and $R_2 = Std_{\mathrm{MC}}/Std_{\mathrm{Fun}}$ is the the standard error reduction ratio of the function CV method compared to the MC simulation. For the function CV method, the expectation of the corresponding CV can be calculated by using Equation (41) and substituting $\sigma_i\sigma_j$ with $\frac{1}{T}\int_0^T E[\sigma_i(t)]E[\sigma_j(t)]dt$, where $E[Y_i(t)] = Y_i(0)e^{\mu_i t}, i = 1, 2$. It is obvious that our martingale CV method has a larger standard reduction ratio than the function CV method. This, again, shows the efficiency and robustness of our method.

5. Conclusions

In the context of European multi-asset options with stochastic volatilities, we propose a dimension and variance reduction Monte Carlo method. A conditional Monte Carlo pricing formula is deduced, and then the martingale representation theorem is proved. A martingale control variate is combined with the conditional Monte Carlo simulation.

Numerical tests on typical multi-asset options—including exchange options, basket options, and currency options—showed that this method yields considerable variance reduction, not only when compared to a traditional Monte Carlo simulation, but also with respect to the function control variate in Ma and Xu [74].

For future research, it would be interesting and challenging to extend the framework in this paper to price more options with stochastic volatilities, not only European options but also exotic options such as American options or barrier options. Furthermore, it would be interesting to study jump diffusion models with stochastic volatilities. Another important approach is to use this framework in empirical financial studies and risk management. After model parameters are calibrated with real market data, our method can be used to accurately and quickly value option prices which can be widely used in areas of economics and finance. We would also like to extend this method to other areas like risk management and civil engineering.

Author Contributions: Y.L. prepared the entire research framework and managed the manuscript. X.X. programmed the numerical tests.

Abbreviations

The following abbreviations are used in this manuscript:

MC   Monte Carlo
CV   control variate
CMC   conditional Monte Carlo
FFT   fast Fourier transformation
FX   foreign exchange

References

1. Hull, J.C. *Options, Futures and Other Derivatives*, 10th ed.; Pearson Education: New York, NY, USA, 2018.
2. Kim, Y.; Shin, K.; Ahn, J.; Lee, E.-B. Probabilistic Cash Flow-Based Optimal Investment Timing Using Two-Color Rainbow Options Valuation for Economic Sustainability Appraisement. *Sustainability* **2017**, *9*, 1781. [CrossRef]
3. Yoo, J.-I.; Lee, E.-B.; Choi, J.-W. Balancing Project Financing and Mezzanine Project Financing with Option Value to Mitigate Sponsor's Risks for Overseas Investment Projects. *Sustainability* **2018**, *10*, 1498. [CrossRef]
4. Black, F.; Scholes, M. The Pricing of Options and Corporate Liabilities. *J. Political Econ.* **1973**, *81*, 637–654. [CrossRef]
5. Merton, R.C. Theory of Rational Option Pricing. *Bell J. Econ. Manag. Sci.* **1973**, *4*, 141–183. [CrossRef]
6. Rubinstein, M. Nonparametric tests of alternative option pricing models using all reported trades and quotes on the 30 most active CBOE option classes from August 23, 1976 through August 31, 1978. *J. Financ.* **1985**, *40*, 455–480. [CrossRef]
7. Andersen, L.; Andreasen, J. Jump-diffusion processes: Volatility smile fitting and numerical methods for option pricing. *Rev. Deriv. Res.* **2000**, *4*, 231–262. [CrossRef]
8. Hull, J.; White, A. The pricing of options on assets with stochastic volatilities. *J. Financ.* **1987**, *42*, 281–300. [CrossRef]
9. Scott, L.O. Option pricing when the variance changes randomly: Theory, estimation, and an application. *J. Financ. Quant. Anal.* **1987**, *22*, 419–438. [CrossRef]
10. Stein, E.M.; Stein, J.C. Stock price distributions with stochastic volatility: An analytic approach. *Rev. Financ. Stud.* **1991**, *4*, 727–752. [CrossRef]
11. Ball, C.A.; Roma, A. Stochastic volatility option pricing. *J. Financ. Quant. Anal.* **1994**, *29*, 589–607. [CrossRef]
12. Heston, S.L. A closed solution for options with stochastic volatility with applications to bond and currency options. *Rev. Financ. Stud.* **1993**, *6*, 327–343. [CrossRef]
13. Schöbel, R.; Zhu, J. Stochastic volatility with an Ornstein-Uhlenbeck process: An extension. *Eur. Financ. Rev.* **1999**, *3*, 23–46. [CrossRef]
14. Hagan, P.S.; Kumar, D.; Lesniewski, A.S.; Woodward, D.E. Managing smile risk. *Wilmott Mag.* **2002**, *1*, 249–296.
15. Fouque, J.P.; Papanicolaou, G.; Sircar, K.R. Mean-reverting stochastic volatility. *Int. J. Theor. Appl. Financ.* **2000**, *3*, 101–142. [CrossRef]
16. Fouque, J.P.; Tullie, T.A. Variance reduction for Monte Carlo simulation in a stochastic volatility environment. *Quant. Financ.* **2002**, *2*, 24–30. [CrossRef]
17. Fouque, J.P.; Han, C.H. Variance reduction for Monte Carlo methods to evaluate option prices under multi-factor stochastic volatility models. *Quant. Financ.* **2004**, *4*, 597–606. [CrossRef]
18. Fouque, J.P.; Han, C.H. A martingale control variate method for option pricing with stochastic volatility. *ESAIM Probab. Stat.* **2007**, *11*, 40–54. [CrossRef]
19. Fouque, J.P.; Papanicolaou, G.; Sircar, R. *Derivatives in Financial Markets with Stochastic Volatility*; Cambridge University Press: Cambridge, UK, 2000.
20. Jiang, L.S. *Mathematical Models and Methdods for Options Prcing*, 2nd ed.; China Higher Education Press: Beijing, China, 2014.
21. Turnbull, S.; Wakeman, L. A quick algorithm for pricing European average options. *J. Financ. Quant. Anal.* **1991**, *26*, 377–389. [CrossRef]

22. Curran, M. Valuing Asian and portfolio options by conditioning on the geometirc mean price. *Manag. Sci.* **1994**, *40*, 1705–1711. [CrossRef]

23. Milevsky, M.A.; Posner, S.E. A closed-form approximation for valuing basket options. *J. Deriv.* **1998**, *5*, 54–61. [CrossRef]

24. Ju, N. Pricing Asian and basket options via Taylor expansion. *J. Comput. Financ.* **2002**, *5*, 79–103. [CrossRef]

25. Zhou, J.; Wang, X. Accurate closed-form approximation for pricing Asian and basket options. *Appl. Stoch. Model. Bus. Ind.* **2008**, *24*, 343–358. [CrossRef]

26. Alexander, C.; Venkatramanan, A. Analytic approximations for multi-asset option pricing. *Math. Financ.* **2012**, *22*, 667–689. [CrossRef]

27. Datey, J.Y.; Gauthier, G.; Simonato, J.G. The performance of analytical approximations for the computation of Asian quanto-basket option prices. *Multinat. Financ.* **2003**, *7*, 55–82. [CrossRef]

28. Brigo, D.; Mercurio, F.; Rapisarda, F.; Scotti, R. Approximated momentmatching dynamics for basket-options pricing. *Quant. Financ.* **2004**, *4*, 1–16. [CrossRef]

29. Borovkova, S.; Permana, F.J.; Weide, H.V.D. A closed form approach to the valuation and hedging of basket and spread option. *J. Deriv.* **2007**, *14*, 8–24. [CrossRef]

30. Deelstra, G.; Liinev, J.; Vanmaele, M. Pricing of arithmetic basket options by conditioning. *Insur. Math. Econ.* **2004**, *34*, 55–77. [CrossRef]

31. Deelstra, G.; Diallo, I.; Vanmaele, M. Moment matching approximation of Asian basket option prices. *J. Comput. Appl. Math.* **2010**, *234*, 1006–1016. [CrossRef]

32. Li, M.; Deng, S.; Zhou, J. Closed-Form Approximations for Spread Option Prices and Greeks. 2010. Available online: https://ssrn.com/abstract=952747 (accessed on 30 December 2018).

33. Carr, P.; Madan D B. Option valuation using the fast Fourier transform. *J. Comput. Financ.* **1999**, *2*, 61–73. [CrossRef]

34. Carr, P.; Wu, L. Time-changed Lévy processes and option pricing. *J. Financ. Econ.* **2004**, *71*, 113–141. [CrossRef]

35. Grzelak, L.A.; Oosterlee, C.W.; Weeren, S.V. The affine Heston model with correlated gaussian interest rates for pricing hybrid derivatives. *Quant. Financ.* **2011**, *11*, 1647–1663. [CrossRef]

36. Grzelak, L.A.; Oosterlee, C.W. On cross-currency models with stochastic volatility and correlated interest rates. *Appl. Math. Financ.* **2012**, *19*, 1–35. [CrossRef]

37. Grzelak, L.A.; Oosterlee, C.W. On the Heston model with stochastic interest rates. *SIAM J. Financ. Math.* **2012**, *2*, 255–286. [CrossRef]

38. He, X.J.; Zhu, S.P. A closed-form pricing formula for European options under the Heston model with stochastic interest rate. *J. Comput. Appl. Math.* **2018**, *335*, 323–333. [CrossRef]

39. Glasserman, P. *Monte Carlo Methods in Financial Engineering*; Springer: New York, NY, USA, 2004.

40. Kemna, A.G.Z.; Vorst, A.C.F. A pricing method for options based on average asset values. *J. Bank. Financ.* **1990**, *14*, 113–129. [CrossRef]

41. Barraquand, J. Numerical valuation of high dimensional multivariate European securities. *Manag. Sci.* **1995**, *41*, 1882–1891. [CrossRef]

42. Pellizari, P. Efficient Monte Carlo pricing of European options using mean value control variates. *Decis. Econ. Financ.* **2001**, *24*, 107–126. [CrossRef]

43. Borogovac, T.; Vakili, P. Control variate technique: A constructive approach. In Proceedings of the 2008 Winter Simulation Conference, Miami, FL, USA, 7–10 December 2008; IEEE: Piscataway, NJ, USA, 2008; pp. 320–327.

44. Dingeç, K.D.; Hörmann, W. Control variates and conditional Monte Carlo for basket and Asian options. *Insur. Math. Econ.* **2013**, *52*, 421–434. [CrossRef]

45. Liang, Y.; Xu C.; Ma J. An efficient pricipal component Monte Carlo method for pricing European options with multi-factors. *J. Southwest Univ.* **2018**, *40*, 88–97.

46. Sun, Y.; Xu, C. A hybrid Monte Carlo acceleration method of pricing basket options based on splitting. *J. Comput. Appl. Math.* **2018**, *342*, 292–304. [CrossRef]

47. Fang, K.; Hickernell, F.J.; Niederreiter, H. *Monte Carlo and Quasi-Monte Carlo Methods*; Springer: Berlin, Germany, 2000.

48. Dahl, L.O.; Benth, F.E. Valuation of Asian basket options with Quasi-Monte Carlo techniques and singular value decomposition. *Pure Math.* **2001**, *5*, 1–21.

49. Wang, X. Variance reduction techniques and quasi-Monte Carlo methods. *J. Comput. Appl. Math.* **2001**, *132*, 309–318. [CrossRef]

50. Wang, X.; Fang, K.T. The effective dimension and quasi-Monte Carlo integration. *J. Complex.* **2003**, *19*, 101–124. [CrossRef]

51. Wang, X. On the effects of dimension reduction techniques on some high-dimensional problems in finance. *Oper. Res.* **2006**, *54*, 1063–1078. [CrossRef]

52. Wang, X. Dimension reduction techniques in quasi-Monte Carlo methods for option pricing. *INFORMS J. Comput.* **2009**, *21*, 488–504. [CrossRef]

53. Abbas-Turki, L.A.; Lapeyre, B. American options pricing on multi-core graphic cards. In Proceedings of the Second International Conference on Business Intelligence and Financial Engineering (BIFE2009), Beijing, China, 24–26 July 2009; IEEE: Piscataway, NJ, USA, 2009; pp. 307–311.

54. Abbas-Turki, L.A.; Vialle, S.; Lapeyre, B.; Mercier, P. High dimensional pricing of exotic European contracts on a GPU cluster, and comparison to a CPU cluster. In Proceedings of the IEEE International Symposium on Parallel and Distributed Processing (IPDPS 2009), Rome, Italy, 23–29 May 2009; IEEE: Piscataway, NJ, USA; 2009; pp. 1–8.

55. Lee, M.; Jeon, J.; Bae, J.; Jang, H.S. Parallel implementation of a financial application on a GPU. In Proceedings of the 2nd International Conference on Interaction Sciences: Information Technology, Culture and Human, Seoul, Korea, 24–26 November 2009; ACM: New York, NY, USA, 2009; pp. 1136–1141.

56. Surkov, V. Parallel option pricing with Fourier space time-stepping method on graphics processing units. *Parallel Comput.* **2010**, *36*, 372–380. [CrossRef]

57. Dang, D.M.; Christara, C.C.; Jackson, K.R. An efficient graphics processing unit-based parallel algorithm for pricing multi-asset American options. *Concurr. Comp. Pract. E* **2012**, *24*, 849–866. [CrossRef]

58. Hu, Y.; Li, Q.; Cao, Z.; Wang, J. Parallel simulation of high-dimensional American option pricing based on CPU versus MIC. *Concurr. Comp. Pract. E* **2015**, *27*, 1110–1121. [CrossRef]

59. Du, K.; Liu, G.; Gu, G. Accelerating Monte Carlo method for pricing multi-asset options under stochastic volatility models. *IAENG Int. J. Appl. Math* **2014**, *44*, 62–70.

60. Antonelli, F.; Ramponi, A.; Scarlatti, S. Exchange option pricing under stochastic volatility: A correlation expansion. *Rev. Deriv. Res.* **2010**, *13*, 45–73. [CrossRef]

61. Shiraya, K.; Takahashi, A. Pricing multiasset cross-currency options. *J. Futures Mark.* **2014**, *34*, 1–19. [CrossRef]

62. Park, J.; Lee, Y.; Lee, J. Pricing of quanto option under the Hull and White stochastic volatility model. *Commun. Korean Math. Soc.* **2013**, *28*, 615–633. [CrossRef]

63. Liang Y.; Xu C. Efficient accelerating method of conditional Monte-Carlo simulation for two-factor option pricing model. *J. Tongji Univ.* **2014**, *42*, 645–650.

64. Willard, G.A. Calculating prices and sensitivities for path-independent derivative securities in multifactor models. *J. Deriv.* **1997**, *5*, 45–61. [CrossRef]

65. Drimus, G.G. Options on realized variance in Log-OU models. *Appl. Math. Financ.* **2012**, *19*, 477–494. [CrossRef]

66. Boyle, P.; Broadie, M.; Glasserman, P. Monte Carlo methods for security pricing. *J. Econ. Dyn. Control* **1997**, *21*, 1267–1321. [CrossRef]

67. Broadie, M.; Kaya, Ö. Exact simulation of stochastic volatility and other affine jump diffusion processes. *Oper. Res.* **2006**, *54*, 217–231. [CrossRef]

68. Yang, Y.; Ma, J.; Liang, Y. The Research on the Calculation of Barrier Options under Stochastic Volatility Models Based on the Exact Simulation. *IAENG Int. J. Appl. Math.* **2018**, *48*, 112–124.

69. Ross, S. *A First Course in Probability*, 9th ed.; Pearson: Boston, MA, USA, 2014.

70. Margrabe, W. The value of an option to exchange one asset for another. *J. Financ.* **1978**, *33*, 177–186. [CrossRef]

71. Feller, W. Two singular diffusion problems. *Ann. Math.* **1951**, *54*, 173–182. [CrossRef]

72. Andersen, L.B.G. Efficient simulation of the Heston stochastic volatility model. *J. Comput. Financ.* **2008**, *11*, 1–42. [CrossRef]

73. Lord, R.; Koekkoek, R.; Dijk, D.V. A comparison of biased simulation schemes for stochastic volatility models. *Quant. Financ.* **2010**, *10*, 177–194. [CrossRef]

74. Ma, J.; Xu, C. An efficient control variate method for pricing variance derivatives. *J. Comput. Appl. Math.* **2010**, *235*, 108–119. [CrossRef]

7

An Analysis of Gains to US Acquiring REIT Shareholders in Domestic and Cross-Border Mergers before and after the Subprime Mortgage Crisis

Alan T. Wang [1], Yu-Hong Liu [1,*] and Yu-Chen Chang [2]

1   Institute of Finance, National Cheng Kung University, Tainan City 70101, Taiwan; wangt@mail.ncku.edu.tw
2   JP Morgan, 8F No. 108, Sec. 5, Xinyi Road., Xinyi Dist., Taipei City 11047, Taiwan; a0981103127@gmail.com
*   Correspondence: yuhong@mail.ncku.edu.tw

Abstract: This paper examines the abnormal returns of acquiring real estate investment trusts (REITs) around the announcement of acquisitions before and after the subprime mortgage crisis. Based on 182 domestic and cross-border US REIT acquisition announcements from 2005 to 2010, the acquiring trusts experienced a 0.73% abnormal return, on average. When the sample was divided into pre-crisis, crisis, and after-crisis subsamples, the acquiring trusts enjoyed the largest abnormal returns (1.86%) for domestic acquisitions during the crisis period. Before the crisis, when the acquisition was cross-border, the target was private, or the transaction was cash-financed, the acquiring trust experienced larger abnormal returns. During the crisis period, the acquiring trust gained larger abnormal returns when the transaction value was larger. After the crisis period, the acquiring trust achieved less abnormal returns in cross-border mergers. For both pre- and after-crisis periods, the shareholders of the acquirer enjoyed larger abnormal returns when the mergers were cash-financed, regardless of whether the target was public or privately held. Neither the blockholder monitoring nor the signaling hypothesis can explain such value gains. The structural changes in the acquirer's abnormal returns are possibly due to the increased risk aversion of the market participants following the crisis.

Keywords: merger; subprime mortgage crisis; event study

1. Introduction

In the early period of the 2000s, the U.S. was experiencing mild economic growth and rising housing prices when the interest rates were low. Because of the rising home prices later on, bankers were encouraged to make more loans for higher compensations, and the quality of the mortgage loans started to deteriorate, especially when the mortgage rates started to rise. The first disruption of the credit market can be dated back to 7 August 2007, when the French bank BNP Paribas suspended the redemption of the shares held in some of its money market funds [1]. Furthermore, on 15 September 2018, the investment bank Lehman Brothers filed for the largest bankruptcy in U.S. history due to its loss during the subprime mortgage market. Reinhart and Rogoff [2] stated that the aftermath of the crisis has three characteristics: the asset market collapses are prolonged, the banking crisis is associated with profound declines in output and employment, and the level of government debt tends to explode. The outbreak of the global financial crisis in 2008 has reshaped the landscape of the financial markets as well. Investors have become more risk-averse, and that has changed the corporate strategies in business activities. It is important to examine how corporations have adjusted their mergers and acquisitions strategies since the crisis and to explore how market participants perceive the acquisition activities. To keep corporations sustainable, acquirers must identify the right targets from long-term perspectives. For example, are the prices of the targets appropriate during the normal periods or the crisis periods? Will the acquisitions help the corporations grow? If the acquisitions are favorable, the market participants will revalue the acquirer's stock price.

Acquisitions may benefit shareholders from different sources, such as revenue enhancement from marketing gains and market monopoly power, cost reductions from economies of scale and the elimination of inefficient management, tax gains, and a reduced cost of capital. The wealth effect of the acquisition has been well documented in the corporate finance literature. A stylized fact concerning mergers is that the shareholders of bidding firms suffer wealth loss at the announcement of stock-financed merger transactions. This is consistent with the information asymmetry hypothesis, in which the manager considers the firm's stocks overvalued, and stock instead of cash is chosen as the payment method for a merger transaction. Jensen and Ruback [3] reported the short-run evidence from studies that used event studies and looked at the effect of a merger announcement on abnormal stock returns. The abnormal returns associated with successful corporate takeover bids for the target firms are 30%, 20%, and 8% in the cases of a tender offer, merger, and proxy contest, respectively. However, for the bidding firms, the abnormal returns are much smaller or close to zero.

On the other hand, other corporate finance literature has documented the opposite results for the acquirer's abnormal returns. For example, Asquith et al. [4] concluded that bidding firms gain during the 21 days before the announcements of merger bids. Bidders' abnormal returns are positively related to the relative size of the merger partners, and the gains around the announcement period are larger for successful mergers. They concluded that their findings are consistent with the value-maximization behavior of the management of the bidding firms. The inconclusive results documented in earlier studies for the gains or losses of bidding firms around the merger announcement are partially explained by the relative size of the merger partner and the time period of the merger.

The purpose of this study is to reexamine the effects of real estate investment trust (REIT) acquisitions on the wealth of the shareholders of the acquiring trust before and after the subprime mortgage crisis. REITs allow investors to indirectly invest in professionally managed commercial real estate portfolios and then distribute rents and capital gains to their investors. REITs have unique institutional settings characterized by very codified and transparent corporate governance. Since REITs do not normally pay federal income taxes and are required to distribute at least 90% of their taxable income, they are highly dependent on their ability to access external capital. Thus, REITs are especially vulnerable during a credit crisis [5]. There are several advantages for a REIT to acquire another trust. For example, net operating losses can be used to offset capital gains tax liabilities from the sale of trust property, making an existing trust an attractive target. Furthermore, the merger may replace existing inefficient management in the acquired trust and result in better utilization of assets (see Allen and Sirmans [6] for detailed descriptions of the institutional background of REITs).

The gains to the bidders from mergers when both the buyer and seller are REITs have also been examined in previous studies. The short-run evidence from the studies using event studies and looking at the effects of mergers on abnormal stock returns for REITs is also inconclusive. For example, with a sample of REIT mergers over the period of 1977–1983, Allen and Sirmans [6] concluded that REIT acquisitions significantly increased the wealth of the acquirer's shareholders, and they argued that the value gain comes from the improved management of the acquired trusts' assets, rather than the tax benefits.

Campbell et al. [7] examined the information content of the method of payment in REIT mergers from 1994 to 1998. They documented that, when the target firm is publicly held, the transactions are always stock-financed, and the acquiring firm's shareholders sustain small negative returns around the announcement date. The explanation for the negative returns is that the acquirer's stock is overvalued. When the target is privately held, the acquirer returns are positive in stock-financed mergers. Their finding may be explained by two hypotheses: the blockholder monitoring hypothesis and the signaling hypothesis. Chang [8] argued that this value enhancement may be caused by the monitoring benefits provided by new blockholders often observed in public-private mergers (blockholder monitoring hypothesis). Alternatively, the owners of private targets are also expected to be better informed about the prospects of the acquiring firm, and their willingness to hold the acquirer's stock provides a positive signal to the market (signaling hypothesis). Campbell et al. [7] concluded that the information signaling hypothesis is the dominant explanation. Sahin [9] examined the performance of acquisitions in the REIT industry from 1994 to 1998. The results indicated that the acquiring REITs suffer statistically significant negative abnormal returns, while the target REITs earn statistically significant positive returns around the announcement date.

To further explore the wealth effect of REIT mergers on the acquiring trust, this study examines the short-run performance of the acquirer in 182 REIT mergers around the announcement dates in the period of 2005Q4–2010Q4 from the perspectives of domestic versus cross-border mergers. Unlike the previous studies, our sample period spans the subprime mortgage crisis period, and we try to highlight the importance of the change in the risk appetite of market participants due to the subprime mortgage crisis by distinguishing domestic from cross-border mergers.

Unlike previous REIT merger literature, there are considerably more REIT merger events in our sample. By considering domestic and cross-border REIT merger announcements over different subperiods, we found that the shareholders of the acquirer achieved significant value gains from cross-border mergers during the crisis period only. The gain is attributable to the lower stock prices of the target trusts. From a cross-sectional analysis, we found that, before the crisis period, if the merger was cross-border, the target trust was privately held, or the merger was cash-financed, the acquirer achieved larger abnormal returns. During the crisis period, a larger acquisition value was associated with a larger value gain to the acquirer. This finding reinforces the hypothesis that the gains come from the undervalued assets of the target REITs during the crisis period. Following the onset of the subprime mortgage crisis, the acquirer achieved more value gain when the target was domestic (rather than cross-border), the acquisition was cash-financed, or there were more states in which the acquirer had properties. This evidence suggests that investors increased their degree of risk aversion after the subprime mortgage crisis because cross-border acquisitions are associated with higher risk resulting from corporate governance, cultural differences, information asymmetries, and valuation issues. If the acquirer has properties in more states, the acquirer's sources of future cash flows are more geographically diversified. The remainder of this paper is organized as follows. Section 2 reviews the literature concerning the wealth effect in merger transactions. The data and research methodology are detailed in Section 3. An empirical analysis is given in Section 4. The final section concludes this paper.

2. Literature Review

2.1. Cross-Border Mergers

Internationalization theory suggests that cross-border acquisitions result in gains from diversification when a business seeks synergies from intangible assets, such as information-based assets [10,11]. Quah and Young [12] asserted that the management of both cultural and organizational integrations in cross-border mergers will tend to make acquisitions successful, but poor attention to these issues will destroy synergistic gains. Cross-border mergers are affected by factors such as cultural identity, physical distance, corporate governance, and equity market valuation differences [13]. In terms of valuation differences, if the difference is temporary, the cross-border acquisitions effectively arbitrage these differences. The valuation difference can also be permanent. Kindleberger [14] argued that cross-border acquisitions can occur because the expected earnings are larger or the cost of capital is lower. For example, if a firm is involved in overseas sales or imports, the firm can acquire a foreign target when the target currency depreciates.

With a sample of 4430 corporate acquisitions for the period of 1985–1995, Moeller and Schlingemann [15] found that US firms who acquire cross-border targets relative to those that acquire domestic targets suffer significantly lower announcement stock returns of approximately 1%. Moeller and Schlingemann [15] summarized several disadvantages of market integration, including increases in competition in the market for corporate control, increases in hubris and agency problems, the cost of internalization, and a decrease in value from diversification.

Other evidence of bidders' abnormal stock returns in cross-border merger announcements is, however, mixed. Dutta et al. [16] found that bidders in the United States had positive cumulative abnormal returns in cross-border mergers. Martynova and Renneboog [17] documented that acquirers engaging in cross-border bids experienced fewer announcement effects than those associated with domestic acquisitions (0.4% and 0.6%, respectively). However, Aybar and Ficici [18] and Chakrabarti et al. [19] found negative cumulative abnormal returns.

2.2. REIT Mergers

Allen and Sirmans [6] conducted the first study concerning the wealth effects of REIT mergers by examining 38 successful REIT–REIT mergers from 1977 to 1983. They found significant positive abnormal returns for the acquirers, which is in contrast to the small negative return from corporate deals. Extending the research of Allen and Sirmans [6], McIntosh et al. [20] examined the return for 27 target REITs over the period of 1962–1986, finding a positive and significant average abnormal return of 2.16%. They concluded that the results are consistent with the hypothesis that target REITs achieve a positive wealth effect due to a merger announcement.

With a REIT merger sample over the period of 1994–1998, Campbell et al. [7] found that, when the target REIT was public, the transactions were always stock-financed, and the shareholders of the acquiring REITs suffered negative returns around the announcement. When the target REIT was privately held, cash financing, mixed financing, and the placement of the acquirer's stock with target owners were more prevalent. Acquirer shareholders achieved positive abnormal returns around the announcement of stock-financed mergers when the target was private, which is consistent with the monitoring by blockholders hypothesis and information signaling hypothesis. Sahin [9] also examined the performance of acquisitions in the REIT industry around the acquisition announcement. The results indicated that the acquiring REITs suffered statistically significant negative abnormal returns. This finding is in line with the research by Campbell et al. [7] but inconsistent with the finding of Allen and Sirmans [6]. The difference is argued to be due to the different environments in the 1980s and 1990s.

Ooi, Ong, and Neo [21] investigated 228 merger announcements in the Japanese and Singaporean REIT markets from 2002 to 2007, suggesting that aggressive growth acquisitions by Asian REITs were a result of improved economies of scale and better management practices. Their results showed that the bidding REITs earned positive and significant abnormal returns of 0.21%. Finally, Ling, and Petrova [22] examined the wealth effects of public-public and public-private REIT merger announcements from 1994 to 2007 and found that targets in public-private mergers earned higher abnormal returns than those in public-public announcements (cumulative abnormal returns were 10.38% and 7.7%, respectively).

2.3. Mergers in the Subprime Mortgage Crisis

Numerous studies examined the wealth effects of mergers during the subprime mortgage crisis period. Berger and Bouwman [23] indicated that healthy banks, particularly from the point of view of capital and liquidity, have an opportunity to improve their market share and profitability during a crisis by making acquisitions. Thus, this implies positive abnormal returns because acquirers can acquire other banks at lower prices and also benefit from portfolio diversification [24] and market power [25]. Furthermore, Reddy et al. [26] examined 26 countries' cross-border mergers from 2004 to 2010 and found that, following the onset of the crisis, companies in emerging countries took advantage of attractive asset prices by acquiring firms in developed countries. Beltratti and Paladino [27] also showed that investors attached significant uncertainty to the completion of deals and rewarded successful acquisitions with delayed abnormal returns during the crisis period.

3. Data and Methodology

3.1. Data

The sample consists of 182 merger announcements made by 229 publicly traded REITs on NYSE between 2005Q4 and 2010Q4. The data were collected from SDC Platinum and Datastream. Of the 182 merger announcements, there are 106 cash-financed, 4 stock-financed, and 10 hybrid transactions. For the rest of the transactions, they are indicated as "unknown" in SDC Platinum.

The 182 transaction announcements have a total value equivalent to 22062.59 million dollars. Table 1 illustrates the distribution of the number of REIT merger announcements for each year. Table 2 shows the compositions of REIT merger announcements for domestic and cross-border transactions before the subprime mortgage crisis period (2005Q4–2007Q1), during the subprime mortgage crisis period (2007Q2–2009Q1), and after the subprime mortgage crisis period (2009Q2–2010Q4).

Table 1. Number of acquisitions from 2005 to 2010 and corresponding transaction value.

Year	Total Number of Acquisitions	Total Transaction Value (US$ million)
2005	17	$1817.22
2006	39	$5165.38
2007	35	$8817.75
2008	30	$2201.90
2009	16	$445.74
2010	45	$3614.60
Total	182	$2,2062.59

Table 2. Profile of domestic and cross-border mergers and acquisitions (M&A) announcements made before, during and after the subprime mortgage crisis.

	Before the Crisis (1 October 2005–31 March 2007)	During the Crisis (1 April 2007–31 March 2009)	After the Crisis (1 April 2009–31 December 2010)
Number (%) of domestic M&A	56 (35%)	54 (34%)	50 (31%)
Number (%) of cross-border M&A	9 (41%)	7 (32%)	6 (27%)

3.2. Methodology

3.2.1. Measuring Abnormal Returns

This study followed the standard event study methodology of Brown and Warner [28,29] to analyze the effect of the merger announcement on REIT acquirers' stock price returns. We followed the market model approach to assume a linear relationship between the expected return on a security and the return on the market portfolio. Specifically, for each security i, the market model assumes the return on security, given by:

$$R_{it} = \alpha_i + \beta_i R_{mt} + \varepsilon_{it}, \tag{1}$$

where R_{it} is the return on security i at time t. R_{mt} is the return on the market portfolio at period t. The linearity and normality of returns are assumed, and ε_{it} is the error. α_i and β_i are coefficients. The market model expressed in Equation (1) is used to compute the expected return on the stock on the day of the event or during a selected event window. Equation (1) is first estimated with the sample observed during the 89-day estimation window from $t = -94$ to $t = -6$, where $t = 0$ is the event day.

The abnormal return (AR) due to the announcement on any given day, therefore, equals the actual return minus the predicted normal return:

$$AR_{it} = R_{it} - (\alpha_i + \beta_i R_{mt}). \tag{2}$$

To obtain a general insight into the abnormal return observations for a sample of N firms, the average abnormal returns (AAR) for each day t are averaged as follows:

$$AAR_t = \frac{1}{N} \sum_{i=1}^{N} AR_{it}. \tag{3}$$

The event window is the period between τ days prior to the event and τ days after the event. The expected returns on the stock calculated from Equation (1) for the security during the event window $(-\tau, +\tau)$ are compared with the actual returns on each day in the event window. The cumulative difference between the predicted return and the actual return in the event window is called the cumulative abnormal return and is calculated as follows:

$$CAR_i(-\tau, +\tau) = \sum_{t=-\tau}^{+\tau} AR_{it} \tag{4}$$

The last step is to calculate the t-value. First, the standard deviation (S) is calculated as follows:

$$S = \sqrt{\frac{\sum_{i=1}^{N}(CAR_i - CAAR_i)^2}{N-1}}, \tag{5}$$

where $CAAR_i$ is the average value of CAR_i, and N is the total number of firms. Then, the t-value is calculated as follows:

$$t = \frac{CAAR_i - 0}{S/\sqrt{N}}, \tag{6}$$

where N is the total number of firms.

3.2.2. Cross-Sectional Regression Models

A cross-sectional regression was applied to identify the sources of cumulative abnormal returns from merger announcements. The dependent variable is the 2-day CAR (0, +1) for all regression models. The independent variables in the regression models are listed and illustrated in Table 3.

Table 3. Definition and summary statistics for the explanatory variables.

Variable	Definition	Mean	Std dev.
DOMES	Type dummy, equals one for domestic M&A and zero otherwise.	0.87	0.34
CRISIS	Subprime dummy, equals one for M&As made during 2007Q2 and 2009Q1, and zero otherwise.	0.33	0.47
DOMES*CRISIS	Interacting dummy, equals one for domestic M&As made during subprime and zero otherwise.	0.29	0.45
STATUS	Target public status dummy, equals one for privately held and zero otherwise.	0.66	0.47
STRUCTURE	Method of payment dummy, equals one for all cash-financed and zero otherwise.	0.44	0.50
R_SIZE	Deal value divided by market capitalization of acquirers.	0.09	0.22
ROE	Return of equity from acquirers.	0.08	0.13
EQUITY	Equity divided by total assets from acquirers.	0.38	0.18
STATES	The number of states that the REITs firm has properties in.	13.84	11.07

182 domestic and cross-border REITs M&A announcements from October 2005 to December 2010.

The major independent variable is domestic merger (*DOMES*), which is a dummy variable equaling one for a domestic merger and zero otherwise. If the cross-border merger announcements consist of additional information, the coefficient of *DOMES* is expected to be statistically significant. The regression models control for the other acquisition attributes: public or private target (*STATUS*), payment structure (*STRUCTURE*), size of the transaction relative to the acquiring REIT (*R_SIZE*), return on equity of the acquiring REIT (*ROE*), the ratio of equity to total assets (*EQUITY*), and the number of states in which the acquiring REIT has properties (*STATES*).

STATUS equals one if the target REIT is privately held and zero if it is publicly held. It is expected to positively influence the abnormal return because privately held firms are frequently controlled by fewer investors who are easier to negotiate with than those in publicly held firms [30]. Also, in the corporate finance literature, Chang [8] concluded that the acquirer achieves positive abnormal returns in the announcement period of public-private mergers when the transaction is stock-financed. The wealth gain is argued to come from the monitoring by blockholders and the reduced information asymmetry.

STRUCTURE is also a dummy variable that controls for the method of payment of merger deals. *STRUCTURE* equals one if the merger deal is cash-financed and zero otherwise. It is expected to positively influence the abnormal return because acquirers prefer a cash payment when their stock is undervalued [31]. Previous studies, such as Campbell et al. [7], concluded that the acquiring REIT achieves positive abnormal returns during the announcement period in public-private mergers when the transaction is stock-financed. Although our data do not contain information on whether the merger transaction was stock-financed, we incorporated the cross-product term, *STATUS × STRUCTURE*, to examine whether the acquirer will experience a positive or negative effect in a cash-financed merger transaction when the target REIT is private. *R_SIZE* is the relative value of both the target and acquiring firms. It is expected to positively influence the abnormal return due to the value-maximizing behavior exhibited by the management of bidding firms [4].

The variable *ROE* measures the acquirers' profitability and is expected to positively affect the abnormal returns, because the bidding firms with better profitability are better equipped to restructure the target firms [27]. *EQUITY* measures the capital strength of acquirers and is expected to have a positive influence because more leveraged firms are susceptible to a greater degree of investor sentiment [32].

STATES is a proxy variable of geographic diversification. Geringer et al. [33] considered the ratio of a company's foreign subsidiaries' sales to its total worldwide sales as the internationalization variable. Kim et al. [34] measured the degree of global diversification by the number of employees in foreign countries. Due to the characteristics of REIT firms having properties in states other than their asset portfolio, the number of states in which a REIT has properties was used as a proxy for the degree of geographic diversification. The cross-sectional regression model of the 2-day CAR is characterized as follows:

$$CAR\,(0,+1) = \beta_0 + \beta_1 DOMES + \beta_2\,STATUS + \beta_3 STRUCTURE$$
$$+ \beta_4 STATUS \times STRUCTURE + \beta_5 R_{SIZE} + \beta_6 ROE \qquad (7)$$
$$+ \beta_7 EQUITY + \beta_8 STATES + \varepsilon$$

4. Empirical Results

4.1. Abnormal Returns of the Acquiring REITs in Domestic and Cross-Border Merger Announcements

Table 4 shows the *CAAR* around the merger announcements. *CAAR*s are reported for the three different event windows: *CAAR* (−1, 1), *CAAR* (0, 1), and *CAAR* (0, 2). Overall, the average return from all merger announcements was 0.8% surrounding a 3-day window (from day 0 to + 2) and 0.73% between day 0 and 1.

Our results are consistent with Allen and Sirmans [6], in which the acquirer had a positive abnormal return around the merger announcement. Campbell et al. [35] also found positive excess return for REIT bidders for the 3-day announcement period following public-private mergers. Overall, our findings support previous evidence in the real estate literature that indicate that bidding firms enjoy more excess in their returns in mergers compared with findings from general corporate finance literature.

Table 4. Cumulative average abnormal returns for the acquiring trusts in REIT merger announcements.

Day/window	Domestic M&A	Cross-Border M&A	All M&A Announcements
CAAR (−1,1)	0.67%**	0.21%	0.61%**
CAAR (0,1)	0.78%**	0.41%	0.73%**
CAAR (0,2)	0.82%*	0.66%	0.80%**
Obs.	160	22	182

** and * indicate significant at 5% and 10% significance levels, respectively. *CAAR* denotes the average value of the cumulative abnormal return (*CAR*).

Table 5 shows the mean cumulative abnormal returns for the acquiring trusts in domestic and cross-border REIT merger announcements from day 0 to day 1, *CAAR* (0, 1), during the three subperiods: before-the-crisis, during-the-crisis, and after-the-crisis periods. Only the *CAAR* for domestic merger announcements during the crisis period is positive and significant. Our results contrast with those reported by Amewu [36] and Beltratti and Paladino [27], who concluded that there was no significant change in abnormal returns on bidding firms' shares following the onset of the global financial crisis. The reason for the positive and significant abnormal returns for the acquiring REITs could be the value gains from investing in the distressed stock price of the target REITs during the crisis period.

The short-term wealth effects of the acquirers around the announcements of the domestic and cross-border mergers have also been documented in the corporate finance literature. Moeller and Schlingemann [15] provided evidence that U.S. firms who acquire cross-border targets relative to those that acquire domestic targets experience significantly lower announcement stock returns of approximately 1%. Acquirers' stock returns are negatively associated with global and industrial diversification. They concluded that the bidder return is positively associated with the legal system favoring strong shareholder rights and negatively associated with restrictive target countries. Mateev and Andonov [37] also found that bidding firms engaging in cross-border bids suffer lower announcement effects than those undertaking domestic acquisitions. They also provided evidence that cross-border bidding firms tend to suffer lower returns when the targets are located in countries with stronger investor protection mechanisms.

Furthermore, Table 5 shows that the average acquirers' *CAAR* was larger for cross-border merger announcements than that for domestic merger announcements before the crisis period, although neither is significant. During the crisis period, acquirers' *CAAR* was positive and statistically significant for domestic merger announcements only. In the aftermath of the crisis period, the acquirers' *CAAR* became smaller and insignificant for domestic mergers and negative for cross-border mergers, although neither is statistically significant.

We can summarize the findings for the short-term wealth effect of the REIT acquirers as follows. First, the acquirers achieved higher returns for domestic mergers than cross-border mergers. Acquirers realize a lower wealth effect from cross-border mergers. This is consistent with the argument in the literature that when the targets are in countries with more economic restrictions, such as investor protection mechanisms, which is likely true in general when compared with the U.S., the U.S. acquirers suffer lower returns than the returns in the case of domestic mergers. Second, acquirers achieved positive and statistically significant abnormal returns during the crisis period only. The gains in wealth were mainly from the distressed prices of the targets.

Table 5. Cumulative average abnormal returns for domestic and cross-border merger announcements during subperiods.

	Before the Crisis		During the Crisis		After the Crisis	
	CAAR(0,1)	t-stats	CAAR(0,1)	t-stats	CAAR(0,1)	t-stats
Domestic	0.13%	0.43	1.86%	2.89 ***	0.34%	0.55
Cross-border	0.58%	1.47	1.28%	0.62	−0.83%	−0.85
All	0.19%	0.71	1.79%	2.92 ***	0.21%	0.37

*** indicates significant at 1% significance level.

4.2. Cross-Sectional Analysis of Abnormal Returns

Table 6 shows the results of the regressions of CAR from day 0 to day 1 for the acquiring firm during the three subperiods: before the crisis, during the crisis, and after the crisis, respectively. Before the crisis, when the target was domestic, the acquiring REIT achieved lower announcement returns than when the target was cross-border. This is consistent with the finding in Sahin [9] and with the internationalization theory, in which gains are from diversification when businesses seek synergies from intangible assets, such as information-based assets [10,11].

Second, the CAR of the acquiring REIT was larger when the target firm was private and when the merger transaction was cash-financed. Campbell et al. [7] concluded that acquirer returns were positive in stock-financed mergers when the target is private. Our results indicate that when the merger was cash-financed, the acquirer returns were positive, regardless of the public or private status of the target. This can be explained by the undervalued stocks of the acquiring REITs [31]. This finding—that when the target was private, the acquirer announcement returns were positive regardless of the method of payment—needs to be explained. In the corporate finance literature, Chang [8] concluded the acquirer achieves positive abnormal returns in the announcement period of public-private mergers when the transaction is stock-financed. He concluded that the wealth gain comes from the monitoring by blockholders and the reduction in information asymmetry. Campbell et al. [7] argued that the acquiring REIT valuation gain from the merger announcement when the target is private is better explained by the signaling effect.

However, the signaling effect cannot explain why the acquirer achieves a positive wealth effect from the merger announcement when the merger transaction is not stock-financed. For corporate acquisitions, Conn et al. [30] concluded that both domestic and cross-border private acquisitions result in positive announcement returns. They discussed several potential explanations for positive acquisition announcement returns when the target is private. For example, the process of making private bids is less exposed to the public gaze, and the acquirer can end the negotiation without loss of face. Poor acquisition outcomes due to hubris are less likely when the target is private. Also, the stocks of the private target are at a discount because of the illiquidity and other trading frictions. When the public acquirer purchases the assets of the private target, the potential value gain of the private target can be realized by the management of the public acquirer.

Finally, the size of the merger relative to the capitalization of the acquiring firm was marginally negatively associated with CAR, which contradicts our expectation. When we incorporate the interaction term of STATUS and R_SIZE, the coefficient of R_SIZE remains negative but becomes insignificant. The coefficient of the above interaction term is positive but, again, is insignificant (to save space, it is not reported in Table 6).

During the crisis period, only the size of the merger transaction relative to the capitalization of the acquiring firm was positively associated with the CAR. This finding is consistent with the finding in Table 5, in which the reason for the positive and significant abnormal returns for the acquiring firms could be the value gains from investing in the undervalued stocks of the target REITs during the crisis period. This is supported by the argument of Reddy et al. [26]. As the deal size becomes larger, the gains from the merger for the acquiring firm become larger.

During the after-crisis period, the acquiring firms' *CAR* was larger when the target was domestic compared with the cross-border target. This reverses the finding from the pre-crisis period, but this is consistent with the finding of Conn et al. [30], who concluded that both the announcement and long-run returns of cross-border mergers are lower than those of domestic mergers. That is, before the crisis, synergies from international diversification dominates the effects of the aforementioned cross-border cultural differences, corporate governance, and valuation differences. However, following the crisis, the latter effects dominate the synergies from international diversification. This may suggest that since market participants became more risk-averse after the onset of the crisis, the market reacted to cross-border merger announcements less favorably than domestic mergers due to uncertainty and information asymmetries.

Furthermore, unlike the case for the pre-crisis period, when the target firm was private, the *CAR* became smaller, although it was not statistically significant. This corresponds to the increase in risk aversion of the market participants following the onset of the crisis: private target firms had more information asymmetry, and the stock prices of the acquiring REITs reacted to the merger announcement less favorably.

In the after-crisis period, when the acquisition was cash-financed, like the case for the pre-crisis period, the *CAR* was larger than that for other methods of payment. Finally, the number of states in which the acquirer had properties also positively affected the acquirer's *CAR*. This again corresponds to the argument of the increase in market participants' risk aversion. If the acquirer's properties had more geographic diversification, the acquirer's announcement return was higher. This effect of the number of states in which the acquirer has properties had no effect on the acquirer's merger announcement return before the crisis or during the crisis periods.

Table 6. Cross-sectional analysis: regressions of cumulative abnormal returns from day 0 to day 1.

Independent Variable	Before the Crisis	During the Crisis	After the Crisis
DOMES	−0.0109 (−1.44)	0.0158 (0.82)	0.0426 ** (2.11)
STATUS	0.0145 ** (2.22)	−0.01687 (−1.20)	−0.0283 ** (−2.00)
STRUCTURE	0.0092 * (1.66)	−0.01221 (−0.80)	0.0215 * (1.83)
R_SIZE	−0.0124 * (−1.79)	0.2101 ** (2.44)	−0.0238 (−0.44)
ROE	0.0246 (1.17)	−0.0436 (−1.14)	−0.0566 (−0.89)
STATES	-1.2×10^{-5} (−0.05)	−0.0005 (−0.96)	0.0011 * (1.91)
Constant	−0.0124 (−1.19)	−0.0051 (−0.20)	−0.0524 ** (−2.27)
Obs.	65	59	54
Adj. *R*-square	0.02	0.07	0.11

Numbers in parentheses are t-statistics. ** and * indicate significant at 5% and 10% significance levels, respectively.

5. Conclusions

A stylized fact concerning corporate acquisitions is that bidding firms experience much smaller returns than the target firms around the acquisition announcement date. This study examined the short-term wealth effect of the merger announcement on the acquiring REIT. Both domestic and cross-border mergers were considered. We tried to reconcile our findings of the wealth effect from a merger announcement on the acquiring REITs with the existing theories and hypotheses on mergers and acquisitions in the corporate finance literature.

When the sample period was divided into pre-crisis, crisis, and after-crisis periods, we found that the acquiring trusts achieved positive and significant abnormal returns around the acquisition announcement date for domestic mergers during the crisis period only. This finding supports the argument that the acquiring REITs took advantage of attractive asset prices during the crisis period [26].

The cross-sectional analysis shows that, before the crisis period, privately held targets and cash-financed deals were positively associated with abnormal returns for the acquiring trusts. Chang [8] argued that when public -private mergers are stock-financed, the acquiring firms achieve positive returns due to the effects of the monitoring hypothesis and the signaling hypothesis. However, our finding cannot be explained by these hypotheses, because acquiring REITs achieved larger abnormal returns when the acquisition was cash-financed rather than stock-financed. During the crisis period, the size of the merger transaction relative to the capitalization of the acquiring trust became positively associated with the abnormal returns to the acquiring trusts. This finding reinforces the argument of the undervalued assets of the target. For example, Reddy et al. [26] found that emerging countries increased their foreign acquisitions in developed countries because of the more attractive asset prices. Following the crisis, the acquiring trusts achieved larger abnormal returns from domestic mergers around the announcement date than that associated with cross-border mergers. Furthermore, if the target trust was privately-held, the acquiring trust achieved smaller abnormal returns around the merger announcement date. Finally, when the acquiring trust had properties in more states, the trust achieved more abnormal returns following the crisis period.

Overall, this study provides evidence which sheds light on the changes in investors' risk preferences after the subprime mortgage crisis. Before the crisis, the acquirer achieved a larger wealth effect from a cross-border merger announcement than that from a domestic merger. This indicates that the benefits resulting from international diversification dominated the losses resulting from cultural differences, investor protection, corporate governance, and valuation differences. During the crisis period, the acquiring REIT achieved larger abnormal returns from the advantage of the undervalued assets of the target REIT. After the crisis, investors became more risk-averse such that the losses resulting from cultural differences, investor protection, corporate governance, and valuation differences dominated the benefits resulting from international diversification. The acquiring REIT also achieved larger abnormal returns around the acquisition announcement date when the acquiring trust had properties in more states.

Author Contributions: Conceptualization, A.T.W. and Y.-H.L.; Methodology, A.T.W. and Y.-H.L.; Software, A.T.W.; Validation, A.T.W., Y.-H.L. and Y.-C.C.; Formal Analysis, A.T.W.; Investigation, Y.-H.L.; Resources, A.T.W. and Y.-H.L.; Data Curation, Y.-C.C.; Writing—Original Draft Preparation, A.T.W. and Y.-C.C.; Writing—Review & Editing, A.T.W.; Visualization, A.T.W.; Supervision, Y.-H.L.; Project Administration, A.T.W.; Funding Acquisition, Y.-H.L.

References

1. Mishkin, F.S. Over the cliff: From the subprime to the global financial crisis. *J. Econ. Perspect.* **2011**, 25, 49–70. [CrossRef]
2. Reinhart, C.M.; Rogoff, K.S. The aftermath of financial crises. *Am. Econ. Rev.* **2009**, 99, 466–472. [CrossRef]
3. Jensen, M.C.; Ruback, R. The market for corporate control: The scientific evidence. *J. Financ. Econ.* **1983**, 11, 5–50. [CrossRef]
4. Asquith, P.; Bruner, R.F.; Mullins, D.W. The gains to bidding firms from merger. *J. Financ. Econ.* **1983**, 11, 121–139. [CrossRef]
5. Ooi, J.T.L.; Wong, W.C.; Ong, S.E. Can bank lines of credit protect REITs against a credit crisis? *Real Estate Econ.* **2011** 40, 285–316. [CrossRef]

6.   Allen, P.R.; Sirmans, C.F. An analysis of gains to acquiring firm's shareholders: The special case of REITs. *J. Financ. Econ.* **1987**, *18*, 175–184. [CrossRef]

7.   Campbell, R.D.; Ghosh, C.; Sirmans, C.F. The information content of method of payment in mergers: Evidence from real estate investment trust (REITs). *Real Estate Econ.* **2001**, *29*, 361–387. [CrossRef]

8.   Chang, S. Takeovers of privately held targets, method of payment, and bidder returns. *J. Financ.* **1998**, *53*, 773–784. [CrossRef]

9.   Sahin, O. The performance of acquisitions in the real estate investment trust industry. *J. Real Estate Res.* **2005**, *27*, 321–342.

10. Baldwin, J.R.; Caves, R.E. Foreign Multinational Enterprises and Merger Activity in Canada. In *Corporate Globalisation Through Mergers and Acquisitions*; Waverman, L., Ed.; The University of Calgary Press: Calgary, AB, USA, 1991.

11. Morck, R.; Yeung, B. *Why Firms Diversify: Internalization vs. Agency Behavior*; Hand, J., Lev, B., Eds.; Oxford University Press: Oxford, UK, 2003.

12. Quah, P.; Young, S. Post-acquisition management: A phases approach for cross-border MERGERs. *Eur. Manag. J.* **2005**, *23*, 65–75. [CrossRef]

13. Erel, I.; Liao, R.C.; Weisbach, M.S. Determinants of cross-border mergers and acquisitions. *J. Financ.* **2012**, *67*, 1045–1082. [CrossRef]

14. Kindleberger, C.P. *American Business Abroad*; Yale University Press: New Heaven, CN, USA, 1969.

15. Moeller, S.B.; Schlingemann, F.P. Global diversification and bidder gains: A comparison between cross-border and domestic acquisitions. *J. Bank. Financ.* **2005**, *29*, 533–564. [CrossRef]

16. Dutta, S.; Saadi, S.; Zhu, P.C. Does payment method matter in cross-border acquisitions? *Int. Rev. Econ. Financ.* **2013**, *25*, 91–107. [CrossRef]

17. Martynova, M.; Renneboog, L. Mergers and acquisitions in Europe. In *Advances in Corporate Finance and Asset Pricing*; Renneboog, L., Ed.; Elsevier: Amsterdam, The Netherlands, 2006; pp. 13–75.

18. Aybar, B.; Ficici, A. Cross-border acquisitions and firm value: An analysis of emerging-market multinationals. *J. Int. Bus. Stud.* **2009**, *40*, 1317–1338. [CrossRef]

19. Chakrabarti, R.; Jayaraman, N.; Mukherjee, S. Mars-Venus marriages: Culture and cross-border merger. *J. Int. Bus. Stud.* **2005**, *40*, 216–236. [CrossRef]

20. McIntosh, W.; Officer, D.; Born, J. The wealth effects of merger activities: Further evidence from real estate investment trusts. *J. Real Estate Res.* **1989**, *4*, 141–155.

21. Ooi, J.T.L.; Ong, S.E.; Neo, P.H. The wealth effects of property acquisitions: Evidence from Japanese and Singaporean REITs. *Real Estate Econ.* **2011**, *39*, 487–505. [CrossRef]

22. Ling, D.C.; Petrova, M. Why do REITs go private? Differences in target characteristics, acquirer motivations, and wealth effects in public and private acquisitions. *J. Real Estate Financ. Econ.* **2011**, *43*, 99–129. [CrossRef]

23. Berger, A.N.; Bouwman, C.H.S. Bank liquidity creation. *Rev. Financ. Stud.* **2009**, *22*, 3779–3837. [CrossRef]

24. Emmons, W.R.; Gilbert, R.A.; Yeager, T.J. Reducing the risk at small community banks: Is it size or geographic diversification matters? *J. Financ. Serv. Res.* **2004**, *25*, 259–281. [CrossRef]

25. Hankir, Y.; Rauch, C.; Umber, M.P. Bank merger: A market power story? *J. Bank. Financ.* **2011**, *35*, 2341–2354. [CrossRef]

26. Reddy, K.S.; Nangia, V.K.; Agrawal, R. The 2007–2008 global financial crisis, and cross-border mergers and acquisitions: A 26-nation exploratory study. *Saga Publ.* **2014**, *6*, 257–281. [CrossRef]

27. Beltratti, A.; Paladino, G. Is merger different during a crisis? Evidence from the European banking sector. *J. Bank. Financ.* **2013**, *37*, 5394–5405. [CrossRef]

28. Brown, S.; Warner, J. Measuring security price performance. *J. Financ. Econ.* **1980**, *8*, 205–258. [CrossRef]

29. Brown, S.; Warner, J. Using daily stock returns: The case of event studies. *J. Financ. Econ.* **1985**, *14*, 3–31. [CrossRef]

30. Conn, R.L.; Cosh, A.; Guest, P.M.; Hughes, A. The impact on UK acquirers of domestic, cross-border, public and private acquisitions. *J. Bank. Financ. Account.* **2005**, *32*, 815–870. [CrossRef]

31. Loughran, T.; Vijh, A.M. Do long-term shareholders benefit from corporate acquisitions? *J. Financ.* **1997**, *52*, 1765–1790. [CrossRef]

32. Nnadi, M.; Tanna, S. Analysis of cross-border and domestic mega-mergers of European commercial banks. *Manag. Financ.* **2013**, *39*, 848–862.

33. Geringer, J.M.; Beamish, P.W.; Da Costa, R.C. Diversification strategy and internationalization: Implications for MNE performance. *Strateg. Manag. J.* **1989**, *10*, 109–119. [CrossRef]

34. Kim, W.C.; Hwang, P.; Burgers, W.P. Global diversification strategy and corporate profit performance. *Strateg. Manag. J.* **1989**, *10*, 45–57.

35. Campbell, R.D.; Ghosh, C.; Sirmans, C.F. Value creation and governance structure in REIT mergers. *J. Real Estate Financ. Econ.* **2005**, *31*, 225–239. [CrossRef]

36. Amewu, G. Implication of mergers and acquisitions on stock returns before and during the 2007–2009 credit crunch: An event study. *Afr. Rev. Econ. Financ.* **2014**, *6*, 102–119.

37. Mateev, M.; Andonov, K. Do cross-border and domestic bidding firms perform differently? New evidence from continental Europe and the UK. *Res. Int. Bus. Financ.* **2016**, *37*, 327–349. [CrossRef]

8

Financial Credit Risk Evaluation Based on Core Enterprise Supply Chains

WeiMing Mou [1], **Wing-Keung Wong** [2] and **Michael McAleer** [3,4,5,6,*]

[1] College of Economics and Management, Changzhou Institute of Technology, Changzhou 213022, China; muwm@czu.cn
[2] Department of Finance, Fintech Center Big Data Research Center, Asia University, Taichung 41354, Taiwan; wong@asia.edu.tw
[3] Department of Finance, Asia University, Taichung 41354, Taiwan
[4] Econometric Institute, Erasmus School of Economics, Erasmus University Rotterdam, 3000 Rotterdam, The Netherlands
[5] Department of Economic Analysis and ICAE, Complutense University of Madrid, 28040 Madrid, Spain
[6] Institute of Advanced Sciences, Yokohama National University, Yokohama 240-8501, Japan
* Correspondence: michael.mcaleer@gmail.com

Abstract: Supply chain finance has broken through traditional credit modes and advanced rapidly as a creative financial business discipline. Core enterprises have played a critical role in the credit enhancement of supply chain finance. Through the analysis of core enterprise credit risks in supply chain finance, by means of a 'fuzzy analytical hierarchy process' (FAHP), the paper constructs a supply chain financial credit risk evaluation system, making quantitative measurements and evaluation of core enterprise credit risk. This enables enterprises to take measures to control credit risk, thereby promoting the healthy development of supply chain finance. The examination of core enterprise supply chains suggests that a unified information file should be collected based on the core enterprise, including the operating conditions, asset status, industry status, credit record, effective information to the database, collecting related data upstream and downstream of the archives around the core enterprise, developing a data information system, electronic data information, and updating the database accurately using the latest information that might be available. Moreover, supply chain finance and modern information technology should be integrated to establish the sharing of information resources and realize the exchange of information flows, capital flows, and logistics between banks. This should reduce a variety of risks and improve the efficiency and effectiveness of supply chain finance.

Keywords: supply chain finance; core enterprises; financial credit risk evaluation; fuzzy analytical hierarchy process (FAHP)

1. Introduction

Small and medium-sized enterprises (SMEs) have generally played the most significant role in the development of the national and provincial economies in China. SMEs have made great strides that have accounted for over 98% of all enterprises, contributed more than 60% of growth in GDP and foreign trade for economic development nationwide, provided over 80% of job opportunities, and more than 50% of business revenues. Although SMEs have experienced an overall performance that would be characterized as excellent and have an irreplaceable role in promoting the national economy, their financial environment has been, and remains, susceptible and sensitive to changing financial conditions at all levels.

Overall, SMEs face greater financial constraints than do larger firms. There are measures that are intended to alleviate the financial constraints of SMEs, such as leasing and factoring that are helpful in facilitating access to finance in the absence of well-developed financial institutions. Numerous studies have argued that SMEs are financially more constrained than large firms.

SMEs are major players in the economy, such that the current financial market failure is an obstacle to their expansion and growth. For this reason, SMEs need administrative and financial support from governments at all levels. However, despite the growing interest in subsidizing SMEs, there are concerns about whether these measures are helpful and sufficient. According to statistics from the People's Bank of China, SMEs have obtained bank loans that account for 16% of the loans of financial institutions, and bank supporting loans to SMEs lie in the range 30–40%. Moreover, virtually 80% of SMEs are experiencing capital circulation problems.

As SMEs have not received financial support relative to the contribution they have made to the economy, their financial problems have become a barrier that affects the sustainable development of SMEs. Given this background, the financial supply chain enters as an important participant to the financial system, with associated financial credit risks.

The remainder of the paper is as follows. Section 2 gives a literature review, including the definition of supply chain finance, credit risk evaluation of supply chain finance, and risk control for supply chain finance. The theory of supply chain financial core enterprise risks is discussed in Section 3, including credit, guarantee, and operational risk. Section 4 presents the fuzzy analytical hierarchy process (FAHP) framework, including the fuzzy judgment matrix and a check for its consistency, the weight vector, and composite weight vector. The empirical analysis is evaluated in Section 5, including a discussion of core enterprises, an evaluation system of the core enterprise credit risk, and model construction and solution. Some concluding remarks are presented in Section 6.

2. Literature Review

International research on supply chain finance started before similar developments in China, the mode of operation is more mature, and the achievements are relatively advanced. Regarding relationship between supply chain and financing, Berger et al. (2006) [1] advanced the conceptual framework for the development and financing of global small and medium-sized enterprises and established the idea of supply chain finance. Klapper (2005) [2] analyzed the principles underlying the inventory financing model, and the functions that small and medium-sized enterprises had adopted in the supply chain.

The development of China's supply chain finance began around 2000. In 2005, the financing mode of "1 plus N" implemented by the Shenzhen Development Bank (since renamed the Ping An Bank) offered a $250 billion credit line, making 25% profit, with the non-performing loans accounting for 0.57% of all supply chain finance.

In recent years, supply chain finance has been developing rapidly. Statistics show that by the end of 2015, 60% of SMEs had chosen supply chain finance to alleviate the shortage of business liquidity. However, as an innovative financing method, supply chain finance also has certain risks, such as the financing of small and medium-sized enterprise core banks, whereby one party's credit problems can lead to the failure of supply chain financing and the loss of other participants. While SMEs are undoubtedly the engine of economic growth, their speed of growth will be dampened by market imperfections and institutional weaknesses (for further details, see [3] Beck and Demirguc-Kunt (2006)).

In [4] Shi et al. (2014), the fuzzy analytical hierarchy process was applied for risk evaluation in model building of logistics financial business for banks. The information asymmetry between banks and enterprises and imperfect mechanism bring some risk to banks carrying out the logistics and financial business. Using logistics financial risk indicators, the risk evaluation index system of logistics finance from the pledge risk, financing enterprise credit risk, logistics enterprise risk, and regulatory risk, the risk evaluation model of logistics financial business for the bank is established by using fuzzy mathematics theory and an analytic hierarchy process.

Further to the above, [5] Shi et al. (2015) evaluated the credit risk of online supply chain finance based on third-party B2B e-commerce platform for China. The system applies the multi-level gray evaluation model based on the Theil index to make a comprehensive evaluation on the credit of the loan enterprise and tests the model's feasibility through the analyses of a numerical example. The evaluation model overcomes the subjectivity of weight distribution to index and presents the degree of the indices on each hierarchy distinctly so as to enable banks to take risk control specifically in operation.

Through the analysis of core enterprise credit risks in supply chain finance, by means of a 'fuzzy analytical hierarchy process' (FAHP), the paper constructs a supply chain financial credit risk evaluation system. This paper extends the work of the two papers just mentioned by discussing the fuzzy judgment matrix, developing a fuzzy Judgment matrix consistency check, weight vector of index layer C, weight vector of index layer C to criterion layer B, and composite weight vectors. The paper also provides a detailed empirical example that highlights the novelty of the model construction and solution. These are the primary and novel purposes of the paper.

2.1. Definition of Supply Chain Finance

The definition of supply chain finance will cover significant contributions from 2005 until the present. According to the definition of supply chain finance (SCF) in [6] Hofmann (2005), it relies on two or more organizations in the supply chain to cooperate on financial resources to create extra values jointly, although these organizations remain independent. Pfohl and Gomm (2009) [7] argued that SCF could raise the value of participating firms in the supply chain, in addition to the value of leading firms in the supply chain.

Several years later, according to [8] Gupta and Dutta (2011), with increasingly fierce competition, it becomes more important to improve the efficiency of working capital by using cash that is trapped in the financial supply chain (FSC). Mathis and Cavinato (2010) [9] argued that banks should play a more active role in the FSC to integrate the resources in the chain. Silvestro and Lustrato (2014) [10] showed that banks are key players that can offer alternative supply chain solutions in the FSC.

More recently, in a related development, [11] Blackman et al. (2013) proposed a formal definition that a 'financial supply chain' is the network of organizations and banks that coordinate the flow of financial transactions through shared information systems to facilitate a product supply chain between trading partners.

SCF can be defined in many ways, depending on perspective and orientation. The analysis of the different definitions and conceptual contributions highlights two major perspectives on SCF, which can be identified as 'financial-oriented' from which a further 'buyer-driven perspective' can be identified) and 'supply chain-oriented'. The financial perspective interprets SCF as a set of (innovative) financial solutions (for further details, see [12] Caniato et al., 2016).

SCF has increasingly become a hot topic in supply chain management and a growing product category of financial institutions (FIs). In China, SCF is experiencing a rapid development stage, and numerous FIs have begun to focus on developing and designing new SCF services and products to solve the financing issues facing SMEs. SCF is a channel for financing, which manages, plans, and controls all cash flows across supply chain members to improve the turnover efficiency of working capital. In SCF, SMEs obtain loans with looser constraints from banks through expanded credit lines. Core enterprises (CEs) alleviate the pressure of funding, and financial intermediaries dramatically increase their incomes.

More specifically, SCF significantly decreases the credit risk of SMEs for FIs. Nevertheless, SCF cannot completely eliminate credit risk, which continues to be one of the major threats to FIs. Moreover, SCF has been promoted for almost 10 years and has experienced slow development in China because there is not as yet an appropriate SME credit risk evaluation index system, or an outstanding prediction model, which hinders SCF (for further details, see [13] Zhu et al., 2016)).

SCF is concerned with the capital flows within a supply chain, an area that has often been neglected in the past. Nevertheless, SCF does have an impact on a firm's capability for adopting sustainable supply chain management (SCM) practices (for further details, see [14] Liu et al. (2015)).

2.2. Credit Risk Evaluation of Supply Chain Finance

In China, SMEs are the main applicants of SCF, so that banks suffer from credit risk in SCF when the SMEs cannot honor agreements and contracts. It is generally agreed that structuring the SME credit risk evaluation index system is the greatest and most critical challenge to bank management of SCF, and that it is fundamental to credit loan decision making. A good credit risk evaluation index system can guarantee profitability and stability of a FI, whereas a poor system can potentially lead to significant losses (for further details, see [13] Zhu et al., 2016).

In previous studies, experts and scholars paid greater attention to the credit risk of SMEs, while neglecting the credit risk of core enterprises, which is one of the main financial entities of the supply chain. In fact, the core enterprises' credit risk is the key to influence the effective implementation of supply chain finance.

Feldmann and Müller (2003) [15] emphasized the role of asymmetric information held by supply chain partners who are opportunistically behaved. Silvestro and Lustrato (2014) [10] argued that the factors that could affect the risk of SCF include supply chain co-ordination, cooperation, and information sharing.

In a much earlier contribution, [16] Berger and Udell (1998) found that small firms have limited access to external financing, and were more tightly constrained in their operations, both in developing and developed countries. Galindo and Schiantarelli (2003) [17] drew the same conclusion for countries in Latin America.

Schiffer and Weder (2001) [18] found that small firms consistently face greater growth obstacles than do large firms, which implies that size is one of the most reliable factors for financing obstacles confronting firms, except for age and ownership of firms (for further details, see [19] Beck et al., 2006).

Song and Zipkin (2009) [20] analyzed the methods for determining the quality of goods in the pawn financing process. Moreover, an investigation by [21] Wuttke et al. (2013) indicated that it is better for the supply chain enterprises of SMEs to adopt a "pre–shipment" financing model in preference to a "post-shipment" funding model. Furthermore, both corporations and banks have shown great interest in using SCF techniques to ease their tensions in the supply chain, and also in making large corporations shorten the payment periods for their key suppliers (for further details, see [22] Randall et al, 2009)).

Very recently, [13] Zhu et al. (2016) proposed an SME credit risk evaluation index system specifically designed for SCF. This system is used to evaluate the credit risks from different points of view, which not only consist of financial and non-financial conditions of SMEs, but also contain the financial and non-financial conditions of CEs, the operational status of the entire supply chain, and the transactional relationship between SMEs and CEs (for further details, see [13] Zhu et al., 2016)).

Therefore, measuring and evaluating the credit level of core enterprises, and controlling the credit risk of core enterprises, are the keys to using supply chain finance in an efficient manner.

2.3. Risk Control for Supply Chain Finance

As mentioned above, there has been substantial and informative research on supply chain finance for SMEs. Nevertheless, there remain some limitations. There has been little research on collaborative supply chain finance for SMEs, and the research has not necessarily been systematic.

In 1931, the British Financial Industry Council established the Macmillan Committee—officially known as the [23] Committee on Finance and Industry (1931)—and presented the Macmillan Report after investigating the British financial industry, and industry and commerce. The report noted that, in the UK financial system, there is a gap between SMEs and financial institutions (for further details, see [24] Stamp (1931)). To date, no research has considered a systematic analysis for the overall optimization of supply chain finance for SMEs in attempting to solve the "Macmillan gap".

Lee and Rhee (2011) [25] demonstrated that, through the coordination and establishment of commercial credit among SMEs, the results of risk control for supply chain finance of SMEs are better than those of financial risk control by financial institutions for the individual companies.

The apparent ability of some supply chains to recover from inevitable risk events more effectively than do others has recently triggered a debate about supply chain resilience (SCRES). While SCRM focuses on the identification and management of risks for the supply chain in order to reduce its vulnerability, SCRES aims at developing the adaptive capability to prepare for unexpected and contingent events, to respond to disruptions, and subsequently recover from them (for further details, see [26] Jüttner and Maklan, 2011)).

3. Theory of Supply Chain Financial Core Enterprise Risks

In supply chain finance, core enterprises are the exchange center of capital flows, information flows, and logistics, and play an important role in the supply chain financing. The risks can vary, including three major risks—namely credit, guarantee, and operational risks—which are discussed below.

3.1. Credit Risk

Core enterprises play an important role in supply chain finance, and play key roles in connecting the supply chain capital flows, information flows and logistics. Banks are based on the core enterprise's strength and credit guarantee and select the upstream and downstream enterprises to perform credit activities. Therefore, the core enterprise conditions and development prospects determine the smooth operation of the supply chain. The credit status of core business problems will inevitably spread to the supply chain with the upstream and downstream enterprises, thereby affecting the overall supply chain finance security and operational efficiency, leading to supply chain financing failure.

Core enterprise credit risk manifests itself in two respects. The core enterprise can undertake the entire supply chain finance guarantee function when they are experiencing poor management themselves. Moreover, the core enterprise may be confronted with a credit crisis due to bonding credit which exceeds its credit capacity, resulting in financing failure. As the core enterprise development prospects are not encouraging, their power is diminished.

A core enterprise may conceal their real transaction records with different parties in the supply chain, which leads to false financing. This can affect their actual performance, so that they will not be able to satisfy the conditions of the agreement with the bank, in which case the SMEs financing will eventually fail.

3.2. Guarantee Risk

For the core enterprise, the so-called guarantee risk arises in financing when SMEs break a contract. When SMEs cannot continue payments of bank loans, the core enterprise, as a guarantor of SMEs, has to bear the associated bank losses. In supply chain finance, guarantees by the core enterprise of the credit situation of SMEs leads to a greater strength of SMEs, and the possibility of reducing the risk of banks in lending money to SMEs through promoting enterprise production and business development. If the core enterprise intends to give credit to SMEs, the core enterprise should be careful in selecting SMEs in the supply chain that are financially strong so as to reduce guarantee risk.

3.3. Operational Risk

In the process of supply chain financing, many of the required steps need to be confirmed manually, so operational risk needs to be accommodated. The operation of the three main financing risk are also different. For example, the operational risk of accounts receivable financing mode focuses primarily on the management of accounts receivable.

The existence of sales discounts will lead to errors when the accounts receivable are checked. Moreover, given the fact that receivables financing is a repeatedly regular procedure, the payments and actual deviations occur when the core enterprises are confirming such payments. In addition, the accounts receivable settlements involve enterprises and many settlement accounts. As the procedures for repayment can be complicated, especially when the methods for the accounts receivable transfer payments change, operational errors are more prone to occur, thereby leading to greater operational risk.

Overall, the greatest influence on the supply chain of the three different types of risks mentioned above is financial credit risk. As the main participant in the supply chain, the core enterprise credit level has a significant influence on the success in financing. In order to reduce the financial risks of the supply chain, the effective control of core enterprise credit risk is fundamental.

4. Fuzzy Analytical Hierarchy Process (FAHP) Framework

Saaty (1990) [27] introduced a multi-factors decision making approach, in which factors are arranged in a hierarchical structure. In order to apply the FAHP method, it is necessary to construct a hierarchy that expresses the relative values of a set of attributes. Decision makers evaluate the relative importance of the attributes in each level based on the FAHP scale which, in turn, is used to direct them to express their preferences between each pairwise comparison. Then the decision makers are required to determine whether the element is of equal importance, somewhat more important, much more important, very much more important, or absolutely important, relative to another element.

These important intensities are, respectively, converted to numeral values in the FAHP scale as 1, 3, 5, 7, 9 and 2, 4, 6, 8, as the intermediate values (see Table 1). By using this scale, the qualitative judgments of evaluators are converted into quantitative values, which enable construction of a pairwise comparison matrix. The pairwise comparison matrix is made for all elements to be considered in the construct hierarchy. The results from these comparisons are used to calculate a list of admittedly arbitrary though reasonable weights, and importance of the factors (eigenvectors) based on the rapid application development (RAD) method. Arbitrary means that mathematical optimization for determining the weights was not used as it would have required a mathematical model to have been imposed on the structure of the model.

Table 1. FAHP Scale.

Intensity of AHP Scale	Linguistic Variable	Positive Value	Positively Reciprocal Value
1	Same importance	$(1, 1, 1)$	$(1, 1, 1)$
3	Weakly more important	$(2, 3, 4)$	$(1/4, 1/3, 1/2)$
5	Fairly more important	$(4, 5, 6)$	$(1/6, 1/5, 1/4)$
7	Strongly more important	$(6, 7, 8)$	$(1/8, 1/7, 1/6)$
9	Absolutely more important	$(8, 9, 10)$	$(1/10, 1/9, 1/8)$
2, 4, 6, 8	Intermediate values		

4.1. Fuzzy Judgment Matrix

Fuzzy judgment matrix can be used to compare the importance of different indicators. The level of importance of two elements are assumed to be incorporated into an index labelled as T, and the hierarchical elements, $a_1, \ldots, a_n$ represent the existing fuzzy relation, all of which constitute a fuzzy matrix, as given below:

$$
\begin{array}{c|ccccc}
T & a_1 & a_2 & \cdots & a_n \\
\hline
a_1 & r_{11} & r_{12} & \cdots & r_{1n} \\
a_2 & r_{21} & r_{22} & \cdots & r_{2n} \\
\\
a_n & r_{n1} & r_{n2} & \cdots & r_{nn}
\end{array}
\tag{1}
$$

In the fuzzy T index matrix, r_{ij} denotes a judgment value which represents the extent to which a_i is much more important than a_j, when the two elements a_i and a_j are compared.

Pairwise comparisons among the main factors, sub-factors, and alternatives are produced based on the typical nine-point scale combined with fuzzy numbers. The next step is to calculate the admittedly arbitrary priority weights of factors, sub-factors, and alternatives by adopting the FAHP approach.

The idea of calculating the priority weights of attributes is based on the pairwise comparisons given in the questionnaire (for further details, see Appendix A). In doing so, a set of comparison questions are proposed in order to ask the experts their opinions. The higher the evaluation is, the greater the importance of a factor will be.

Corresponding to three levels of the hierarchical model, the experts first evaluate the four main factors in the second level with respect to the overall goal. In the third level, pairwise comparisons of alternatives are made with respect to the overall goal.

In order to obtain the quantitative value of the compared importance between each two indicators, fuzzy numerical values from 1 to 9 are employed, as shown in Table 1. With such comparisons between each two factors, the fuzzy judgment matrix can be constructed.

4.2. Fuzzy Judgment Matrix Consistency Check

A consistency check is the first condition for calculating the weights. Only if the consistency meets the requirements can the model be solved. A relatively simple judgment method is based on the following formula.

$$\mathrm{CI}(A, W) = \frac{1}{n^2} \sum_{i=1}^{n} \sum_{j=1}^{n} \left| a_{ij} - \omega_{ij} \right| \tag{2}$$

The acceptable condition for the consistency judgment is $\mathrm{CI}(A, W) \leq \alpha$, where the implication of α is the attitude of the decision maker. The higher is the consistency of the fuzzy judgment matrix required by the decision maker, the smaller will be the value of α. The value of α is most suitable when it is set to 0.01.

4.3. Weight Vector of Criterion Layer B

The determination of the weight vector is the key to the fuzzy judgment matrix which can be obtained after sorting out the results of the questionnaire given by the experts. The formula given in Equation (3) is used to solve the weight vector for each criterion layer. The weight given to each expert is multiplied by the weight vector, and the weight vector of the elements at the B layer, such that $\omega_B = (\omega_1, \ldots, \omega_n)$, can be obtained as

$$\omega_i = \frac{\sum\limits_{j=1}^{n} a_{ij} + 1 - \frac{n}{2}}{n} \quad \text{for any i} = 1, 2, \ldots, \text{n}. \tag{3}$$

4.4. Weight Vector of Index Layer C to Criterion Layer B

Each decision-making expert takes the B layer elements as the criterion, and gives the fuzzy judgment matrix, which is obtained by the C layer elements, compares two fuzzy judgment matrix, by using the same method, and thereby obtains the weight vector of each element of the C layer.

4.5. Composite Weight Vector

After calculating the priority weight vectors of the B and C layers, the following formula in Equation (4)

$$\omega_j = \sum_{i=1}^{n} w_i w_j \tag{4}$$

This equation is used to compute the composite weight vector and the priority weight vector of the different indexes to obtain the credit risk. The key risk factors can then be identified. In the formula, ω_j is the index values of no. j element and w_i w_i is the weight vector. No. i criterion layer, w_{ij} is the weight vector of the no. i criterion layer of the no. j index value.

5. Empirical Analysis

5.1. Introduction to Core Enterprises

The Wuhan Iron and Steel Group is affiliated to the state-owned SASAC important backbone enterprises, has a good credit rating, and substantial financial strength. It is among the core enterprises in the supply chain finance. The Wuhan Iron and Steel Group is in the production stage of the three stages of product supply, production, and sales.

The upstream enterprises act primarily as steel materials suppliers, which are responsible for the mining of steel. The Wuhan Iron and Steel Group has applied to various banks for financial loans by means of the receivables documents in the financing process.

Downstream enterprises are mainly steel dealers, which are responsible for the sales of steel. During the financing process, they select the financing mode of prepayment to purchase and apply for loans based on sales contracts.

The China Industrial Bank (CIB) has been cooperating with the Wuhan Iron and Steel Group in the supply chain finance since 2002. Until December 2015, the China Industrial Bank had 53 credit lines among the upstream and downstream dealers of the Wuhan Iron and Steel Group, with a credit amount that exceeded RMB 1.536 billion. The non-performing loan ratio of the upstream and downstream enterprises is very low, almost close to zero, which is a successful case of the implementation of supply chain finance.

5.2. Evaluation System of the Core Enterprise Credit Risk

The core enterprise risk control is the most important factor in the supply chain risk. For this reason, the construction of the core enterprise credit risk system is very important. This paper constructs a layer analysis using four approaches toward risk, namely the core enterprise industry position, management perspective, asset status, and credit record.

5.2.1. Core Enterprise Industry Status (B1)

The achievement of inter-enterprise transactions not only relies on the quality of goods, but also the industry status as the focus of attention. In general, the core enterprise industry status has a significant effect on their business conditions. This paper selects the macroscopic environment and the development situation of the enterprises as the secondary index of industry status evaluation.

5.2.2. Core Enterprise Operations (B2)

Banks are more concerned about the operation of the core enterprise with guarantees. The reason is that the core enterprise needs to assume the guarantee obligation in case of default by the SMEs. If the core enterprises do not have high solvency, the banks will not be in a position to offer loans to the SMEs as they need to consider their own financial interests. The operating performance of the core enterprises is mainly reflected in the three indicators of profitability, operating capacity, and solvency. This paper selects these three indexes as the secondary indicators in the evaluation system.

5.2.3. Asset Status of the Core Enterprises (B3)

The main premise of bank loans is that the core enterprise provides security for SMEs, such that, when SMEs breach their contracts, the core enterprises will accept their responsibility for the guarantees, thereby compensating the banks and reducing bank losses. Therefore, the asset status of the core enterprise is also an important focus of bank inspections. In this way, the ability of the core enterprise to cash financial assets is stronger than that of the monetary funds, receivable accounts, and inventories. This paper will take the three items as the secondary index of the current asset status evaluation.

5.2.4. Core Enterprise Credit History (B4)

The key to the successful financing of SMEs is the core enterprise credit guarantees to be bundled together with SMEs to form the overall credit. However, if the credit situation of the core enterprise is poor, even if the SMEs and the core enterprise credit guarantees are bundled together, the bank will not make the loans accessible. This paper selects the credit rating and the previous performance, namely the credit history, as the secondary index.

The hierarchy of the evaluation system of core enterprise credit risk can constructed, as shown in Figure 1. It is divided into three levels, and arranged in descending order. The first level presents the overall goal, which is the risk evaluation of supply chain financial core enterprises (A) and is situated at the top of the hierarchy. In the second level, four major factors are inserted into the model, namely industry status (B1), operation condition (B2), asset state (B3), and credit record (B4). Each factor includes several sub-factors in the third level of the hierarchy.

The industry status factor is explained by two sub-factors, namely macro-environment (C1) and enterprise development (C2). The operation condition includes operation ability (C3), profitability (C4) and solvency (C5). The asset state consists of monetary fund (C6), accounts receivable (C7), and inventory (C8). The credit history includes enterprise credit rating (C9) and past performance (C10).

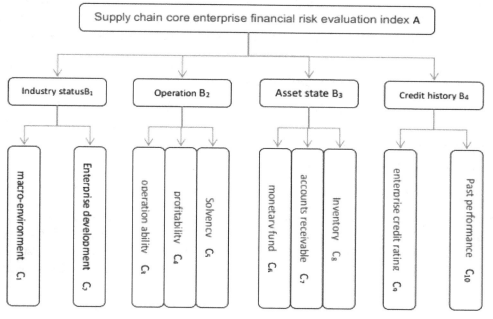

Figure 1. Core enterprise credit risk evaluation system hierarchical graph.

5.3. Model Construction and Solution

By using the risk evaluation system that was described above, including 4 risk categories and 10 risk factors, the risk identification model was constructed using a fuzzy analytic hierarchy process (FAHP), and the model was thereby solved. In this paper, the core enterprise employees are divided into four categories, namely managerial staff, senior engineers, middle-level employees, and general employees. The questionnaire is scored according to four types of employees (see below), with the fuzzy matrices given as B1, B2, B3, and B4.

The four types of employees are given as follows:

Managerial staff: They perform management functions, and direct or coordinate others to complete specific tasks in the organization. Their educational background is relatively good. They are familiar with the work flow of management and have a clearer business operation. Therefore, their assignment weights are 0.3. In this paper, a total of 50 managers were selected by the sampling method. After removing the highest and lowest scores, an average value was obtained.

Senior engineers: They are technical experts or technicians in the engineering field, play an irreplaceable role in the enterprise, and have strong working ability. In the enterprise work, they have a relatively professional technical background and authority, so their assignment weight is 0.3. In this paper, a total of 20 senior engineers were selected by the sampling method. After removing the highest and lowest scores, an average value was obtained.

Middle-level employees: They are managers at one or more intermediate levels between senior managers and grass-roots managers. Their main responsibilities are to implement major decisions made by senior managers, and to supervise and coordinate the work of grass-roots managers. Therefore, their work plays a connecting role. They are not as high as the headquarters management, and may only focus on part of the enterprise, so the assignment weight is 0.2. In this paper, a total of 50 middle-level employees were selected by the sampling method. After removing the highest and lowest scores, an average value was obtained.

General employees: Specifically engaged in various post work, and are at the forefront of staff, but their focus is their own post work. The overall perspective of the problem or risk is relatively small, so the assignment weight is 0.2. In this paper, a total of 50 employees were selected by the sampling method. After removing the highest and lowest scores, an average value was obtained.

These four categories of employees are given different weights, specifically managerial staff 0.3, senior engineers 0.3, middle-level staff 0.2, and general employees 0.2. Various types of employees on the B-layer elements are compared pairwise, and thereby obtain the fuzzy judgment matrix

$$B_1 = \begin{bmatrix} 0.5 & 0.7 & 0.6 & 0.4 \\ 0.3 & 0.5 & 0.4 & 0.4 \\ 0.4 & 0.6 & 0.5 & 0.3 \\ 0.6 & 0.6 & 0.7 & 0.5 \end{bmatrix} \tag{5}$$

$$B_2 = \begin{bmatrix} 0.5 & 0.8 & 0.7 & 0.6 \\ 0.2 & 0.5 & 0.5 & 0.4 \\ 0.3 & 0.5 & 0.5 & 0.3 \\ 0.4 & 0.6 & 0.7 & 0.5 \end{bmatrix} \tag{6}$$

$$B_3 = \begin{bmatrix} 0.5 & 0.7 & 0.8 & 0.6 \\ 0.3 & 0.5 & 0.6 & 0.4 \\ 0.2 & 0.4 & 0.5 & 0.3 \\ 0.4 & 0.6 & 0.7 & 0.5 \end{bmatrix} \tag{7}$$

$$B_4 = \begin{bmatrix} 0.5 & 0.8 & 0.9 & 0.5 \\ 0.2 & 0.5 & 0.7 & 0.2 \\ 0.1 & 0.3 & 0.5 & 0.3 \\ 0.5 & 0.8 & 0.7 & 0.5 \end{bmatrix} \tag{8}$$

The fuzzy judgment matrix is used to determine the fuzzy consistency of the four matrices, namely B1, B2, B3, B4, and the weight order vectors, that is, $\omega B1$, $\omega B2$, $\omega B3$, $\omega B4$, can be solved. By taking B1 as an example, the solution is given as

$$\begin{aligned} \omega_{B11} &= \tfrac{1}{4}\left(0.5 + 0.3 + 0.4 + 0.6 + 1 - \tfrac{4}{2}\right) = 0.2 \\ \omega_{B12} &= \tfrac{1}{4}\left(0.7 + 0.5 + 0.6 + 0.6 + 1 - \tfrac{4}{2}\right) = 0.35 \\ \omega_{B13} &= \tfrac{1}{4}\left(0.6 + 0.4 + 0.5 + 0.7 + 1 - \tfrac{4}{2}\right) = 0.3 \\ \omega_{B14} &= \tfrac{1}{4}\left(0.4 + 0.4 + 0.3 + 0.5 + 1 - \tfrac{4}{2}\right) = 0.15 \end{aligned} \tag{9}$$

Therefore:

$$\omega B1 = (0.2\ 0.35\ 0.3\ 0.15) \tag{10}$$

Similarly:

$$\omega B2 = (0.1\ 0.35\ 0.35\ 0.2)$$
$$\omega B3 = (0.1\ 0.3\ 0.4\ 0.2) \tag{11}$$
$$\omega B4 = (0.075\ 0.35\ 0.45\ 0.125)$$

Given the above, the weight of the four categories of employees can be added, and the B-level weight vector can be obtained as:

$$
\begin{aligned}
\omega_{B1} &= 0.3 \times 0.2 + 0.3 \times 0.1 + 0.2 \times 0.1 + 0.2 \times 0.075 = 0.125 \\
\omega_{B2} &= 0.3 \times 0.35 + 0.3 \times 0.35 + 0.2 \times 0.4 + 0.2 \times 0.35 = 0.34 \\
\omega_{B3} &= 0.3 \times 0.3 + 0.3 \times 0.35 + 0.2 \times 0.4 + 0.2 \times 0.45 = 0.365 \\
\omega_{B4} &= 0.3 \times 0.15 + 0.3 \times 0.2 + 0.2 \times 0.2 + 0.2 \times 0.125 = 0.17
\end{aligned}
\tag{12}
$$

As a result, the weight vector of the criterion layer to the target layer is $(0.125, 0.34, 0.36, 0.17)$. Given the construction, the total weight vector of the criterion layer to the target layer can be determined, as follows: the core enterprise asset weight is 0.365, and is ranked first; the operating weight is 0.33, which is ranked second; the credit record weight is 0.17, thereby being ranked third; the industry position weight is 0.125, and is ranked fourth.

The ranking constructed above shows that commercial banks are primarily concerned with the asset status of the core enterprise, followed by the core enterprise operation, then the credit record of the core enterprise, and finally the core enterprise industry status.

Under the premise of calculating the weight of the criterion layer, the weight value of each risk factor in the index layer can also be obtained. According to the questionnaire survey results of the 4 kinds of employees, the 10 risk factors in the index layer are compared with each other, the fuzzy judgment matrix is constructed, and the single ranking weight vector is obtained according to the judgment matrix.

In this paper, the weight vector of the criterion layer B to each element in the C layer is taken as an example. The fuzzy judgment matrix, C1k(k = 1, 2, 3, 4), is constructed, as given in Appendix B.

The same method is used to obtain the weight vector, namely,

$$
\begin{aligned}
\omega_{C11} &= \tfrac{1}{10}\left(0.5 + 0.6 + 0.7 + 0.5 + 0.3 + 0.7 + 0.5 + 0.8 + 0.6 + 0.5 + 1 - \tfrac{10}{2}\right) = 0.17 \\
\omega_{C12} &= \tfrac{1}{10}\left(0.4 + 0.5 + 0.4 + 0.6 + 0.4 + 0.7 + 0.7 + 0.3 + 0.5 + 0.6 + 1 - \tfrac{10}{2}\right) = 0.11 \\
\omega_{C13} &= \tfrac{1}{10}\left(0.3 + 0.6 + 0.5 + 0.4 + 0.7 + 0.5 + 0.4 + 0.2 + 0.5 + 0.4 + 1 - \tfrac{10}{2}\right) = 0.05 \\
\omega_{C14} &= \tfrac{1}{10}\left(0.5 + 0.4 + 0.6 + 0.5 + 0.3 + 0.2 + 0.8 + 0.6 + 0.7 + 0.5 + 1 - \tfrac{10}{2}\right) = 0.11 \\
\omega_{C15} &= \tfrac{1}{10}\left(0.7 + 0.6 + 0.3 + 0.7 + 0.5 + 0.5 + 0.8 + 0.1 + 0.5 + 0.7 + 1 - \tfrac{10}{2}\right) = 0.14 \\
\omega_{C16} &= \tfrac{1}{10}\left(0.3 + 0.3 + 0.5 + 0.8 + 0.5 + 0.5 + 0.4 + 0.7 + 0.2 + 0.5 + 1 - \tfrac{10}{2}\right) = 0.07 \\
\omega_{C17} &= \tfrac{1}{10}\left(0.5 + 0.3 + 0.6 + 0.2 + 0.2 + 0.6 + 0.5 + 0.7 + 0.8 + 0.6 + 1 - \tfrac{10}{2}\right) = 0.1 \\
\omega_{C18} &= \tfrac{1}{10}\left(0.2 + 0.7 + 0.8 + 0.4 + 0.9 + 0.8 + 0.3 + 0.5 + 0.3 + 0.5 + 1 - \tfrac{10}{2}\right) = 0.14 \\
\omega_{C19} &= \tfrac{1}{10}\left(0.4 + 0.5 + 0.5 + 0.3 + 0.3 + 0.3 + 0.2 + 0.7 + 0.5 + 0.5 + 1 - \tfrac{10}{2}\right) = 0.02 \\
\omega_{C10} &= \tfrac{1}{10}\left(0.5 + 0.4 + 0.6 + 0.5 + 0.3 + 0.5 + 0.4 + 0.5 + 0.5 + 0.5 + 1 - \tfrac{10}{2}\right) = 0.07
\end{aligned}
\tag{13}
$$

Therefore:

$$\omega C1 = (0.17\ 0.11\ 0.05\ 0.11\ 0.14\ 0.07\ 0.1\ 0.14\ 0.02\ 0.07) \tag{14}$$

Similarly:

$$\omega C2 = (0.1\ 0.11\ 0.15\ 0.15\ 0.09\ 0.12\ 0.06\ 0.1\ 0.09\ 0.03)$$
$$\omega C3 = (0.08\ 0.06\ 0.13\ 0.11\ 0.16\ 0.12\ 0.14\ 0.07\ 0.06\ 0.07) \quad (15)$$
$$\omega C4 = (0.08\ 0.07\ 0.15\ 0.06\ 0.14\ 0.17\ 0.12\ 0.09\ 0.04\ 0.08)$$

Based on the weight vector of the four kinds of employee fuzzy judgment matrix, the weight coefficients of four kinds of employees are added to obtain the group weight vector as

$$
\begin{aligned}
\omega C1 &= 0.3 \times 0.17 + 0.3 \times 0.1 + 0.2 \times 0.08 + 0.2 \times 0.08 = 0.113 \\
\omega C2 &= 0.3 \times 0.11 + 0.3 \times 0.11 + 0.2 \times 0.06 + 0.2 \times 0.07 = 0.092 \\
\omega C3 &= 0.3 \times 0.05 + 0.3 \times 0.15 + 0.2 \times 0.13 + 0.2 \times 0.15 = 0.116 \\
\omega C4 &= 0.3 \times 0.11 + 0.3 \times 0.15 + 0.2 \times 0.11 + 0.2 \times 0.06 = 0.112 \\
\omega C5 &= 0.3 \times 0.14 + 0.3 \times 0.09 + 0.2 \times 0.16 + 0.2 \times 0.14 = 0.129 \\
\omega C6 &= 0.3 \times 0.07 + 0.3 \times 0.12 + 0.2 \times 0.12 + 0.2 \times 0.17 = 0.115 \\
\omega C7 &= 0.3 \times 0.1 + 0.3 \times 0.06 + 0.2 \times 0.14 + 0.2 \times 0.12 = 0.1 \\
\omega C8 &= 0.3 \times 0.14 + 0.3 \times 0.1 + 0.2 \times 0.07 + 0.2 \times 0.09 = 0.104 \\
\omega C9 &= 0.3 \times 0.02 + 0.3 \times 0.09 + 0.2 \times 0.06 + 0.2 \times 0.04 = 0.044 \\
\omega C10 &= 0.3 \times 0.07 + 0.3 \times 0.03 + 0.2 \times 0.07 + 0.2 \times 0.08 = 0.075
\end{aligned}
\quad (16)
$$

Therefore, the weight vector of the criterion layer B1 to the index layer is given as

$$\omega C1 = (0.113\ 0.092\ 0.116\ 0.112\ 0.129\ 0.115\ 0.1\ 0.104\ 0.044\ 0.075) \quad (17)$$

Similarly, the weight vectors of the criterion layers B2, B3, B4 to the index layer C can be summarized, as given below.

The weight vector of the criterion layer B2 to the index layer is given as

$$\omega C2 = (0.078\ 0.072\ 0.127\ 0.12\ 0.095\ 0.135\ 0.102\ 0.094\ 0.072\ 0.105) \quad (18)$$

The weight vector of criterion layer B3 to the index layer is given as

$$\omega C3 = (0.79\ 0.072\ 0.125\ 0.141\ 0.116\ 0.112\ 0.097\ 0.08\ 0.079\ 0.099) \quad (19)$$

The weight vector of criterion layer B4 to the index layer is given as

$$\omega C4 = (0.085\ 0.089\ 0.129\ 0.125\ 0.107\ 0.111\ 0.092\ 0.116\ 0.079\ 0.067) \quad (20)$$

The weight vector ωC of the target layer can be obtained by calculating the criterion layer weight vector for the target layer and the index layer. Taking C1 as the index, the weight vector of the operating capacity is calculated as

$$0.125 \times 0.133 + 0.34 \times 0.078 + 0.365 \times 0.079 + 0.17 \times 0.085 = 0.08393 \quad (21)$$

Similarly, we can derive the weight vector of 10 risk factors in the index layer as

$$\omega C = (0.0839\ 0.0774\ 0.1252\ 0.1275\ 0.109\ 0.120\ 0.0982\ 0.0939\ 0.0723\ 0.0926) \quad (22)$$

According to the degree of importance, 10 risk factors were ranked, as follows profitability (0.1275), operating capacity (0.1252), monetary fund (0.120), solvency (0.109), accounts receivable (0.0982), inventory (0.0939), past performance (0.0926), macro-enterprise environment (0.0839), enterprise development (0.0774), and enterprise credit rating (0.0723).

Based on the importance ranking, the index C layer of the ranking of the indicators and the importance of evaluating the standard level is basically the same. The indicators of business performance and asset status are at the forefront of the core corporate credit risk and are the two factors affecting core enterprise credit risk the most. Therefore, by means of a fuzzy analytic hierarchy process, a quantitative risk assessment can be performed. This approach can be very helpful in conducting key analysis observations for financial institutions to provide supply chain financing for purposes of determining the key financial indicators.

6. Concluding Remarks

The primary purpose of the paper was to analyze core enterprise credit risks in supply chain finance, by means of a 'fuzzy analytical hierarchy process' (FAHP), and to construct a supply chain financial credit risk evaluation system. This paper extended earlier work discussing the fuzzy judgment matrix, developing a fuzzy Judgment matrix consistency check, weight vector of index layer C, weight vector of index layer C to criterion layer B, and composite weight vectors. The paper also provides a detailed empirical example that highlights the novelty of the model construction and solution.

Supply chain finance is 'good medicine' to solve the financing problem of small and medium-sized enterprises, which can effectively alleviate the capital constraints of SMEs and achieve benefits for many participants in the supply chain. Therefore, core enterprises should improve their economic strength by adjusting their business strategies and innovation to enhance enterprise competitiveness, improving their asset quality and credit records to enhance their industry status and core competitiveness.

Core enterprises should also carefully select SMEs in the supply chain; choosing those with good credit status, higher industry position, and strong profitability, to ensure the overall security and stability of the supply chain, reduce credit risks, and enhance the overall competitiveness.

There are several suggestions regarding balancing the development of supply chain finance, building and dynamic improvements of the supply chain financial risk evaluation and control system, and establishing electronic databases by commercial banks. At present, supply chain finance is mainly used in automobile, steel, and other industries, which have large industry limitations.

As important participants in the supply chain, core enterprises strengthen the strategic cooperative relationship of the supply chain members, so that supply chain financing can be extended to other industries to solve the financing constraints of SMEs. The core enterprises can also use their own advantages to expand supply chain financing to other industries to maximize the profits among different industry groups. In this way, core enterprises can play an important role in supply chain finance.

Supply chain finance is involved in the exchange of capital flows, information flows, and logistics. The major participants include banks, core enterprises and SMEs. In order to maintain the interests of all parties, it is necessary to construct and perfect the risk evaluation and control system. This requires establishing a scientific concept of risk management and risk assessment based on real transactions. The main business objects involved in supply chain financing should be strictly controlled to control a variety of risks, dynamic adjustments of the arbitrary but reasonable weights, and improving the supply chain financial risk assessment system.

A unified information file should be collected based on the core enterprise, including the operating conditions, asset status, industry status, credit record, effective information to the database, collecting related data upstream and downstream of the archives around the core enterprise, developing a data information system, electronic data information, and updating the database accurately using the latest information that might be available.

Finally, through the establishment of a database on the supply chain finance, supply chain finance and modern information technology are integrated to establish the sharing of information resources, and realize the exchange of information flows, capital flows, and logistics between banks. The core enterprises and small and medium-sized enterprises will thereby function more smoothly, which not only improves the efficiency of the supply chain operation, but should also reduce a variety of risks, and improve the efficiency and effectiveness of supply chain finance.

Author Contributions: Data curation, W.M.; Formal analysis, W.M., W.-K.W. and M.M.; Methodology, M.M.; Project administration, W.-K.W.; Software, W.M.; Validation, W.-K.W. and M.M.; Writing—original draft, W.M.; Revisions M.M.; Writing—review & editing, W.-K.W. and M.M.

Acknowledgments: The authors are grateful for the very helpful comments and suggestions of three reviewers. For financial support, the third author wishes to acknowledge the Australian Research Council and Ministry of Science and Technology (MOST), Taiwan.

Appendix A. Questionnaire

The research in this paper is based on the data of the questionnaire and the case enterprise, which are objective. The data of the questionnaire have certain subjective components.

The questionnaires were based on random sampling and they did not have any economic interest in the study. In terms of economic characteristics, the sample is divided into four levels, namely management personnel, senior engineers, middle-level employees, and general employees. They have a certain degree of representation which guarantees the objectivity and reliability of the research.

The latter is aligned with the mean, so this contingency does not affect the results of the study as the focus of the study is the mean.

The questionnaire is conducted using sampling methods, and there is no conflict of interest as the employees did not have any economic interest in this study.

The paper uses a simple averaging method to take values, which should not have a significant impact on the results of the study. The data obtained from the entire questionnaire are processed in advance during the writing process. Given space limitations, the data aggregation and processing are not presented in detail.
Business friends:

First of all, thank you for completing this questionnaire. We are conducting an academic study to study the financial credit risk of supply chain. We guarantee that all survey data are for academic research only, and will not involve the trade secrets of the unit. The information obtained will not be used for any commercial purpose. We hope you will take the time to provide us with the following information. The investigation is not registered, and answers are neither right nor wrong. If there is a problem that does not fully express your opinion, please choose the answer that is closest to your opinion. Thank you for your help!

Basic Information

1. Your gender is (   ).
   A. Male   B. Female
2. Your age is (   ).
   A. 20–30 years old   B. 31–40 years old   C. 41–50 years old   D. 51–60 years old
3. Your working life in this unit is (   ).
   A. 5 years or less   B. 5–10 years   C. 10–20 years   D. 20 years or more
4. Your position in this unit is (   ).
   A. General employees   B. Middle-level employees   C. Senior engineers   D. Managers
5. Your department in the unit is (   ).
   A. Purchasing department   B. Production department   C. Sales department
   D. Finance department   E. Personnel Department   F. Logistics Department   G. Others
6. The industry of the unit is (   ).
   A. Steel industry   B. Textile industry
   C. Home appliance manufacturing   D. Medical machinery industry
7. Your academic qualifications (   ).
   A. High School   B. Undergraduate   C. Master/Dr.   D. Specialist

Credit Risk Survey

The following is a description of the financial risk indicators for the supply chain.

Please make your choices for each of the influencing factors according to your company's situation and your personal experience.

The larger is the number, the higher is the risk. For example, the choice of 1, which indicates that the risk level is very low: the choice of 2, indicating a low degree of risk; the choice of 3, indicating a moderate degree of risk; the choice of 4, indicating a high degree of risk: the choice of 5, indicating a high degree of risk. Please mark '$\sqrt{}$' on the corresponding number.

1. Criteria Layer Risk

Risk factor	Risk level				
	1	2	3	4	5
Industry status					
Operation					
Asset state					
Credit history					

2. Risks of Each Indicator Layer Under the Criteria Layer

Risk factor	Risk level				
	1	2	3	4	5
Macro environment					
Enterprise development					
Operation ability					
Profitability					
Solvency					
Monetary fund					
Accounts receivable					
Inventory					
Enterprise credit rating					
Past performance					

Appendix B. Calculation of the Fuzzy Judgment Matrices

$$C_{11} = \begin{bmatrix} 0.5 & 0.4 & 0.3 & 0.5 & 0.7 & 0.3 & 0.5 & 0.2 & 0.4 & 0.5 \\ 0.6 & 0.5 & 0.6 & 0.4 & 0.6 & 0.3 & 0.3 & 0.7 & 0.5 & 0.4 \\ 0.7 & 0.4 & 0.5 & 0.6 & 0.3 & 0.5 & 0.6 & 0.8 & 0.5 & 0.6 \\ 0.5 & 0.6 & 0.4 & 0.5 & 0.7 & 0.8 & 0.2 & 0.4 & 0.3 & 0.5 \\ 0.3 & 0.4 & 0.7 & 0.3 & 0.5 & 0.5 & 0.2 & 0.9 & 0.5 & 0.3 \\ 0.7 & 0.7 & 0.5 & 0.2 & 0.5 & 0.5 & 0.6 & 0.8 & 0.3 & 0.5 \\ 0.5 & 0.7 & 0.4 & 0.8 & 0.8 & 0.4 & 0.5 & 0.3 & 0.2 & 0.4 \\ 0.8 & 0.3 & 0.2 & 0.6 & 0.1 & 0.2 & 0.7 & 0.5 & 0.7 & 0.5 \\ 0.6 & 0.5 & 0.5 & 0.7 & 0.5 & 0.7 & 0.8 & 0.3 & 0.5 & 0.5 \\ 0.5 & 0.6 & 0.4 & 0.5 & 0.7 & 0.5 & 0.6 & 0.5 & 0.5 & 0.5 \end{bmatrix} \tag{23}$$

$$C_{12} = \begin{bmatrix} 0.5 & 0.4 & 0.7 & 0.6 & 0.5 & 0.3 & 0.4 & 0.5 & 0.7 & 0.4 \\ 0.6 & 0.5 & 0.9 & 0.5 & 0.2 & 0.5 & 0.3 & 0.4 & 0.5 & 0.5 \\ 0.3 & 0.1 & 0.5 & 0.5 & 0.4 & 0.7 & 0.6 & 0.4 & 0.5 & 0.5 \\ 0.4 & 0.5 & 0.5 & 0.5 & 0.5 & 0.6 & 0.5 & 0.3 & 0.3 & 0.4 \\ 0.5 & 0.8 & 0.6 & 0.5 & 0.5 & 0.4 & 0.5 & 0.4 & 0.6 & 0.3 \\ 0.7 & 0.5 & 0.3 & 0.4 & 0.6 & 0.5 & 0.2 & 0.5 & 0.6 & 0.5 \\ 0.6 & 0.7 & 0.4 & 0.5 & 0.5 & 0.8 & 0.5 & 0.4 & 0.6 & 0.4 \\ 0.5 & 0.6 & 0.6 & 0.7 & 0.6 & 0.5 & 0.6 & 0.5 & 0.1 & 0.3 \\ 0.3 & 0.5 & 0.5 & 0.7 & 0.4 & 0.4 & 0.4 & 0.9 & 0.5 & 0.5 \\ 0.6 & 0.5 & 0.5 & 0.6 & 0.7 & 0.5 & 0.6 & 0.7 & 0.5 & 0.5 \end{bmatrix} \tag{24}$$

$$C_{13} = \begin{bmatrix} 0.5 & 0.3 & 0.4 & 0.5 & 0.5 & 0.7 & 0.6 & 0.4 & 0.8 & 0.5 \\ 0.7 & 0.5 & 0.6 & 0.9 & 0.4 & 0.7 & 0.5 & 0.3 & 0.3 & 0.4 \\ 0.6 & 0.4 & 0.5 & 0.2 & 0.5 & 0.3 & 0.6 & 0.6 & 0.5 & 0.3 \\ 0.5 & 0.1 & 0.8 & 0.5 & 0.6 & 0.8 & 0.7 & 0.5 & 0.4 & 0.5 \\ 0.5 & 0.6 & 0.5 & 0.4 & 0.5 & 0.6 & 0.7 & 0.2 & 0.2 & 0.4 \\ 0.3 & 0.3 & 0.7 & 0.2 & 0.4 & 0.5 & 0.3 & 0.5 & 0.6 & 0.5 \\ 0.4 & 0.5 & 0.4 & 0.3 & 0.3 & 0.7 & 0.5 & 0.6 & 0.5 & 0.6 \\ 0.6 & 0.7 & 0.4 & 0.5 & 0.8 & 0.5 & 0.4 & 0.5 & 0.3 & 0.4 \\ 0.5 & 0.7 & 0.5 & 0.6 & 0.8 & 0.4 & 0.5 & 0.7 & 0.5 & 0.7 \\ 0.2 & 0.6 & 0.7 & 0.5 & 0.6 & 0.5 & 0.4 & 0.6 & 0.3 & 0.5 \end{bmatrix} \tag{25}$$

$$C_{14} = \begin{bmatrix} 0.5 & 0.3 & 0.4 & 0.6 & 0.5 & 0.5 & 0.7 & 0.4 & 0.6 & 0.7 \\ 0.7 & 0.5 & 0.5 & 0.3 & 0.6 & 0.9 & 0.5 & 0.3 & 0.5 & 0.6 \\ 0.6 & 0.5 & 0.5 & 0.6 & 0.5 & 0.6 & 0.2 & 0.4 & 0.3 & 0.5 \\ 0.4 & 0.7 & 0.4 & 0.5 & 0.4 & 0.3 & 0.7 & 0.6 & 0.5 & 0.4 \\ 0.5 & 0.4 & 0.5 & 0.6 & 0.5 & 0.4 & 0.4 & 0.5 & 0.4 & 0.2 \\ 0.5 & 0.1 & 0.4 & 0.7 & 0.6 & 0.5 & 0.7 & 0.4 & 0.5 & 0.4 \\ 0.3 & 0.5 & 0.8 & 0.3 & 0.6 & 0.3 & 0.5 & 0.2 & 0.6 & 0.5 \\ 0.6 & 0.7 & 0.6 & 0.4 & 0.5 & 0.6 & 0.8 & 0.5 & 0.4 & 0.2 \\ 0.4 & 0.5 & 0.7 & 0.5 & 0.6 & 0.5 & 0.4 & 0.6 & 0.5 & 0.7 \\ 0.3 & 0.4 & 0.5 & 0.6 & 0.8 & 0.6 & 0.5 & 0.8 & 0.3 & 0.5 \end{bmatrix} \tag{26}$$

References

1. Berger, A.N.; Udell, G.F. A more complete conceptual framework for SME finance. *J. Bank Financ.* **2006**, *30*, 2945–2966. [CrossRef]
2. Klapper, L. The role of factoring for financing small and medium enterprises. *J. Bank Financ.* **2006**, *30*, 3111–3130. [CrossRef]
3. Beck, T.; Demirguc-Kunt, A. Small and medium-size enterprises: Access to finance as a growth constraint. *J. Bank Financ.* **2006**, *30*, 2931–2943. [CrossRef]
4. Shi, Y.L.; Guan, Z.G.; Xie, X. Risk evaluation model building of logistics financial business for the bank and empirical research. *J. Syst. Manag. Sci.* **2014**, *4*, 53–61.
5. Shi, J.Z.; Guo, J.E.; Wang, S.B.; Wang, Z.H. Credit risk evaluation of online supply chain finance based on third-party B2B e-commerce platform: An exploratory research. International Journal of u- and e-Service. *Sci. Technol.* **2015**, *8*, 93–104.
6. Hofmann, E. Supply chain finance: Some conceptual insights. Logistic Management. In *Logistik Management—Innovative Logistikkonzepte*; Lasch, R., Janker, C.G., Eds.; Deutscher Universitätsverlag: Wiesbaden, Germany, 2005.
7. Pfoh, H.; Gomm, M. Supply chain finance: Optimizing financial flows in supply chains. *Logist. Res.* **2009**, *1*, 149–161. [CrossRef]
8. Gupta, S.; Dutta, K. Modeling of financial supply chain. *Eur. J. Oper. Res.* **2011**, *211*, 47–56. [CrossRef]
9. Mathis, F.J.; Cavinato, J. Financing the global supply chain: Growing need for management action. *Thunderbird Int. Bus. Rev.* **2010**, *52*, 467–474. [CrossRef]
10. Silvestro, R.; Lustrato, P. Integrating financial and physical supply chains: The role of banks in enabling supply chain integration. *Int. J. Oper. Prod. Manag.* **2014**, *34*, 298–324. [CrossRef]
11. Blackman, I.D.; Holland, C.P.; Westcott, T. Motorola's global financial supply chain strategy. *Supply Chain Manag.* **2013**, *18*, 132–147. [CrossRef]
12. Caniato, F.; Gelsomino, L.M.; Perego, A.; Ronchi, S. Does finance solve the supply chain financing problem? *Supply Chain Manag.* **2016**, *21*, 534–549. [CrossRef]
13. Zhu, Y.; Xie, C.; Sun, B.; Wang, G.J.; Yan, X.G. Predicting China's SME credit risk in supply chain financing by logistic regression, artificial neural network and hybrid models. *Sustainability* **2016**, *8*, 433. [CrossRef]
14. Liu, X.; Zhou, L.; Wu, Y.C.J. Supply chain finance in China: Business innovation and theory development. *Sustainability* **2015**, *7*, 14689–14709. [CrossRef]

15.   Feldmann, M.; Müller, S. An incentive scheme for true information providing in Supply Chains. *Omega* **2003**, *31*, 63–73. [CrossRef]

16.   Berger, A.N.; Udell, G.F. The economics of small business finance: The roles of private equity and debt markets in the financial growth cycle. *J. Bank Financ.* **1998**, *22*, 613–673. [CrossRef]

17.   Ganlindo, A.; Schiantarelli, F. (Eds.) *Credit Constraints and Investment in Latin America*; Inter-American Development Bank: Washington, DC, USA, 2003.

18.   Schiffer, M.; Weder, B. *Firm Size and the Business Environment: Worldwide Survey Results*; Discussion Paper No. 43; International Finance Corporation: Washington, DC, USA, 2001.

19.   Beck, T.; Demirguc-Kunt, A.; Laeven, L.; Maksimovic, V. The determinants of financing obstacles. *J. Int. Money Financ.* **2006**, *25*, 932–952. [CrossRef]

20.   Song, J.S.; Zipkin, P. Inventories with multiple supply sources and networks of queues with overflow bypasses. *Manag. Sci.* **2009**, *55*, 362–372. [CrossRef]

21.   Wuttke, D.A.; Blome, C.; Henke, M. Focusing the financial flow of supply chains: An empirical investigation of financial supply chain management. *Inter. J. Prod. Econ.* **2013**, *145*, 773–789. [CrossRef]

22.   Randall, W.S.; Farris, M.T. Supply chain financing: Using cash-to-cash variables to strengthen the supply chain. International Journal of Phys. *Distrib. Logist. Manag.* **2009**, *39*, 669–689. [CrossRef]

23.   Committee on Finance and Industry (1931), Report of Committee on Finance and Industry. Cmd 3897; p. 322. Available online: http://discovery.nationalarchives.gov.uk/details/r/C1851842 (accessed on 20 September 2018).

24.   Stamp, J.C. The report of the Macmillan Committee. *Econ. J.* **1931**, *41*, 424–435. [CrossRef]

25.   Lee, C.H.; Rhee, B.D. Trade credit for supply chain coordination. *Eur. J. Oper. Res.* **2011**, *214*, 136–146. [CrossRef]

26.   Jüttner, U.; Maklan, S. Supply chain resilience in the global financial crisis: An empirical study. *Supply Chain Manag.* **2011**, *16*, 246–259.

27.   Saaty, T.L. How to make a decision: The Analytic Hierarchy Process. *Eur. J. Oper. Res.* **1990**, *48*, 9–26. [CrossRef]

9

Fake News and Propaganda: Trump's Democratic America and Hitler's National Socialist (Nazi) Germany

David E. Allen [1,2,3] **and Michael McAleer** [2,4,5,6,7,8,*]

1   Department of Finance, School of Mathematics and Statistics, University of Sydney, Sydney, NSW 2006, Australia; profallen2007@gmail.com
2   Department of Finance, College of Management, Asia University, Wufeng 41354, Taiwan
3   School of Business and Law, Edith Cowan University, Joondalup, WA 6027, Australia
4   Discipline of Business Analytics, University of Sydney Business School, NSW 2006, Australia
5   Econometric Institute, Erasmus School of Economics, Erasmus University, 3062 Rotterdam, The Netherlands
6   Department of Economic Analysis and ICAE, Complutense University of Madrid, 28040 Madrid, Spain
7   Department of Mathematics and Statistics, University of Canterbury, Christchurch 8041, New Zealand
8   Institute of Advanced Sciences, Yokohama National University, Yokohama, Kanagawa 240-8501, Japan
*   Correspondence: michael.mcaleer@gmail.com

Abstract: This paper features an analysis of President Trump's two State of the Union addresses, which are analysed by means of various data mining techniques, including sentiment analysis. The intention is to explore the contents and sentiments of the messages contained, the degree to which they differ, and their potential implications for the national mood and state of the economy. We also apply Zipf and Mandelbrot's power law to assess the degree to which they differ from common language patterns. To provide a contrast and some parallel context, analyses are also undertaken of President Obama's last State of the Union address and Hitler's 1933 Berlin Proclamation. The structure of these four political addresses is remarkably similar. The three US Presidential speeches are more positive emotionally than is Hitler's relatively shorter address, which is characterised by a prevalence of negative emotions. Hitler's speech deviates the most from common speech, but all three appear to target their audiences by use of non-complex speech. However, it should be said that the economic circumstances in contemporary America and Germany in the 1930s are vastly different.

Keywords: text mining; sentiment analysis; word cloud; emotional valence

JEL Classification: C19; C65; D79

1. Introduction

President Trump continues to attract controversy in the media and in political commentary, partly because of his attitude to "fake news", combined with his own lavish use of his Twitter account and lack of attention to the verification of some of his more extreme pronouncements. In 2018, the President used Twitter to announce the "winners" of his "fake news" awards, most frequently naming the New York Times and CNN for a series of perceived transgressions which varied from minor errors by journalists on social media to news reports that later invited corrections.

Given his predilection for criticising the media, the authors have previously analysed his pronouncements on climate change [1], on nuclear weapons and [2], and contrasted his first State of the Union Address (SOU) with the previous one by President Obama [3].

Given the controversy about the timing and delivery of his most recent SOU address, the authors thought it might be of interest to subject both of his SOU addresses to textual analysis using data mining techniques, so as to explore whether his political addresses are typical or whether they deviate markedly from those of other political leaders, specifically, Obama and Hitler, the latter being selected as an extreme benchmark. The null hypothesis is that political speeches are essentially similar.

We decided to analyse both Trump's 2018 State of the Union Address (SOU1), and 2019 address (SOU2) to assess whether there had been any change in the structure and emotional tenor of his two addresses in response to changing political and economic circumstances, at the end of the second year of his term in office. To provide a contrast, one contemporary and another more historically extreme, we also analyse President Obama's last SOU and Hitler's 1933 Berlin Proclamation.

The contents of these speeches are analysed using a variety of R packages, including several in data mining: "tm" a text mining package, created by Feinerer and Hornik [4]. We also used "syuzhet", a sentiment extraction tool, originally developed in the NLP group at Stanford University, and then incorporated into an R package by Jockers [5], and "wordcloud" by Fellows [6].

Data mining refers to the process of analysing datasets to reveal patterns, and usually involves methods that are drawn from statistics, machine learning, and database systems. Text data mining similarly involves the analysis of patterns in text data. Sentiment analysis is concerned with the emotional context of a text, and seeks to infer whether a section of text is positive or negative, or the nature of the emotions involved. There is a variety of methods and dictionaries that exist for undertaking sentiment analysis of a piece of text.

Although sentiment is often framed in terms of being a binary distinction (positive versus negative), it can also be analysed in a more nuanced manner. We decided to apply the R package "syuzhet", which distinguishes between eight different emotions, namely trust, anticipation, fear, joy, anger, sadness, disgust and surprise. There are many different forms of sentiment analyses, but most use the same basic approach. They begin by constructing a list of words or dictionary associated with different emotions, count the number of positive and negative words in a given text, and then analyse the mix of positive and negative words to assess the general emotional tenor of the text.

Clearly, there are considerable limitations to the basic approach adopted in the paper. Pröllochs et al. [7] discussed the difficulties in processing negations, which invert the meanings of words and sentences. Equally problematic are sarcasm, backhanded compliments, and inflammatory gibberish, such as "Pocahontas" and "Crooked Hillary", in the context of President Trump's tweets. Nevertheless, sentiment analysis can reveal the general emotional direction of a piece of text, and machine-based learning systems are well-established methods for the sifting and interpretation of digital information. This tool has numerous applications in, for example, financial markets.

We can now apply machine learning techniques to news feeds to determine what average opinion is. For example, the Thomson Reuters News Analytics (TRNA) series could be termed news sentiment, and is produced by the application of machine learning techniques to news items. The TRNA system can scan and analyse stories on thousands of companies in real time, and translate the results into a series that can be used to help model and inform quantitative trading strategies. RavenPack is another example of a commercial news analytics product that has applications to financial markets. There is now considerable evidence about the commercial relevance of financial news analysed using machine learning methods.

Allen, McAleer and Singh [8,9] analysed the economic impact of the TRNA sentiment series. The first of these papers examines the influence of the Sentiment measure as a factor in pricing DJIA constituent company stocks in a Capital Asset Pricing Model (CAPM) context. The second uses these real time scores, aggregated into a DJIA market sentiment score, to analyse the relationship between financial news sentiment scores and the DJIA return series, using entropy-based measures. Both studies find that the sentiment scores have a significant information component which, in the former, is priced as a factor in an asset pricing context.

Allen, McAleer and Singh [10] used the Thomson Reuters News Analytics (TRNA) dataset to construct a series of daily sentiment scores for Dow Jones Industrial Average (DJIA) stock index constituents. The authors used these daily DJIA market sentiment scores to study the influence of financial news sentiment scores on the stock returns of these constituents using a multi-factor model. They augmented the Fama–French three-factor model with the day's sentiment score along 20 with lagged scores to evaluate the additional effects of financial news sentiment on stock prices in the context of this model. Estimation is based on Ordinary Least Squares (OLS) and Quantile Regression (QR) to analyse the effects around the tails of the returns distribution. The results suggest that, even when market factors are taken into account, sentiment scores have a significant effect on Dow Jones constituent returns, and that lagged daily sentiment scores are also often significant.

Other research on this topic argues that news items from different sources influence investor sentiment, which feeds into asset prices, asset price volatility and risk (see, among others, Tetlock [11] Tetlock, Macskassy and Saar-Tsechansky [12] (2008), Da, Engleberg and Gao, [13], Barber and Odean [14], diBartolomeo and Warrick [15], Mitra, Mitra and diBartolomeo [16], and Dzielinski, Rieger and Talpsepp [17]. The diversification benefits of the information impounded in news sentiment scores provided by RavenPack were demonstrated by Cahan, Jussa and Luo [18], and Hafez and Xie [19], who examined the benefits in the context of popular asset pricing models.

Several papers provide surveys of this burgeoning literature. Kearney and Lui [20] concentrated on sentiment analysis and provided an analysis of methods and the related literature. Loughran and McDonald [21] provided a survey of the accounting, finance, and economics literature on textual analysis, plus a description of some of its methods, together with potential pitfalls in its application.

In the current paper, the focus is on the actual content of President Trump's 2018 SOU1, and his subsequent 2019 SOU2 address. The intention is to explore whether there are any systematic differences in the sentiments of these two SOUs, and whether there is any evidence of a tendency by President Trump to generate a "positive" spin for the benefit of his voter base. A contrast is provided by parallel analyses of President Obama's last SOU and Hitler's 1933 Berlin Proclamation.

Could President Trump's addresses be fairly described as constituting "propaganda"? This has been defined as being the presentation of information, ideas, opinions, or images, which may only present one part of an argument, and which are broadcast, published, or in some other way spread with the intention of influencing people's opinions. Sentiment analysis will not give a clear answer as to whether content represents propaganda per se, but it will give an indication as to the emotional tenor of a text or speech. It will reveal correlations between the use of words, changes in sentiment, and any patterns revealed through time in the presentation of a speech.

An alternative approach to the analysis of language as a whole, was first suggested by Zipf (1932, p. 1) [22], who applied a concept of relative frequency which suggested that: "the accent or degree of conspicuousness of any word, syllable, or sound is inversely proportionate to the relative frequency of that word, syllable, or sound, among its fellow words, syllables, or sounds in the stream of spoken language. As any element's usage becomes more frequent, its form tends to become less accented, or more easily pronounceable, and vice versa. He analysed whether the modern vernacular of Beijing, China, was consistent with Indo-European tongues in substantiating his "Principle of Relative Frequency".

Zipf [22] suggested that there are four important characteristics that are recognisable in words: The first is meaning, an elusive concept which is difficult to describe. The second he described as being "quality", by which he meant positive or negative qualities. These are the subject of sentiment analysis in the current paper. The third he described as being "emotional intensity", which could also be related to the degree to which sentiment is espoused. The fourth he described as being "order", which is related to semantic change and the relative frequency of use of different words. Order is also related to the probability of occurrence of different words. Zipf suggested that the formula for abbreviation is $ab^2 = k$.

Mandelbrot [23] expanded on this approach, refining Zipf's theory by suggesting that human languages evolved over time to optimise the capacity to convey information from the sender to receiver. He couched his analysis in terms of Shannon's [24] "information theory". Mandelbrot suggested that, as a first approximation, $i(r,k)/k$, which he defines as the relative number of repetitions of the word $W(r)$ in a sample of length k, is inversely proportional to 10 times r, $i(r,k)/k = 1/10r$.

Shannon ([24], p. 6) suggested that it is possible to use artificial languages to approximate natural languages. The zero-order approximation is to choose all letters with the same probability and independently. The first-order approximation is to choose each letter independently but with the same probability of occurrence as would apply in the relevant natural language. In a third-order approximation, a trigram structure is adopted with the probability of each letter dependent on the preceeding two letters.

Shannon [24] suggested that we let $p(B_i)$ be the probability B_i of a sequence of symbols from a source text. Let:

$$G_N = -\frac{1}{N}\sum_i p(B_i) log p(B_i), \tag{1}$$

where the sum is over all sequences B_i containing N symbols. This suggests that G_N is a monotonically decreasing function of N, and that:

$$\underset{N\to\infty}{Lim}\, G_N = H.$$

Shannon lets $p(B_i, S_j)$ be the probability of sequence B_i being followed by symbol S_j and $p_{B_i}S_j = p(B_i, S_j)/p(B_i)$ be the conditional probability of S_j after B_i. Then, let:

$$F_N = -\sum p(B_i, S_j) log p_{B_i}(S_j), \tag{2}$$

where the summation is over all blocks B_i of $N-1$ symbols and over all symbols S_j; then, F_N is a monotonically decreasing function of N:

$$F_N = NG_N - (N-1)G_{N-1},$$

$$G_N = \frac{1}{N}\sum_{N=1}^{N} F_N,$$

$$F_N \leq G_N,$$

and, $Lim_{N\to\infty}F_N = H$.

Shannon [24] stated that F_N is the entropy of the Nth-order approximation to the source of the type discussed above. Mandelbrot [23] suggested that his derivation of the law of word frequencies was characterised by maximising Shannon's "quantity of information" under certain constraints.

We use some of these concepts in the subsequent analysis of the political addresses featured in this paper to explore how far they deviate from standard patterns of language. The most recent comprehensive use of this type of analysis is that of Ficcadenti et al. [25], which also features a lengthy review of the relevant literature. However, there is no sentiment analysis of Presidential speeches in their study.

The remainder of the paper is divided into four sections. An explanation of the research method is given in Section 2. Section 3 presents the results. Section 4 provides some concluding comments.

2. Research Method

The analysis features the use of a number of R libraries which facilitate data mining and sentiment analysis, namely word cloud, tm and syuzhet, plus a variety of graphics packages. The R package tm has a focus on extensibility based on generic functions and object-oriented inheritance, and provides a basic infrastructure required to organise, transform, and analyse textual data. The basic document is imported into a "corpus", which is then transformed into a suitable form for analysis using stemming, stopword removal, and so on. Then, we can create a term-document matrix from a corpus which can be used for analysis.

Once we have the text in matrix form, a huge amount of R functions (e.g., clustering, classifications, among others) can be applied. We can explore the associations of words, correlations, and so forth, and screen the text for frequently occurring words. The analysis can be used to create a word cloud of the most frequently used words. Feinerer and Hornik [4] provided an introduction to the package.

The R package wordcloud by Fellows [6] provides functionality to create word clouds, visualise differences and similarity between documents, and avoid over-plotting in scatter plots with text. We use the R package "syuzhet" for sentiment analysis. The package comes with four sentiment dictionaries, and provides a method for accessing the robust, but computationally expensive, sentiment extraction tool developed in the NLP group at Stanford University. We transform the text in character vectors. Once we have the vector, we can select which of the four sentiment extraction methods available in "syuzhet" to employ. We use the default syuzet lexicon, which was developed in the Nebraska Literary Lab under the direction of Jockers [5].

The name "Syuzhet" comes from the Russian Formalists Shklovsky [26] and Propp [27], who divided narrative into two components, the "fabula" and the "syuzhet". "Syuzhet" refers to the "device" or technique of a narrative, whereas "fabula" is the chronological order of events. 'Syuzhet", therefore, is concerned with the manner in which the elements of the story (fabula) are organised (syuzhet). The R syuzhet package attempts to reveal the latent structure of narrative by means of sentiment analysis, and we can construct global measures of sentiment into eight constituent emotional categories, namely trust, anticipation, fear, joy, anger, sadness, disgust and surprise.

While these global measures of sentiment can be informative, they tell us very little in terms of how the narrative is structured and how these positive and negative sentiments are activated across the text. To explore this, we plot the values in a graph where the x-axis represents the passage of time from the beginning to the end of the text, and the y-axis measures the degrees of positive and negative sentiment.

President Trump's first SOU in 2018 contained 5169 words and 30,308 characters, while his second SOU in 2019 contained 5493 words and 32,204 characters. Therefore, the two addresses were of similar size.

We use the R package "tm" and develop the appropriate R code to undertake the Zipf and Mandelbrot power law distribution analysis to assess the degree to which the four political addresses deviate from common language.

The limitations of the analysis should be borne in mind. The context of "natural language processing", of which sentiment analysis is a component, is important. The use of sarcasm and other types of ironic language are inherently problematic for machines to detect, especially when viewed in isolation.

3. Results and Interpretation of the Analysis

3.1. Sentiment Analysis

Figure 1 presents a word cloud analysis of President Trump's two SOUs. In his first 2018 SOU, depicted in Figure 1A, the most frequently occurring word is "American", followed by the symbol $ae\bullet$, which is a generic representation of different dollar amounts mentioned at various stages in his address. Other words emphasised include "will", "year", "one", "tonight", "people", "new", "year", "america", "together", 'great", "home", "tax" "congress", "families", "countries", "proud", "just", "job", and "citizen".

The second and most recent SOU by President Trump is shown in Figure 1B. This is dominated by the words "will", "American", "years", "one", "new", "thank", "americans", "tonight", "now", "can", 'must", "congress", "border", "last", "time", "also", and "country".

(A)

(B)

Figure 1. Word Cloud representing President Trump's two SOU addresses: **(A)** Word Cloud SOU2018; and **(B)** RplotTRUMPSOU1CLOUD. The aₑ is a symbol representing different dollar amounts.

To provide a further contrast, the authors thought it might be instructive to compare this SOU with President Obama's last SOU. Moreover, to provide an extreme contrast, we undertook an analysis of Hitler's Proclamation to the German nation, in Berlin on 1 February 1933. The intention was to see whether a political speech has typical common elements, or whether more extreme National Socialist (Nazi) proclamations have a different structure and emotional tenor. A further caveat is that the analysis is undertaken on an English translation of Hitler's 1933 proclamation, and not on the original German version.

It must be borne in mind that the economic circumstances in Germany in 1933 were markedly different from those in the USA in recent years. The German economy experienced the effects of the Great Depression, with unemployment soaring around the Wall Street Crash of 1929. When Adolf Hitler became Chancellor in 1933, he introduced policies aimed at improving the economy, including privatisation of state industries. National Socialist (or Nazi) Germany increased its military spending faster than any other state in peacetime, and the military eventually came to represent the majority of the German economy by the 1940s.

Figure 2 presents a word cloud analysis of both President Obama's last SOU plus Hitler's 1933 Berlin proclamation. The word cloud for President Obama's last SOU, shown in Figure 2A, displays that "will", "American", and "year" received the greatest emphases in terms of their frequency of use. These words were closely followed by "work", "America", "now", "change", "people", and "just". Further prominent words include "world", "want", "job", "can" and "need".

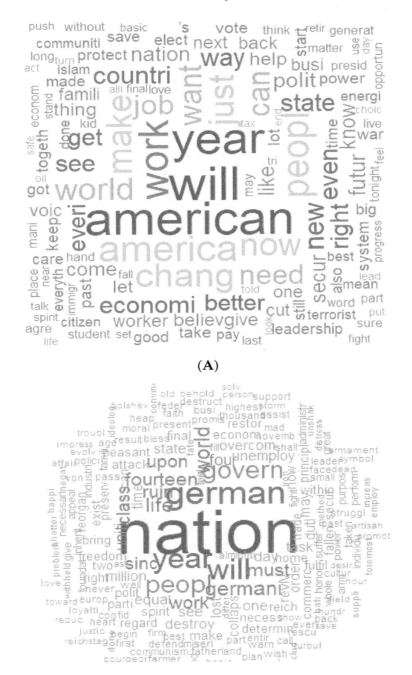

(A)

(B)

Figure 2. Word Cloud Analysis of President Obama's last SOU and Hitlers 1933 Berlin Proclamation: (**A**) President Obama's last SOU; and (**B**) Hitler's 1933 Proclamation.

Hitler's 1933 proclamation, as represented by the word cloud depicted in Figure 2B, reveals that the most frequently occurring word is "nation", followed by "German", "year", "will", "govern", "people", "work", 'class", "must", "world", "fourteen", "life", "upon", and so on.

Figure 3 provides bar plots of the words used most frequently in President Trump's two SOUs. The bar charts reinforce the word cloud analysis, but provide an indication of the relative frequency of use of the twenty most frequently occurring words. Figure 3A shows that, in the first SOU, "American" occurs over 50 times, followed by various indications of dollar amounts, "will" occurs more than thirty times, while "great", "last", "together" and "tax" occur around twenty times each.

In Trump's second SOU, depicted by the bar chart in Figure 3B, "will" becomes the most frequently occurring word, followed by "years", "one" and "American", but the top few words are less frequent in President Trump's second SOU than in his first. "American" is now the fourth most frequent word rather than the first, as in the previous SOU. Perhaps surprisingly, given the political battles enveloping the topic, "border" is the twentieth most frequently used word.

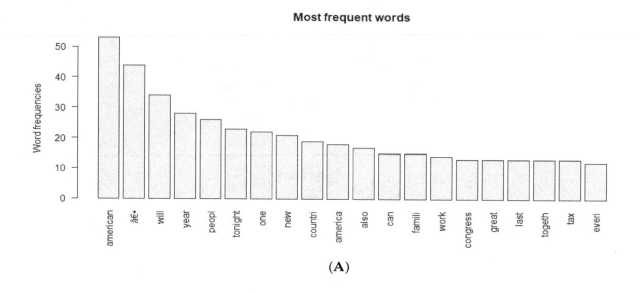

(A)

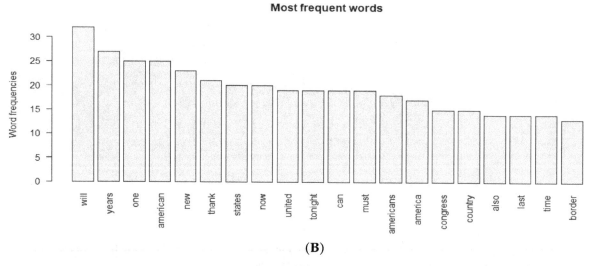

(B)

Figure 3. Bar Plots of words used frequently in President Trump's two SOUs: (**A**) President Trump SOU1; and (**B**) President Trump SOU2.

Figure 4 provides a similar analysis for President Obama's last SOU and for Hitler's 1933 Proclamation. Figure 4A reveals that the most frequently used word in President Obama's last SOU was "will", which occurred 38 times, closely followed by "American" 37 times, and "year" 35 times. "Work", "America" and "people" were the next most frequently occurring words.

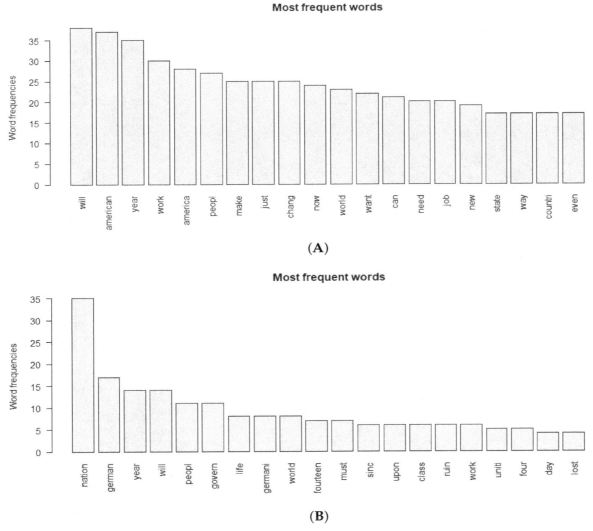

Figure 4. Bar Plots of most frequently used words in President Obama's last SOU and in Hitler's 1933 Proclamation: (**A**) President Obama's last SOU; and (**B**) Hitler's 1933 Proclamation.

Hitler's 1933 Proclamation was a much shorter speech than the SOUs just considered. However, it was relatively dominated by the word "nation", which occurred 35 times, while the next most frequently used word was "German", mentioned 17 times, while "year" and "will" occurred 14 times each.

Patriotism and nationalism appear to be frequently occurring themes in these four very different political addresses. "American" is the first and fourth most frequently occurring words in President Trump's two SOUs, and it is the second most frequently used word in President Obama's last SOU. The most frequently used word in Hitler's 1933 Proclamation was "Nation", which had double the frequency of any other words mentioned, followed by "German". There is clearly a strong nationalistic tone in his 1933 address.

The other recurrent theme in these four political speeches is the importance of intention, as captured by the use of the word "will". It is the third and first most frequently occurring word used in President Trump's two SOUs, respectively. It is the most frequent word in President Obama's last SOU and the fourth most frequently occurring word in Hitler's 1933 Proclamation.

Table 1 shows the words most highly correlated with President Trump's frequently used words in his two SOUs. "American" is the most frequently used word in his first SOU. Its use is most highly correlated with: "bridge", "gleam", "grit", "heritage", "highway", "railway", "reclaim", "waterway", "background", "color", "creed", "dreamer", "official", "religion", and "sacred".

Table 1. Words highly correlated with frequently used words in President Trump's SOUs.

Word	Trump SOU2018		Word	Trump SOU2019	
	Correlated Words	**Correlation**		**Correlated Words**	**Correlation**
American	bridge	0.34	Will	never	0.49
	gleam	0.34		Afghan	0.41
	grit	0.34		constructive	0.41
	heritage	0.34		counter terrorism	0.41
	highway	0.34		focus	0.41
	railway	0.34		groups	0.41
	reclaim	0.34		indeed	0.41
	waterway	0.34		taliban	0.41
	background	0.34		talks	0.41
	color	0.34		troop	0.41
	creed	0.34		agreement	0.38
	dreamer	0.34		achieve	0.37
	official	0.34		make	0.37
	religion	0.34		progress	0.37
	sacred	0.34		proudly	0.37
	dream	0.33		dream	0.37
	hand	0.33		holding	0.37
	land	0.31		whether	0.35
	duty	0.31		incredible	0.32
	right	0.31	American	back	0.51
will	arsenal	0.44		soldiers	0.40
	deter	0.44		astronauts	0.37
	magic	0.44		Buzz	0.37
	part	0.44		space	0.37
	someday	0.44		intellectual	0.37
	unfortunate	0.44		property	0.37
	use	0.44		Dachau	0.37
	weapon	0.44		second	0.37
	yet	0.44			
	aggression	0.40			
	moment	0.32			
	modern	0.32			

A second frequently used word is "will", which is highly correlated with "deter", "magic", "part", "someday", "unfortunate", "use", "weapon", and "yet". The same two words are reversed in relative frequency of use in the second SOU. "Will" is most highly correlated with "never", followed by "Afghan", "constructive", "counter-terrorism", "focus", "groups", "indeed", "Taliban", "talks", and "troop". "American is most highly correlated with "back" and "soldiers".

The analysis is concerned with an examination of the extent to which political speeches by different political leaders differ. We would expect to see similarities in the two speeches by President

Trump. This includes similarities in the usage of words and correlations between pairs of words when they are made by the same politician.

Table 2 provides an analysis of the words most highly correlated with frequently used words in President Obama's last SOU and Hitler's 1933 Proclamation. The analysis of President Obama's last SOU reveals the weaknesses of a statistical analysis of individual words used as components of a particular address. The words most correlated with the word "American" were individual dollar amounts. "Will" is highly correlated with "preserve", "status-quo", and "planet".

Table 2. Words highly correlated with frequently used words in President Obama's last SOU and Hitler's 1933 Proclamation.

Obama SOU			Hitler 1933		
Word	**Correlated Words**	**Correlation**	**Word**	**Correlated Words**	**Correlation**
American	various numbers	n.a.		life	0.42
will	preserve	0.44	Nation	will	0.40
	status-quo	0.44		govern	0.37
	planet	0.30		regard	0.32
America	George Washington Carver	0.36	will	health	0.50
	Katherine Johnson	0.36		lead	0.40
	Sally Ride	0.36		nation	0.40
	unit	0.35		back	0.33
			German	assist	0.33
				work	0.34
				rescue	0.32
				support	0.32

"America" is highly correlated with individual names, the components of which the program picked up individually, and it was not until the authors analysed the original text that the analysis made sense. In the speech, President Obama stated: "Now, that spirit of discovery is in our DNA. America is Thomas Edison and the Wright Brothers and George Washington Carver. America is Grace Hopper and Katherine Johnson and Sally Ride. America is every immigrant and entrepreneur from Boston to Austin to Silicon Valley racing to shape a better future".

The analysis of Hitler's 1933 Berlin Proclamation was more revealing. "Nation", the most frequently used word, is highly correlated with "life", "will", "govern", and "regard". "Will" is highly correlated with "health", "lead", "nation", "back", and "assist". Finally, "German" is highly correlated with "work", "rescue", and "support". This supports the national rebuilding of the German economy and the promotion of employment that was part of Hitler's agenda in the early 1930s. He adopted the view that the natural unit of mankind was the Volk ("the people"), of which the German people was the greatest. He also believed that the state existed to serve the Volk. This leads to a consideration of "National Socialism" (or "Nazism").

Smith ([28], pp. 18–19) suggested that "... nationalists have a vital role to play in the construction of nations, not as culinary artists or social engineers, but as political archaeologists rediscovering and reinterpreting the communal past in order to regenerate the community. Their task is indeed selective—they forget as well as remember the past—but to succeed in their task they must meet certain criteria. Their interpretations must be consonant not only with the ideological demands of nationalism, but also with the scientific evidence, popular resonance and patterning of particular ethnohistories".

Nationalism holds that each nation should govern itself, free from outside interference (self-determination), and that the nation is the only rightful source of political power (popular sovereignty). It usually involves the maintenance of a single national identity, which would be based on shared social characteristics, such as shared history culture, language, religion, and politics. President Trump, with his slogan "MAGA" (make America great again), espouses a form of Nationalism.

President Obama's last SOU is not free of nationalistic sentiment. He stated that: "I told you earlier all the talk of America's economic decline is political hot air. Well, so is all the rhetoric you hear about our enemies getting stronger and America getting weaker. Let me tell you something. The United States of America is the most powerful nation on Earth, period. Period. It is not even close. It is not even close. We spend more on our military than the next eight nations combined."

However, as the mechanical and statistical form of textmining used in this paper, though revealing, is not suited to teasing out the nuances in meaning of different forms of nationalism, emphasis is placed on a statistical analysis of the text.

We also used the R package "syuzhet" to examine the the sentiment of each string of words or sentences. We calculated the overall score and the mean or average sentiment score. The results vary slightly, depending on which lexicon or base dictionary is used. Syuzhet incorporates four sentiment lexicons. The default "syuzhet" lexicon was developed in the University of Nebraska Literary Lab under the direction of Jockers [5], the creator of the R syuzhet package. This is the default lexicon. We also cross-checked using the nrc lexicon developed by Mohammad, who is a research scientist at the National Research Council Canada (NRC) (see: http://saifmohammad.com). However, the results were quantitatively similar, and hence are not reported in the paper.

The analysis tells us whether the speech has a predominantly positive or negative score in emotional tenor. In the case of President Trumps first SOU, the total score was 113.75 and the mean score was 0.02196. This positive sentiment score is consistent with Allen, McAleer and Reid [3], who reported similarly positive results for President Trump's first SOU, on the basis of an application of the R package "sentiment", which used a different lexicography. In the previous analysis, on the basis of a primary binary division into positive and negative sentiments, 60 per cent of the first SOU, in cases where sentiment could be ascribed, was recorded as being positive.

In his second SOU in 2019, the address had a total score of 139.85 and a mean score of 0.02557. His first SOU contained 5190 words and 30,271 characters, while his second SOU was slightly larger at 5442 words and 32,045 characters. President Obama's last SOU had a total score of 169.8 and a mean score of 0.02712. President Obama's last SOU was quite a large speech, containing 6233 words and 34,634 characters. In the case of Hitler's 1933 Proclamation, the sum is 8.4 and the mean is 0.0053, but Hitler's parsimonious proclamation only contained 1578 words and 9286 characters.

An interesting feature of these various speeches is the degree to which they contained predominantly positive or negative emotions. These are plotted in Figures 5 and 6. In both of President Trump's SOUs, "Trust" is the predominant emotion displayed. In all speeches, apart from President Trump's second SOU, it accounts for more than 25 per cent of the total emotional content. This is also the case in President Obama's last SOU, and in Hitler's 1933 Proclamation. In all four speeches, "Trust" dominates by a large margin in the order of 10 per cent, though it is slightly lower in President Trump's second SOU.

"Fear" is the second dominant emotion in Trump's SOU, and drops to third in his second SOU. "Fear" is the third emotion in President Obama's last SOU, accounting for about 14 per cent of the emotional content, but it is more prominent in Hitler's 1933 proclamation, in which it is the second ranked emotion, and accounts for about 18 per cent of the emotional content.

"Anticipation" plays a large role in President Trump's and Obama's addresses, in which it always accounts for around 15 per cent of the total emotional content; indeed, it is slightly more than 15 per cent in the case of President Obama. It is much less prominent in Hitler's Proclamation, where it is the fifth most frequently occurring emotion, accounting for about 12 per cent of the total emotional content. Indeed, a feature of Hitler's address is the predominance of negative emotions, with "fear", "sadness" and "anger" taking precedence after "trust".

In contrast, "anticipation" and "joy" are much more predominant in the two US President's SOUs, never dropping below 13 per cent in emotional content, and always ranking in the top four emotions. In Hitler's speech, "anticipation" is the fifth ranked emotion.

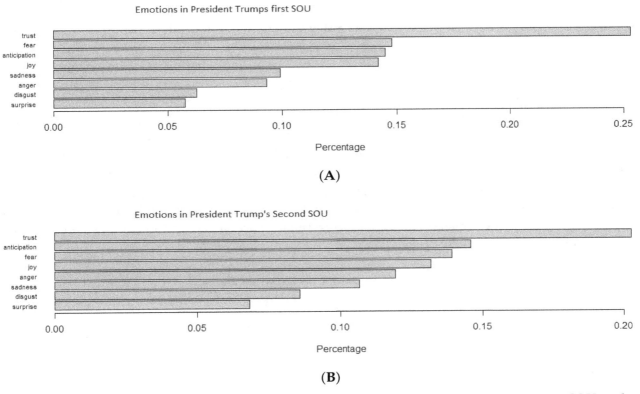

(A)

(B)

Figure 5. The Emotional Tenor of President Trumps two SOUs: (**A**) President Trump's First SOU; and (**B**) President Trump's Second SOU.

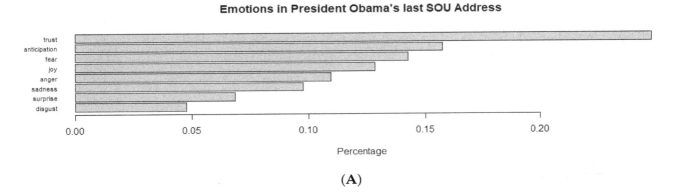

(A)

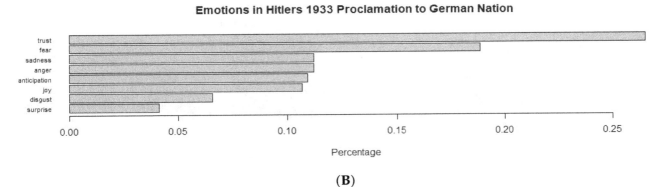

(B)

Figure 6. The Emotional Tenor of President Obama's last SOU and Hitler's 1933 Berlin Proclamation: (**A**) President Obama's last SOU; and (**B**) Hitler's 1933 Proclamation.

Another interesting feature of the four speeches is their "emotional valence", or the pattern of sequential positive and negative emotions displayed as the speech unfolds through time. Plots of these patterns are shown in Figures 7 and 8. There is a distinct change in pattern in the emotional valence of President Trump's two SOUs, as shown in Figure 7A,B. In the first, he commences on a positive emotional tone and is fairly upbeat in the first part of the speech, but then has multiple negative drops in the second half of the speech, before ending on a positive emotional note. In his second SOU, the pattern is roughly reversed, and there are more emotional negative points in the first half of the SOU, whereas the emotional volatility increases in the second half of the speech, with more frequent extreme highs and lows, and a predominantly positive tone at the end of the speech.

Figure 8A reveals that President Obama, in his last SOU, commences on a predominantly positive note, with some pronounced positive spikes, becomes more measured and negative in the middle of the speech, and ends on a predominantly positive note, with multiple positive peaks towards the end of his speech. Figure 8B shows that Hitler's much shorter 1933 Proclamation is quite volatile in the first part of the speech, becomes more measured in the second half, with fewer extreme peaks and troughs, and finishes on a positive note.

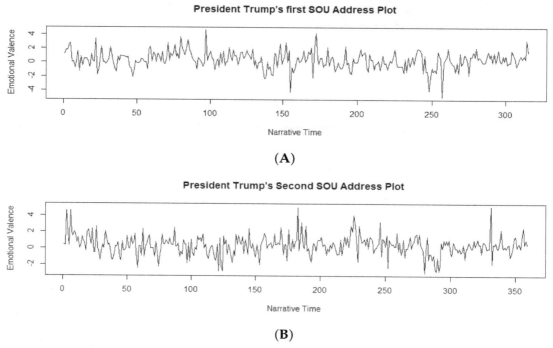

Figure 7. The Emotional Valence of President Trumps two SOUs: (**A**) President Trump's first SOU; and (**B**) President Trump's second SOU.

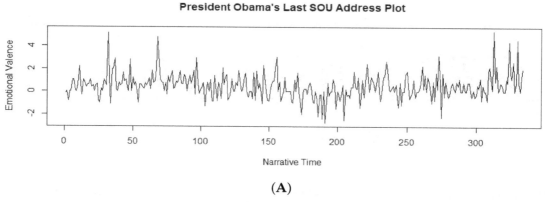

Figure 8. *Cont.*

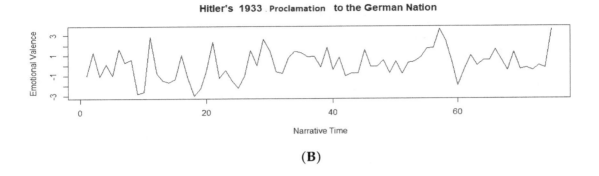

(B)

Figure 8. The Emotional Valence of President Obama's last SOU and Hitler's 1933 Berlin Proclamation: (**A**) President Obama's last SOU; and (**B**) Hitler's 1933 Berlin Proclamation.

3.2. Zipf Mandelbrot Analysis

Zipf [22] suggested that his "Theory of Relative Frequency" is a statistical law which falls within the laws of probability. Zipf's law is an experimental law which is often applied to the study of the frequency of words in a corpus of natural language utterances. The law suggests that the frequency of any word is inversely proportional to its rank in the frequency table. In the case of the English language, the two most common words are "the" and "of", and Zipf's law states that "the" is twice as common as "of".

Figure 9 shows plots of the application of Zipf's law to the four speeches considered. The scales are in natural logarithms on both axes. A theoretical application of Zipf's law would show a slope of negative one in the plots in Figure 9, running from top left to bottom right. All plots deviate from this concept, but the greatest deviation, from the theoretical concept, is in Hitler's 1933 address, which is the most concave.

A flatter Zipf slope can indicate a more random signal, but it can also indicate a broader vocabulary that conveys a more precisely worded message. Zipf suggests that attempts to remove ambiguities should produce a flatter slope that favours the recipient. Mandelbrot [23] suggested that human languages have a slope of around 1. These political speeches are framed to favour the recipient. Hitler's is the most extreme, but this is in translation. Obama's is the closest to normal language, but is still some distance from it.

To further explore the degree of deviation in the context of these four speeches, we ran Ordinary Least Squares regressions of the log of rank regressed on the log of frequency. The results of these regressions are shown in Table 3.

The regression results in Table 3 reveal that all four regressions have F-Statistics that are highly significant, and Adjusted-R squares of 0.94, 0.94, 0.94, and 0.91, in the cases of President Trump's two speeches, President Obama's speech, and Hitler's speech, respectively. The values of the slope coefficients, all of which are significant at the one per cent level, are Trump SOUA1 slope -0.67, Trump SOUA2 slope -0.71, Obama last SOUA slope -0.74, and Hitler 1933 slope -0.57.

These results suggest that all four political speeches are framed to favour the recipient. Hitler's is the most extreme, but this is in translation. Obama's is the closest to normal language but is still some distance from it. The most simplified and audience targeted is Hitler's 1933 speech. Trump and Obama are close together, with Trump's SOUAs showing slightly greater audience targeting.

Zipf Frequency Rank Trump First SOUA

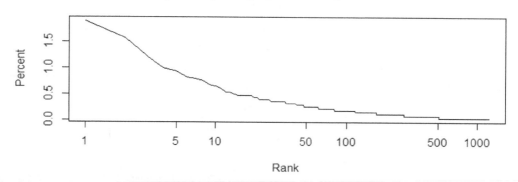

Zipf Frequency Rank Trump SOU2019

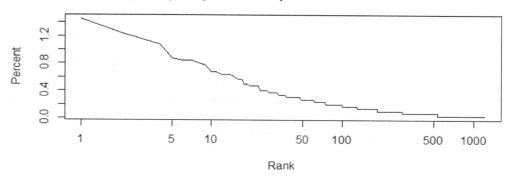

Zipf Frequency Rank OBAMA LAST SOUA

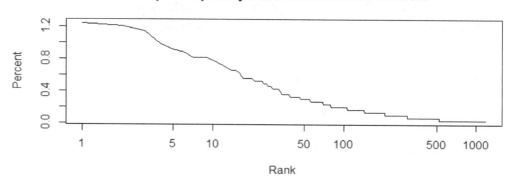

Zipf Frequency Rank Hitler 1933 Proclamation

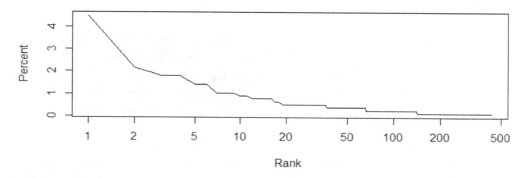

Figure 9. Zipf Plots.

Table 3. OLS, using Observations 1–1233 Dependent variable: l_freqT1.

	Coefficient	Std. Error	t-Ratio	p-Value
const	4.60818	0.0301961	152.6	0.0000
l_RankT1	−0.674643	0.00487040	−138.5	0.0000
Mean dependent var	0.478800	S.D. dependent var		0.687286
Sum squared resid	35.08483	S.E. of regression		0.168823
R^2	0.939712	Adjusted R^2		0.939663
$F(1, 1231)$	19187.55	P-value(F)		0.000000
Log-likelihood	444.8414	Akaike criterion		−885.6829
Schwarz criterion	−875.4484	Hannan–Quinn		−881.8328

OLS, using Observations 1–1227 Dependent variable: l_freqT2

	Coefficient	Std. Error	t-Ratio	p-value
const	4.83631	0.0306320	157.9	0.0000
l_RankT2	−0.706661	0.00494454	−142.9	0.0000
Mean dependent var	0.514392	S.D. dependent var		0.718456
Sum squared resid	35.80636	S.E. of regression		0.170967
R^2	0.943419	Adjusted R^2		0.943373
$F(1, 1225)$	20425.42	P-value(F)		0.000000
Log-likelihood	427.1954	Akaike criterion		−850.3908
Schwarz criterion	−840.1661	Hannan–Quinn		−846.5434

OLS, using Observations 1–433 Dependent variable: l_freqH1

	Coefficient	Std. Error	t- Ratio	p-Value
const	3.21372	0.0434618	73.94	0.0000
l_RankH	−0.565233	0.00840317	−67.26	0.0000
Mean dependent var	0.342408	S.D. dependent var		0.575778
Sum squared resid	12.45621	S.E. of regression		0.170002
R^2	0.913026	Adjusted R^2		0.912824
$F(1, 431)$	4524.478	P-value(F)		1.1e−230
Log-likelihood	153.8538	Akaike criterion		−303.7076
Schwarz criterion	−295.5661	Hannan–Quinn		−300.4936

OLS, using Observations 1–1189 Dependent variable: l_freqO

	Coefficient	Std. Error	t-Ratio	p-value
const	5.05132	0.0326043	154.9	0.0000
l_RankO	−0.740851	0.00528936	−140.1	0.0000
Mean dependent var	0.543524	S.D. dependent var		0.753179
Sum squared resid	38.44997	S.E. of regression		0.179979
R^2	0.942946	Adjusted R^2		0.942898
$F(1, 1187)$	19618.01	P-value(F)		0.000000
Log-likelihood	352.9148	Akaike criterion		−701.8296
Schwarz criterion	−691.6679	Hannan–Quinn		−698.0000

4. Conclusions

In this paper, we have analysed President Trump's two SOUs and contrasted the content with those of the last SOU of President Obama and that of Hitler's 1933 Berlin Proclamation. All four are political speeches, and share a great deal of commonality. The sentiment analysis showed that they emphasize the nation, America and American, in the case of the two US Presidents, and Nation and German, in the case of Hitler. The word "will" features prominently in all four speeches, and relates to the respective political agendas of the speakers. The emotional tenor of the speeches of the two US Presidents is more positive than adopted by Hitler in his 1933 Berlin Proclamation. All speakers chose to end their speeches on a positive emotional note, and all four speeches contain Nationalistic elements.

The analysis also includes an application of the Zipf and Mandelbrot laws. The fact that all four had a slope of less then negative one, which would be standard speech in this framework, indicates that all three speakers had targeted their audiences and simplified the language used in their speeches. Hitler's use of language was the most distant from standard speech with a score of negative 0.57. This suggests his status as a skillful mob-orator is justified. Presidents Trump and Obama were less extreme but still had slope coefficients with values around negative 0.7, suggesting that they also target their audiences carefully.

The limitation of the text-mining approach adopted in the analysis of the contents of these four speeches is that it does not feature a verification of the statements made, and cannot pick up nuances in meaning and context. However, the approach does provide a broad indication of the structure and emotional flavour of the content, subject to the limitations of the lexicon applied. The Zipf analysis highlights the degree to which speech patterns within the speeches deviate from normal language values.

Author Contributions: D.E.A. and M.M. conceptualization and methodology, D.E.A. software, investigation and formal analysis, data curation, writing–original draft preparation, M.M. resources, writing–review and editing.

Acknowledgments: For financial support, the first author acknowledges the Australian Research Council, and the second author is most grateful to the Australian Research Council; Ministry of Science and Technology (MOST), Taiwan; and the Japan Society for the Promotion of Science. The authors wish to thank four reviewers for helpful comments and suggestions.

References

1. Allen, D.E.; McAleer, M. Fake News and Indifference to Scientific Fact: President Trump's Confused Tweets on Global Warming, Climate Change and Weather. *Scientometrics* **2018**, *117*, 625–629. [CrossRef]

2. Allen, D.E.; McAleer, M. President Trump Tweets Supreme Leader Kim Jong-Un on Nuclear Weapons: A Comparison with Climate Change. *Sustainability* **2018**, *10*, 2310. [CrossRef]

3. Allen, D.E.; McAleer, M.; Reid, D.M. Fake News and Indifference to Truth: Dissecting Tweets and State of the Union Addresses by Presidents Obama and Trump. *Adv. Dec. Sci.* **2018**, *22*. [CrossRef]

4. Feinerer, I.; Hornik, K. Tm: Text Mining Package. R Package Version 0.7-6. 2018. Available online: https://CRAN.R-project.org/package=tm (accessed on 27 August 2019).

5. Jockers, M.L. Syuzhet: Extract Sentiment and Plot Arcs from Text. 2015. Available online: https://github.com/mjockers/syuzhet (accessed on 27 August 2019).

6. Fellows, I. Wordcloud. 2018. Available online: https://CRAN.R-project.org/package=wordcloud (accessed on 27 August 2019).

7. Pröllochs, N.; Fuerriegel, S.; Neumann, D. *Understanding Negations in Information Processing: Learning from Replicating Human Behaviour*; Working Paper; Information Systems Research, University of Freiburg: Freiburg im Breisgau, Germany, 2017. Available online: https://ssrn.com/abstract=2954460 (accessed on 27 August 2019).

8. Allen, D.E.; McAleer, M.; Singh, A.K. Machine News and Volatility: The Dow Jones Industrial Average and the TRNA Real-Time High Frequency Sentiment Series. In *Handbook of High Frequency Trading*, Gregoriou, G.N., Ed.; Academic Press: Cambridge, MA, USA, 2015; Chapter 19.

9. Allen, D.E.; McAleer, M.; Singh, A.K. An Entropy-based Analysis of the Relationship Between the DOW JONES Index and the TRNA Sentiment series. *Appl. Econ.* **2017**, *49*, 677–692. [CrossRef]

10. Allen, D.E.; McAleer, M.; Singh, A.K. Daily Market News Sentiment and Stock Prices. *Appl. Econ.* **2018**, doi:10.1080/00036846.2018.1564115 [CrossRef]

11. Tetlock, P.C. Giving Content to Investor Sentiment: The Role of Media in the Stock Market. *J. Financ.* **2007**, *62*, 1139–1167. [CrossRef]

12. Tetlock, P.C.; Macskassy, S.A.; Saar-Tsechansky, M. More than Words: Quantifying Language to Measure Firms' Fundamentals. *J. Financ.* **2008**, *63*, 1427–1467. [CrossRef]

13. Da, Z.H.I.; Engelberg, J.; Gao, P. In Search of Attention. *J. Financ.* **2011**, *66*, 1461–1499. [CrossRef]

14. Barber, B.M.; Odean, T. All that Glitters: The Effect of Attention and News on the Buying Behaviour of Individual and Institutional Investors. *Rev. Financ. Stud.* **2008**, *21*, 785–818. [CrossRef]

15. diBartolomeo, D.; Warrick, S. *Making Covariance Based Portfolio Risk Models Sensitive to the Rate at Which Markets React to New Information*; Knight, J., Satchell, S., Eds.; Linear Factor Models; Elsevier Finance: Amsterdam, The Netherlands, 2005.

16. Mitra, L.; Mitra, G.; diBartolomeo, D. Equity Portfolio Risk (Volatility) Estimation using Market Information and Sentiment. *Quant. Financ.* **2009**, *9*, 887–895. [CrossRef]

17. Dzielinski, M.; Rieger, M.O.; Talpsepp, T. Volatility Asymmetry, News, and Private Investors. In *Handbook of News Analytics in Finance*; Wiley: Hoboken, NJ, USA, 2011; pp. 255–270.
18. Cahan, R.; Jussa, J.; Luo, Y. *Breaking News: How to Use News Sentiment to Pick Stocks*; MacQuarie US Research Report: New York, NY, USA, 2009.
19. Hafez, P.; Xie, J. Factoring Sentiment Risk into Quant Models, RavenPack International S.L. *J. Investig.* **2012**, *25*. [CrossRef]
20. Kearney, C.; Lui, S. Textual Sentiment in Finance: A Survey of Methods and Models. *Int. Rev. Financ. Anal.* **2014**, *33*, 171–185. [CrossRef]
21. Loughran, T.; McDonald, B. Textual Analysis in Accounting and Finance: A Survey. *J. Account. Res.* **2016**, *54*, 1187–1230. [CrossRef]
22. Zipf, G.K. *Selected Studies of the Principle of Relative Frequency in Language*; Harvard University Press: Cambridge, UK, 1932.
23. Mandelbrot, B. Information Theory and Psycholinguistics. In *Chapter in Scientific Psychology*; Wolman, B.B., Ed.; Basic Books: New York, NY, USA, 1965.
24. Shannon, C. A Mathematical Theory of Communication. *Bell Syst. Tech. J.* **1948**, 379–423, 623–656. [CrossRef]
25. Ficcadenti, V.; Cerqueti, R.; Ausloos, M. A Joint Text Mining-rank Size Investigation of the Rhetoric Structures of the US Presidents' Speeches. *Expert Syst. Appl.* **2019**, *123*, 127–142 [CrossRef]
26. Shklovsky, V. Art as Technique. In *Russian Formalist Criticism*; Lemon, L.T., Reis, M., Eds.; University of Nebraska Press: Lincoln, NE, USA, 1965.
27. Propp, V. *Morphology of the Folk Tale*; English Trans; First Published in Moscow in 1928; University of Texas Press: Laurence Scott, TX, USA, 1968.
28. Smith, A.D. Gastronomy or Geology? The role of Nationalism in the Reconstruction of Nations. *N. Natl.* **1994**, *1*, 3–23. [CrossRef]

10

Equity Return Dispersion and Stock Market Volatility: Evidence from Multivariate Linear and Nonlinear Causality Tests

Riza Demirer [1,*], **Rangan Gupta** [2], **Zhihui Lv** [3] **and Wing-Keung Wong** [4,5,6]

[1] Department of Economics & Finance, Southern Illinois University Edwardsville, School of Business, Edwardsville, IL 62026-1102, USA

[2] Department of Economics, University of Pretoria, Pretoria 0002, South Africa; rangan.gupta@up.ac.za

[3] KLASMOE & School of Mathematics and Statistics, Northeast Normal University, Changchun 130024, China; luzh694@nenu.edu.cn

[4] Department of Finance, Fintech Center, and Big Data Research Center, Asia University, Taichung 41354, Taiwan; wong@asia.edu.tw

[5] Department of Medical Research, China Medical University Hospital, Taichung 40402, Taiwan

[6] Department of Economics and Finance, Hang Seng University of Hong Kong, Shatin, Hong Kong 999077, China

* Correspondence: rdemire@siue.edu

Abstract: We employ bivariate and multivariate nonlinear causality tests to document causality from equity return dispersion to stock market volatility and excess returns, even after controlling for the state of the economy. Expansionary (contractionary) market states are associated with a low (high) level of equity return dispersion, indicating asymmetries in the relationship between return dispersion and economic conditions. Our findings indicate that both return dispersion and business conditions are valid joint forecasters of stock market volatility and excess returns and that return dispersion possesses incremental information regarding future stock return dynamics beyond that which can be explained by the state of the economy.

Keywords: equity return dispersion; stock market volatility; business cycle; multivariate causality

JEL Codes: C32; E32; G10

1. Introduction

Numerous catalysts, ranging from discount rate factors to cash flow and other related variables, can drive fluctuations in stock markets. While stock market fluctuations do not always signal bad news for investors, monitoring and modelling stock market volatility is crucial, not only for investors in their portfolio management and risk assessment models, but also for policy makers in their assessment of financial fundamentals and investor sentiment. Recent literature has documented that equity return dispersion, measured by the cross-sectional standard deviation of stock returns, either at the individual stock or disaggregate portfolio level, carries reliable information regarding the state of the economy and future stock market volatility [1–3]. In another strand of the literature, however, stock market volatility is linked to economic fundamentals [4,5] and the business cycle [6].

Given the ample evidence on the predictive power of equity return dispersion on stock market volatility and the evidence of causality between stock market volatility and the business cycle, a natural research question is whether the predictive power of return dispersion is driven by a common fundamental factor that drives both stock market volatility and the dispersion of stock returns. To that end, multivariate causality tests provide a valuable avenue for empirical analysis as we are able to test for causality between return dispersion and stock market premium and volatility after controlling for the state of the economy.

This paper contributes to the literature on stock market predictability by exploring the causal relationship between return dispersion and stock market volatility and excess returns via multivariate nonlinear causality tests recently developed by Bai et al. [7–9] and Chow et al. [10]. The advantage of multivariate causality tests, as opposed to bivariate alternatives that are often employed in the literature, is that it allows us to control for business cycles via the business conditions index that we use in our tests and to examine the causality relationship that bivariate alternatives cannot detect. Given the recent evidence by Choudhry et al. [6] of a bidirectional causal relationship between stock market volatility and the business cycle, the multivariate causality tests that control for business cycles in the causal relationship between return dispersion and stock market volatility allow us to explore whether return dispersion possesses any incremental information regarding stock market return dynamics even after controlling for business cycles, and thus enlarges our understanding of the role of return dispersion as an economic state variable. The issue is of interest not only from the perspective of stock market predictability, but it also has significant applicability to the pricing of derivatives, and hedging and portfolio diversification, as volatility forecasts are an integral part of these exercises. On the other hand, bivariate causality tests could detect the causality relationship between any pair of variables that multivariate causality tests cannot detect. Thus, we employ both bivariate and multivariate causality tests in this study.

Performing a combination of linear vs. nonlinear and bivariate vs. multivariate causality tests, we show that linear causality tests generally fail to detect causal effects from return dispersion to excess market returns and volatility. While observing some evidence of causality from return dispersion to both stock market volatility and excess returns, we observe that causality disappears when we control for the business conditions via the Aruoba–Diebold–Scotti business conditions index. Furthermore, we find that the predictive power of business conditions on return dispersion is concentrated on contractionary periods only, suggesting the presence of asymmetric causal interactions between business conditions, equity return dispersion, and stock market volatility.

Both bivariate and multivariate nonlinear causality tests, however, yield significant evidence of causality from return dispersion to both stock market volatility and equity premium. While detecting significant causality from business conditions to return dispersion, we observe that expansionary (contractionary) market states are associated with a low (high) level of equity return dispersion, in line with the findings in Angelidis et al. [2] that high return dispersion is associated with a deterioration of business conditions. Overall, our findings suggest that both return dispersion and business conditions are valid joint forecasters of both the stock market volatility and excess market return and that return dispersion indeed possesses incremental information regarding future stock return dynamics beyond that which can be explained by the state of the economy. The results have significant implications for stock market forecasting models as well as for policy makers to take into account the cross-sectional variation in stock returns and nonlinearities when assessing the predictors of stock market dynamics.

The rest of the paper is organized as follows. Section 2 provides a brief review of the literature on equity return dispersion in asset pricing and investments. Section 3 presents the data and the methodology for linear and nonlinear multivariate causality tests. Section 4 presents the empirical findings and Section 5 concludes the paper.

2. Literature Review

The literature provides ample evidence that associates equity return dispersion with different aspects of risk. In earlier studies focusing on the U.S. stock returns, Christie and Huang [11] and Duffee [12] associated return dispersion with economic expansions and recessions, documenting asymmetries in the cross-sectional dispersion of stock returns with respect to stock market movements and business cycles. Similarly, Loungani et al. [13] found that an index that measures the dispersion among stock prices from different industries has predictive power over unemployment. To that end, early research established evidence of an association between equity return dispersion and macroeconomic indicators.

In other works on return dispersion, studies including those of Stivers [14] and Connolly and Stivers [1] established a link between return dispersion, aggregate market volatility, and idiosyncratic volatility, implying that return dispersion provides signals about future aggregate stock market volatility. Further extending the role of return dispersion to asset pricing models, Stivers and Sun [15] and Bhootra [16] associated the time variation in the value and momentum premia with the variation in the market's cross-sectional return dispersion. Similarly, studies including those of Jiang [17], Demirer and Jategaonkar [18], and Demirer et al. [19] showed that return dispersion serves as a systematic risk factor, carrying a positive price of risk in the cross-section of stock returns, while Demirer and Jategaonkar [18] showed that return dispersion risk is asymmetrically priced, conditional on the market return. In a more recent application to G7 countries, Angelidis et al. [2] further supported the role of return dispersion as an economic state variable and showed that return dispersion reliably predicts the time-variation in stock market returns, volatility, as well as the value and momentum premia observed in the cross-section of stock returns. Similarly, Maio [3] showed that return dispersion consistently forecasts a decline in the excess market returns, with superior out-of-sample performance in predicting the equity premium, compared to alternative predictors, including the dividend yield, term spread, etc.

In another strand of the literature that is related to portfolio management, studies including those of Lillo and Mantegna [20], Solnik and Roulet [21], Baur [22], Statman and Scheid [23,24], and Demirer [25] related return dispersion to the association of asset returns and examined the statistic in the context of portfolio diversification. While Baur [22] noted that return dispersion can be used to obtain additional information about market linkages that is not provided by correlation, Eiling and Gerard [26] used a variant of the dispersion measure in order to examine the time variation in linkages among global stock markets.

Meanwhile, another strand of the literature provides ample evidence linking stock market volatility to real economic activity [4,5] and stock market volatility to future aggregate stock returns [27–30]. In a recent study, applying linear and nonlinear causality tests, Choudhry et al. [6] showed that a bidirectional causal relationship exists between stock market volatility and the business cycle in a sample of four major economies without using return dispersion in their multivariate tests.

Building on the recent evidence from asset pricing tests, Chichernea et al. [31] further supported the role of return dispersion as a systematic risk factor and document that return dispersion has explanatory power for accrual and investment anomalies, associating a high level of return dispersion exposure with conditions that are not conducive to growth and investment. A natural research question, therefore, is what drives the predictive value of return dispersion for future returns and volatility and whether this predictive ability is indeed driven by the information return dispersion possesses regarding the state of the economy. To that end, multivariate causality tests provide an interesting opening as they allow us not only to account for possible nonlinearities in the time series, but also to examine the causal associations between return dispersion and stock market return and volatility after controlling for business conditions.

3. Data and Methodology

3.1. Data

The primary variables of interest in our causality tests are equity return dispersion and stock market volatility, with the Aruoba–Diebold–Scotti business conditions index used as a control variable in our multivariate tests. The sample period covers July 1963 to February 2017, including 13,508 observations of stock and market returns, the Center for Research in Security Prices (CRSP) value-weighted index return, and the one-month Treasury bill rate. From the data, we compute equity return dispersion (RD_t) for day t as the cross-sectional standard deviation of daily stock returns calculated as:

$$RD_t = \sqrt{w_{i,t} \sum_{i=1}^{N} (r_{i,t} - r_{m,t})^2},$$ (1)

where $r_{i,t}$ and $r_{m,t}$ are the return for stock i and the market for day t, respectively; $w_{i,t} = 1/N$ for the equally-weighted cross-sectional dispersion of equity returns; and N is the number of stocks. Following Stivers and Sun [15], Angelidis et al. [2], and Maio [3], we compute the cross-sectional standard deviation of daily returns on 100 portfolios sorted on size and book-to-market ratios, obtained from Ken French's website as an estimate for equity return dispersion. Maio [3] argues that the use of portfolios in the computation of return dispersion mitigates estimation errors due to the presence of illiquid and small stocks in the cross-section of individual stocks. Likewise, we obtain data for daily excess returns on the market, defined as the CRSP value-weighted index return minus the one-month Treasury bill rate, from Ken French's website. Please note that as our study builds on the previous studies regarding the predictive power of return dispersion, in particular Angelidis et al. [2] and Maio [3], we compute return dispersion consistent with these studies. This allows us to compare our findings to previous results and focus on the new insight multivariate tests provide; that is, after controlling for business conditions.

Solnik and Roulet [21] used the market model benchmark to show that return dispersion relates to the cross-sectional correlation of asset returns. However, unlike traditional measures of correlation and volatility, return dispersion provides an aggregate measure of co-movement in a portfolio for a given time period. To that end, the equity return dispersion measure in Equation (1) can be regarded as a measure of directional similarity in stock returns for a given day. In the case of stock market volatility, we follow Choudhry et al. [6] and estimate stock market volatility (SV) by means of the univariate generalized autoregressive conditional heteroskedasticity (GARCH (1,1)) model of CRSP market index returns. Consistent with Choudhry et al. [6], the computation of SV allows us to compare our findings to the previous findings and provide further insight by adding return dispersion to the multivariate tests. It must be noted that we also tried several alternative models, including the exponential GARCH (EGARCH) and Glosten-Jagannathan-Runkle-GARCH (GJR-GARCH) models, to estimate stock market volatility, and the EGARCH model was found to fit the data better than the GARCH and GJR-GARCH models. However, the results using the EGARCH-based estimates of stock market volatility yielded similar findings for the linear and nonlinear causal relationships in both bivariate and multivariate situations (available upon request).

Figure 1 presents the time series plots for daily equity return dispersion (RD) and stock market volatility (SV) during the sample period. Not surprisingly, we observe several notable spikes in both series, particularly during the Asian crisis period in the late 1990s and the global financial crisis periods, in line with the previous studies associating high stock market volatility with recessionary periods and periods of market stress [4,5]. It is interesting that return dispersion values also exhibit similar spikes during these periods. Demirer et al. [32] note that these periods were also associated with spikes observed in the level of global risk aversion, driving equity market correlations higher globally. To that end, the high level of equity return dispersion observed in Figure 1 during periods when stock market volatility also rises suggests that these two series are possibly driven by a common fundamental factor related to the economy.

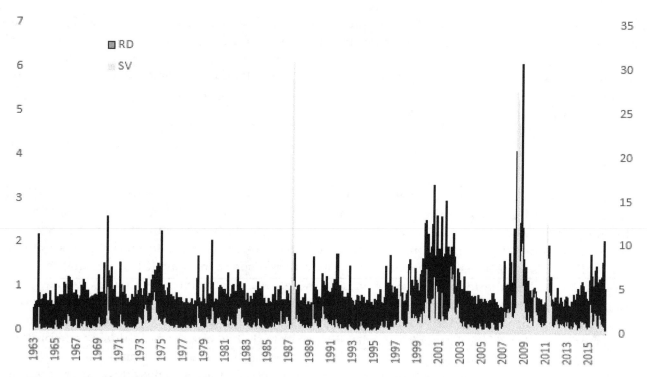

Figure 1. Daily equity return dispersion (RD) and stock market volatility (SV). Note: RD and SV are equity return dispersion and stock market volatility, respectively.

Motivated by studies, including those of Stivers and Sun [15] and Angelidis et al. [2], suggesting that equity return dispersion can predict the time-variation in economic activity, we supplement our multivariate causality tests with the Aruoba–Diebold–Scotti business conditions index (ADS) in order to account for economic conditions in the causal effect of return dispersion on stock market return and volatility. The ADS index developed in Aruoba et al. [33] measures economic activity at high frequency using a dynamic factor model that includes a number of economic variables. We obtain the data for the ADS index from the Philadelphia Fed's website and use this index in our multivariate causality tests in order to track the predictive ability of business conditions along with return dispersion over stock market volatility and premium.

3.2. Methodology

3.2.1. Bivariate Linear Causality Tests

In order to examine the bivariate linear causal relationship between any pair of equity return dispersion (RD_t), stock market volatility (SV_t), equity market premium (MP_t), business conditions index (ADS_t), and the positive (negative) ADS business conditions index values ($ADS1_t$) [($ADS2_t$)], we let x_t and y_t present any pair of RD_t, SV_t, MP_t, ADS_t, $ADS1_t$, and $ADS2_t$ that we are interested in studying and used the widely accepted vector autoregression (VAR) specification and the corresponding Granger causality test [34]. Consider the following two-equation model:

$$x_t = a_1 + \sum_{i=1}^{p} \alpha_i x_{t-i} + \sum_{i=1}^{p} \beta_i y_{t-i} + \varepsilon_{1t}, \tag{2a}$$

$$y_t = a_2 + \sum_{i=1}^{p} \gamma_i x_{t-i} + \sum_{i=1}^{p} \delta_i y_{t-i} + \varepsilon_{2t}, \tag{2b}$$

where x_t and y_t are stationary variables, p is the optimal lag in the system based on the well-known information criteria, such as the Akaike information criterion (AIC), and ε_{1t} and ε_{2t} are the disturbances satisfying the regularity assumptions of the classical linear normal regression model. The variable $\{y_t\}$ is said not to Granger cause $\{x_t\}$ if $\beta_i = 0$ in Equation (2a), for any $i = 1, \ldots, p$. In other words, the past values of $\{y_t\}$ do not provide any additional information on $\{x_t\}$. Similarly, $\{x_t\}$ does not Granger cause $\{y_t\}$ if $\gamma_i = 0$ in Equation (2b), for any $i = 1, \ldots, p$. In order to test for Granger causality, we used the following null hypotheses separately:

$$H_0^1 : \beta_1 = \beta_2 = \cdots = \beta_p = 0, \tag{3a}$$

$$H_0^2 : \gamma_1 = \gamma_2 = \cdots = \gamma_p = 0, \tag{3b}$$

and used the standard F-test to empirically test them.

There are four different situations for the causality relationships between RD_t and SV_t in Equations (2a) and (2b): (a) Rejecting H_0^1 but not rejecting H_0^2 implies a unidirectional causality from SV_t to RD_t; (b) rejecting H_0^2 but not rejecting H_0^1 implies a unidirectional causality from RD_t to SV_t; (c) rejecting both H_0^1 and H_0^2 implies the existence of feedback relations; and (d) not rejecting both H_0^1 and H_0^2 implies that RD_t and SV_t are not rejected to be independent. Readers may refer to Bai et al. [7–9], Chow et al. [10], and the references therein for the details of testing H_0^1 and/or H_0^2.

3.2.2. Nonlinearity Tests

In this paper, we first perform a linear causality test and thereafter conduct nonlinear causality tests to test whether there is any linear and nonlinear causality among RD_t, SV_t, MP_t, ADS_t, $ADS1_t$, and $ADS2_t$. If it is necessary to conduct nonlinear causality tests on the variables, we believe that the residuals obtained from performing the linear causality should contain nonlinearity. In addition, RD_t, SV_t, MP_t, ADS_t, $ADS1_t$, and $ADS2_t$ should contain some nonlinear elements so that linear causality cannot eliminate nonlinearity. Thus, in this paper, we conduct a nonlinear test on RD_t, SV_t, MP_t, ADS_t, $ADS1_t$, and $ADS2_t$. We let Y_t represent RD_t, SV_t, MP_t, ADS_t, $ADS1_t$, and. In order to test for nonlinearity in the variable Y_t, we first remove the linear components in the series $\{Y_t\}$ using an autoregressive (AR) specification and compute the residuals series of $\{Y_t\}$ without loss of generality; we also let $\{Y_t\}$ be the residuals series of $\{Y_t\}$ if there is no confusion. The series $\{Y_t\}$ does not possess any nonlinearity if and only if, for any t, the law of corresponding residuals $\{Y_t\}$ satisfies $L(Y_t|Y_{t-1}) = L(Y_t)$ and we define $C_1(\tau) \equiv \Pr(Y_{t-1} < \tau, Y_t < \tau)$, $C_2(\tau) \equiv \Pr(Y_{t-1} < \tau)$, and $C_3(\tau) \equiv \Pr(Y_t < \tau)$. Since $\Pr(Y_t < \tau | Y_{t-1} < \tau) = \frac{C_1(\tau)}{C_2(\tau)}$, we can test the following hypothesis when testing the existence of the nonlinear of a sequence $\{Y_t\}$:

$$H_0 : \frac{C_1(\tau)}{C_2(\tau)} - C_3(\tau) = 0, \tag{4}$$

For a residual sequence $\{Y_t\}$, the dependence test statistic is given by:

$$T_n = \sqrt{n}\left(\frac{C_1(\tau, n)}{C_2(\tau, n)} - C_3(\tau, n)\right), \tag{5}$$

where:

$$C_1(\tau, n) \equiv \frac{1}{n}\sum_{t=2}^{T} I_{(y_{t-1}<\tau)} \cdot I_{(y_t<\tau)},$$

$$C_2(\tau, n) \equiv \frac{1}{n}\sum_{t=2}^{T} I_{(y_{t-1}<\tau)},$$

$$C_1(\tau, n) \equiv \frac{1}{n}\sum_{t=2}^{T} I_{(y_t<\tau)},$$

$n = T - 1$, and T is the length of residual $\{Y_t\}$. Under this condition, if the residual $\{Y_t\}$ is iid, then the test statistic $T_n \to N(0, \sigma^2(\tau))$, as n is large enough and the hypothesis: $H_0 : \frac{C_1(\tau)}{C_2(\tau)} - C_3(\tau) = 0$ is rejected at level α if $|T_n| / \hat{\sigma}^2(\tau) > z_{\frac{\alpha}{2}}$. In this situation, the series $\{Y_t\}$ possesses any nonlinearity. We note that the nonlinear test takes GARCH effects into consideration in the test (Hui et al. [35] and Bai et al. [9]).

3.2.3. Multivariate Granger Causality tests

In this section, we review the theory of both linear and nonlinear causality and discuss how to apply the linear and nonlinear Granger causality tests to identify the causality relationships among RD_t, ADS_t, $ADS1_t$, and $ADS2_t$ to SV_t and MP_t. To test the linear and nonlinear causality relationship between a vector of stationary variables from RD_t, ADS_t, $ADS1_t$, and $ADS2_t$ and another vector of stationary variable of either SV_t and MP_t, we let $x_t = (x_{1,t}, \ldots, x_{n_1,t})'$ and $y_t = (y_{1,t}, \ldots, y_{n_2,t})'$ with $n_1 = 2$ and $n_2 = 1$, $x_{1,t} = RD_t$, $x_{2,t} = ADS_t$, $ADS1_t$, or $ADS2_t$, $x_{1,t} = SV_t$ or MP_t, and $n_1 + n_2 = n$ series in total.

Multivariate Linear Causality

To test the linear causality relationship between a vector of stationary variables from $x_t = (x_{1,t}, \ldots, x_{n_1,t})'$ and $y_t = (y_{1,t}, \ldots, y_{n_2,t})'$, one could construct the following $n-$ VAR equations:

$$\begin{pmatrix} x_t \\ y_t \end{pmatrix} = \begin{pmatrix} A_{x[n_1 \times 1]} \\ A_{y[n_2 \times 1]} \end{pmatrix} + \begin{pmatrix} A_{xx}(L)_{[n_1 \times n_1]} & A_{xy}(L)_{[n_1 \times n_2]} \\ A_{yx}(L)_{[n_2 \times n_1]} & A_{yy}(L)_{[n_2 \times n_2]} \end{pmatrix} \begin{pmatrix} x_{t-1} \\ y_{t-1} \end{pmatrix} + \begin{pmatrix} e_{x,t} \\ e_{y,t} \end{pmatrix}, \tag{6}$$

where $A_{x[n_1 \times 1]}$ and $A_{y[n_2 \times 1]}$ are two vectors of intercept terms, and $A_{xx}(L)_{[n_1 \times n_1]}$, $A_{yx}(L)_{[n_2 \times n_1]}$, $A_{xy}(L)_{[n_1 \times n_2]}$, and $A_{yy}(L)_{[n_2 \times n_2]}$ are matrices of lag polynomials.

In order to test the following null hypotheses separately:

(1) $H_0^1 : A_{xy}(L) = 0$,
(2) $H_0^2 : A_{yx}(L) = 0$, and,
(3) both $H_0^1 : A_{xy}(L) = 0$ and $H_0^2 : A_{yx}(L) = 0$,

We should obtain the residual covariance matrix Σ from the full model using an ordinary least squares estimation (OLSE) for each equation without imposing any restriction on the parameters, compute the residual covariance matrix Σ_0 from the restricted model in Equation (6) using OLSE for each equation with the restriction on the parameters imposed by the null hypothesis H_0^1, H_0^2 or both H_0^1 and H_0^2, and obtain the following statistic:

$$(T - c)(\log|\Sigma_0| - \log|\Sigma|) \tag{7}$$

where T is the number of usable observations, c is the number of parameters estimated in each equation of the unrestricted system, and $\log|\Sigma_0|$ and $\log|\Sigma|$ are the natural logarithms of the determinants of restricted and unrestricted residual covariance matrices, respectively. When the null hypothesis is true, this test statistic has an asymptotic χ^2 distribution with the degree of freedom equal to the number of restrictions on the coefficients in the system.

Multivariate Nonlinear Causality

After applying the VAR model to identify the linear causality relationships from RD_t, ADS_t, $ADS1_t$, and $ADS2_t$ to SV_t and MP_t, we obtain their corresponding residuals $\{\hat{\varepsilon}_{1t}\}$ and $\{\hat{\varepsilon}_{2t}\}$ to test the nonlinear causality with the residual series. For simplicity, in this section, we denote $X_t = (X_{1,t}, \ldots, X_{n_1,t})'$ and $Y_t = (Y_{1,t}, \ldots, Y_{n_2,t})'$ to be the corresponding residuals of any two vectors of variables to be examined. We define the lead vector and lag vector of a time series, say $X_{i,t}$, as follows: for $X_{i,t}$, $i = 1, \ldots, n$, the m_{x_i}-length lead vector, and the L_{x_i}-length lag vector of $X_{i,t}$ to be:

$$X_{i,t}^{m_{x_i}} \equiv \left(X_{i,t}, X_{i,t+1}, \ldots, X_{i,t+m_{x_i}-1} \right), m_{x_i} = 1, 2, \ldots, t = 1, 2, \ldots,$$

$$X_{i,t-L_{x_i}}^{L_{x_i}} \equiv \left(X_{i,t-L_{x_i}}, X_{i,t-L_{x_i}+1}, \ldots, X_{i,t-1} \right), L_{x_i} = 1, 2, \ldots, t = L_{x_i} + 1, L_{x_i} + 2, \ldots, \text{respectively.}$$

We denote $M_x = \left(m_{x1}, \ldots, m_{x_{n_1}} \right)$, $L_x = \left(L_{x1}, \ldots, L_{x_{n_1}} \right)$, $m_x = \max(m_{x1}, \ldots, m_{n_1})$, and $l_x = \max \left(L_{x1}, \ldots, L_{x_{n_1}} \right)$. The m_{y_i}-length lead vector, $Y_{i,t}^{m_{y_i}}$, the L_{y_i}-length lag vector, $Y_{i,t-L_{y_i}}^{L_{y_i}}$, of $Y_{i,t}$, and $M_y, L_y, m_y,$ and l_y can be defined similarly.

To test the null hypothesis, H_0, that Y_t does not strictly Granger cause $X_t = (X_{1,t}, \ldots, X_{n_1,t})\prime$ under the assumptions that the time series vector variables $X_t = (X_{1,t}, \ldots, X_{n_1,t})\prime$ and $Y_t = (Y_{1,t}, \ldots, Y_{n_2,t})\prime$ are strictly stationary, weakly dependent, and satisfy the mixing conditions stated in Denker and Keller [36], we first defined the following four events given that m_x, m_y, L_x, L_y, and $e > 0$:

$$\left\{ \| X_t^{M_x} - X_s^{M_x} \| < e \right\} \equiv \left\{ \| X_{i,t}^{M_{x_i}} - X_{i,s}^{m_{x_i}} \| < e, \text{ for any } i = 1, \ldots, n_1 \right\};$$

$$\left\{ \| X_{t-L_x}^{L_x} - X_{s-L_x}^{L_x} \| < e \right\} \equiv \left\{ \| X_{i,t-L_{x_i}}^{L_{x_i}} - X_{i,s-L_{x_i}}^{L_{x_i}} \| < e, \text{ for any } i = 1, \ldots, n_1 \right\};$$

$$\left\{ \| Y_t^{M_y} - Y_s^{M_y} \| < e \right\} \equiv \left\{ \| Y_{i,t}^{m_{y_i}} - Y_{i,s}^{m_{y_i}} \| < e, \text{ for any } i = 1, \ldots, n_2 \right\}; \text{ and}$$

$$\left\{ \| Y_{t-L_y}^{L_y} - Y_{s-L_y}^{L_y} \| < e \right\} \equiv \left\{ \| Y_{i,t-L_{y_i}}^{L_{y_i}} - Y_{i,s-L_{y_i}}^{L_{y_i}} \| < e, \text{ for any } i = 1, \ldots, n_2 \right\};$$

where $\|\cdot\|$ denotes the maximum norm which is defined as $\| X - Y \| = \max(|x_1 - y_1|, |x_2 - y_2|, \ldots, |x_n - y_n|)$ for any two vectors $X = (x_1, \ldots, x_n)$ and $Y = (y_1, \ldots, y_n)$. The vector series $\{Y_t\}$ is said not to strictly Granger cause another vector series $\{X_t\}$ if:

$$\Pr\left(\| X_t^{M_x} - X_s^{M_x} \| < e \Big| \| X_{t-L_x}^{L_x} - X_{s-L_x}^{L_x} \| < e, \| Y_{t-L_y}^{L_y} - Y_{s-L_y}^{L_y} \| < e, \right)$$
$$= \Pr\left(\| X_t^{M_x} - X_s^{M_x} \| < e \Big| \| X_{t-L_x}^{L_x} - X_{s-L_x}^{L_x} \| < e \right) \tag{8}$$

where $Pr(\cdot|\cdot)$ denotes conditional probability.

If the null hypothesis, H_0, is true, the test statistic:

$$\sqrt{n} \left(\frac{C_1(M_x + L_x, L_y, e, n)}{C_2(L_x, L_y, e, n)} - \frac{C_3(M_x + L_x, e, n)}{C_4(L_x, e, n)} \right), \tag{9}$$

is distributed as $N\left(0, \sigma^2(M_x, L_x, L_y, e)\right)$. When the test statistic is too far away from zero, we reject the null hypothesis. Readers may refer to Bai et al. [7–9] and Chow et al. [10] for the definitions of $C_1, C_2, C_3,$ and $C_4,$ and more information on the estimates of Equation (9).

4. Empirical Results

Although not reported due to space considerations, the summary statistics reveal evidence of non-normality, indicated by highly significant Jarque–Bera statistics, with all four-time series (i.e., RD_t, SV_t, ADS_t and equity market premium, MP_t) exhibiting significant kurtosis. We also observe significant skewness for both RD_t and SV_t, suggesting greater likelihood of experiencing large values for these variables. Finally, in unreported findings, unit root tests based on the augmented Dickey and Fuller [37] show that the series are stationary.

4.1. Descriptive Statistics and Stationarity Test

Before describing the nonlinear causality tests, we first report in Table 1 the basic descriptive statistics and the most commonly used stationarity test, the augmented Dickey–Fuller test, for all the variables RD_t, ADS_t, SV_t and MP_t, examined in our paper. From the table, we find that the means of all the variables are significantly positive at the 1 percent level except ADS_t that is significantly negative at the 1 percent level. The skewness estimates show that RD_t and SV_t are positively skewed while ADS_t and MP_t are negatively skewed. Among them, RD_t, ADS_t, and MP_t are significant at the 1 percent, while the skewness of SV_t is not significant. We also find that all variables have positive excess kurtosis at the 1 percent level. Furthermore, from the skewness, kurtosis, and Jarque–Bera (J–B) test statistics, we conclude that the variables are obviously not normally distributed. The results of the augmented Dickey–Fuller test exhibited in Table 1 do not reject that all variables are strictly stationary. Thus, on the premise of the strictly stationary series, we proceed with the causality analysis.

Table 1. Descriptive statistics and the augmented Dickey–Fuller (ADF) test.

	Mean	Stdev	Skewness	Kurtosis	J-B	ADF Test
RD_t	0.627 ***	0.275	4.057 ***	35.136 ***	732,071.353 ***	−8.9165 ***
SV_t	1.000 ***	1.778	8.723	101.069 ***	5,921,984.155 ***	−9.4998 ***
MP_t	0.025 ***	0.988	−0.508 ***	15.633 ***	138,157.710 ***	−82.3209 ***
ADS_t	−0.018 ***	0.876	−1.206 ***	3.921 ***	11,929.823 ***	−7.7651 ***

Note: RD_t, SV_t, MP_t, and ADS_t refer to equity return dispersion, stock market volatility, equity market premium, and business conditions index, respectively. This table reports the summary statistics including the mean, standard deviation (s.d.), skewness, excess kurtosis, Jarque–Bera (JB) test, and the augmented Dickey–Fuller test. The symbols *, **, and *** denote the significance at the 10%, 5%, and 1% levels, respectively.

4.2. Bivariate Causality Tests

We begin our discussion by presenting the findings from bivariate causality tests. Table 2 presents the findings for the bivariate linear Granger causality tests. The optimal lag length for each case based on the well-known information criteria, such as Bayesian Information Criterion (BIC) and Akaike Information Criterion(AIC), are also presented along with the test statistics. Examining the findings in Panel A, we observe significant causality from equity return dispersion to both the stock market volatility and equity market premium, consistent with the evidence in Angelidis et al. [2]. Interestingly, however, we see that the causality from return dispersion becomes insignificant after controlling for business conditions measured by the ADS_t index. Following the suggestion by Angelidis et al. [2] that a relatively high return dispersion predicts a deterioration in business conditions, we distinguished between good and bad business conditions and created two additional variables $ADS1_t$ ($ADS2_t$) representing the positive (negative) ADS_t business conditions index values, respectively. However, we see in Panel A that differentiating between good and bad business conditions still yields insignificant causal effects from return dispersion, suggesting that business conditions serve as the primary driver of stock market volatility, rendering the predictive power of return dispersion insignificant.

The findings in Panel B further support these observations, suggesting that business conditions have significant predictive power over both stock market volatility and equity return dispersion. However, interestingly, the predictive power of business conditions is concentrated on contractionary periods only, suggesting asymmetric causal interactions between business conditions, equity return dispersion and stock market volatility. Overall, the findings in Table 2 show that the level of economic activity plays a significant role in studying linear causality from return dispersion to both stock market volatility and equity market premium.

Table 2. Bivariate linear causality tests.

	Panel A: The Predictive Power of Equity Return Dispersion			
	$RD_t \rightarrow SV_t$	$RD_t \rightarrow MP_t$	$RD_t \rightarrow SV_t \mid ADS_t$	$RD_t \rightarrow MP_t \mid ADS_t$
Lags	15	9	16	16
F-Stat	188.760 ***	3.196 ***	9.716×10^{-7}	1.136×10^{-8}
	$RD_t \rightarrow SV_t \mid ADS1_t$	$RD_t \rightarrow SV_t \mid ADS2_t$	$RD_t \rightarrow MP_t \mid ADS1_t$	$RD_t \rightarrow MP_t \mid ADS2_t$
Lags	9	9	9	9
F-Stat	1.729×10^{-6}	1.714×10^{-6}	1.744×10^{-8}	1.749×10^{-8}
	Panel B: The Predictive Power of Business Conditions			
	$ADS1_t \rightarrow SV_t$	$ADS2_t \rightarrow SV_t$	$ADS1_t \rightarrow MP_t$	$ADS2_t \rightarrow MP_t$
Lags	16	16	9	9
F-Stat	1.146	3.579 ***	0.738	1.768
	$ADS_t \rightarrow RD_t$	$ADS1_t \rightarrow RD_t$	$ADS2_t \rightarrow RD_t$	
Lags	9	9	9	
F-Stat	4.068 ***	0.513	5.967 ***	

Note: RD_t, SV_t, MP_t and ADS_t refer to equity return dispersion, stock market volatility, equity market premium, and business conditions index, respectively. $ADS1_t$ ($ADS2_t$) represents the positive (negative) business conditions index values, respectively. The notation "$\rightarrow$" indicates causality and "$RD_t \rightarrow SV_t \mid ADS_t$" indicates causality from RD_t to SV_t after controlling for ADS_t. *, **, *** indicate significance at 5, 1, and 0.1 percent level, respectively.

Table 3 presents the results from the nonlinearity tests based on Hui et al. [35] presented in Section 3.2.2. The tests indicate significant evidence of nonlinearity in all-time series at the highest significance level, justifying the use of subsequent nonlinear causality tests. Table 4 presents the results from bivariate nonlinear causality tests. Examining the results in Panels A and B, we observe a significant linear causal relationship from return dispersion to both stock market volatility and equity market premium even after including the ADS_t business conditions index. Furthermore, we observe in Panel C that there exists significant causality from business conditions to return dispersion, but with some degree of asymmetry such that expansionary (contractionary) market states are associated with a low (high) level of equity return dispersion, indicating a higher (lower) degree of directional similarity in stock returns, respectively. To that end, the findings from bivariate tests clearly indicate that the predictive power of equity return dispersion over stock market volatility and equity premium is largely asymmetric with regime specific patterns. This finding is indeed significant for not only stock market forecasting models, but also in the pricing of stock options, as volatility forecasts are crucial in pricing derivatives as well as the estimation of optimal hedge ratios.

Table 3. Nonlinearity Tests.

	ADS_t	$ADS1_t$	$ADS2_t$	RD_t	SV_t	MP_t
Lags	11	10	16	10	15	2
T-Stat	7.734 ***	7.845 ***	7.893 ***	8.970 ***	3.574 ***	8.547 ***

Note: RD_t, SV_t, MP_t and ADS_t refer to equity return dispersion, stock market volatility, equity market premium, and business conditions index, respectively. $ADS1_t$ ($ADS2_t$) represents the positive (negative) business conditions index, respectively; *** indicate significance at 0.1 percent level.

Table 4. Bivariate nonlinear causality tests.

	Panel A: The Predictability of Stock Market Volatility			
Lags	$RD_t \rightarrow SV_t$	$RD_t \rightarrow SV_t \mid ADS_t$	$RD_t \rightarrow SV_t \mid ADS1_t$	$RD_t \rightarrow SV_t \mid ADS2_t$
1	7.879 ***	7.8190 ***	7.758 ***	7.824 ***
2	7.718 ***	7.665 ***	7.533 ***	7.525 ***
3	7.637 ***	7.659 ***	7.533 ***	7.621 ***
4	7.908 ***	7.871 ***	7.745 ***	7.772 ***
5	7.461 ***	7.484 ***	7.309 ***	7.449 ***
6	7.155 ***	7.207 ***	7.141 ***	7.279 ***
7	6.770 ***	6.813 ***	6.611 ***	6.662 ***
8	6.617 ***	6.721 ***	6.461 ***	6.535 ***
9	5.984 ***	6.169 ***	5.741 ***	5.884 ***
10	5.918 ***	6.067 ***	5.646 ***	5.742 ***

	Panel B: The Predictability of Equity Market Premium			
Lags	$RD_t \rightarrow MP_t$	$RD_t \rightarrow MP_t \mid ADS_t$	$RD_t \rightarrow MP_t \mid ADS1_t$	$RD_t \rightarrow MP_t \mid ADS2_t$
1	11.365 ***	11.379 ***	11.363 ***	11.302 ***
2	12.910 ***	13.079 ***	12.904 ***	12.877 ***
3	12.878 ***	13.053 ***	12.867 ***	12.928 ***
4	13.357 ***	13.643 ***	13.364 ***	13.428 ***
5	13.275 ***	13.693 ***	13.272 ***	13.420 ***
6	12.519 ***	12.931 ***	12.527 ***	12.694 ***
7	11.823 ***	12.206 ***	11.844 ***	12.038 ***
8	11.805 ***	12.155 ***	11.807 ***	12.048 ***
9	11.716 ***	11.996 ***	11.695 ***	11.950 ***
10	11.104 ***	11.405 ***	11.068 ***	11.321 ***

	Panel C: The Predictive Power of Business Conditions		
Lags	$ADS_t \rightarrow RD_t$	$ADS1_t \rightarrow RD_t$	$ADS2_t \rightarrow RD_t$
1	−1.122	−5.676 ***	1.755 *
2	−1.366	−6.626 ***	1.808 *
3	−1.352	−6.930 ***	2.627 **
4	−2.015 *	−6.917 ***	2.317 *
5	−0.820	−4.650 ***	2.711 **
6	−1.718 *	−5.231 ***	2.311 *
7	−2.147 *	−5.412 ***	2.425 **
8	−2.148 *	−4.913 ***	1.708 *
9	−1.919 *	−4.669 ***	1.928 *
10	−1.987 *	−4.427 ***	1.053

Note: RD_t, SV_t, MP_t and ADS_t refer to equity return dispersion, stock market volatility, equity market premium, and business conditions index, respectively. The notation "$\rightarrow$" indicates causality and "$RD_t \rightarrow SV_t \mid ADS_t$" indicates causality from RD_t to SV after controlling for ADS_t. *, **, *** indicate significance at 5, 1, and 0.1 percent level, respectively.

4.3. Multivariate Granger Causality Tests

Having established evidence suggesting that the level of economic activity plays a significant role in studying causality from return dispersion to both stock market volatility and equity market premium, we now proceed with the multivariate causality tests. Table 5 presents the findings for the multivariate linear Granger causality tests explained in Section 3.2.3. We observe in Panel A that multivariate linear Granger causality exists from the return dispersion and business conditions to stock market volatility at the highest significance level, while the same does not hold for equity market premium, regardless of the distinction between expansionary or contractionary business conditions.

Table 5. Multivariate linear causality tests.

	Panel A: The Predictability of Stock Market Volatility		
	$RD_t+ADS_t{\rightarrow}SV_t$	$RD_t+ADS1_t{\rightarrow}SV_t$	$RD_t+ADS2_t{\rightarrow}SV_t$
Lags	10	9	9
LR	535.909 ***	560.136 ***	573.599 ***
	Panel B: The Predictability of Equity Market Premium		
	$RD_t+ADS_t{\rightarrow}MP_t$	$RD_t+ADS1_t{\rightarrow}MP_t$	$RD_t+ADS2_t{\rightarrow}MP_t$
Lags	10	9	9
LR	37.812	37.456	39.096

Note: RD_t, SV_t, MP_t and ADS_t refer to equity return dispersion, stock market volatility, equity market premium, and business conditions index, respectively. $ADS1_t (ADS2_t)$ represents the positive (negative) business conditions index values, respectively. The notation "$RD_t+ADS_t{\rightarrow}X$" indicates RD_t and ADS_t together predict variable X. *, **, *** indicate significance at 5, 1, and 0.1 percent level, respectively.

On the other hand, similar to the findings observed for the bivariate case, when we examine the findings from the multivariate nonlinear tests, presented in Table 6, we observe that equity return dispersion and business conditions together have significant predictive power over both the stock market volatility and equity market premium at the highest statistical significance level. The predictive power of RD_t and ADS_t together is robust regardless of the state of economic activity, implied by significant findings for both $ADS1_t$ and $ADS2_t$. To that end, our findings underline the significance of nonlinearity in the causal relationship between return dispersion and stock market premium and volatility but also suggest that equity return dispersion along with a measure of economic conditions can be used to improve forecasting models for both return and volatility of stock market returns.

Table 6. Multivariate nonlinear causality tests.

	Panel A: The Predictability of Stock Market Volatility		
Lags	$RD_t+ADS_t{\rightarrow}SV_t$	$RD_t+ADS1_t{\rightarrow}SV_t$	$RD_t+ADS2_t{\rightarrow}SV_t$
1	7.706 ***	7.661 ***	7.614 ***
2	7.529 ***	7.454 ***	7.217 ***
3	7.140 ***	7.286 ***	7.037 ***
4	6.736 ***	7.496 ***	6.565 ***
5	6.321 ***	6.954 ***	5.967 ***
6	5.818 ***	6.610 ***	5.694 ***
7	5.380 ***	6.107 ***	4.963 ***
8	5.447 ***	6.016 ***	4.969 ***
9	4.731 ***	5.387 ***	4.095 ***
10	4.665 ***	5.168 ***	4.108 ***
	Panel B: The Predictability of Equity Market Premium		
Lags	$RD_t+ADS_t{\rightarrow}MP_t$	$RD_t+ADS1_t{\rightarrow}MP_t$	$RD_t+ADS2_t{\rightarrow}MP_t$
1	11.271 ***	11.296 ***	11.260 ***
2	12.523 ***	12.655 ***	12.280 ***
3	12.557 ***	12.594 ***	12.370 ***
4	13.092 ***	12.988 ***	12.846 ***
5	12.590 ***	12.727 ***	11.980 ***
6	11.753 ***	11.797 ***	11.288 ***
7	10.6764 ***	10.733 ***	10.478 ***
8	10.749 ***	10.493 ***	10.584 ***
9	10.662 ***	10.577 ***	10.141 ***
10	10.075 ***	9.923 ***	9.601 ***

Note: RD_t, SV_t, MP_t and ADS_t refer to equity return dispersion, stock market volatility, equity market premium, and business conditions index, respectively. $ADS1_t (ADS2_t)$ represents the positive (negative) business conditions index values, respectively. The notation "$RD_t+ADS_t{\rightarrow}X$" indicates RD_t and ADS_t together predict variable X. *, **, *** indicate significance at 5, 1, and 0.1 percent level, respectively.

Angelidis et al. [2] showed that a relatively high return dispersion predicts a deterioration in business conditions, establishing a link between return dispersion and the business cycle. Therefore, one might be tempted to conclude that the predictive power of return dispersion over stock market volatility is, in fact, driven by its predictive power over the business cycle, which, in turn, is shown to have predictive power over stock market volatility (Choudhry et al. [6]). To this end, multivariate tests allow us to check the robustness of the predictive power of return dispersion by controlling for business conditions in our tests. Therefore, the evidence of causality from return dispersion to stock market volatility even after controlling for business conditions suggests that return dispersion conveys incremental information over stock market volatility beyond which is captured by business conditions. In this sense, it supports the previous findings in Demirer and Jategaonkar [18] and others that return dispersion is more likely to capture shocks related to fundamental economic restructuring, rather than the business cycle. Overall, multivariate tests add new insight that one cannot capture via bivariate counterparts, suggesting that return dispersion possesses incremental predictive content over stock market volatility that business conditions alone cannot capture, and this is an important consideration to improve the accuracy of volatility forecasting models.

5. Conclusions

This paper contributes to the literature on stock market predictability by exploring the causal relationships between equity return dispersion, stock market volatility, and excess returns via multivariate nonlinear causality tests recently developed by Bai et al. [7–9]. Performing a combination of linear vs. nonlinear and bivariate vs. multivariate causality tests, we show that linear causality tests generally fail to detect causal effects from return dispersion to excess market returns and volatility. Both bivariate and multivariate nonlinear causality tests, however, yield significant evidence of causality from return dispersion to both stock market volatility and equity premium, even after controlling for the state of the economy. Overall, our findings suggest that both return dispersion and business conditions are valid joint forecasters of both the stock market volatility and excess market return and that return dispersion indeed possesses incremental information regarding future stock return dynamics beyond which can be explained by the state of the economy.

The findings have significant practical implications for the forecasting of stock market volatility dynamics with a possible extension to forecasting risk premia along the lines of Stivers and Sun [15]. As Angelidis et al. [2] note, return dispersion provides a timely and model free estimation of risk. Considering our finding that return dispersion captures incremental information about stock market volatility beyond which can be captured by the level of economic activity, one can use this model-free statistic to improve volatility forecasting models; however, that can only be achieved using nonlinear specifications, as our findings imply. Similarly, the fact that return dispersion offers a timely estimate of risk also allows one to update volatility forecasts in a timely and relatively model-free framework. Furthermore, given the integrated nature of global markets, one can also use return dispersion measures across markets in order to use cross-market dispersion information to improve volatility forecasts in a multi-market setting. This could also lead the path to improved models of co-movement in which return dispersion is used across multiple markets.

There are many directions in which our paper can be extended. One possible extension could include forecasting stock market volatility from equity return dispersion. Future studies could also apply the Copulas approach or other approaches to examine the relationship between equity return dispersion and stock market volatility. So far, to the best of our knowledge, there is no theory explaining whether it is equity return dispersion that causes stock market volatility or it is stock market volatility that causes equity return dispersion or other variables that cause both equity return dispersion and stock market volatility. Thus, another interesting extension is to develop an economic theory to explain the causality between equity return dispersion and stock market volatility. One possible explanation is that it is due to investors' conservative and representative heuristics that relate to the causality of both equity return dispersion and stock market volatility; see, for example, Lam et al. [38,39], Fung et al. [40], Guo et al. [41], and the references therein for more information.

Author Contributions: All authors contributed equally in the paper.

Acknowledgments: The authors are grateful to the Editor-in-Chief, and anonymous referees for substantive comments that have significantly improved this manuscript. The fourth author would like to thank Robert B. Miller and Howard E. Thompson for their continuous guidance and encouragement. This research has been partially supported by grants from Southern Illinois University Edwardsville, University of Pretoria, Northeast Normal University, Asia University, China Medical University Hospital, The Hang Seng University of Hong Kong, the Research Grants Council of Hong Kong (Project Number 12500915), and Ministry of Science and Technology (MOST, Project Numbers 106-2410-H-468-002 and 107-2410-H-468-002-MY3), Taiwan.

References

1. Connolly, R.; Stivers, C. Information content and other characteristics of the daily cross-sectional dispersion in stock returns. *J. Empir. Financ.* **2006**, *13*, 79–112. [CrossRef]
2. Angelidis, T.; Sakkas, A.; Tessaromatis, N. Stock market dispersion, the business cycle and expected factor returns. *J. Bank. Financ.* **2015**, *59*, 265–279. [CrossRef]
3. Maio, P. Cross-sectional return dispersion and the equity premium. *J. Financ. Mark.* **2016**, *29*, 87–109. [CrossRef]
4. Hamilton, J.D.; Lin, G. Stock market volatility and the business cycle. *J. Appl. Econ.* **1996**, *11*, 573–593. [CrossRef]
5. Schwert, G.W. Stock Volatility during the Recent Financial Crisis. *Eur. Financ. Manag.* **2011**, *17*, 789–805. [CrossRef]
6. Choudhry, T.; Papadimitriou, F.I.; Shabi, S. Stock market volatility and business cycle: Evidence from linear and nonlinear causality tests. *J. Bank. Financ.* **2016**, *66*, 89–101. [CrossRef]
7. Bai, Z.D.; Wong, W.K.; Zhang, B.Z. Multivariate linear and nonlinear causality tests. *Math. Comput. Simul.* **2010**, *81*, 5–17. [CrossRef]
8. Bai, Z.D.; Li, H.; Wong, W.K.; Zhang, B.Z. Multivariate Causality Tests with Simulation and Application. *Stat. Probab. Lett.* **2011**, *81*, 1063–1071. [CrossRef]
9. Bai, Z.; Hui, Y.; Jiang, D.; Lv, Z.; Wong, W.K.; Zheng, S. A new test of multivariate nonlinear causality. *PLoS ONE* **2018**, *13*, e0185155. [CrossRef]
10. Chow, S.C.; Cunado, J.; Gupta, R.; Wong, W.K. Causal Relationships between Economic Policy Uncertainty and Housing Market Returns in China and India: Evidence from Linear and Nonlinear Panel and Time Series Models. *Stud. Nonlinear Dyn. Econom.* **2018**, *22*. [CrossRef]
11. Christie, W.; Huang, R. *Equity Return Dispersions*; Work Paper; Vanderbilt University: Nashville, TN, USA, 1994.
12. Duffee, G.R. *Asymmetric Cross-Sectional Dispersion in Stock Returns: Evidence and Implications*; U.C. Berkeley: Berkeley, CA, USA, 2001.
13. Loungani, P.; Rush, R.; Tave, W. Stock market dispersion and unemployment. *J. Monet. Econ.* **1990**, *25*, 367–388. [CrossRef]
14. Stivers, C.T. Firm-level return dispersion and the future volatility of aggregate stock market returns. *J. Financ. Mark.* **2003**, *6*, 389–411. [CrossRef]
15. Stivers, C.; Sun, L. Cross-Sectional Return Dispersion and Time Variation in Value and Momentum Premiums. *J. Financ. Quant. Anal.* **2010**, *45*, 987–1014. [CrossRef]
16. Bhootra, A. Are momentum profits driven by the cross-sectional dispersion in expected stock returns? *J. Financ. Mark.* **2011**, *14*, 494–513. [CrossRef]
17. Jiang, X. Return dispersion and expected returns. *Financ. Mark. Portfol. Manag.* **2010**, *24*, 107–135. [CrossRef]
18. Demirer, R.; Jategaonkar, S. The Conditional Relation Between Dispersion and Return. *Rev. Financ. Econ.* **2013**, *22*, 125–134. [CrossRef]
19. Demirer, R.; Jategaonkar, S.P.; Khalifa, A.A. Oil price risk exposure and the cross-section of stock returns: The case of net exporting countries. *Energy Econ.* **2015**, *49*, 132–140. [CrossRef]
20. Lillo, F.; Mantegna, R.N. Variety and Volatility in Financial Markets. *Phys. Rev. E* **2000**, *62*, 6126–6134. [CrossRef]

21. Solnik, B.; Roulet, J. Dispersion as cross-sectional correlation. *Financ. Anal. J.* **2000**, *56*, 54–61. [CrossRef]
22. Baur, D. Multivariate market association and its extremes. *J. Int. Financ. Markets Inst. Money* **2006**, *16*, 355–369. [CrossRef]
23. Statman, M.; Scheid, J. Global Diversification. *J. Invest. Manag.* **2005**, *3*, 55–63. [CrossRef]
24. Statman, M.; Scheid, J. Correlation, Return Gaps, and the Benefits of Diversification. *J. Portfol. Manag.* **2008**, *34*, 132–139. [CrossRef]
25. Demirer, R. Can Advanced Markets Help Diversify Risks in Frontier Markets? Evidence from Gulf Arab Stock Markets. *Res. Int. Bus. Financ.* **2013**, *29*, 77–98. [CrossRef]
26. Eiling, E.; Gerard, B. *Dispersion, Equity Return Correlations and Market Integration*; University of Toronto: Toronto, ON, Canada, 2011.
27. Goyal, A.; Santa-Clara, P. Idiosyncratic risk matters. *J. Financ.* **2003**, *58*, 975–1006. [CrossRef]
28. Bali, T.; Cakici, N.; Yan, X.; Zhang, Z. Does idiosyncratic risk really matter? *J. Financ.* **2005**, *60*, 905–929. [CrossRef]
29. Pollet, J.; Wilson, M. Average correlation and stock market returns. *J. Financ. Econ.* **2010**, *96*, 364–380. [CrossRef]
30. Garcia, R.; Mantilla-Garcia, D.; Martellini, L. A model-free measure of aggregate idiosyncratic volatility and the prediction of market returns. *J. Financ. Quant. Anal.* **2014**, *49*, 1133–1165. [CrossRef]
31. Chichernea, D.C.; Holder, A.D.; Petkevich, A. Does return dispersion explain the accrual and investment anomalies? *J. Account. Econ.* **2015**, *60*, 133–148. [CrossRef]
32. Demirer, R.; Omay, T.; Yuksel, A.; Yuksel, A. Global Risk Aversion and Emerging Market Return Comovements. *Econ. Lett.* **2018**, *173*, 118–121. [CrossRef]
33. Aruoba, S.; Diebold, F.; Scotti, C. Real-time measurement of business condition. *J. Bus. Econ. Stat.* **2009**, *27*, 417–427. [CrossRef]
34. Granger, C.W. Investigating causal relations by econometric models and cross-spectral methods. *Econometrica* **1969**, *37*, 424–438. [CrossRef]
35. Hui, Y.C.; Wong, W.K.; Bai, Z.D.; Zhu, Z.Z. A New Nonlinearity Test to Circumvent the Limitation of Volterra Expansion with Application. *J. Korean Stat. Soc.* **2017**, *46*, 365–374. [CrossRef]
36. Denker, M.; Keller, G. On U-statistics and v. mise'statistics for weakly dependent processes. *Zeitschrift für Wahrscheinlichkeitstheorie und verwandte Gebiete* **1983**, *64*, 505–522. [CrossRef]
37. Dickey, D.A.; Fuller, W.A. Distribution of the estimators for autoregressive time series with a unit root. *J. Am. Stat. Assoc.* **1979**, *74*, 427–431.
38. Lam, K.; Liu, T.S.; Wong, W.K. A pseudo-Bayesian model in financial decision making with implications to market volatility, under- and overreaction. *Eur. J. Oper. Res.* **2010**, *203*, 166–175. [CrossRef]
39. Lam, K.; Liu, T.S.; Wong, W.K. A New Pseudo Bayesian Model with Implications to Financial Anomalies and Investors' Behaviors. *J. Behav. Financ.* **2012**, *13*, 93–107. [CrossRef]
40. Fung, E.S.; Lam, K.; Siu, T.K.; Wong, W.K. A New Pseudo Bayesian Model for Financial Crisis. *J. Risk Financ. Manag.* **2011**, *4*, 42–72. [CrossRef]
41. Guo, X.; McAleer, M.; Wong, W.K.; Zhu, L.X. A Bayesian approach to excess volatility, short-term underreaction and long-term overreaction during financial crises, North American. *J. Econ. Financ.* **2017**, *42*, 346–358.

11

Relationship among HIV/AIDS Prevalence, Human Capital, Good Governance and Sustainable Development: Empirical Evidence from Sub-Saharan Africa

Jamiu Adetola Odugbesan [1] and Husam Rjoub [2,*]

[1] Department of Business Administration, Faculty of Economics and Administrative Sciences, Cyprus International University, Haspolat, Mersin 10, Turkey; odugbesanadetola@gmail.com

[2] Department of Accounting and Finance, Faculty of Economics and Administrative Sciences, Cyprus International University, Haspolat, Mersin 10, Turkey

* Correspondence: hrjoub@ciu.edu.tr

Abstract: Sub-Saharan Africa is regarded as the region that accommodates about 75% of the world HIV/AIDS prevalence as of 2016. Research on the relationship between the epidemic and sustainable development is scant in this part of the world, as available literature is dominated by studies that focus on HIV and economic growth. Therefore, this study examines the relationship between sustainable development and HIV/AIDS prevalence, along with other determinants of sustainable development, such as good governance and human capital in 26 sub-Saharan Africa countries over a 27-year period from 1990—2016. The pooled mean group (PMG) estimator was employed for analysis after it was confirmed by the Hausman test for the estimation of the relationship among the variables. The results revealed a unidirectional long-run and significant relationship between HIV/AIDS prevalence and sustainable development, human capital and good governance, and human capital and sustainable development. Also, a bidirectional long-run relationship was found between good governance and HIV/AIDS prevalence. Estimation of subgroups provides a robustness check for our findings. Therefore, the paper gives new insight to the government of sub-Saharan Africa countries and major stakeholders about how to attain sustainable development in the region, while intensifying efforts on reducing HIV/AIDS prevalence, and at the same time ensuring effective good governance and human capital development.

Keywords: sustainable development; HIV/AIDS; human capital; good governance; sub-Saharan Africa

1. Introduction

Globally, the prevalence of HIV/AIDS constitutes a hindrance to the advancement of human development and remains a major concern for researchers, stakeholders, and policymakers [1]. With reference to the report of Joint United Nations Programme on HIV/AIDS [2], it was estimated at the end of 2016 that 34.5 million adults globally have been infected with HIV/AIDS virus, while about one million died from AIDS-related diseases. In the same year, about 25.73 million (almost 75% of the world HIV/AIDS prevalence) people were HIV/AIDS carrier in Africa, out of which 741,000 died as a result of AIDS-related illnesses. [2].

Today, the HIV/AIDS epidemics remains one of the challenges facing Africa continent, as it is far more than a health issue, and still requires more efforts so as not to hinder the sustainable development of the region [3,4]. However, in order to avert the reverse of the development, the issue of sustainable development has taken a center stage position, both in the academia and among various stakeholders and policymakers.

It was noted that the world is facing great challenges in terms of development sustainability. On one part, there is a high number of people that are living below standard, even when there is overdependence on natural resources, most especially in the developing countries. On the other part, there are an important economic (poverty, inequality, etc.), social (health), and environmental (climate change) crises, which sometimes culminate into an epidemic and result in death [5,6].

Though studies abound on the definition of sustainable development, a definition by World Bank simply put it as development path or structured principles that could be maintained to ensure that total welfare of the people does not decline along the development path [7]. An important point of reference for sustainable development is the report published in 1987 by Brundtland Commission entitled *Our Common Future* [8]. According to this report, sustainable development is conceptualized as the actions or principles put in place that will enable the people to meet their present needs without compromising the ability of future generations to meet their own needs [8].

Achieving sustainable development involves economic, social, and quality environment. These three pillars must be evenly and wholly integrated within the process of improving development. In respect of social dimension, *Our Common Future* reports argue that sustainable development requires meeting the requisite needs of the citizens and extending to them the opportunity to accomplish their aspirations for a better life [9]. It is worthy to note that the report did not limit the pillars of sustainable development to the economic, social, and environment, but also includes other aspects that were not broadly considered, for instance, good governance. It is believed that such equity in achieving sustainable development will be enhanced by an effective political system and rule of law that secure effective citizen participation in decision-making.

The sustainable development agenda for 2030 has a health issue at the center [10]. One of the goals of this agenda is "to ensure healthy lives and promote well-being for all citizens at all ages." In order to meet this target, there is a need to examine the various factors that could hinder the achievement of the goals. Among the ones highlighted which could do this is the infectious disease (e.g. HIV/AIDS) [10]. Health is as inherently significant as human rights and is also important to achieving the pillars of sustainable development (economic development, environmental sustainability, social inclusion, and good governance). Sustainable development will be elusive in the absence of health and productive population. There is a report which details that combating the spread of HIV/AIDS is critical to human progress, as this disease disproportionately affect the development potential of dozens of countries [11]. HIV/AIDS has a complex linkage with poverty and, in turn, to the larger sustainable development [12].

There is no doubt that the consequences of the epidemic in sub-Saharan Africa would have a great impact on sustainable development in the region if the scenario continues.

2. Literature Review

The studies on HIV/AIDS and economic growth have been prolific. Among them is the one on HIV and economic growth in 30 sub-Saharan Africa countries, which revealed that AIDS has a significant negative impact on GDP [13]. Reference [13] found that the negative impact of the epidemic will reduce the growth rate of per capital income in the average number of countries studied and concluded that the larger impact will be felt on the 10 countries with the highest HIV prevalence in those 30 sub-Saharan Africa countries. A similar study was conducted in South Africa, which is among the countries with the highest HIV prevalence in sub-Saharan Africa. The study corroborated over Reference [13] and concluded that in the presence of HIV prevalence, South Africa economic growth will decline in GDP by about 17% [14]. This finding was corroborated by subsequent studies [15,16]. In 2000, a similar study was conducted which forecasted that the situation of HIV in Lesotho will cause the GDP of the country to decline by 2010 [17]. Meanwhile, Maijama and Samusidin [16] found in their study that the current HIV prevalence in sub-Saharan Africa has a negative effect on GDP per capital growth. A similar study was previously conducted by Augier and Yaly [18], which modeled diseases with the highest mortality rates, among which is AIDS as it affects economic growth. The result showed that poor health due to these infectious diseases has effects on decreasing economic growth of any country where the epidemic is prevalent. However, a contrary view was held by another author on HIV/AIDS. His study found no statistically significant impact of HIV/AIDS on GDP [19]. Meanwhile, Afawubo and Mathey [20] conducted a study on the factors influencing HIV/AIDS prevalence. The study found that human capital has a short-run causal impact on HIV prevalence but found a negative relationship between HIV and economic growth and concluded that GDP growth is not a driver for HIV prevalence across the West African countries [20]. Alemu et al. investigated the effect of HIV on the manufacturing sector in Lesotho and South Africa. The study concluded that there is a negative significant impact of the HIV on the productivity growth of the two countries [21]. This study was in agreement with Young, who revealed a significant impact of HIV/AIDS on human capital which, in turn, affects economic growth in sub-Saharan Africa [22]. The subsequent study established a long-term impact of HIV/AIDS on economic growth [23]. However, contrary results were found when studies were conducted on how much of a threat a mature AIDS epidemic is to economic growth. The study revealed that AIDS is not likely to threaten economic growth, either through human capital or accumulation channels. [17,19,24]. The relationship between HIV/AIDS prevalence and human capital in sub-Saharan Africa was found to be negative and statistically significant [25]. These findings were not different from the findings of other authors, who concluded in their studies that poor health as a result of an infectious disease has an impact on the economic growth of any country where it is prevalent [18,26].

In a more recent study, several authors empirically established the impact of HIV/AIDS prevalence on economic growth [15,16,27,28]. Their studies found a long-run relationship between HIV/AIDS prevalence and economic growth and argued that, in the long-run, HIV/AIDS will have a devastating impact on economic growth. In another dimension, the impact of HIV/AIDS on human capital was empirically examined and the results showed that HIV/AIDS prevalence have a long-run impact on human capital [16,20]. The argument from the studies was that as the HIV/AIDS prevalence increases, the country human capital decreases. Meanwhile, Shuaibu and Oladapo [29] were able to establish a long-run relationship between human capital economic growth and good governance in their study on Africa countries using a panel model. The study argued that economic growth and good governance are drivers for human capital development. In all the reviewed literature, none of the studies attempted to model the HIV and sustainable development.

Meanwhile, there are multiple dimension of views on sustainable economic development and good governance. Of importance to this study is the view of Brautigam on governance and economy which put it as a neutral concept, meaning "the political direction and control exercised over the actions of the members, citizens or inhabitants of communities, societies and states" [30] (p.3). The author argued in his book that the impact of good governance on a country economic growth cannot be neglected. In his view, political accountability, an effective rule of law, and transparency are some of the significant ingredients of good governance that impact on economic development. Good governance is considered to be the recent concept that recognized the functions of the state in the economy, where the involvement of all stakeholders is significant in the process of achieving sustainable economic development [7]. Stojanovic et al. noted that the central place of development policy is occupied with the model of good governance, which has become the cornerstone of sustainable development [31].

The relationship between good governance and development sustainability received great attention in scholarly enquiry [7,31]. The literature on the relationship is mixed, as there are both opposing and supporting views on the issue. An observation was made that, while few studies addressed the influence of good governance on sustainable development, some authors found that good governance is not a determinant factor for sustainable development [7]. Those studies found that relationship opined that good governance to demand voice and accountability to the citizen and rule of law guiding economic transactions, regulatory quality, control of corruption, the ability of the government to be effective, and an environment devoid of war/terrorism.

Various studies established a relationship between sustainable economic development and good governance [7,32,33], while some show no relationship between the two variables [34,35]. Though Stojanovic et al. revealed a statistical significance, direction, and significance of the effect of good governance, the study, however, suggested that there is no "one size fits all" model of good governance [31]. In view of the mixed results on the relationship between good governance and sustainable development, it is pertinent to follow the findings of Stojanovic et al. and examine the relationship between good governance and sustainable development in different regions.

The impact of human capital on sustainable development cannot be downplayed. Various literature abound on the human capital and sustainable development. The linkage among population, economic growth, employment, education, and sustainable development was examined and the study revealed that human capital is significant to sustainable development and efforts to ensure the synergy depends on the effective approach adopted [36]. This was corroborated by another author who opined that human capital faster rate of development of the society contributes to the sustainability of the society and ensures equitable distribution of development benefits [37]. Scicchitano [38] demonstrated in his study that human capital composition (research and development), which was in the past not considered in the endogenous growth model, was found to be significant in determining economic growth rate. Also, it was found in the recent studies that human capital increase led to sustainable economic growth [39,40]. Similarly, in EU states, a study was conducted and found that human capital is directly influencing sustainable development [41]. In a reversed case, Shuaibu and Oladapo [29] found economic growth as one of the drivers for human capital development.

It is evident from the literature reviewed that studies on sustainable economic development and human capital has not been well researched in sub-Saharan Africa countries. The available ones are country-specific and are primarily focused on the traditional parameters of measuring country economic development (i.e., GDP); human development index (HDI), and educational attainment for human capital [42]. The study of Shuaibu and Oladayo was tilted study toward determining factors contributing to human capital development using 33 African countries. The study confirmed a significant long-run relationship between health and human capital development and also institutions (good governance) [29]. However, it argues that short-term gains may be achieved through enhanced institutional quality.

The idea that HIV/AIDS may have a significant impact on sustainable development is understandable, for the simple reason that "health is wealth." As a consequence, one would expect HIV/AIDS to have an influence on sustainable development. It is therefore surprising that although there is an extensive empirical literature on sustainable development, HIV/AIDS prevalence, and economic growth in developing countries, most especially African countries where the epidemic is ravaging, research on how the HIV/AIDS could impact on sustainable development are scant.

To date, however, and to the best of our knowledge, the relationship between HIV/AIDS and sustainable economic growth in sub-Saharan Africa countries has not been thoroughly dealt with in empirical literature, and this study will contribute to the literature on this important topic.

The main thrust of this paper is to analyze the relationships among HIV/AIDS, good governance, human capital, and sustainable development in sub-Saharan Africa. This study will investigate through the long and short-run dynamic relationship following the sustainable development framework proposed by World Bank. Consequently, it will contribute empirically to the literature on the relationship between HIV/AIDS and sustainable development in sub-Saharan Africa by employing a more recent panel data estimator by Pesaran et al.

3. Data and Methods

3.1. Data

In order to achieve the objective of the study, variables such as HIV/AIDS prevalence rate, country-level governance index, and human capital index were selected to examine their relationship with sustainable economic development. The adjusted net savings was measured as the gross national savings, less the value of consumption of fixed capital. This variable was established to be a good indicator for sustainable development [43–46]. Prevalence of HIV/AIDS, measured as the percentage of people aged between 15—49 who are infected with HIV, was utilized in previous studies [1,3,13–15,19]. The country-level governance index was measured with six indices: Voice and accountability, rule of law, regulatory quality, control of corruption, government effectiveness and political stability, and absence of violence/terrorism (see Table 1). In order to compute the indices into a single variable, the average rank of each country in the panel for the six indices was computed for individual years. This index was used by previous researchers [7,31]. For measuring human capital, we employed human capital index [47]. This was employed based on the arguments in the literature on the non-consensus on the human capital index, which prompted the Penn World Table to introduce another index in PWT version 8 that was computed using the data from Barro and Lee and an assumed rate of return to education based on Mincer equation estimates [47,48].

These variables are sourced from the World Development Bank Indicator [49], Word Governance Indicator [50], and Penn World Table [47]. The data are yearly and cover the period 1990—2016. The countries included in the panel are 26 sub-Saharan African countries (see Appendix Table A1). The choice of countries in the panel was based on the availability of data for the variables included in the study during the observed period.

Table 1. Description of variables.

Code Name	Variable	Proxy	Definition	Measurement Unit	Source
HPREV	HIV/AIDS	HIV/AIDS prevalence	Prevalence of HIV refers to the percentage of people ages 15—49 who are infected with HIV	Percentage	World Bank Development Indicators
HCI	Human Capital	Human capital index	Human capital is measured as the discounted value of earnings over a person's lifetime	Based on average years of schooling and returns to education	World Penn Table
CLG	Good governance	Country level governance	It is the perception on the efficiency of government in the following areas: Voice and Accountability, Rule of Law, Regulatory Quality, Control of Corruption, Government Effectiveness, and Political stability and absence of Violence/Terrorism.	Percentile Rank	World Governance Indicator
ANS	Sustainable development	Adjusted net saving	Adjusted net savings are equal to net national savings plus education expenditure and minus energy depletion, net forest depletion, and carbon dioxide	Percentage	World Bank Development Indicator

3.2. Method

Following the sustainable development framework developed by the World Bank, this paper follows the one released by the World Bank and it's based on the crude estimate as follows:

ANS = NNS + E − R − P

where ANS is the adjusted net saving, NNS is the Net National Saving, E is the Current education expenditure, R is the Resource rents, and P is the Carbon dioxide (CO_2) damage.

In the calculation of sustainable development (ANS) in this study, current expenditure is treated as saving rather than consumption, since it increases the country's human capital (human capital is being considered here as a proxy), and pollution damages seek to reflect losses of welfare in the form of human sickness (HIV/AIDS prevalence as a proxy). Energy depletion is the depletion of oil, coal, and natural gas. A measure of depletion stands for the management of the natural resources (country-level governance index as a proxy).

For the empirical analysis, the study is based on Pesaran et al. methodology, which introduced the pooled mean group (PMG) approach in the panel ARDL framework [51]. This estimator was settled as a result of its advantages in comparison with other panel estimators. First, PMG/panel ARDL does not require a formal test for cointegration. Second, PMG minimizes the endogeneity problems and all the variables are considered to be endogenous. Third, the testing for the order of variables integration is not generally required, i.e either the variable is I(0) or I(1) is not an issue in PMG. Last, the long-run and short-run variables are estimated simultaneously, lessening problems of omitted variables and autocorrelation.

Therefore, based on Pesaran et al. methodology, the panel ARDL model for this study including the long-run relationship between the variables is presented as follows:

$$\Delta ANS_{it} = \alpha_i + \sum_{j=1}^{p-1}\beta_{ij}\Delta ANS_{i,t-j} + \sum_{r=0}^{n-1}\gamma_{ir}\Delta HCI_{i,t-r} + \sum_{i=0}^{q-1}\varphi_{il}\Delta HPREV_{i,t-l} + \sum_{c=0}^{m-1}\tau_{ic}\Delta CLG_{i,t-c} + \delta_1 ANS_{i,t-1} + \delta_2 HCI_{i,t-1} + \delta_3 HPREV_{i,t-1} + \delta_4 CLG_{i,t-1} + \varepsilon_{1i,t} \tag{1}$$

$$\Delta HCI_{it} = \alpha_i + \sum_{j=1}^{p-1}\beta_{ij}\Delta HCI_{i,t-j} + \sum_{i=0}^{q-1}\varphi_{il}\Delta ANS_{i,t-l} + \sum_{r=0}^{n-1}\gamma_{ir}\Delta HPREV_{i,t-r} + \sum_{c=0}^{m-1}\tau_{ic}\Delta CLG_{i,t-c} + \omega_1 HCI_{i,t-1} + \omega_2 ANS_{i,t-1} + \omega_3 HPREV_{i,t-1} + \omega_4 HPREV_{i,t-1} + \varepsilon_{2i,t} \tag{2}$$

$$\Delta HPREV_{it} = \alpha_i + \sum_{j=1}^{p-1}\beta_{ij}\Delta HPREV_{i,t-j} + \sum_{i=0}^{q-1}\varphi_{il}\Delta HCI_{i,t-l} + \sum_{r=0}^{n-1}\gamma_{ir}\Delta ANS_{i,t-r} + \sum_{c=0}^{m-1}\tau_{ic}\Delta CLG_{i,t-c} + \pi_1 HPREV_{,t-1} + \pi_2 HCI_{i,t-1} + \pi_3 ANS_{i,t-1} + \pi_4 CLG + \varepsilon_{3i,t} \tag{3}$$

$$\Delta CLG_{it} = \alpha_i + \sum_{j=1}^{p-1}\beta_{ij}\Delta CLG_{i,t-j} + \sum_{i=0}^{q-1}\varphi_{il}\Delta HCI_{i,t-l} + \sum_{r=0}^{n-1}\gamma_{ir}\Delta ANS_{i,t-r} + \sum_{c=0}^{m-1}\tau_{ic}\Delta HPREV_{i,t-c} + \Omega_1 CLG_{,t-l} + \Omega_2 HCI_{i,t-l} + \Omega_3 ANS_{i,t-l} + \Omega_4 HPREV + \varepsilon_{4i,t} \tag{4}$$

where *ANS*, *HPREV*, *HCI*, and *CLG* are adjusted net saving (a proxy for sustainable development), HIV/AIDS prevalence rate, human capital index, and country-level governance. Δ and $\sum k_{it}$ *(k = 1, 2, 3, 4)* are the first difference operator and a white noise term. Also, in Equations (1—4), α_1 denotes a country-specific intercept. The subscript *I* denotes a specific unit and varies from *1* to *N*. A reasonable generalization of cointegration test from time series to panel data may formulate the H_0 of no cointegration between the four variables in Equation (1) as follows: H_0: $\delta_1 = \delta_2 = \delta_3 = \delta_4 = 0$, while H_1: At least one $\delta k \neq 0$ *(k = 1,2,3,4)*.

Similarly, the null hypothesis of no cointegration in Equation (2) may be written as H_0: $\omega_1 = \omega_2 = \omega_3 = \omega_4 = 0$. Also, in Equation (3,4), the H_0 of no cointegration between the four variables may be formulated as H_0: $\pi_1 = \pi_2 = \pi_3 = \pi_4 = 0$, and $\Omega_1 = \Omega_2 = \Omega_3 = \Omega_4 = 0$

Subsequently, if the null hypothesis of cointegration is rejected, we estimate the long-run relationship for the first panel ARDL described in Equation (1) is presented as follows:

$$ANS_{it} = \mu_i + \sum_{j=1}^{p-1}\lambda_{1j}ANS_{i,t-j} + \sum_{i=0}^{q-1}\lambda_{2j}HCI_{i,t-l} + \sum_{r=0}^{n-1}\lambda_{3j}HPREV_{i,t-r} + \sum_{c=0}^{m-1}\lambda_{4j}CLG_{i,t-c} + v_{1i,t} \tag{5}$$

Consequent to the above model specification, the assumption of PMG estimator of the coefficient of the long-run relationship to be the same for every country in the panel were considered. Meanwhile, the assumption is also considered in the null hypothesis of no cointegration model specification for the four models. Similarly, the remaining three models were specified in line with Equation (5).

The error correction models for the ARDL models described above are constructed as follows:

$$\Delta ANS_{it} = \alpha_i + \sum_{j=1}^{p-1}\beta_{ij}\Delta ANS_{i,t-j} + \sum_{i=0}^{q-1}\varphi_{il}\Delta HCI_{i,t-l} + \sum_{r=0}^{n-1}\gamma_{ir}\Delta HPREV_{i,t-r} + \\ \sum_{c=0}^{m-1}\tau_{ic}\Delta CLG_{i,t-c} + aECT_{t-1} + e_{1i,t}$$

(6)

$$\Delta HCI_{it} = \alpha_i + \sum_{j=1}^{p-1}\beta_{ij}\Delta HCI_{i,t-j} + \sum_{i=0}^{q-1}\varphi_{il}\Delta ANS_{i,t-l} + \sum_{r=0}^{n-1}\gamma_{ir}\Delta HPREV_{i,t-r} + \\ \sum_{c=0}^{m-1}\tau_{ic}\Delta CLG_{i,t-c} + bECT_{t-1} + e_{2i,t}$$

(7)

$$\Delta HPREV_{it} = \alpha_i + \sum_{j=1}^{p-1}\beta_{ij}\Delta HPREV_{i,t-j} + \sum_{i=0}^{q-1}\varphi_{il}\Delta ANS_{i,t-l} + \sum_{r=0}^{n-1}\gamma_{ir}\Delta HCI_{i,t-r} + \\ \sum_{c=0}^{m-1}\tau_{ic}\Delta CLG_{i,t-c} + cECT_{t-1} + e_{3i,t}$$

(8)

$$\Delta CLG_{it} = \alpha_i + \sum_{j=1}^{p-1}\beta_{ij}\Delta CLG_{i,t-j} + \sum_{i=0}^{q-1}\varphi_{il}\Delta HCI_{i,t-l} + \sum_{r=0}^{n-1}\gamma_{ir}\Delta ANS_{i,t-r} + \\ \sum_{c=0}^{m-1}\tau_{ic}\Delta HPREV_{i,t-c} + dECT_{t-1} + e_{4i,t}$$

(9)

where the error term $e_{ki,t}$ (k = 1,2,3,4) is independently and normally distributed with zero mean and constant variance, and ECT_{t-1} is the error correction term specified from the long-run equilibrium relationship. The coefficient of a, b, c, d shows the speed of adjustment to the equilibrium level in the presence of shock.

In addition to the specified model above, Pesaran et al. proposed two other estimators that could be applied when both time and cross sections are large. Pooled mean group (PMG) and mean group (MG) difference are that MG estimator is more effective when there is variation in the slope and intercept among the countries in the panel, whereas PMG assumed homogeneity of slope and intercepts among the countries. Also, dynamic fixed effect (DFE) was proposed to be considered where the slope is constant, but the intercept could vary across the countries.

In order to enhance the robustness of our findings, the panel was subdivided into subgroups. This classification into subgroup (upper middle income –UMIC, low middle income – LMIC, and low income – LIC) was based on the 2018 World Bank country's classification according to level of economies.

Meanwhile, it is often assumed that errors in panel data are cross-sectional independent in most cases when the cross-section dimension (N) is large [52]. Evidence abounds in the literature that proved the presence of cross-sectional dependence (CD) in panel model. Pesaran et al. [52] argued that failing to give adequate consideration to cross-sectional dependence in estimation could give loss of estimator efficiency and insignificant test statistics. In view of these, Pesaran's CD test was employed to test for cross-sectional dependency in our data. Moreover, Westerlund [53] observed that many studies failed to reject the no-cointegration hypothesis, which was centered on the fact that most residuals-based cointegration tests require that the long-run parameters for the variables in their levels are equal to the short-run parameters for the variables. In view of the above, this study employed Westerlund's [53] error-correction-based cointegration tests that are based on structural, instead of residual, dynamic, which do not enforce any common-factor restriction to examine the existence of long-run relationship among our variables.

Having specified the models according to Pesaran et al., the next step is to give descriptive statistics on the data, which will enable us to show and explain the characteristics of each variable in the model. Subsequently, the unit root test was conducted to ascertain that no variable is integrated of order two. This is to ensure that the model does not violate the assumption of PMG [51]. Last, analysis was done and inferences from the analysis were made to draw a conclusion.

4. Empirical Findings

4.1. Descriptive Statistics

As revealed in Table 2, while the average adjusted net savings (ANS) in the group panel is -3.62, the UMIC group has the highest mean value for ANS, followed by LIC and LMIC groups. However, greater variation was observed in LMIC, which shows a standard deviation value of 32.81 compared to the group panel, UMIC, and LIC, which have 21.96, 13.75, and 11.49, respectively.

Table 2. Characteristics of the variables.

	Statistics	ANS	HIVPREV	HCI	CLG
Group Panel	Mean	−3.62	5.19	1.62	−0.56
	Max.	47.93	29.4	2.91	0.99
	Min.	−210.90	0.1	1.03	−2.1
	Std.Dev	21.96	6.61	0.40	0.56
	Obs.	697	702	702	624
UMIC	Mean	11.60	12.34	2.26	0.24
	Max.	37.58	27	2.81	0.88
	Min.	−26.99	0.6	1.77	−0.67
	Std.Dev.	13.75	8.03	0.27	0.43
	Obs.	105	108	108	96
LMIC	Mean	−9.21	5.25	1.67	−0.81
	Max.	47.83	28.4	2.38	0.12
	Min.	−210.90	0.2	1.14	−1.66
	Std.Dev.	32.81	7.18	0.29	0.42
	Obs.	231	216	216	192
LIC	Mean	−4.73	3.11	1.40	−0.64
	Max.	36.06	14.9	2.17	0.05
	Min.	−47.21	0.1	1.03	−2.1
	Std.Dev.	11.49	3.81	0.24	0.46
	Obs.	369	378	378	336

ANS = Adjusted net savings, HIVPREV = HIV/AIDS Prevalence, HCI = Human capital index, CLG = Country-level governance. UMIC = Upper-middle income countries, LMIC = Low-middle income countries, LIC = Low income countries.

The average mean value of HIV/AIDS prevalence for the group panel is 5.19, UMIC has a 12.34 mean value for HIV/AIDS, while LMIC and LIC have 5.25 and 3.11, respectively. Meanwhile, the standard deviation shows that there is high deviation from the mean value in UMIC with a standard deviation value of 8.03 compared to 6.61, 7.18, and 3.81, which are values for group panel, LMIC, and LIC, respectively.

The average human capital index in UMIC is higher than the other groups. This is expected being an upper-middle income country. However, all the groups show a minimal standard deviation value, which could be an indication that each group possess similar characteristic in terms of human capital. The country level governance could be described to be fair in UMIC by having a mean value of 0.24 compared to the average value for the group panel, which is -0.56, while -0.81 and -0.64 are for LMIC and LIC, respectively.

4.2. Cross-Dependency Test

In line with Pesaran et al. [54] cross-dependency test, the null hypothesis is that there is no cross-section dependence (correlation in residuals). The results from the test presented in Table 3, which shows that this study failed to reject the null hypothesis of no cross-sectional dependency in all the four panels. It implies that the panels are free from the cross-sectional dependency problem.

Table 3. Pesaran cross-sectional dependency test.

	Statistics	Prob.
Group Panel	1.01	0.31
UMIC	−0.63	0.53
LMIC	−1.58	0.12
LIC	1.06	0.29

UMIC = Upper-middle income countries, LMIC = Low-middle income countries, LIC = Low income countries.

4.3. Unit Root Test

Pesaran et al. commented that the variables for PMG estimator could either be integrated on $I(0)$ or $I(1)$ in order for the variable not to lose its predictive power [51]. However, Kumar et al. opined that panel ARDL does not generally require a knowledge of the order of integration of variables [55]. Nevertheless, we apply Im, Pesaran, and Shin (IPS) W-stat test for both levels and their first difference with an intercept and trend. This was done to ascertain the stationary properties of the variable to enhance the robustness of our results and ensure that none of the variables is integrated at order (2). The results as presented in Table 4. The IPS statistics, as revealed in the table, indicate that for the group panel, three out of the four variables are integrated at order (0), while country-level governance is integrated at order (1). In the UMIC panel, HIVPREV and CLG integrated at order (0), while ANS and HCI integrated at order (1). However, the stationary property of the variables in the LMIC panel is a bit different, in the sense that HCI integrated at order (0) only with intercept. Last, in the LIC panel, both ANS and $HIVPREV$ integrated at order (0), while HCI and CLG integrated at order (1). In summary, the variables across the four panel were tested both at intercept, an intercept and trend. The results, as presented in Table 4, indicate that none of the series are integrated at order (2). Therefore, it is safe for us to employ PMG estimator.

Table 4. Im, Pesaran, and Shin (IPS) Panel unit root result.

	Variable	Level		1st Difference	
		Intercept	Intercept and Trend	Intercept	Intercept and Trend
Group Panel	ANS	−5.55*	−4.77*	-	-
	HIVPREV	−20.32*	−20.22*	-	-
	HCI	−2.05**	2.22	-	−5.17*
	CLG	−0.35	−1.37	−17.66*	−15.93*
UMIC	ANS	−0.79	−0.99	−8.42*	−15.93*
	HIVPREV	−16.12*	−10.29*	-	-
	HCI	0.30	0.91	−2.77*	−6.96*
	CLG	−0.39	−2.15*	−9.94*	-
LMIC	ANS	−4.28*	−5.10*	-	-
	HIVPREV	−8.21*	−6.14*	-	-
	HCI	−2.32*	1.87	-	−0.66
	CLG	−0.98	−2.65*	−9.91*	-
LIC	ANS	-3.92*	−2.03**	-	-
	HIVPREV	−13.31*	−17.92*	-	-
	HCI	−1.20	1.10	−5.89*	−4.71*
	CLG	0.49	1.43	−11.30*	−9.98*

*, ** indicates 1% and 5% significance level respectively. UMIC = Upper-middle income countries, LMIC = Low-middle income countries, LIC = Low income countries.

4.4. Cointegration Analysis

The Westerlund ECM panel cointegration tests consists of four tests designed to test cointegration in panel data. The first two tests were to test the alternative hypothesis that the panel is cointegrated as whole, while the other two tests were to test that at least one unit is cointegrated. However, the results from the test, as shown in Table 5, reveals that the three tests out of four in group panel strongly reject the null hypothesis of no cointegration among the variables. Two tests accepted alternative hypothesis that there is cointegration among the variables in UMIC panel, and three tests strongly rejected null hypothesis of no cointegration in LMIC panel. Meanwhile, the test results failed to reject the null hypothesis of no cointegration in LIC panel. In summary, there is strong evidence that there is cointegration among the variables, which was as a result of similar outcome for the cointegration found among variables in the subgroups.

Table 5. Westerlund ECM Panel Cointegration test.

Test	Group Panel	UMIC	LMIC	LIC
Gt	−2.27 *	−2.73 **	−3.27 *	−1.57
Ga	−5.45	−7.02	−5.11	−5.19
Pt	−23.39 *	−5.26 **	−16.29 *	−4.69
Pa	−9.64 *	−6.61	−9.39 **	−3.80

*, ** indicate 1% and 5% significance level respectively. UMIC = Upper-middle income countries, LMIC = Low-middle income countries, LIC = Low income countries.

4.5. Hausman Test

Table 6 reports the results of Hausman test statistics for all the three predictor variable used in the study. The Hausman test statistics fail to decline the homogeneity of long-run coefficients because the chi2 value is greater than 0.05 in absolute value. Hence, the model supports the PMG estimator.

Table 6. Hausman Test.

	PMG	MG	DFE	PMG/MG	PMG/DFE
HIVPREV	1.12	3.18	0.23		
HCI	−10.08	−1.30	−0.75		
CLG	11.09	12.07	17.06		
Hausman Test				−0.90	−5.75

4.6. Long- and Short-Run Estimates

The analysis results from Table 7 indicate that when *ANS* is the dependent variable (Equation (1)), HIVPREV has a positive and significant long-run relationship with *ANS* at 1% significance level. However, when *HIVPREV* is the dependent variable (Equation (2)), *ANS* does not show any significant relationship with *HPREV*. This implies that the relationship between sustainable development and HIV/AIDS is unidirectional, which means that there is only effect running from *HIVPREV* to sustainable development, but not vice versa. Similarly, the relationship between human capital *(HCI)* and sustainable development is unidirectional. The results in Table 7 reveal a negative and significant relationship between the two variables. However, good governance (CLG) according to the estimate shows a positive and statistically significant long-run relationship with sustainable development.

Moreover, the results, as revealed in Table 7, show that HIV/AIDS has a negative and significant long-run relationship with human capital. It also worthy to note that the relationship is bidirectional. There is also a unidirectional long-run relationship between human capital and good governance. The result also established a bidirectional long-run relationship between HIV/AIDS and good governance. Meanwhile, all the results were supported with the estimates from the subgroup estimations. Table 8 shows the coefficients for the cointegration vectors for *ANS, HIVPREV, HCI,* and *CLG,* respectively. It is sufficient to say that the signs and intervals of *ECTs* from Table 8 are consistent with theory, meaning that a negative ECT ranges between 0 and 1 and is imperative for a stable error correction mechanism [54]. A positive *ECT* implies deviation from the equilibrium, while a negative ECT is important for the restoration of equilibrium following an exogenous shock.

Table 7. Long-run causality estimates.

		Independent Variables			
	Dep. Var.	ΔANS	ΔHIVPREV	ΔHCI	ΔCLG
Group Panel	ΔANS	-	1.12*(0.32)	−10.05**(4.28	11.11*(2.50)
	ΔHIVPREV	−0.001(0.004)	-	−23.11*(0.84)	2.12*(0.23)
	ΔHCI	0.0002(0.0002)	0.01**(0.002)	-	−0.05***(0.03)
	ΔCLG	0.001(0.001)	0.01**(0.01)	0.04(0.07)	-
UMIC	ΔANS	-	1.70**(0.77)	−7.33(7.85)	16.21***(9.17)
	ΔHIVPREV	−0.08**(0.04)	-	−26.81*(3.80)	1.85(2.81)
	ΔHCI	−0.003**(0.002)	−0.02*(0.006)	-	0.23***(0.13)
	ΔCLG	0.001(0.002)	−0.002(0.004)	−0.42*(0.07)	-
LMIC	ΔANS	-	−1.04(0.65)	37.06*(10.09)	22.41**(7.86)
	ΔHIVPREV	−0.004(0.01)	-	19.60*(4.99)	−8.96**(3.20)
	ΔHCI	0.001***(0.0003)	0.03**(0.01)	-	−0.11***(0.07)
	ΔCLG	0.001(0.001)	0.02***(0.01)	0.19(0.16)	-
LIC	ΔANS	-	1.24*(0.38)	−10.17***(5.72)	9.90*(2.75)
	ΔHIVPREV	0.08*(0.02)	-	0.67(0.69)	3.45*(0.75)
	ΔHCI	−0.02(0.01)	0.10(0.07)	-	−1.01***(0.60)
	ΔCLG	−0.001(0.003)	0.01(0.01)	0.10(0.10)	-

*, **, *** indicates 1%, 5% and 10% significance levels, respectively. Values in parentheses are standard error. UMIC = Upper-middle income countries, LMIC = Low-middle income countries, LIC = Low income countries.

Table 8. Short-run estimates (koint causality).

		Independent variables				
	Dep. Var.	ΔANS	ΔHIVPREV	ΔHCI	ΔCLG	ECT(-1)
Group Panel	ΔANS	-	9.82(10.16)	12.22(38.54)	0.94(3.04)	−0.50*
	ΔHIVPREV	0.001(0.002)	-	1.64(1.24)	−0.05(0.06)	−0.07*
	ΔHCI	0.0003(0.0003)	0.001(0.01)	-	0.01(0.01)	−0.05*
	ΔCLG	−0.0002(0.001)	0.06(0.07)	−0.25(0.70)	-	−0.36*
UMIC	ΔANS	-	−1.75(3.31)	37.96(62.63)	4.81(4.01)	−0.43**
	ΔHIVPREV	0.004(0.01)	-	−5.76***(3.10)	−0.15(0.19)	−0.10**
	ΔHCI	−0.000**(0.001)	−0.06***(0.04)		0.01(0.03)	−0.11*
	ΔCLG	−0.0001(0.002)	0.002(0.04)	0.10(0.37)	-	−0.62*
LMIC	ΔANS	-	38.28(33.90)	−66.22(41.21)	−5.98(8.06)	−0.53*
	ΔHIVPREV	0.0004(0.001)	-	2.19(3.82)	0.42(0.32)	−0.01
	ΔHCI	−0.0001(0.0001)	0.02(0.02)	-	0.02(0.02)	−0.07*
	ΔCLG	0.003(0.002)	0.17(0.13)	−1.19(1.25)	-	−0.49*
LIC	ΔANS	-	0.01(3.56)	39.80(55.81)	1.11(3.53)	−0.52*
	ΔHIVPREV	−0.003(0.002)	-	3.62**(1.62)	−0.04(0.08)	−0.03
	ΔHCI	0.001(0.001)	0.02(0.01)	-	0.01(0.01)	−0.01
	ΔCLG	−0.001(0.002)	0.0004(0.09)	0.09(1.09)	-	−0.25**

*, **, *** indicates 1%, 5% and 10% significance levels, respectively. Values in parentheses are standard error. UMIC = Upper-middle income countries, LMIC = Low-middle income countries, LIC = Low income countries.

The ECT coefficient from Table 8 shows that sustainable development, HIV/AIDS, human capital, and good governance can be restored to long-run equilibrium. The analysis of Equation (6), as presented in Table 7, indicates that there is long-run cointegration among the variables at 1% significance level, and the ECT coefficient of (–0.50) revealed in Table 8 implies that any deviation from the long-run equilibrium is corrected at 50% adjustment speed. This also indicates a strong and joint causality of the three variables on sustainable development.

From Tables 7 and 8 and Equation (7), the results show a long-run cointegration among the variables at 1% significance level. The results also reveal a strong and joint causality of sustainable development, HIV/AIDS prevalence, and good governance on human capital. Human capital could be significantly restored to its long-run equilibrium at 5% adjustment speed in the presence of a shock. Analysis for Equation (8), as presented in Table 8, indicates that sustainable development, human capital, and good governance have a joint causal effect on HIV/AIDS prevalence, while Table 7 reveals that there is long-run cointegration which is statistically significant at 1% level. In presence of a shock, *HIV/AIDS* could be significantly restored to its long-run equilibrium at 7% adjustment speed. Similarly, in reference to Equation (9), sustainable development, HIV/AIDS prevalence, and human capital have a joint and strong causal effect on good governance, which is depicted in Table 8. In case of any shock in the system, it could be adjusted at 36% adjustment speed.

For upper-middle income economies, a long-run bidirectional causal relationship was found to exist between sustainable development and HIV/AIDS and human capital, and sustainable development and country-level governance. Meanwhile, a unidirectional long-run causal relationship was found to exist between human capital and country-level governance, and human capital and sustainable development. However, a bidirectional short-run causality was found between HIV/AIDS and human capital, and a unidirectional short-run causality was found between sustainable development and human capital.

As for the joint causality, the results are summarized in Table 8. The results show that HIV/AIDS, country-level governance, and human capital have joint causality on sustainable development. The model has about 43% speed of adjustment to return back to equilibrium in the presence of shock. Similarly, sustainable development, human capital, and country-level governance show a strong joint causality on HIV/AIDS with 10% speed of adjustment. HIV/AIDS, country-level governance, and sustainable development were found to have a strong joint causal long-run relationship on human capital, while HIV/AIDS, sustainable development, and human capital were also found to have a strong long-run causal relationship with country-level governance.

In a similar result to that obtained with respect to the group panel, we found bidirectional long-run causal relationship between HIV/AIDS and human capital, sustainable development and human capital, and HIV/AIDS and country-level governance. A unidirectional long-run causal relationship was found between human capital and country-level governance, and sustainable development and country-level governance. The results are presented in Table 7. Further estimates, as shown in Table 8, reveal that HIV/AIDS, country-level governance, and human capital were found to have joint long-run causal relationship with sustainable development. Sustainable development, HIV/AIDS, and human capital also have a joint long-run causal relationship with country-level governance.

As for the low income economies, the results as shown in Tables 7 and 8 are not significantly different from the other three panesl. As summarized in Table 7, a bidirectional long-run causal relationship was found to exist between sustainable development and HIV/AIDS, while a unidirectional relationship was found to exist between sustainable development and human capital, human capital and country-level governance, country-level governance and HIV/AIDS, and country-level governance and sustainable development. Meanwhile, a joint long-run causal relationship was found between country-level governance, HIV/AIDS, and human capital on sustainable development, and between sustainable developments, HIV/AIDS, and human capital on country-level governance (Table 8).

4.7. Robustness Check

We considered dividing the group panel into subgroups (upper-middle income, low-middle income, and low income countries) for analysis using PMG estimator. The results are summarized in Tables 7 and 8. First, we estimated the cointegration across the subgroup. The results, as presented in Table 5, supported our findings for the whole group panel that a long-run relationship exists among the sustainable development (ANS) and the variables considered. Meanwhile, the short-run relationship varies across the subgroups (Table 8). Human capital was found to have a short-run negative causal relationship with HIV/AIDS prevalence in upper-middle income countries (UMIC), while it was positive for low income countries (LIC). However, it has no short-run relationship in low-middle income countries (LMIC), which is similar to the results obtained for the group panel.

5. Summary and Conclusion

This study empirically examined the relationship among sustainable development, HIV/AIDS prevalence, human capital, and good governance in 26 sub-Saharan Africa countries using dynamic heterogeneous panel estimation. In the present globalized era, the issue of sustainable development is critical to measure the progress of any country's development, which will not only account for the economic development, but other factors that will account for the general improved welfare of the citizen. It has become essential to understand the underlying fundamental factors that influence the achievement of sustainable development in the region. Thus, variables like HIV/AIDS, which have been a great challenge to Africa countries, human capital, and country-level governance are taken as the independent variables, which are measured using yearly data from 1990 to 2016 and were analyzed using pooled mean group estimator. To ensure the robustness of the findings, the panel was subdivided into three panels based on the World Bank level of economies categorization. The three categories are upper-middle income (UMIC), low-middle income (LMIC), and low income (LIC) countries.

For the group panel, a bidirectional long-run causal relationship was found between HIV/AIDS and human capital, and HIV/AIDS prevalence and country-level governance. A unidirectional long-run causal relationship was found to exist between human capital and country-level governance, while a bidirectional long-run causal relationship was found between sustainable development and country-level governance, human capital, and sustainable development, and sustainable development and HIV/AIDS.

The positive and significant long-run causal relationship between HIV/AIDS and sustainable development is in line with some previous studies [19,24], which argued that in the future, HIV/AIDS is not likely to threaten economic growth in Africa. Sustainable development and good governance according to the estimated results reveal a positive and significant long-run relationship. This result is in line with previous studies. Previous studies found that the central place of development policy is occupied with the model of good governance [7,31–33], which has become the cornerstone of sustainable development. However, the result is in contrast to some previous studies [34,35], which found no relationship between sustainable development and good governance. The result from the estimates implies that to achieve sustainable development in sub-Saharan Africa countries, there is a need for a concerted effort on the part of the continent country's government to ensure effective good governance. However, while a unidirectional long-run causal relationship was found between sustainable development and HIV/AIDS in the group panel, a bidirectional long-run causal relationship was found between sustainable development and HIV/AIDS in UMIC and LIC respectively. The difference could be attributed to the heterogeneous nature of the countries included in the panel.

A disturbing result from the study is the coefficient sign of a human capital long-run relationship with sustainable development. The authors hypothesized a positive relationship, but the result turned out to be negative, although the significant long-run relationship found in this study is in line with some authors, who inferred human capital to have a significant long-run relationship with the sustainable development of any country [37–40]. However, the negative sign of the result is not surprising in reference to the study of Quadri and Waheed [56], who observed that the contribution of human capital to sustainable development is more in the theoretical realm than the empirical. The study submitted that the theoretical contribution of human capital is clear, but empirical findings are mixed [56].

An interesting finding from this study is the significant strong joint causality of sustainable development, good governance, and human capital on HIV/AIDS prevalence, and in case of any shock, it could be restored back to equilibrium at 7% adjustment speed. This is an indication that, the threat of HIV/AIDS prevalence on sustainable development could be curtailed by putting effective policies and programs in place. There is also a bi-directional long-run relationship between HIV/AIDS prevalence and good governance. It is of importance to note that in sub-Saharan Africa countries, an effective good governance would enhance significant reduction in the prevalence of HIV/AIDS in the region.

The study estimated the relationship among sustainable development, HIV/AIDS prevalence, human capital, and good governance. It found that all the variables are cointegrated, which implies a long-run relationship. The estimation of the long-run slope coefficient restricted it to be homogenous across countries. This is because the authors expect that the long-run equilibrium relationship between the variables will be similar across countries in sub-Saharan Africa. Future studies can do a comparative study of countries with high HIV/AIDS prevalence in African regions to confirm the outcome of these results. Also, there is a need for a robustness test to explore the mixed result on the relationship between sustainable development and human capital. Based on the findings of this study, it is imperative for the government and stakeholders in the region to pursue policies that will enhance sustainable development with expected long-term results, rather than short-term gains. First, there is a need to improve the country-level governance policy, development of human capital, and improve on the policies and programs targeted toward the prevention and eradication of HIV/AIDS in sub-Saharan Africa countries. Second, human capital needs to be more developed to drive down the effects of HIV/AIDS prevalence. Lastly, good governance, found to have a long-run relationship with sustainable development, should be strengthened to ensure that the rule of law prevailed, transparency in their dealings, corruption to be eradicated, conducive business regulatory environment, and a country free of war/terrorism. However, sustainable development is achievable in sub-Saharan Africa countries if an adequate research grounded policy is put in place to address the challenges as revealed by this study.

Author Contributions: The individual author's contributions are as follows: J.A.O. conceived the idea, H.R. designed the statistical data base, J.A.O. and H.R. performed the data base and analyzed the data. H.R. contributed the analysis tools, J.A.O. wrote the paper.

Acknowledgments: We acknowledge the insightful comments from the reviewers on this manuscript, which have enhanced the quality of the article.

Appendix A

Table A1. List of countries in the panel.

S/No	Country	Classification	S/No	Country	Classification
1	Angola	LMIC	14	Madagascar	LIC
2	Benin	LIC	15	Malawi	LIC
3	Bostwana	UMIC	16	Mali	LIC
4	B/Faso	LIC	17	Mauritania	LMIC
5	Burundi	LIC	18	Mozambique	LIC
6	Cameroon	LMIC	19	Namibia	UMIC
7	Congo DR	LIC	20	Niger	LIC
8	Congo R	LMIC	21	Nigeria	LMIC
9	C/Ivoire	LMIC	22	Senegal	LIC
10	Eswatini	LMIC	23	S/Leone	LIC
11	Gabon	UMIC	24	S/Africa	UMIC
12	Gambia	LIC	25	Togo	LIC
13	Ghana	LMIC	26	Uganda	LIC

UMIC = Upper-middle income countries, LMIC = Low-middle income countries, LIC = Low income countries.

References

1. Mondal, M.N.I.; Shitan, M. Factors affecting the HIV/AIDS epidemic: An ecological analysis of global data. *Afr. Health Sci.* **2013**, *13*, 301–310. [CrossRef] [PubMed]
2. UNAIDS. UNAIDS Data 2017. 2017. Available online: www.unaids.org (accessed on 16 June 2018).
3. Djukpen, R.O. Mapping the HIV/AIDS epidemic in Nigeria using exploratory spatial data analysis. *GeoJournal* **2012**, *77*, 555–569. [CrossRef]
4. Erinosho, O.; Dike, N.; Joseph, R.; Isiugo-Abanihe, U.; Aderinto, A.A. Methodological Issues in HIV-Related Social Research in Nigeria. *Afr. J. Reprod.* **2013**, *17*, 146–155.
5. Milanovic, B. Global inequality recalculated and updated: The effect of new PPP estimates on global inequality and 2005 estimates. *J. Econ. Inequal.* **2012**, *10*, 1–18. [CrossRef]
6. UNEP (United Nations Environment Programme). *Global Environment Outlook: Environment for the Future We Want—GE05*; UNEP: Nairobi, Kenya, 2012.
7. Boţa-Avram, C.; Groşanu, A.; Răchişan, P.R.; Gavriletea, M.D. The Bidirectional Causality between Country-Level Governance, Economic Growth and Sustainable Development: A Cross-Country Data Analysis. *Sustainability* **2018**, *10*, 502. [CrossRef]
8. Mignaqui, V. Sustainable development as a goal: Social, environmental and economic dimensions. *Int. J. Soc. Qual.* **2014**, *4*, 57–77. [CrossRef]
9. World Bank. *Inclusive Green Growth: The Pathway to Sustainable Development*; World Bank: Washington, DC, USA, 2012.
10. WHO. Health in the Sustainable Development Goals. 2016. Available online: http://www.searo.who.int/entity/health_situation_trends/health_in_sustainable_devlop_goals.pdf (accessed on 12 December 2017).
11. Sustainable Development Solutions Network (SDSN). Health in the Framework of Sustainable Development. 2014. Available online: http://unsdsn.org/wp-content/uploads/2014/02/Health-For-All-Report.pdf (accessed on 17 July 2017).
12. UNAIDS. The Sustainable Development Goals and the HIV Response. 2018. Available online: www.unaids.org/sites/default/files/media_asset/SDGsandHIV_en.pdf (accessed on 6 August 2018).
13. Over, M. *The macroeconomic impact of AIDS in Sub-Saharan Africa*; AFTN Technical Working Paper 3; Population, Health and Nutrition Division, Africa Technical Department, World Bank: Washington, DC, USA, 1992.

14. Arndt, C.; Lewis, J.D. The macro implications of HIV/AIDS in South Africa: A preliminary assessment. *S. Afr. J. Econ.* **2000**, *68*, 380–392. [CrossRef]

15. Maijama'a, D.; Samsudin, S. HIV/AIDS and economic growth: Empirical evidence from sub-Saharan Africa. *Res. Appl. Econ.* **2015**, *7*, 30–47. [CrossRef]

16. Essig, A.; Kang, S.; Sellers, R. *The Relationship between HIV Infection Rates and GDP Per Capita in African Countries*; Georgia Institute of Technology: Atlanta, GA, USA, 2015.

17. Sackey, J.; Raparla, T. *Lesotho, The Development Impact of HIV/AIDS—Selected Issues and Options*; AFTMI Report, No. 21103; LSO, Macroeconomic Technical Group, Africa Region, World Bank: Washington, DC, USA, 2000.

18. Augier, L.; Yaly, A. Economic growth and disease in the OLG model: The HIV/AIDS case. *Econ. Model.* **2013**, *33*, 471–481. [CrossRef]

19. Kirigia, J.M.; Sambo, L.G.; Okorosobo, T.; Mwabu, G.M. Impact of HIV/AIDS on Gross Domestic Product (GGP) in the WHO Africa Region. *Afr. J. Health Sci.* **2002**, *9*, 27–39. [CrossRef] [PubMed]

20. Afawubo, K.; Mathey, S. Employment and education effects on HIV/AIDS prevalence rate and economic growth: Empirical investigation in ECOWAS. *Appl. Econ. Lett.* **2014**, *21*, 755–759. [CrossRef]

21. Alemu, Z.G.; Roe, T.L.; Smith, R.B. *The Impact of HIV on Total Factor Productivity*; Working Paper; Economic Development Center, University of Minnesota: Minneapolis, MN, USA, 2005.

22. Young, A. The gift of the dying: The tragedy of AIDS and the welfare of future African generations. *Q. J. Econ.* **2005**, *120*, 423–466.

23. Couderc, N.; Ventelou, B. AIDS, economic growth and the epidemic trap in Africa. *Oxf. Dev. Stud.* **2005**, *33*, 417–426. [CrossRef]

24. Cuesta, J. How much of a threat to economic growth is a mature AIDS epidemic? *Appl. Econ.* **2010**, *42*, 3077–3089. [CrossRef]

25. Fortson, J.G. Mortality risk and human capital investment: The Impact of HIV/AIDS in Sub-Saharan Africa. *Rev. Econ. Stat.* **2011**, *93*, 1–15. [CrossRef]

26. Frimpong, P.B.; Adu, G. Population health and economic growth in Sub-Saharan Africa: A panel cointegration analysis. *J. Afr. Bus.* **2014**, *15*, 36–48. [CrossRef]

27. Roy, S. The effects of HIV/AIDS on economic growths and human capitals: A panel study evidence from Asian countries. *AIDS Care* **2014**, *26*, 1568–1575. [CrossRef] [PubMed]

28. Asiedu, E.; Jin, Y.; Kanyama, I.K. The impact of HIV/AIDS on foreign direct investment: Evidence from Sub-Saharan Africa. *J. Afr. Trade* **2015**, *2*, 1–17. [CrossRef]

29. Shuaibu, M.; Oladayo, P.T. Determinants of human capital development in Africa: A panel data analysis. *Oeconomia Copernic.* **2016**, *7*, 523–549. [CrossRef]

30. Brautigam, D. *Governance and Economy: A Review*; World Bank Publications: Washington, DC, USA, 1991; Volume 815.

31. Stojanović, I.; Ateljević, J.; Stević, R.S. Good governance as a tool of sustainable development. *Eur. J. Sustain. Dev.* **2016**, *5*, 558–573. [CrossRef]

32. Wilson, R. Does governance cause growth? Evidence from China. *World Dev.* **2016**, *79*, 138–151. [CrossRef]

33. Leal Filho, W.; Platje, J.; Gerstlberger, W.; Ciegis, R.; Kääriä, J.; Klavins, M.; Kliucininkas, L. The role of governance in realizing the transition towards sustainable societies. *J. Clean. Prod.* **2016**, *113*, 755–766. [CrossRef]

34. Rodrik, D. Thinking about Governance. In *Governance, Growth and Development Decision-Making*; North, D.C., Daron, A., Francis, F., Dani, R., Eds.; The World Bank: Washington, DC, USA, 2008.

35. Khan, M.H. *Governance, Economic Growth and Development Since the 1960s*; UNDESA Working Paper No. 54, ST/ESA/2007/DWP/54; UNDESA: New York, NY, USA, 2007.

36. Šlaus, I.; Jacobs, G. Human capital and sustainability. *Sustainability* **2011**, *3*, 97–154. [CrossRef]

37. Jakimhovski, J. The human capital as a factor in the sustainable development. *Škola Biznia* **2011**, *3*, 72–85.

38. Scicchitano, S. Complementarity between heterogeneous human capital and R&D: can job-training avoid low development traps? *Empirica* **2010**, *37*, 361–380.

39. Absalyamova, S.G.; Absalyamov, T.B.; Mukhametgalieva, C.F.; Khusnullova, A.R. Management of the sustainable development of human capital in the terms of macroeconomic instability. *Procedia Econ. Financ.* **2015**, *24*, 13–17. [CrossRef]

40. Ekperiware, M.C.; Olatayo, T.O.; Egbetokun, A.A. *Human Capital and Sustainable Development in Nigeria: How Can Economic Growth Suffice Environmental Degradation?* (No. 2017-29); Economics Discussion Papers; Kiel Institute for the World Economy (IfW): Kiel, Germany, 2017.

41. Diaconu, L.; Popescu, C.C. Human capital—A pillar of sustainable development. Empirical evidences from the EU states. *Eur. J. Sustain. Dev.* **2016**, *5*, 103–112.

42. Eigbiremolen, G.O.; Anaduka, U.S. Human Capital Development and Economic Growth: The Nigeria experience. *Int. J. Acad. Res. Bus. Soc. Sci.* **2014**, *4*, 4. [CrossRef]

43. Nourry, M. Measuring sustainable development: Some empirical evidence for France from eight alternative indicators. *Ecol. Econ.* **2008**, *67*, 441–456. [CrossRef]

44. Gnègnè, Y. Adjusted net saving and welfare change. *Ecol. Econ.* **2009**, *68*, 1127–1139. [CrossRef]

45. Thiry, G.; Cassiers, I. Alternative indicators to GDP: Values behind numbers. Adjusted net savings in question. *Appl. Res. Qual. Life* **2010**, *23*, 1–23.

46. Lange, G.M.; Wodon, Q.; Carey, K. (Eds.) *The Changing Wealth of Nations 2018: Building a Sustainable Future*; The World Bank: Washington, DC, USA, 2018.

47. Feenstra, R.C.; Inklaar, R.; Timmer, M.P. The Next Generation of the Penn World Table. *Am. Econ. Rev.* **2015**, *105*, 3150–3182. [CrossRef]

48. Barro, R.J.; Lee, J.W. A new data set of educational attainment in the world, 1950–2010. *J. Dev. Econ.* **2013**, *104*, 184–198. [CrossRef]

49. Pesaran, M.H.; Shin, Y.; Smith, R.J. Pooled mean group estimation of dynamic heterogeneous panels. *J. Am. Stat. Assoc.* **1999**, *94*, 621–634. [CrossRef]

50. World Governance Indicators. 2018. Available online: www.govindicators.org (accessed on 16 June 2018).

51. World Bank. World Band Development Indicators. 2018. Available online: http://databank.worldbank.org/data/home.aspx (accessed on 16 June 2018).

52. Pesaran, M.H.; Schuermann, T.; Weiner, S.M. Modeling regional interdependencies using a global error-correcting macroeconometric model. *J. Bus. Econ. Stat.* **2004**, *22*, 129–162. [CrossRef]

53. Persyn, D.; Westerlund, J. Error-correction-based cointegration tests for panel data. *Stata J.* **2008**, *8*, 232–241. [CrossRef]

54. Asongu, S.; El Montasser, G.; Toumi, H. Testing the relationships between energy consumption, CO_2 emissions, and economic growth in 24 African countries: A panel ARDL approach. *Environ. Sci. Pollut. Res.* **2016**, *23*, 6563–6573. [CrossRef] [PubMed]

55. Kumar, S.; Webber, D.J.; Fargher, S. Wagner's Law revisited: Cointegration and causality tests for New Zealand. *Appl. Econ.* **2012**, *44*, 607–616. [CrossRef]

56. Qadri, F.S.; Waheed, A. Human capital and economic growth: Cross-country evidence from low-, middle-and high-income countries. *Prog. Dev. Stud.* **2013**, *13*, 89–104. [CrossRef]

12

Confucius and Herding Behaviour in the Stock Markets in China and Taiwan

Batmunkh John Munkh-Ulzii [1], Michael McAleer [2,3,4,5,6,*], Massoud Moslehpour [7] and Wing-Keung Wong [2]

[1] Department of International Relations, National University of Mongolia, Ulaanbaatar 14200, Mongolia; ulzii03@gmail.com
[2] Department of Finance, Asia University, Taichung 41354, Taiwan; wong@asia.edu.tw
[3] Discipline of Business Analytics, University of Sydney Business School, Sydney, NSW 2006, Australia
[4] Econometric Institute, Erasmus School of Economics, Erasmus University Rotterdam, 3000 Rotterdam, The Netherlands
[5] Department of Economic Analysis and ICAE, Complutense University of Madrid, 28040 Madrid, Spain
[6] Institute of Advanced Sciences, Yokohama National University, Yokohama 240-8501, Japan
[7] Department of Business Administration, Asia University, Taichung 41354, Taiwan; writetodrm@gmail.com
[*] Correspondence: michael.mcaleer@gmail.com

Abstract: It has been argued in the literature that financial markets with a Confucian background tend to exhibit herding behaviour, or correlated behavioural patterns in individuals. This paper applies the return dispersion model to investigate financial herding behaviour by examining index returns from the stock markets in China and Taiwan. The sample period is from 1 January 1999 to 31 December 2014, and the data were obtained from Thomson Reuters Datastream. Although the sample period finishes in 2014, the data are more than sufficient to test the three hypotheses relating to the stock markets in China and Taiwan, both of which have Confucian cultures. The empirical results demonstrate significant herding behaviour under both general and specified markets conditions, including bull and bear markets, and high-low trading volume states. This paper contributes to the herding literature by examining three different hypotheses regarding the stock markets in China and Taiwan, and showing that there is empirical support for these hypotheses.

Keywords: herding behaviour; Confucian background; emerging market; frontier market; China market; Taiwan market

JEL Classification: B26; C58; D53; P34

1. Introduction

Herding is typically associated with a correlated behavioural pattern across individuals, and hence represents human behaviour that mimics the actions of other individuals. Numerous studies have emphasised that herding behaviour can be rational as well as irrational. Moreover, there are alternative types of such behaviour, such as information-based, reputation-based, compensation-based, and spurious herding forms [1,2].

Sequential decision theory states that each trader observes decisions made by others in making their own decisions. This is rational as the decisions of others can include useful information [3–10].

This paper is concerned with the stock markets of China and Taiwan. Stock markets in China provide an interesting insight for the analysis of herding behaviour. Since the establishment of the Shanghai Stock Exchange and the Shenzhen Stock Exchange in December 1990, two classes of shares have been issued, namely: (i) A-shares, which can be purchased and traded only by Chinese domestic investors, and are denominated in the local currency, the Renminbi; and (ii) B-shares, which were sold only to foreign investors before February 2001, after which they have been sold to both foreign and domestic investors. A-shares and B-shares are traded simultaneously on the Shanghai and Shenzhen exchanges.

The characteristics of investors of A-shares and B-shares are very different. A-shares are used by domestic individuals, who typically lack significant knowledge and experience in financial investments. The market for B-shares is dominated by foreign institutional investors, who tend to be more knowledgeable and sophisticated than A-share investors. The different characteristics of A-share and B-share investors may result in differences in the level of herding in each market, especially as the A-share market is relatively immature compared to its B-share counterparts [1,11,12].

Having been established in 1961, which is much earlier than the creation of the stock markets in China, the Taiwan stock market is dominated by domestic individual investors, rather than institutional and foreign investors. Most individual investors tend to have less professional knowledge and cannot access information accurately and easily. However, there has been an increasing interest in the Taiwan stock market by foreign investors in recent years, following the lifting of trading restrictions on qualified foreign institutional investors in 2000 [13,14].

In a market that is dominated by domestic individual investors with limited access to information, it might be argued that the resulting information asymmetry would lead such individual investors to follow the actions of other investors, with the latter including more well-informed domestic and foreign institutional investors. Despite being what might be described as an emerging market, the Taiwan stock market is nevertheless highly developed (for further details, see Ref. [15]).

Moreover, a common characteristic of the stock markets in China and Taiwan is that they arise from Chinese culture, where Confucian management philosophy has been dominant. In this context, Ref. [16,17] argue that Confucian markets tend to exhibit herding behaviour.

This study has two main contributions to herding literature. First, in addition to Confucian culture, these markets have specific common and contradictory characteristics; specifically, both are Chinese societies, though one has a free market economy under democratic governance, while the other has a market economy supervised under a communist regime. Furthermore, Taiwan is one of the four Tiger economies, whereas China has become the second largest economy in the world. Therefore, we feel that it is worth discussing and comparing these two markets. Second, the paper uses daily trading data covering a period of 16 years.

Although stock markets can and do differ across those that have a Confucian culture and those that do not, the primary purpose of this paper is to compare the stock markets in China and Taiwan, both of which have Confucian cultures. The issue of a control group would be important if the paper were to compare stock markets in countries that have a Confucian culture and those that do not.

For these reasons, this paper examines whether herding exists for China and Taiwan under both general and specific markets conditions, including bull and bear markets, and high-low trading volumes states.

The remainder of the paper is presented as follows. A literature review is given in Section 2. Methodological issues and the data to be used in the empirical analysis are discussed in Section 3, including the cross-sectional standard deviation model, the cross-sectional absolute deviation model, herding in up and down markets, and herding in high and low trading volumes. Three hypotheses are presented in Section 4, namely, whether herding exists in China and Taiwan, the existence of asymmetric herding in bull and bear markets, and also in high and low trading volumes. The empirical analysis is conducted in Section 5, where the outcomes of testing the three hypotheses are analysed. Some concluding remarks are given in Section 6.

2. Literature Review

Parts of the review follow the presentation in Ref. [5,18] examine herding in several international markets, specifically the USA, Hong Kong, Japan, South Korea, and Taiwan, by using daily stock price data from January 1963 to December 1997. The authors use the cross-sectional absolute deviation method, as an extension of Ref. [19]. They find no evidence of herding from the US and Hong Kong markets, and only a small amount from Japan. However, they find significant herding from the markets in South Korea and Taiwan.

The authors also find that macroeconomic information affects the formation of herding behaviour more significantly than firm-specific information. Furthermore, they suggest that stock return dispersion, as a function of market returns, is greater in up markets than in down markets. They also test the model suggested by Ref. [19] and find herding only for the Taiwan market.

Using the model of Ref. [5,12] find evidence of herding behaviour in Chinese A-shares. Owing to issues relating to the acquisition of accurate estimates of beta, as suggested in Ref. [5], the authors use the standard deviation in estimating the return dispersion, as in Ref. [12,19] also test the asymmetric impact of herding behaviour by varying returns, trading volumes, and volatility. They find herding behaviour in A-shares in the Shanghai market under rising market circumstances, with high volumes of trading of stocks and volatility. However, they find no evidence of herding in B-shares.

The main participants of A-share markets, which are considered as frontier markets, are local investors, who tend to lack sufficient talent and experience in finance. Investors in B-share markets, which are considered as emerging markets, are primarily foreigners with greater skills and knowledge of finance than investors in A-shares. For these reasons, Tan et al. [12] argue that the differences between A-shares and B-shares may affect the variance in herding. The authors also test herding and the cross-market information effect, but find no evidence of herding. Accordingly, the dissimilarity can be explained due to differences in the samples.

Lin and Swanson [20] also examine herding behaviour in the Taiwan stock market for 1996–2003, using one of the methods discussed in this paper. However, the authors focus only on foreign investors and the most liquid stocks, without classifying them into sectoral groups. They find no evidence to support the proposition that foreign investors display herding behaviour in this market. Lin et al. [21] examine daily trading data by foreign and domestic institutional investors for the fifty stocks that are most actively traded by institutional investors in Taiwan. The authors find the herding tendencies of stocks to be more prominent for small capitalized stocks with high share turnovers and high return volatility, thereby suggesting that market conditions and firm characteristics are significant factors driving herding behaviour.

Using buying and selling volume data, Chen, Wang, and Lin [13] find that qualified foreign institutional investors demonstrate herding behaviour in the Taiwan stock market. The authors show that industry effects, in addition to firm characteristics such as high previous returns and large market capitalization, explain the herding behaviour of foreign institutional investors.

Demirer, Kutan, and Chen [22] measure herding behaviour with daily data regarding stock returns for 689 stocks on the Taiwan Stock Exchange from January 1995 to December 2006. The authors use the models of Ref. [4,19] in addition to state space models. They find no evidence of herding in the model of Ref. [19], but find significant evidence in the non-linear model of Ref. [4] and the state space-based models in Ref. [23]. The authors also find that herding behaviour is stronger during periods of market losses than market gains.

Consequently, this paper suggests that investors need more diversified opportunities in periods of market losses. The authors emphasise the following in their analysis: (i) interesting and novel empirical results for an emerging yet relatively sophisticated Taiwan stock market at the sectoral level with firm-level data; (ii) an application of different models; and (iii) an analysis of the practical implications of different herding measures for investors who face both systematic and unexpected risks.

Yao, Ma, and He [24] measure the existence of herding behaviour in the China A-share and B-share markets. They use daily and weekly firm-level and market-level data of equity prices for all firms and indexes that are listed on the Shanghai Stock Exchange and the Shenzhen Stock Exchange from January 1999 to December 2008. Monthly data are also collected for all firms included in the data set. For the empirical analysis in testing herding behaviour, the authors use a modified version of the models of Ref. [4,19].

The empirical results show that herding behaviour is heterogeneous, so that herding is stronger in Chinese B-shares. In addition, the authors find that cross-market herding behaviour is stronger at the industry level, for the largest and smallest stocks, and for growth stocks relative to value stocks. The empirical results show that herding behaviour is greater when share prices are declining. Finally, the authors find that herding behaviour is affected by the regulatory reforms in China that are intended to increase investment efficiency.

In exploring the determinants of investment decision-making in international stock markets, Chang and Lin [16] analyse herding in daily market returns data and industrial index data for 50 stock markets for the cross-sectional absolute deviation of returns. The analysis uses an extended version of the model in Ref. [4]. In order to investigate the influence of culture on herding behaviour, the authors examine the Hofstede national culture indexes for the empirical analysis. In order to test behavioural pitfalls on the herding tendency, the authors use daily data of price-to-book ratios as proxies for excessive optimism, and daily trading volumes data are used as proxies for overconfidence and disposition.

The data set ranges from January 1965 to July 2011. The authors argue that their research examines the effects of culture and behavioural pitfalls in investments, and show that herding is exhibited in Confucian, as well as in less sophisticated stock markets. Moreover, the authors find that some cultural indexes have a high degree of correlation with herding behaviour.

3. Methodology and Data

3.1. Data

Ref. [12,19] find that the average cross-sectional absolute deviation (CSAD) calculated with the use of daily data is smaller than with the use of weekly or monthly data. This difference reflects the fact that, with weekly or monthly data, individual returns have a greater opportunity to stray further from the mean. Consequently, herding is less likely to be detected with weekly or monthly data. For this reason, this paper uses daily stock returns data for all firms on the Shanghai Stock Exchange (SSE), the Shenzhen Stock Exchange (SZSE), and the Taiwan Stock Exchange.

There are 425 Shanghai A-share firms (SHA) and 50 Shanghai B-share firms (SHB) at the SSE, 415 Shenzhen A-share firms (SZA) and 45 Shenzhen B-share firms (SZB) at the SZSE, and 455 firms comprising the Taiwan Capitalization Weighted Stock Index (TAIEX). In addition, we use daily index price data in each corresponding market. The data period spans from 1 January 1999 to 1 January 2015. A-share markets are considered as frontier markets, while both B-share markets and TAIEX are classified as emerging markets. The data are obtained from the Thomson Reuters Datastream database. The simple return method is used to calculate market returns and stock returns.

3.2. Methodology

The return dispersion method is a widely-used approach in most herding studies because it is a reliable method to measure herding behaviour. In the following subsections, we discuss several return dispersion models that are used in this paper.

3.2.1. Cross-Sectional Standard Deviation Model

Ref. [4,19] use individual stock returns and market returns to detect herding behaviour. Christie and Huang [19] propose the following cross-sectional standard deviation (CSSD) model to detect herding behaviour:

$$CSSD_t = \alpha + \beta^L D_t^L + \beta^U D_t^U + \varepsilon_t \tag{1}$$

where

$$CSSD_t = \sqrt{\frac{\sum_{i=1}^{N}(R_{i,t} - R_{m,t})^2}{(N-1)}}$$

at time t is the cross-sectional standard deviation; D_t^L is a dummy variable of unity when market returns at t lie in the extreme lower tail returns, and zero otherwise; D_t^U is a dummy variable of one when market returns at t lie in the extreme upper tail returns, and zero otherwise; α is a constant, both β^L and β^U are coefficients of D_t^L and D_t^U, respectively; ε_t is a random error term; N is the number of firms; and $R_{i,t}$ and $R_{m,t}$ are individual stock returns of stock i and market returns, respectively.

The model argues that if herding occurs when market returns lie in the extreme lower tail returns, then the estimate of β^L will be significantly negative. On the other hand, if herding occurs when market returns lie in the extreme upper tail returns, then the estimate of β^U will be significantly negative.

3.2.2. Cross-Sectional Absolute Deviation Model

One of the challenges associated with the CSSD model is that it must define extreme returns. Arguing that the definition in the CSSD model is arbitrary, Christie and Huang [19] suggest using 1% and 5% as the cut-off points of the upper and lower tails of returns. In practice, investors may have different opinions regarding extreme returns, and it is possible that the returns will change dynamically.

In addition, herding behaviour may occur for the return distribution, but become more pronounced with market stress. Consequently, Christie and Huang [19] suggest that herding might be captured only for extreme returns. Ref. [4,25] suggest that Christie and Huang's [19] approach is too stringent to discover any empirical evidence of herding.

3.2.3. Herding Behaviour

Ref. [4,12,25] suggest using the following cross-sectional absolute deviation (CSAD) model:

$$CSAD_t = \alpha + \gamma_1|R_{m,t}| + \gamma_2(R_{m,t})^2 + \varepsilon_t \tag{2}$$

to facilitate the detection of herding for all returns where, at time t, the cross-sectional absolute deviation given by:

$$CSAD_t = \frac{1}{N}\sum_{i=1}^{N}|R_{i,t} - R_{m,t}|$$

is a measure of the average absolute return dispersion from $R_{m,t}$ to measure the return dispersion, and $|R_{m,t}|$ and $R_{i,t}$ are the absolute value of market returns and individual stock returns of stock i, respectively.

If one analyses more than one financial market, it is possible to use the following model:

$$CSAD_{i,t} = \alpha + \gamma_1|R_{i,m,t}| + \gamma_2(R_{i,m,t})^2 + \varepsilon_{i,t} \tag{3}$$

where, for market i at time t, $CSAD_{i,t}$ is the return dispersion calculated according to Equation (2), α is a constant, $|R_{i,m,t}|$ is the absolute value of market returns, $(R_{i,m,t})^2$ is the squared value of market returns, and $\varepsilon_{i,t}$ is a random error term.

3.2.4. Herding Behaviour in Up and Down Markets

As the direction of market returns may affect investor behaviour, it is sensible to examine whether there is any asymmetry in herding behaviour, conditional on the market rising or falling. The herding regression model is estimated separately for positive and negative market returns. Specifically, the two-equation system can be written as:

$$CSAD_{i,t}^{UP} = \alpha + \gamma_1^{UP}\left|R_{i,m,t}^{UP}\right| + \gamma_2^{UP}\left(R_{i,m,t}^{UP}\right)^2 + \varepsilon_{i,t} \text{ If } R_{i,m,t} > 0 \tag{4}$$

$$CSAD_{i,t}^{DOWN} = \alpha + \gamma_1^{DOWN}\left|R_{i,m,t}^{DOWN}\right| + \gamma_2^{DOWN}\left(R_{i,m,t}^{DOWN}\right)^2 + \varepsilon_{i,t} \text{ If } R_{i,m,t} < 0 \tag{5}$$

where, for market i at t, $CSAD_{i,t}^{UP}$ is the return dispersion when markets rise, α is a constant, $\left|R_{i,m,t}^{UP}\right|$ is the absolute value of market returns when the market rises, $\left(R_{i,m,t}^{UP}\right)^2$ is the squared value of market returns when the market rises, and $\varepsilon_{i,t}$ is a random error term. Variables with the superscript $DOWN$ in Equation (5) refer to market falls. The variable $CSAD_{i,t}$ for each market in Equations (4) and (5) is defined in Equation (2). A negative and significant estimated coefficient γ_2^{UP} or γ_2^{DOWN} would indicate the presence of herding.

3.2.5. Herding Behaviour in High and Low Trading Volumes

The level of herding behaviour may be associated with the trading volume. For this reason, it is possible to examine any asymmetric effects during periods of high and low trading volume. The trading volume is given the superscript $HIGH$ if the trading volume on day t is greater than the moving average for the previous 30 days. The trading volume is given the superscript LOW if it is less than the moving average for the previous 30 days. We also checked moving averages for periods of 7 and 90 days.

The empirical results of this paper are different from those in Tan et al. (2008), who use longer time periods of 60, 90, and 120 days. We used shorter time periods because many studies (for example, Chang et al. [4] suggest that the sentiment of investors typically occurs in a relatively short period of time. Therefore, we tested the following empirical models:

$$CSAD_{i,t}^{TV-HIGH} = \alpha + \gamma_1^{TV-HIGH}\left|R_{i,m,t}^{TV-HIGH}\right| + \gamma_2^{TV-HIGH}\left(R_{i,m,t}^{TV-HIGH}\right)^2 + \varepsilon_{i,t} \tag{6}$$

$$CSAD_{i,t}^{TV-LOW} = \alpha + \gamma_1^{TV-LOW}\left|R_{i,m,t}^{TV-LOW}\right| + \gamma_2^{TV-LOW}\left(R_{i,m,t}^{TV-LOW}\right)^2 + \varepsilon_{i,t} \tag{7}$$

where, in market i at t, $CSAD_{i,t}^{TV-HIGH}$ is the return dispersion when the trading volume is high, α is an intercept term, $\left|R_{i,m,t}^{TV-HIGH}\right|$ is the absolute value of market returns when the trading volume is high, $\left(R_{i,m,t}^{TV-HIGH}\right)^2$ is the squared value of market returns when the trading volume is high, and $\varepsilon_{i,t}$ is a random error term.

Similarly, variables with the superscript $TV-LOW$ refer to low trading volumes, where the superscript TV refers to trading volume. The variable $CSAD_{i,t}$ in Equations (6) and (7) is calculated using Equation (2). A negative and statistically significant estimated coefficient $\gamma_2^{TV-HIGH}$ or γ_2^{TV-LOW} would indicate herding.

4. Three Hypotheses of Herding Behaviour

There are three hypotheses regarding herding behaviour that will be tested in this paper. They are discussed separately in the following subsections.

4.1. First Hypothesis

Theoreticians and practitioners alike believe that there is herding behaviour in stock markets. It is hypothesised that this phenomenon also holds for the China and Taiwan stock markets. Therefore, we present the following hypothesis to test whether any herding exists in stocks in China and Taiwan:

Hypothesis 1. *Herding behaviour exists in the stock markets in China and Taiwan.*

We note that there are different factors that may induce herding behaviour, including a high degree of government involvement in equity markets and heavy interest rate intervention by the central bank.

In this paper, we use Equation (8) to test Hypothesis 1. A negative and statistically significant estimated coefficient γ_2 would indicate herding. We note that γ_1 in Equation (3) [and also in Equation (2) cannot be used to test Hypothesis 1. However, γ_1 is positive, implying that there is a linear relationship between the cross-sectional absolute deviation of returns, $CSAD_t$, and $|R_{i,m,t}|$. In addition, from Equation (3), we have a quadratic function for $CSAD_t$ and $|R_{i,m,t}|$:

$$CSAD_{i,t} = \alpha + \gamma_1|R_{i,m,t}| + \gamma_2(R_{i,m,t})^2 \tag{8}$$

where $CSAD_t$ reaches its maximum value when:

$$|R_{i,m,t}|^* = -\left(\frac{\gamma_1}{2\gamma_2}\right)$$

If $|R_{i,m,t}|$ increases when the realised average daily returns in absolute terms are less than $|R_{i,m,t}|^*$, $CSAD_t$ is still associated with an increasing trend. However, as $|R_{i,m,t}|$ exceeds $|R_{i,m,t}|^*$, then $CSAD$ starts to increase at a decreasing rate, which is captured by a negative and significant estimated coefficient γ_2. Therefore, the non-linear relationship between the market returns and the return dispersion would indicate herding behaviour. For this reason, a non-linear market return $(R_{i,m,t})^2$ is included in the equation.

However, if market participants tend to follow aggregate market behaviour and ignore their own priors during periods of large average price movements, then the linear and increasing relation between dispersion and market returns will no longer hold. Instead, the proposed relationship could increase non-linearly, or even decrease non-linearly. The empirical model builds on this intuition.

4.2. Second Hypothesis

It is well-known that stock markets perform differently in bull runs and bear markets [26,27]. Some studies, for example, Ref. [28], have found that herding behaviour can be different in bull runs and bear markets. It is common (see Ref. [29,30]) for the negative fear of potential loss when the market crashes to exceed the positive effects of potential gains under market booms. McQueen, Pinegar, and Thorley [31] claim that this is because while all stocks tend to respond quickly to negative macroeconomic news, small stocks tend to be slow in reacting to positive news.

As positive news often entails an increase in stock prices, a slow reaction implies a delay in reacting to good news. Therefore, herding is more pronounced during market downturns than upturns [24,28,32].

It is hypothesised that these phenomena also hold for the stock markets in China and Taiwan. Consequently, we propose the following hypothesis to test whether investors tend to display herding behaviour more in downturns than upturns:

Hypothesis 2. *Asymmetric herding behaviour exists in the stock markets in both China and Taiwan during bull and bear markets.*

Hypothesis 2 states that herding exists in bull and bear markets in the stock markets in China and Taiwan if the estimated coefficients γ_2^{UP} and γ_2^{DOWN} in Equations (4) and (5), respectively, are significantly different from zero. Chang et al. (2000) have shown that when γ_1^{UP} and γ_1^{DOWN} reach a certain value, both $CSAD_{i,t}^{UP}$ and $CSAD_{i,t}^{DOWN}$ start to decrease, or at least increase less proportionately with the market returns because there is a non-linear relationship between return dispersion and market returns. Therefore, γ_1^{UP} and γ_1^{DOWN} cannot be used to test Hypothesis 2, according to which herding exists in both bull and bear markets.

4.3. Third Hypothesis

It is also well-known (see Ref. [33]) that stock returns depend on the magnitude of the trading volume. In addition, the relationship between stock returns and trading volume is different for different levels of herding behaviour under alternative market conditions [24,34].

It is hypothesised that these phenomena also hold for the stock markets in China and Taiwan. Therefore, we propose the following hypothesis to test whether the level of herding behaviour is associated with trading volume:

Hypothesis 3. *Asymmetric herding behaviour exists in the stock markets in both China and Taiwan in high and low trading volumes.*

We confirm Hypothesis 3 that herding exists in the high and low volatility states of the stock markets in China and Taiwan if the estimated coefficients $\gamma_2^{TV-HIGH}$ and γ_2^{TV-LOW} in Equations (6) and (7), respectively, are significantly different from zero. Chang et al. (2000) have shown that when $\gamma_1^{TV-HIGH}$ or γ_1^{TV-LOW} reaches a certain value, $CSAD_{i,t}^{TV-HIGH}$ or $CSAD_{i,t}^{TV-LOW}$ will start to decrease, or at least increase less proportionately with the market returns because there is a non-linear relationship between return dispersion and market returns. Therefore, $\gamma_1^{TV-HIGH}$ or γ_1^{TV-LOW} cannot be used to test Hypothesis 3, according to which herding exists in high and low volatility states in the stock markets in China and Taiwan.

5. Empirical Analysis

5.1. Descriptive Statistics

This paper applies the CSAD return dispersion model, as given in Equations (2)–(7), and tests Hypotheses 1–3 to investigate whether there is any herding behaviour by examining the index returns from the stock markets in China and Taiwan. In order to do so, we first estimated the univariate descriptive statistics for the return dispersion and market returns of the markets in China and Taiwan. By definition, CSAD takes on a minimum value of zero when all individual stock returns move in perfect unison with the market, and increases when the returns of individual stocks deviate from the market returns.

Table 1 shows the descriptive statistics of market returns and CSAD return dispersions for the stock markets in both China and Taiwan. The average daily returns range from a low of 0.0129% for the TAIEX market to a high of 0.0899% for the SZB market. Daily returns of B-share markets consistently have higher mean values than those of A-shares markets, along with higher standard deviations. This evidence is consistent with the findings in Chang et al. (2000) and Tan et al. (2008) in that, in more well-developed markets, the greater the mean values of market returns and the higher the volatility.

The lowest daily returns ($^-$9.780) were observed on 6 August 2001 in the SHB market, while the second lowest minimum daily returns (−9.493) were observed on 6 July 1999 in the SZB market. Maximum daily returns also occurred around the same time. The lowest and highest daily returns were observed in the B-share markets as the B-shares were made accessible to foreign investors from February 2001.

The descriptive statistics show that the mean values of CSAD for A-shares are consistently higher than those of B-shares, and are also accompanied by higher standard deviations. Chiang and Zheng [35] argue that higher standard deviations in similar markets suggest that the markets had unusual cross-sectional variations due to unexpected news or shocks. The TAIEX market also has a relatively high mean returns dispersion, which is accompanied by the lowest standard deviation.

This observation is consistent with the herding behaviour according to which investors in the TAIEX market are more likely to react efficiently to news and diverse shocks. One explanation is that sophisticated investors in emerging markets have more information and analytical tools that allow them to assess and reallocate their investments, thereby leading to a higher dispersion of stock returns and lower standard deviations.

Table 1. Descriptive statistics of cross-sectional absolute deviation (CSAD) and market returns of the stock markets in China and Taiwan.

	SHA		SHB		SZA		SZB		TAIEX	
	CSAD	R_m	CSAD	R_m	CSAD	R_m	CSAD	R_m	CSAD	R_m
Mean	1.504 ***	0.028	1.107 ***	0.076 **	1.453 ***	0.038	1.272 ***	0.089 ***	1.549 ***	0.012
Std. dev.	0.767	1.511	0.686	2.055	0.684	1.656	0.693	1.957	0.656	1.398
Minimum	0	−8.845	0	−9.780	0	−8.539	0	−9.493	0	−9.460
Maximum	7.220	9.856	5.129	9.914	6.678	9.680	5.287	9.857	6.014	6.740
Skewness	0.835 ***	0.066 *	1.132 ***	0.280 ***	0.589 ***	−0.293 ***	0.773 ***	0.385 ***	0.315 ***	−0.149 ***
Kurtosis	6.225 ***	8.048 ***	5.741 ***	8.446 ***	6.833 ***	6.554 ***	5.044 ***	8.391 ***	5.024 ***	6.308 ***
N obs.	3982		4174		3877		4174		3779	
N firms	425		50		415		45		455	

Note: CSAD is defined as cross-sectional absolute deviation. R_m is the market return. SHA, SHB, SZA, SZB, and TAIEX are stated in Section 4.1. ***, **, and * represent statistical significance at the 1%, 5%, and 10% levels, respectively.

In addition to the above results, Ref. [25,31] argue that investors may fear potential losses in downturns more than they enjoy potential gains in upturns. This proposition leads investors to display herding behaviour. The consequence is a reduction in the returns dispersion. The empirical findings in this paper are consistent with such an argument.

The stationarity of the measures of the returns dispersion is evaluated through the implementation of the Augmented Dickey-Fuller (ADF) test. As all the series are found to be stationary, we do not report details of the ADF test results. After reviewing the relevant literature, we have developed the three hypotheses presented in Section 4 to test whether the stock markets in China and Taiwan exhibit herding under different conditions. We discuss each of the hypotheses in the following subsections.

5.2. Testing Herding Behaviour (H1)

In order to test the first proposed hypothesis as to whether there is any herding behaviour in the stock markets in both China and Taiwan, we examined whether the estimated coefficients in Equation (3) are significantly less than zero, as discussed in Section 4.1. The empirical findings are reported in Table 2. According to the definition of the empirical model in Equation (3), a negative and statistically significant estimated coefficient γ_2 would indicate the presence of herding.

Table 2. Results of herding behaviour in the sample stock markets.

Market Name (N)	α	$\gamma 1$	$\gamma 2$	Adj. R^2
SHA (3982)	1.053 (59.32) ***	0.564 (27.33) ***	−0.053 (−15.09) ***	0.249
SHB (4174)	0.668 (48.15) ***	0.479 (32.19) ***	−0.043 (−22.42) ***	0.290
SZA (3877)	1.000 (56.62) ***	0.473 (23.26) ***	−0.035 (−8.55) ***	0.299
SZB (4174)	0.839 (55.36) ***	0.479 (31.15) ***	−0.044 (−21.24) ***	0.273
TAIEX (3779)	1.126 (47.78) ***	0.588 (12.81) ***	−0.072 (−5.47) ***	0.267

Notes: Numbers in parentheses are *t*-statistics from Ref. [36] consistent standard errors. ***, **, and * represent statistical significance at the 1%, 5%, and 10% levels, respectively. This table reports the results of the estimation of the empirical model in Equation (3): $CSAD_{i,t} = \alpha + \gamma_1 |R_{i,m,t}| + \gamma_2 (R_{i,m,t})^2 + \varepsilon_{i,t}$.

Table 2 shows that the estimates of γ_2 are significantly negative in all markets at the 1% level, thereby supporting the first hypothesis and suggesting that there is strong herding behaviour in the Taiwan stock index, TAIEX, and all the Chinese stock indexes, including SHA, SHB, SZA, and SZB. The empirical findings do not reject Hypothesis 1, thereby suggesting that there is significant herding behaviour in the SHB, SZB, and TAIEX stock markets, which are emerging markets. These results are consistent with the empirical findings in Ref. [4,12,16].

The coefficients on the linear component of $|R_{i,m,t}|$ are positive and significant, thereby indicating that there is both a significant and positive linear relationship between $CSAD_{i,t}$ and $|R_{i,m,t}|$. Table 2 shows that the combined effects of the herding effect and the linear relationship between $CSAD_{i,t}$ and $|R_{i,m,t}|$ explain from 24.9% (SHA) to 29.9% (SZA) of the total variation in $CSAD_{i,t}$. In addition, substituting the estimated coefficients for the SHA market ($\gamma_1 = 0.564$ and $\gamma_2 = -0.053$) into the quadratic relationship in Equation (8) indicates that $CSAD_t$ reaches a maximum when the following holds:

$$|R_{i,m,t}| = |R_{i,m,t}|^* = 5.321\%$$

This outcome suggests that, during large price movements in market returns that exceed the threshold level $|R_{i,m,t}|^*$, the $CSAD_t$ increases at a decreasing rate, as in Figure 1.

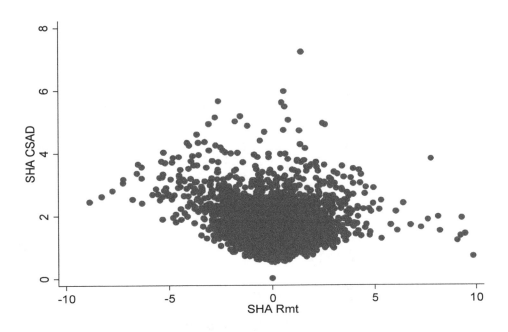

Figure 1. Relationship between the daily return dispersion ($CSAD_{i,t}$) and equally-weighted market return ($R_{i,m,t}$) for the SHA market.

In addition to the negative and statistically significant estimated coefficient, γ_2, the sizes of the coefficient capture the magnitudes of the herding behaviour in each market [34]. As the largest value of the estimated coefficient, γ_2, is found in the TAIEX market (as measured at -0.072), while the smallest value lies in the SZA market (as measured at -0.035), the estimated coefficients show that herding behaviour is greater in the TAIEX market than in the emerging markets in China.

5.3. Testing Herding Behaviour in Up and Down Markets (H2)

The second hypothesis tests whether herding is asymmetric in the stock markets in China and Taiwan when they rise and fall. Table 3 reports the outcomes in testing the second hypothesis. According to the models in Equations (4) and (5), the negative and statistically significant estimated coefficients, γ_2^{UP} and γ_2^{DOWN}, respectively, indicate that there is herding behaviour due to the up and down markets. If the magnitudes of γ_2^{UP} and γ_2^{DOWN} are different, then the additional herding behaviours due to the up and down markets are different, thereby showing that herding behaviour is asymmetric in both up and down markets.

Table 3. Results of herding behaviour in the stock markets in China and Taiwan in up and down markets.

Market Name (N)	UP Market $R_{i,m,t} > 0$				Market Name (N)	DOWN Market $R_{i,m,t} < 0$			
	α	$\gamma 1^{UP}$	$\gamma 2^{UP}$	Adj. R^2		A	$\gamma 1^{DOWN}$	$\gamma 2^{DOWN}$	Adj. R^2
SHA (2224)	0.916 (39.79) ***	0.605 (22.96) ***	−0.066 (−13.97) ***	0.236	SHA (1758)	1.309 (53.61) ***	0.391 (11.65) ***	−0.015 (−2.39) **	0.272
SHB (2314)	0.560 (31.99) ***	0.546 (28.29) ***	−0.051 (−21.42) ***	0.337	SHB (1860)	0.840 (40.19) ***	0.356 (15.46) ***	−0.027 (−8.32) ***	0.227
SZA (2237)	0.862 (38.75) ***	0.551 (22.31) ***	−0.059 (−11.78) ***	0.284	SZA (1640)	1.288 (58.35) ***	0.291 (11.73) ***	−0.000 (−0.01)	0.338
SZB (2372)	0.700 (36.27) ***	0.581 (30.21) ***	−0.056 (−24.63) ***	0.329	SZB (1802)	1.082 (50.06) ***	0.282 (11.34) ***	−0.017 (−4.39) ***	0.197
TAIEX (2058)	0.960 (39.23) ***	0.783 (23.80) ***	−0.111 (−12.78) ***	0.329	TAIEX (1721)	1.332 (50.91) ***	0.381 (8.02) ***	−0.034 (−2.62) ***	0.199

Notes: Numbers in parentheses are t-statistics based on Ref. [36] consistent standard errors. ***, **, and * represent statistical significance at the 1%, 5%, and 10% levels, respectively.

This table reports the results of the estimation of the empirical model in Equations (4) and (5): $CSAD_{i,t}^{UP} = \alpha + \gamma_1^{UP} \left| R_{i,m,t}^{UP} \right| + \gamma_2^{UP} \left(R_{i,m,t}^{UP} \right)^2 + \varepsilon_{i,t}$ if $R_{i,m,t} > 0$ $CSAD_{i,t}^{DOWN} =$

$\alpha + \gamma_1^{DOWN} \left| R_{i,m,t}^{DOWN} \right| + \gamma_2^{DOWN} \left(R_{i,m,t}^{DOWN} \right)^2 + \varepsilon_{i,t}$ if $R_{i,m,t} < 0$.

Table 3 shows that the estimated coefficient, γ_2^{UP}, is negative and statistically significant in all markets at the 1% level, thereby implying that there is herding behaviour due to the up markets in all cases that have been considered. However, the coefficient, γ_2^{DOWN}, is negative and statistically significant at the 1% level only for SHB, SZB, and TAIEX, significant at the 5% level for SHA, and not significant for SZA. These results suggest that there is herding behaviour due to the down markets for SHB, SZB, TAIEX, and SHA, but not for SZA. It follows that Hypothesis 2 is rejected only for the SZA market.

For SZA, as the estimated coefficient γ_2^{UP} is significant, while the estimated coefficient γ_2^{DOWN} is not significant, it follows that herding behaviour is asymmetric in the up and down markets, respectively. In addition, for SHB, SZB, TAIEX, and SHA, as both the estimated coefficients, γ_2^{UP} and γ_2^{DOWN}, are significant, but of different magnitudes, the herding behaviour is asymmetric in the up and down markets. Therefore, Hypothesis 2 is supported empirically for the SHB, SZB, TAIEX, and SHA markets.

The outcomes of the tests of Hypothesis 2 are consistent with the empirical results as reported in Ref. [12,35]. A possible explanation for these findings is that institutional investors in the China and Taiwan stock markets may engage in positive feedback trading by buying additional shares when prices are rising, and selling them when the prices are falling [37,38]. However, the empirical findings in this paper are different from those in Ref. [4,24,31,34], among others, who find that investors behave more homogeneously when stock markets are declining.

Breaking down the up and down markets, the up market states are bull markets that are characterized by optimism under a strong economy, with confident investors who expect stock prices to continue rising [39,40]. On the other hand, down markets are bear markets that are characterized by falling prices and shrouded in pessimism. Bear markets typically occur before the economy starts to contract [15,41].

5.4. Testing Herding Behaviour during HIGH and LOW Trading Volume States (H3)

The third hypothesis conjectures that asymmetric herding exists in the China and Taiwan stock markets during high and low trading volume states. Table 4 reports the empirical results in testing the third hypothesis. According to the definitions in Equations (6) and (7), negative and statistically significant estimated coefficients, $\gamma_2^{TV-HIGH}$ and γ_2^{TV-LOW}, indicate herding behaviour in the high and low trading volume states, respectively.

The results in Table 4 show that the estimated coefficient, $\gamma_2^{TV-HIGH}$, is negative and statistically significant for all the markets, except for SZA.

On the other hand, the estimated coefficient, γ_2^{TV-LOW}, is negative and significant in all markets at the 1% level, thereby implying that there is a strong indication of herding in all markets during the low trading states. For SZA, as the estimated coefficient, $\gamma_2^{TV-HIGH}$, is negative, but not significant, while the estimated coefficient, γ_2^{TV-LOW}, is significantly negative, it follows that herding behaviour is asymmetric in the up and down markets, respectively.

In short, the empirical findings strongly suggest that there is evidence of herding in sample markets when the trading volume is either high or low. Nonetheless, herding is greater when the trading volume is low than when it is high. A possible explanation is that, during low trading volume states, less trading happens, and thus share returns become naturally more homogenous and correlated, which can lead to ineffective herding behaviour.

Ref. [12,24] find that herding is greater when the trading volume is high. It is worth noting that the empirical results in this paper find that herding behaviour is greater when the trading volume is high. However, it is also found that herding is even greater when the trading volume is low, which is also in line with the findings of Ref. [28].

This paper also examines Hypothesis 3 with moving averages of 7 and 90 days. The empirical results show that the 7-day and 90-day moving averages are consistent with the use of 30-day moving averages. In summary, the empirical results provide very strong evidence in favour of Hypothesis 3.

Table 4. Results of herding behaviour in the China and Taiwan stock markets during HIGH and LOW trading volume states.

Market Name (N)	$TV^{HIGH} > TV^{MA}_{t-30}$				Market Name (N)	$TV^{LOW} < TV^{MA}_{t-30}$			
	α	$\gamma1^{TV\text{-}HIGH}$	$\gamma2^{TV\text{-}HIGH}$	Adj. R^2		α	$\gamma1^{TV\text{-}LOW}$	$\gamma2^{TV\text{-}LOW}$	Adj. R^2
SHA (2003)	1.423 (58.53) ***	0.297 (10.03) ***	−0.022 (−3.83) ***	0.111	SHA (1949)	0.790 (34.87) ***	0.800 (25.31) ***	−0.082 (−12.93) ***	0.371
SHB (1783)	0.962 (37.21) ***	0.3224 (14.24) ***	−0.027 (−9.74) ***	0.155	SHB (2361)	0.532 (35.06) ***	0.542 (28.41) ***	−0.052 (−18.29) ***	0.341
SZA (1975)	1.357 (56.70) ***	0.211 (6.85) ***	−0.005 (−0.79)	0.167	SZA (1872)	0.752 (34.08) ***	0.670 (23.93) ***	−0.05 (−8.40) ***	0.421
SZB (1770)	1.150 (45.40) ***	0.319 (14.12) ***	−0.027 (−9.20) ***	0.156	SZB (2374)	0.689 (39.9) ***	0.542 (26.19) ***	−0.054 (−15.88) ***	0.306
TAIEX (1835)	1.382 (55.5) ***	0.416 (10.38) ***	−0.042 (−3.78) ***	0.198	TAIEX (1914)	0.953 (28.32) ***	0.653 (8.38) ***	−0.082 (−14.05) ***	0.307

Notes: Numbers in parentheses are t-statistics based on Ref. [36] consistent standard errors. ***, **, and * represent statistical significance at the 1%, 5%, and 10% levels, respectively. Thirty-day moving averages of trading volume (TV) are given when TV is high and low. This table reports the results of the estimation of Equations (6) and (7): $CSAD^{TV-HIGH}_{i,t} = \alpha + \gamma_1^{TV-HIGH} \left| R^{TV-HIGH}_{i,m,t} \right| + \gamma_2^{TV-HIGH} \left(R^{TV-HIGH}_{i,m,t} \right)^2 + \varepsilon_{i,t}, CSAD^{TV-LOW}_{i,t} = \alpha + \gamma_1^{TV-LOW} \left| R^{TV-LOW}_{i,m,t} \right| + \gamma_2^{TV-LOW} \left(R^{TV-LOW}_{i,m,t} \right)^2 + \varepsilon_{i,t}.$

6. Concluding Remarks

As it has been argued in the literature that markets with a Confucian background are more likely to exhibit herding behaviour, this paper examined the stock markets in China and Taiwan through empirical analysis. There was overwhelming evidence of herding behaviour from the full sample markets. The three hypotheses were tested against empirical evidence, and were all supported by the data.

In respect to the first hypothesis, there was significant herding from all markets, regardless of whether they were emerging or frontier markets.

In addition to testing the second and third hypotheses, it was found that herding is greater in up markets than in down markets, and was also greater during low trading volume states than during high trading volumes. The up markets are positive and profitable for investors, and are key features of bull markets. During a bull market, investors are more optimistic with regards to trading.

However, this does not mean that investors make decisions entirely on they own. When investors are overly optimistic, they exhibit risky behaviour by making risky investment decisions, such as buying too many stocks, based either on their own decisions or by following other traders [40]. Therefore, bull markets might be creating a foundation for possible herding behaviour.

Moreover, previous research has suggested that one of the indicators of down markets is a reduction in trading volume, which follows uncertainty among investors. Investors perceive falls in trading volume with an understandable fear that the market might also fall. Consequently, investors are more likely to convert shares into fast cash [39,42].

Therefore, this sentiment makes the fear among investors contagious, thereby leading to the formation of herding. On the other hand, in bear markets, markets cool down and less trading happens, and thus stock returns become less diverse and more correlated, which may lead to ineffective herding behaviour.

In general, this paper detected overwhelming herding from the entire sample markets. For this reason, all three hypotheses were supported strongly by the data. This paper analysed the stock markets of China and Taiwan empirically based on 15 years of daily observations, which offers another contribution to the literature on herding. Although the sample period finishes in 2014, the data are more than sufficient to test the three hypotheses relating to the stock markets in China and Taiwan, both of which have Confucian cultures.

Although the stock market in Taiwan is relatively developed compared to the markets in China, it still displayed strong herding behaviour. Therefore, further research is necessary to examine herding behaviour beyond the maturity of market settings. Moreover, the authors of this paper intend to include non-Confucian markets as a control group in future research to ascertain if herding behaviour is found in Confucian and non-Confucian countries.

Author Contributions: Conceptualization, B.J.M.-U., M.M. and W.-K.W.; Data curation, B.J.M.-U.; Formal analysis, B.J.M.-U., M.M. and W.-K.W.; Funding acquisition, M.M.; Investigation W.-K.W.; Methodology, M.M.; Project administration, M.M.; Resources, M.M.; Software, B.J.M.-U.; Supervision, M.M., M.M. and W.-K.W.; Writing—original draft, B.J.M.-U.; Writing—review & editing, M.M.

Acknowledgments: The authors are most grateful for the helpful comment s and suggestions of three referees. The second author wishes to thank the Australian Research Council and the Ministry of Science and Technology (MOST), Taiwan, for financial support. The fourth author would like to acknowledge financial support from Asia University, China Medical University Hospital, the Hang Seng University of Hong Kong, the Research Grants Council of Hong Kong (Project Number 12500915), and the Ministry of Science and Technology (MOST, Project Numbers 106-2410-H-468-002 and 107-2410-H-468-002-MY3), Taiwan.

References

1. Zheng, Y.; Chen, H.; Wong, W.-K. China's stock market integration with a leading power and a close neighbor. *J. Risk Financ. Manag.* **2009**, *2*, 38–74.

2. Spyrou, S. Herding in Financial Market: A Review of Literature. *Rev. Behav. Financ.* **2013**, *5*, 175–194. [CrossRef]

3. Bikhchandani, S.; Sharma, S. Herd behavior in financial markets. *IMF Staff Papers* **2000**, *47*, 279–310.

4. Chang, E.C.; Cheng, J.W.; Khorana, A. An examination of herd behaviour in equity markets: An international perspective. *J. Bank. Financ.* **2000**, *24*, 1651–1679. [CrossRef]

5. Chang, W.C.; Wong, W.-K.; Koh, B.K. Chinese values in Singapore: Traditional and modern. *Asian J. Soc. Psychol.* **2003**, *6*, 5–29. [CrossRef]

6. Wong, W.-K.; Penm, J.H.W.; Terrell, R.D.; Lim, K.Y.C. The relationship between stock markets of major developed countries and Asian emerging markets. *Adv. Decis. Sci.* **2004**, *8*, 201–218.

7. Fong, W.M.; Wong, W.-K.; Lean, H.H. International momentum strategies: A stochastic dominance approach. *J. Financ. Mark.* **2005**, *8*, 89–109. [CrossRef]

8. Bikhchandani, S.; Hirshleifer, D.; Welch, I. A theory of fads, fashion, custom, and cultural change as informational cascades. *J. Polit. Econ.* **1992**, *100*, 992–1026. [CrossRef]

9. Scharfstein, D.S.; Stein, J.C. Herd behavior and investment. *Am. Econ. Rev.* **1990**, *80*, 465–479.

10. Devenow, A.; Welch, I. Rational herding in financial economics. *Eur. Econ. Rev.* **1996**, *40*, 603–615. [CrossRef]

11. Demirer, R.; Kutan, A.M. Does herding behavior exist in Chinese stock markets? *J. Int. Financ. Mark. Inst. Money* **2006**, *16*, 123–142. [CrossRef]

12. Tan, L.; Chiang, T.C.; Mason, J.R.; Nelling, E. Herding behaviour in Chinese stock markets: An examination of A and B shares. *Pacific Basin Financ. J.* **2008**, *16*, 61–77. [CrossRef]

13. Chen, Y.F.; Wang, C.Y.; Lin, F.L. Do qualified foreign institutional investors herd in Taiwan's securities market? *Emerg. Mark. Financ. Trade* **2008**, *44*, 62–74. [CrossRef]

14. Chiang, T.C.; Li, J.; Tan, L. Empirical investigation of herding behavior in Chinese stock markets: Evidence from quantile regression analysis. *Global Financ. J.* **2010**, *21*, 111–124. [CrossRef]

15. Clark, E.; Qiao, Z.; Wong, W.K. Theories of risk: Testing investor behaviour on the Taiwan stock and stock index futures markets. *Econ. Inq.* **2016**, *54*, 907–924. [CrossRef]

16. Chang, C.H.; Lin, S.J. The effects of national culture and behavioural pitfalls on investors' decision-making: Herding behaviour in international stock markets. *Int. Rev. Econ. Financ.* **2015**, *37*, 380–392. [CrossRef]

17. Beckmann, D.; Menkhoff, L.; Suto, M. Does culture influence asset managers' views and behaviour? *J. Econ. Behav. Organ.* **2008**, *67*, 624–643. [CrossRef]

18. Munkh-Ulzii, B.; Moslehpour, M.; Van Kien, P. Empirical models of herding behaviour for Asian countries with Confucian Culture. In *Predictive Econometrics and Big Data*; Kreinovich, V., Sriboonchitta, S., Chakpitak, N., Eds.; Studies in Computational Intelligence; Springer Nature: Basingstoke, UK, 2018; Volume 753.

19. Christie, W.G.; Huang, R.D. Following the Pied Piper: Do individual returns herd around the market? *Financ. Anal. J.* **1995**, *51*, 31–37. [CrossRef]

20. Lin, A.Y.; Swanson, P.E. The behaviour and performance of foreign investors in emerging equity markets: Evidence from Taiwan. *Int. Rev. Financ.* **2003**, *4*, 189–210. [CrossRef]

21. Lin, A.Y.; Huang, L.S.; Chen, M.Y. Price co-movement and institutional performance following large market movements. *Emerg. Mark. Financ. Trade* **2007**, *43*, 37–61. [CrossRef]

22. Demirer, R.; Kutan, A.M.; Chen, C.D. Do investors herd in emerging stock markets? *Evidence from the Taiwanese market. J. Econ. Behav. Organ.* **2010**, *76*, 283–295. [CrossRef]

23. Hwang, S.; Salmon, M. Market stress and herding. *J. Empir. Financ.* **2004**, *11*, 585–616. [CrossRef]

24. Yao, J.; Ma, C.; He, W.P. Investor herding behaviour of Chinese stock market. *Int. Rev. Econ. Financ.* **2014**, *29*, 12–29. [CrossRef]

25. Gleason, K.C.; Mathur, I.; Peterson, M.A. Analysis of intraday herding behaviour among the sector ETFs. *J. Empir. Financ.* **2004**, *11*, 681–694. [CrossRef]

26. Pagan, A.R.; Sossounov, K.A. A simple framework for analyzing bull and bear markets. *J. Appl. Econ.* **2003**, *18*, 23–46. [CrossRef]

27. Brown, G.W.; Cliff, M.T. Investor sentiment and the near-term stock market. *J. Empir. Financ.* **2004**, *11*, 1–27. [CrossRef]

28. Mobarek, A.; Mollah, S.; Keasey, K. A cross-country analysis of herd behaviour in Europe. *J. Int. Financ. Mark. Inst. Money* **2014**, *32*, 107–127. [CrossRef]

29. Abolafia, M.Y.; Kilduff, M. Enacting market crisis: The social construction of a speculative bubble. *Adm. Sci. Q.* **1988**, *33*, 177–193. [CrossRef]

30. Drożdż, S.; Grümmer, F.; Górski, A.Z.; Ruf, F.; Speth, J. Dynamics of competition between collectivity and noise in the stock market. *Phys. A Stat. Mech. Appl.* **2000**, *287*, 440–449. [CrossRef]

31. McQueen, G.; Pinegar, M.; Thorley, S. Delayed reaction to good news and the cross-autocorrelation of portfolio returns. *J. Financ.* **1996**, *51*, 889–919. [CrossRef]

32. Drożdż, S.; Grümmer, F.; Ruf, F.; Speth, J. Towards identifying the world stock market cross-correlations: DAX versus Dow Jones. *Phys. A Stat. Mech. Appl.* **2001**, *294*, 226–234. [CrossRef]

33. Lee, B.S.; Rui, O.M. The dynamic relationship between stock returns and trading volume: Domestic and cross-country evidence. *J. Bank. Financ.* **2002**, *26*, 51–78. [CrossRef]

34. Lao, P.; Singh, H. Herding behaviour in the Chinese and Indian stock markets. *J. Asian Econ.* **2011**, *22*, 495–506. [CrossRef]

35. Chiang, T.C.; Zheng, D. An empirical analysis of herd behaviour in global stock markets. *J. Bank. Financ.* **2010**, *34*, 1911–1921. [CrossRef]

36. Newey, W.K.; West, K. A simple positive semi-definite, heteroskedasticity and autocorrelation consistent covariance matrix. *Econometrica* **1987**, *55*, 703–708. [CrossRef]

37. Nofsinger, J.R.; Sias, R.W. Herding and feedback trading by institutional and individual investors. *J. Financ.* **1999**, *54*, 2263–2295. [CrossRef]

38. Koutmos, G. Positive feedback trading: A review. *Rev. Behav. Financ.* **2014**, *6*, 155–162. [CrossRef]

39. Jansen, D.W.; Tsai, C.L. Monetary policy and stock returns: Financing constraints and asymmetries in bull and bear markets. *J. Empir. Financ.* **2010**, *17*, 981–990. [CrossRef]

40. Kurov, A. Investor sentiment and the stock market's reaction to monetary policy. *J. Bank. Financ.* **2010**, *34*, 139–149. [CrossRef]

41. Vieito, J.P.; Wong, W.-K.; Zhu, Z.Z. Could the global financial crisis improve the performance of the G7 stocks markets? *Appl. Econ.* **2016**, *48*, 1066–1080. [CrossRef]

42. Wong, W.-K.; Manzur, M.; Chew, B.K. How rewarding is technical analysis? Evidence from Singapore stock market. *Appl. Financ. Econ.* **2003**, *13*, 543–551. [CrossRef]

13

Information Disclosure Ranking, Industry Production Market Competition and Mispricing

Bing Wang [1], Si Xu [2,*], Kung-Cheng Ho [3], I-Ming Jiang [4] and Hung-Yi Huang [5]

[1] School of Accounting, Fujian Jiangxia University, Fuzhou 350108, China; wangbing@fjjxu.edu.cn

[2] School of Economics & Management, South China Normal University, Guangzhou 510006, China

[3] School of Finance, Collaborative Innovation Center of Industrial Upgrading and Regional Finance (Hubei), Zhongnan University of Economics and Law, Wuhan 430073, China; z0004531@zuel.edu.cn

[4] Faculty of Digital Finance, College of Management, Yuan Ze University, Taoyuan 32003, Taiwan; jiangfinance@saturn.yzu.edu.tw

[5] Department of Business Administration, Soochow University, Taipei 10048, Taiwan; hy.huang@scu.edu.tw

* Correspondence: xusi@m.scnu.edu.cn

Abstract: Improving the transparency of corporate information disclosure is a key principle of corporate governance in Taiwan. This study uses the information disclosure assessment system established by the information disclosure and transparency ranking system to explore whether information transparency can reduce the degree of mispricing. The study uses the data of 10,686 listed companies in Taiwan for the period from 2005 to 2014. We find that a higher information disclosure ranking (IDR) of rated companies corresponds to a more substantial reduction in the degree of mispricing. Moreover, we discover that product market competition affects mispricing in that smaller degrees of mispricing reflect greater exclusivity; this suggests that lower industry transaction and competition costs lead to less substantial mispricing. Finally, we observe that the effect of information disclosure score on the degree of mispricing is lower in more exclusive industries. Furthermore, a regression process using instrumental variables reveals that IDRs have the significant effect of reducing the degree of mispricing.

Keywords: information disclosure ranking; industry production market competition; mispricing; Taiwan stock market

JEL Classification: G18; G30; G34

---

1. Introduction

Financial fraud, such as that committed by Tyco, Enron, and WorldCom, has become prevalent. Some internal managers or shareholders take advantage of their own business operations out of self-interest, leaving investors with insufficient information in a relatively weak position. Detecting fraud that causes loss to investors and corporate decline is difficult [1–3].

Therefore, in addition to a greater amount of attention paid by scholars and people practicing business to the matter of information disclosure, financial supervision agencies in various countries have developed guidelines for measuring transparency when encouraging enterprises to improve information disclosure. In 2003, the Taiwan Stock Exchange Corporation (TSEC) entrusted the Securities and Futures Institute (SFI) with the task of improving the information disclosure system to ensure a reduction in information asymmetry between insiders and outsiders on all companies listed in the TSEC. The purpose of this information disclosure system is to plan and design evaluation indicators that meet the needs of the information disclosure and transparency ranking system (IDTRS).

The investment publication is expected to be capable of easily determining the degree of corporate information asymmetry by publishing evaluation grades for listed companies annually.

Differences in information disclosure often imply that various agency problems [4,5], stock liquidity [6,7], corporate capital costs [8,9], and earnings quality [10] may influence enterprise value. Moreover, the evaluation level naturally becomes an auxiliary reference for investor decisions.

The relationship between information disclosure quality and corporate value is inextricable. Improving the integrity of information disclosure can improve the quality of information disclosure, reduce corporate capital costs, and increase shareholder wealth [11]. This effectively repairs damage caused by information asymmetry between shareholders and operators [12,13]; moreover, it can mitigate the effect of excessive executive compensation on company value and enhance corporate value [14]. Merton [15] indicated that the complete disclosure of information helps investors identify with the company and attract new investors, which can reduce the cost of capital and increase the value of the company. Diamond and Verrecchia [7] also discovered that incensement in response to information disclosure can reduce information asymmetry and transaction costs, improve liquidity, and reduce corporate capital costs [16–18]. Klapper and Love [19] explored 14 emerging markets and discovered that more effective corporate governance corresponds to favorable operational performance and corporate value. Bai et al. [20], Black et al. [21], and Braga-Alves and Shastri [22] have examined corporate governance in China, the Soviet Union, Mexico, and Brazil, respectively, and its relationship with company value, and they have reached the same conclusion as the aforementioned study. Ho et al. [23] applied the data of listed companies in Taiwan for the period from 2005 to 2013 to demonstrate that product market competition is negatively correlated with corporate value and that when product market competition is weak, information disclosure is more conducive to company value.

According to the aforementioned research, information disclosure can effectively reduce information asymmetry, reduce company costs, and enhance company value. However, because information disclosure also has external costs, more disclosure is not always better. Excessive disclosure of information may provide competitors with a better understanding of the company's strategy, profitability, and innovation level as well as weaken competitive advantages [24]. Bloomfield and Fischer [25] explored the effects of information disclosure on capital costs, reporting that corporate capital costs increase when firms believe that investors respond to noncritical disclosures.

Product market competition is often considered an external mechanism that affects information disclosure [23]. Information disclosure is endogenous but also influenced by the market competition environment. One view holds that industries with low levels of competition tend to have excess returns and therefore low levels of information disclosure. Information disclosure can also help sellers to distinguish themselves from competitors. However, the fierce competition in the product market is not always beneficial. Other studies have conducted a relatively comprehensive exploration of market competition level by measuring the degree of market product differentiation; they have discovered that higher levels of competition correspond to lower likelihood of high-quality information disclosure. Research has also demonstrated that if the cost of disclosure is high, companies will disclose higher-quality information. When the market itself is more competitive and disclosure cost is higher, competitors will tend to disclose higher-quality information to mitigate high costs. When the degree of competition in the market is not high, competition will always lead to the disclosure of low-quality information regardless of the level of cost.

The degree of mispricing affects the choice of financing method. Baker et al. [26] indicated that when companies rely heavily on equity financing, the effect of mispricing on equity financing is more obvious. However, even if external financing is not required, mispricing may directly affect company investments. The degree of mispricing is affected by many factors [27]. Sloan [28] proposed that investors do not understand that inherent future earnings information is the primary cause of mispricing. Moreover, because the quality of public information remains at the same level, an increased amount of information does not necessarily correspond to a reasonable equity valuation. Compliance with regulations improves company information environments, reduces mispricing, and increases stock market efficiency. Furthermore, policymakers should consider the quality of information provided when attempting to increase capital market efficiency by forcing more disclosures.

Emerging markets possess the characteristics of rapid economic development and remarkable market potential. However, their market economic system remains in a stage of gradual improvement, their external supervision mechanism is not perfect, their information disclosure mechanism is incomplete, and their internal control system of listed companies is inadequate. Investors are more likely to be in an unfavorable position when investing with limited information acquisition and professional knowledge. Therefore, improving the level of investor protection and exploring the relationship between information disclosure and degree of corporate value is necessary to enable investors to more accurately judge investment value. Some scholars have turned their attention away from mature markets to investigate whether emerging markets are subject to the same phenomenon [29].

Investor relations indicators provided by the Association for Investment Management and Research (AIMR) and the Center for International Financial Analysis and Research (CIFAR) can be used as a measure of information disclosure, in addition to other variables used as information disclosure agents [30,31]. However, the AIMR score is not available after 1996, and the CIFAR indicator system does not include Taiwan. We use the SFI information disclosure ranking (IDR) as a measure of information disclosure quality and expand the scope of application of SFI IDRs. By contrast, SFI forms a research team composed of experts from independent parties—consisting of the accounting and finance profession, academic researchers, in-house research staff, and IT personnel—using 114 measures to evaluate the information quality of all listed firms, except for some firms with inadequate data or under regulatory investigation. Therefore, the disclosure scores are based on the same set of information criteria and are not skewed to large firms and variation in accounting standards. The research results are highly relevant to Taiwan's actual situation and possess certain theoretical value.

We show our main results and contributions. First, using a relatively large sample, this study provides further support for the effectiveness of the information disclosure ranking in reducing information asymmetry between enterprises and investors and reflects the degree of mispricing in emerging markets. Our results show that information disclosure ranking, industry production market competition and their interaction did influence the mispricing of Taiwanese firms between 2005 and 2014. Second, we find unique data that shows the SFI's measurements for information disclosure ranking are negatively associated with mispricing. It suggests that higher levels of information disclosure rankings (transparency) reduce agency problems, thus leading to lower mispricing. Third, we find that the benefits of increased information disclosure rankings levels are significant only for firms that face strong competition in the product market, compared to other firms in less competitive industries. Finally, we solve the endogeneity problem to improve the degree of mispricing, information disclosure may improve the information disclosure score as a result of decreased mispricing. In summary, the primary purpose of the evaluation system is to provide investors with a convenient pipeline for knowing the level of information disclosure of a company, thereby helping investors to make more informed investment decisions. However, the implementation of the system also indirectly forces enterprises to improve the quality of their information disclosure. The information disclosure evaluation system reduces information asymmetry between enterprises and investors and reflects the degree of mispricing. We argue that information disclosure rankings could facilitate managers' forward thinking, and firms with better information disclosure rankings or corporate social responsibility not only aim to reduce short-term mispricing but also focus on long-term sustainable development [32–39]. Moreover, information disclosure rankings firms are found to be more ethical [23,40], and managers are encouraged to undertake actions that boost long-term firm value, thus resulting in less mispricing.

This paper is structured as follows: the first section introduces the research background and literature review, the second section presents the hypothesis development, and the third section explains the sample and the definition of variables required in this study. The fourth section provides an analysis of the empirical results, and the final section presents conclusions drawn on the basis of the empirical findings of this study.

2. Hypothesis Development

2.1. Information Disclosure and Mispricing

Information disclosure is inextricably linked to mispricing. According to Hail [41], the effect of information pre-disclosure is favorable in developing markets because of relatively relaxed regulations and the lack of mandatory public rankings. Conversely, the trading market has higher levels of disclosure and a smaller discrepancy between real values and market expectations. Drake et al. [42] argued that because the quality of disclosed information improves the ability of investors to more accurately assess the sustainability of accruals and cash flow and their effect on future stocks, companies with higher-quality information disclosure experience less mispricing. Jiao [43] suggested that the amount of information disclosure is positively related to return on stocks, which may be because increased information transparency can correct mispricing. Kobayashi et al. [44] indicated that disclosure of patent information can significantly reduce risk and produce a relatively low standard deviation of 9.25%; in other words, disclosure of patent information helps to reduce mispricing. However, some scholars who have conducted research using news reports have reported contradictory results [40,45,46]. It demonstrate that inaccurate news reports make investors more critical and less likely to invest, resulting in mispricing and deviations in company value.

Through the implementation of the information disclosure evaluation system, we explore whether the increase in quality of information disclosure can effectively reduce information asymmetry between enterprises and investors and thus reduce mispricing. We present the following hypothesis:

Hypothesis 1 (H1). *Information disclosure rankings reduce mispricing.*

2.2. Effect of IDR on Mispricing under Different Levels of Industry Product Market Competition

Regarding supplementation and substitution of information disclosure, Bens [47] measured the amount of information that US companies voluntarily disclosed during 1990–1993 and discovered that significantly more information was disclosed when the SEC increased its supervision of restructuring companies at the end of 1993. He found that the positive relationship between amount of information disclosure and shareholder supervision indicates that supervision supplements disclosure.

Another study discerned a different relationship between information disclosure and product market competition. Healy and Palepu [48] suggested that voluntary company disclosure of information such as long-term strategic and nonfinancial indicators may increase the credibility of the financial reports of managers for competitive products. Increasing market disclosure may negatively affect the competitive position of companies. Similarly, Elliott and Jacobson [24] demonstrated that information disclosure can benefit public relations, such as by gaining the trust of investors and creditors. However, because potential competitors can acquire knowledge concerning marketing strategies, segment sales, production cost figures, technology, and management innovations from proprietary information, disclosure can increase competition and undermine the ability of a company to generate future cash flows. Giroud et al. [49] discovered that corporate merger laws weaken corporate governance by reducing the threat of hostile takeovers and prompting insufficient management. Giroud and Mueller [50] reported that in a noncompetitive industry, companies with weak governance are more likely to be investment targets for radical hedge funds, suggesting that investors actively mitigate inefficiencies. Ho et al. [23] investigated whether information disclosure is related to company value in markets with different levels of competition, revealing that information disclosure and product market competition levels affect company value. Consistent with the concept of competition to reduce management slack, companies in noncompetitive industries experienced a significant decline in business performance after the law was enacted, whereas companies in competitive industries were not significantly affected. We present the following hypothesis:

Hypothesis 2 (H2). *The negative relationship between information disclosure and mispricing is stronger for firms in competitive industries.*

3. Research Design

3.1. Sample Selection

Since 2005, the SFI has implemented a public IDTRS for listed companies, thereby determining the information transparency level of companies in the Taiwan stock market. This is based on the discussion of whether the publication of information transparency level forces enterprises to commit to the improvement of information disclosure. After the implementation of the evaluation system, we select the annual data of 10,686 SFI companies for the period from 2005 to 2014 as the research object. The final sample is selected on the basis of the following conditions, as determined by evidence: (1) To ensure data consistency, we omit annual data of enterprises that had not used the calendar system. (2) Furthermore, to estimate the degree of mispricing, we exclude industries with fewer than five sample counts for any year during the sample period. The sample variables used in this study are obtained from the CSMAR and Taiwan Economic Journal.

3.2. Variable Description

3.2.1. IDR Variable

IDRs and information transparency are major concerns in corporate governance. Foreign information disclosure level is assessed using the indices of Standard & Poor and Credit Lyonnais Securities regarding content concerning ownership, inverter, financial transparency, information disclosure, and board of director structure. The corporate governance ranking system has seven principles: management discipline, transparency, independence, accountability, responsibility, fairness, and social responsibility. Until 2014, the evaluation system for the ninth IDRs comprised scores from A++ to C− with seven ranking indices. To assess the level of corporate transparency, information ratings identified 114 indicators as evaluation criteria, which can be further grouped into five sub-categories: (1) compliance with the mandatory information disclosures; (2) timeliness of information reporting; (3) disclosure of financial forecast; (4) disclosure of annual report; and (5) disclosure of corporate website. Each disclosure indicator represents a "yes" or "no" question. One point is given to the question with a "yes" answer and zero otherwise. This study discusses information transparency by categorizing A++ to C− scores from 7 to 1. The 114 questions used to compile the IDR scores for each sample firm are presented in Pan et al. [46].

3.2.2. Industry Product Market Competition

The primary measure of product market competition used in this study is the Herfindahl–Hirschman Index (HHI). The HHI is computed as the sum of squared market shares [50–52]:

$$\text{HHI}_{jt} = \sum_{i=1}^{N_j} S_{ijt}^2 \tag{1}$$

where S_{ijt}^2 is the market share of firm i in industry j in year t. A higher HHI indicates higher industry exclusivity, and a lower HHI reflects a greater likelihood of the industry being a competitive industry.

3.2.3. Mispricing

First, we use Equation (2) provided by Rhodes-Kropf et al. [53] and Chu et al. [40] to predict mispricing:

$$\ln(\text{MV}_{ijt}) = \alpha + \beta_1 \ln(\text{BE}_{ijt}) + \beta_2 \ln(\text{NI}_{ijt}^+) + \beta_3 I_{<0} \ln(\text{NI})_{ijt}^+ + \beta_4 \text{LEV}_{ijt} + \varepsilon_{ijt} \qquad (2)$$

where $\ln(\text{MV})$ is the natural logarithm of market capitalization, $\ln(\text{BE})$ is the natural logarithm of book value of equity, and NI is the absolute value of net income. $I_{<0}$ is a dummy variable that has a value of 1 when the net income is negative and 0 otherwise. LEV is the leverage ratio, calculated as the debt of firm i divided by total assets.

Next, we use Equation (3) to compare corporate predicted and real value and estimate mispricing:

$$Mispricing_{it} = \ln[Real\ value_{it} / Predict\ value_{it}] \qquad (3)$$

where *real value* is the market value of equity plus book value of debt and *predicted value* is the estimated market capitalization of predicted value obtained from Equation (2).

With reference to Berger and Ofek [54] and Chu et al. [40], we predict value by multiplying sales revenue by the median market value for a company in the industry during the sample year and dividing this product by the median sales revenue for the industry. We define mispricing as the value of the sample real market value divided by the predicted market value. A higher difference in value indicates greater mispricing.

3.2.4. Control Variables

We follow Pan et al. [46] to consider firm characteristics and agency-based proxies [40], including the natural logarithm of market capitalization (SIZE), ratio of debt to book value of assets (LEV), total number of annual trading days (Trading), institutional ownership (Inshd), number of analysts providing earnings forecasts (Analyst), illiquidity ratio (Liquidity), shareholding of directors and supervisors (SDS), shareholding of the largest shareholder (SLS), voting rights (TFV), and listed company (TSE). All variables are defined in Table 1.

3.3. Methodology

To assess the influence of IDR on mispricing, we use Equation (4) as follows:

$$\begin{aligned} Mispricing_{it} = \ &\beta_0 + \beta_1 \text{IDR}_{it} + \beta_2 \text{SIZE}_{it} + \beta_3 \text{LEV}_{it} + \beta_4 \ln(\text{Trading})_{it} + \beta_5 \ln(\text{Inshd})_{it} \\ &+ \beta_6 \ln(\text{Liquidity})_{it} + \beta_7 \text{SDS}_{it} + \beta_8 \text{SLS}_{it} + \beta_9 \text{TSV}_{it} + Time\ \text{FE} \\ &+ Industry\ \text{FE} + \varepsilon_{it} \end{aligned} \qquad (4)$$

where *Mispricing* is derived using the two estimation methods proposed by Berger and Ofek [54] and Rhodes-Kropf et al. [53] discussed in Section 3.2.3. *Time* FE is year fixed effects, and *industry* FE is industry fixed effects. These variables are defined in Table 1.

To provide further evidence, this study examines the effect of IDR on mispricing in industries with different levels of product market competition. According to the procedure developed by Giroud and Mueller [50], we use Equation (5) to perform estimates in this study:

$$\begin{aligned} Mispricing_{it} = \ &\gamma_0 + \gamma_1 (\text{IDR}_{it} * \text{HHI}_{it}) + \gamma_2 X_{it} + \gamma_3 \text{SIZE}_{it} + \gamma_4 \text{LEV}_{it} \\ &+ \gamma_5 \ln(\text{Trading})_{it} + \gamma_6 \ln(\text{Inshd})_{it} \\ &+ \gamma_7 \ln(\text{Liquidity})_{it} + \gamma_8 \text{SDS}_{it} + \gamma_9 \text{SLS}_{it} + \gamma_{10} TSV_{it} + Time\ \text{FE} \\ &+ Industry\ \text{FE} + \varepsilon_{it} \end{aligned} \qquad (5)$$

where HHI is a (3×1) vector of HHI dummies for high, medium, and low levels of industry product market competition. X denotes the control variables, which are HHI dummies for medium and low levels of industry product market competition.

Table 1. Definition.

Panel A: Variable definition	
Variable	**Explanation**
Mispricing1	We use Rhodes-Kropf et al. [53] and Chu et al. [40] method to predict mispricing.
Mispricing2	Market value of equity plus book value of debt to imputed value of total capital to sales for the median single-segment firm in industry and year [40,54].
	Industry Characteristics
HHI	Set the product market competition index as the dummy variable and use SALES as the measurement variable. If the HHI index is higher than the average HHI = 1 or else HHI = 0.
	Firm Characteristics
IDR	Information disclosure ranking score, ranging from 1 (the lowest, C−) to 7 (the highest, A++).
ln(BE)	Natural logarithm of book value of equity.
ln(NI)+	Natural logarithm of absolute value of net income.
$I_{<0}$	It is 1 if the net income is negative, or else is 0.
SIZE	Natural logarithm of market capitalization.
LEV	The ratio of debt to book value of assets.
ln(Trading)	Natural logarithm of total number of trading days in a year.
ln(Inshd)	Institutional ownership = natural logarithm of stock ownership of foreign institutions, domestic funds, and securities companies.
ln(1 + Analyst)	Natural logarithm of number of analysts providing earnings forecasts.
ln(Liquidity)	Illiquidity ratio defined as natural logarithm of average daily absolute return divided by dollar trading volume in millions of a year.
	Agency-based measurements
SDS	Percentage of total outstanding shares owned by directors and supervisors.
SLS	Percentage of total outstanding shares owned by largest shareholder.
TFV	Times of seating to voting rights = seating rights %/voting rights %
TSE	It is 1 if the listed company and 0 is OTC firm.

Panel B: Measurements of information disclosure rankings based on five different dimensions [46]				
Dimension	**Item range**	**Total items**	**Percentage of total items represented**	**Items with extra rewards**
(1) Regulatory compliance	1–12	12	11%	None
(2) Timeliness of information disclosure	13–39	27	23%	9 items
(3) Disclosure of financial forecast	40–44	5	4%	5 items
(4) Disclosure of annual report	45–94	50	44%	4 items
(5) Disclosure of firm website	95–114	20	18%	20 items
Total			100%	38 items

3.4. Endogeneity Problem

This section details the endogenous relationship discovered between company information disclosure rankings and mispricing. In addition to improving the degree of mispricing, information disclosure may improve the information disclosure score as a result of decreased mispricing. However, although this study considers factors that may be related to the degree of deviation of information disclosure from corporate value and controls them to mitigate the problem of endogeneity [46,55,56], other endogenous links may exist. Therefore, this study uses a two-stage least squares method with instrumental variables (IVs) to address the endogeneity between information disclosure and mispricing [57–59].

In the selection of IVs, we adopt the method used by Cui et al. [60] and Gong and Ho [52,61] to consider changes in the first two periods of information disclosure (IDR_{t-1} and IDR_{t-2}) and the median information disclosure in each industry ($IDR_{Industry}$) and control other possible corporate governance IVs. We also apply the method presented by Chung et al. [14] and use the following criteria: proportion of shares owned by domestic trst funds (%DTF), family institutional investors (%FI), family-controlled foundations (%FF), and listed companies controlled by family directors (%FL); board independence (ID_Rate); listed companies (TSE); and changes in chairman of the board (Chairman_C), CEO (CEO_C), CFO (CFO_C), spokesman (Spokesman_C), and audit (Audit_C). The first stage of the least squares method entails using the method proposed by Larcker and Rusticus [62] to regress all selected exogenous IVs. The second stage entails the execution of least squares regression using the information disclosure ranking (IDR) valuation (IDR_{2SLS}) estimated in the first stage to identify any influence that helps to reduce the degree of mispricing. Equation (6) represents the first stage of the least squares method:

$$
\begin{aligned}
IDR_{it} = {} & \lambda_0 + \lambda_1 IDR_{i,t-1} \\
& + \lambda_2 IDR_{i,t-2} + \lambda_3 IDR_{Industry,t} + \lambda_4 \%DEF_{it} \\
& + \lambda_5 \%FI_{it} + \lambda_6 \%FF_{it} + \lambda_7 \%FL_{it} + \lambda_8 ID\_Rate_{it} + \lambda_9 Chairman\_C_{it} \\
& + \lambda_{10} CEO\_C_{it} + \lambda_{11} CFO\_C_{it} \\
& + \lambda_{12} Spokeman\_C_{it} + \lambda_{13} Audit\_C_{it} + \lambda_{14} SIZE_{it} + \lambda_{15} LEV_{it} \\
& + \lambda_{16} \ln(Trading)_{it} + \lambda_{17} \ln(Inshd)_{it} + \lambda_{18} \ln(Liquidity)_{it} \\
& + \lambda_{19} SDS_{it} + \lambda_{20} SLS_{it} + \lambda_{21} TSV_{it} + Time\ FE + Industry\ FE + \varepsilon_{it}
\end{aligned}
\tag{6}
$$

3.5. Summary Statistics

As presented in panel A of Table 2, the IDRs of the sample firms are arranged from the lowest score 1 (C−) to the highest score 7 (A++). The average value of IDR is 3.59 and the median is 3. This indicates that the sample firms have lower than average IDRs. The mean and median of HHI are 0.16 and 0.11, respectively, suggesting that industry product market competition is generally high in all sample firms. Panel B of Table 2 presents the distribution of sample corporations according to industry product market competition. Among the 30 industries, we discover that the electronics industry constitutes two-thirds of the sample because this is a major industry in Taiwan. However, some corporations are in oligopoly industries and are involved in the production of cement, food, electric cables, glass ceramics, paper, auto parts, other electronics, oil, gas, or electricity.

Table 2. Summary statistics.

Panel A: Summary statistics of all firms					
	MEAN	**STD**	**Q1**	**MEDIAN**	**Q3**
IDR	3.59	1.18	3.00	3.00	5.00
Mispricing1	0.00	0.43	−0.27	−0.08	0.18
Mispricing2	0.00	0.79	−0.46	−0.03	0.42
HHI	0.16	0.17	0.08	0.11	0.18
SIZE	15.53	1.59	14.43	15.27	16.28
LEV	1.27	2.79	0.39	0.73	1.21
ln(Trading)	5.57	0.17	5.51	5.52	5.53
ln(Inshd)	2.91%	5.77%	0.00%	0.30%	3.50%
ln(1 + Analyst)	1.18	1.33	0.00	0.69	2.20
ln(Liquidity)	0.05%	0.19%	0.00%	0.00%	0.01%
SDS	23.10	14.28	12.62	19.53	29.81
SLS	19.75	11.53	11.77	17.74	25.55
TSV	23.86	17.43	9.90	19.94	34.33

Table 2. *Cont.*

Panel B: Summary statistics of all industries

Classification	Industry	Industrial concentration level	HHI
1	Cement	Oligopoly	0.42
2	Food	Oligopoly	0.39
3	Plastics	General	0.21
4	Textile	General	0.20
5	Electric machinery	General	0.15
6	Electric cables	Oligopoly	0.32
7	Chemical industry	Competition	0.08
8	Biotechnology and medical care	Competition	0.06
9	Glass ceramic	Oligopoly	0.51
10	Paper	Oligopoly	0.28
11	Steel	General	0.21
12	Rubber	Oligopoly	0.25
13	Auto	Oligopoly	0.26
14	Semiconductor	Competition	0.10
15	Computer peripherals	Competition	0.11
16	Photoelectric	Competition	0.12
17	Communications network operator	Competition	0.11
18	Electronic components	Competition	0.03
19	Electronic access	Competition	0.12
20	Information services	Competition	0.09
21	Other electronics	Oligopoly	0.74
22	Building material and construction	Competition	0.04
23	Shipping	General	0.16
24	Sightseeing	General	0.13
25	Finance and insurance	General	0.15
26	Trade department	General	0.20
27	Securities	General	0.15
28	Culture	General	0.22
29	Oil, gas and electricity	Oligopoly	0.85
30	Other	General	0.13

Note: This table reports descriptive statistics of explanatory variables, industry characteristics, firm characteristics, and agency-based proxies for sample firms. The definitions of the variables are shown in detail in Table 1.

To identify potential multicollinearity among the explanatory variables, we examine the correlations and variance inflation factor among all independent variables. Table 3 indicates that there are no multicollinearity problems.

Table 3. Correlation matrix.

	VIF	IDR	HHI	SIZE	LEV	ln(Trading)	ln(Inshd)	ln(1 + Analyst)	ln(Liquidity)	SDS	SLS	TSV
IDR	1.13	1.00										
HHI	1.04	−0.01	1.00									
SIZE	2.17	**0.31**	0.04	1.00								
LEV	1.45	**0.16**	−0.02	**0.49**	1.00							
ln(Trading)	1.22	0.05	−0.05	**0.19**	0.03	1.00						
ln(Inshd)	1.29	**0.22**	0.06	**0.42**	**0.30**	0.05	1.00					
ln(1 + Analyst)	1.56	**0.16**	−0.08	**0.51**	0.07	**0.22**	**0.26**	1.00				
ln(Liquidity)	1.13	−0.05	−0.02	−0.07	0.03	**0.29**	−0.04	−0.07	1.00			
SDS	1.53	−0.01	**0.11**	**−0.11**	0.01	**−0.16**	0.05	**−0.13**	−0.04	1.00		
SLS	1.56	−0.03	0.00	−0.02	0.04	−0.08	0.00	**−0.13**	−0.01	**−0.17**	1.00	
TSV	1.83	**−0.11**	**0.10**	**−0.13**	0.01	**−0.13**	−0.08	**−0.23**	−0.03	**0.40**	**0.45**	1.00

Note: This table reports the Pearson correlation coefficients and Variance Inflation Factor (VIF) between independent variables. The definitions of the variables are shown in detail in Table 1. The boldfaced numbers denote statistical significance below 10%.

4. Empirical Results

4.1. Effect of IDR on Mispricing

In this study, we refer to the methods presented by Berger and Ofek [54], Rhodes-Kropf et al. [53], and Chu et al. [40] to estimate the degree of mispricing of the sample companies. In Table 4, empirical results reveal the effect of IDR on the degree of mispricing; the coefficient is −0.008 (t-statistic = −2.64) in the Mispricing1 regression and −0.032 (t-statistic = −5.04) in the Mispricing 2 regression. The IDR score is significantly representative because the different methods for estimating the degree of mispricing all maintain a significance level of less than 1%, even after we control for both the year and industry fixed effects. Therefore, we standardize annual IDRs by using the following formula: (original IDR—average annual information disclosure)/standard deviation of IDRs. The standard deviation of IDRs is calculated from the standardized information disclosure score. This result is consistent with those of previous analyses [46]. The regression analysis results verify that IDRs effectively reduce the degree of mispricing, which supports the findings of Lee and Lee [45] and Chu et al. [40]. The higher quality is the disclosed information, the better investors can evaluate firms, and hence the stock price is closer to the firm's true fundamentals. On the other hand, if the information disclosed to investors is inaccurate, incomplete, late or even fraudulent, the market valuation will hardly be accurate hence the stock price is likely to deviate much form the firm's true fundamental.

Table 4. Effect of IDR on mispricing.

Dependent Variable	Mispricing1	Mispricing2
Intercept	1.713 ***	1.539 ***
	(14.37)	(6.18)
IDR	−0.008 ***	−0.032 ***
	(−2.64)	(−5.04)
SIZE	−0.121 ***	−0.105 ***
	(−37.23)	(−15.57)
LEV	0.073 ***	0.036 ***
	(38.98)	(9.31)
ln(Trading)	−0.005	0.031
	(−0.23)	(0.75)
ln(Inshd)	0.183 ***	1.373 ***
	(2.93)	(10.56)
ln(1 + Analyst)	0.114 ***	0.071 ***
	(34.24)	(10.27)
ln(Liquidity)	−13.617 ***	−14.129 ***
	(−6.78)	(−3.37)
SDS	0.002 ***	0.001
	(6.59)	(1.39)
SLS	0.002 ***	0.006 ***
	(6.45)	(7.90)
TSV	−0.001 ***	0.000
	(−4.83)	(−0.57)
Year FE	YES	YES
Industry FE	YES	YES
Adj R^2	0.43	0.18
N	10,686	10,686

Note: This table reports the impact of IDR on mispricing. All models are based on Equation (4). The definitions of the variables are shown in detail in Table 1. The t-statistics are based on standard errors clustered by industry and year and reported in the parenthesis. *, **, *** denote statistical significance at 10%, 5%, and 1%, respectively.

4.2. Effect of IDR on Mispricing in Industries with Different Levels of Product Market Competition

Table 5 presents the results of investigating the effect of IDR on the degree of mispricing in industries with different levels of market competition (HHI). We conduct a test using the method presented by Giroud and Mueller [50]. The empirical results indicate a (3×1) vector interaction between IDR and HHI, and the HHI can be divided into three distinct groups: high HHI (33%), median HHI (34%), and low HHI (33%). In Mispricing1, the coefficient for the interaction between IDR and HHI (high) is -0.006 (t-statistic = -0.83), that for the interaction between IDR and HHI (median) is 0.006 (t-statistic = 1.38), and that for the interaction between IDR and HHI (low) is -0.019 (t-statistic = -4.69). The Mispricing2 regression indicates that the (3×1) vector coefficient for the interaction between IDR and HHI (high) is -0.025 (t-statistic = -1.59), that for the interaction between IDR and HHI (median) is -0.010 (t-statistic = -1.04), and that for the interaction between IDR and HHI (low) is -0.049 (t-statistic = -5.75). All interactions between IDR and HHI (high or median) are nonsignificant, and the interaction between IDR and HHI (low) is significantly negative. IDRs do not exhibit an influence on mispricing in oligopoly industries. However, regarding the interaction between IDR and the lowest HHI (competitive industries), financial risk and default probability are higher for these industries compared with others; therefore, investors should consider information transparency prior to investing. If a firm has higher information disclosure quality, then investors will have more confidence when investing in the firm, which reduces mispricing.

Table 5. The impact of IDR on mispricing under different industry product market competition level.

Dependent Variable	Mispricing1	Mispricing2
Intercept	1.801 ***	1.650 ***
	(15.00)	(6.58)
IDR*HHI(high)	−0.006	−0.025
	(−0.83)	(−1.59)
IDR*HHI(median)	0.006	−0.010
	(1.38)	(−1.04)
IDR*HHI(low)	−0.019 ***	−0.049 ***
	(−4.69)	(−5.75)
HHI(median)	−0.137 ***	−0.177 ***
	(−5.56)	(−3.42)
HHI(high)	−0.104 ***	−0.168 **
	(−2.71)	(−2.09)
SIZE	−0.120 ***	−0.105 ***
	(−37.21)	(−15.56)
LEV	0.073 ***	0.036 ***
	(38.91)	(9.25)
ln(Trading)	−0.007	0.028
	(−0.33)	(0.68)
ln(Inshd)	0.195 ***	1.388 ***
	(3.13)	(10.67)
ln(1 + Analyst)	0.113 ***	0.070 ***
	(33.87)	(10.08)
ln(Liquidity)	−13.881 ***	−14.414 ***
	(−6.92)	(−3.44)
SDS	0.002 ***	0.001
	(6.54)	(1.36)
SLS	0.002 ***	0.006 ***
	(6.50)	(7.93)
TSV	−0.001 ***	0.000
	(−4.85)	(−0.55)
Year FE	YES	YES
Industry FE	YES	YES
Adj R^2	0.43	0.18
N	10,686	10,686

Note: This table reports the impact of information disclosure ranking on mispricing under different industry product market competition levels. All models are based on Equation (5). The definitions of the variables are shown in detail in Table 1. The t-statistics are based on standard errors clustered by industry and year and reported in the parenthesis. *, **, *** denote statistical significance at 10%, 5%, and 1%, respectively.

4.3. Tests of the Endogeneity Effect

Table 6 presents the results obtained from the use of the two-stage least square method to solve the problem of endogeneity. We use the method proposed by Larcker and Rusticus [62] to regress all selected exogenous IVs in the first stage of the least squares regression to estimate IDRs. The IDRs estimated in first stage of the least squares regressions are then used to evaluate the effect of IDR on mispricing. Using the methods presented by Chung et al. [14] and Cui et al. [60], we regress IVs on IDRs in the first stage of the least squares regression. We discover that the coefficient of the estimated IDRs in the second-stage regression on Mispricing1 is −0.008 (t-statistic = −1.76). In the Mispricing2 regression, the coefficient of the estimated IDRs is −0.048 (t-statistic = −5.16). The empirical results indicate that the IDRs estimated using IVs significantly reduce mispricing. Moreover, we use this method to solve the problem of endogeneity. Another analysis confirms the robustness of this result. According to the method presented by Gong and Ho [61], we use the Generalized Method of Moments (GMM) approach to solve the problem of endogeneity, and the consistent results support our findings.

Table 6. Two-stage least squares (2SLS) regression analysis for the relationship between mispricing and IDR.

Dependent Variable	First Stage: IDR	Second Stage: Mispricing1	Second Stage: Mispricing2
Intercept	−1.976 ***	1.569 ***	1.434 ***
	(−5.13)	(12.17)	(5.26)
IDR_{t-1}	0.635 ***		
	(69.73)		
IDR_{t-2}	0.119 ***		
	(13.41)		
$IDR_{Industry}$	0.727 ***		
	(12.74)		
%DTF	0.000		
	(−0.11)		
%FI	0.001		
	(1.00)		
%FF	0.001		
	(0.61)		
%FL	0.002		
	(1.45)		
ID_Rate	0.080 *		
	(1.87)		
Chairman_C	−0.005		
	(−0.17)		
CEO_C	0.014		
	(0.63)		
CFO_C	−0.001		
	(−0.03)		
Spokeman_C	0.004		
	(0.19)		
Aduit_C	−0.040 **		
	(−2.21)		
TSE	−0.103 ***		
	(−5.25)		

Table 6. *Cont.*

Dependent Variable	First Stage: IDR	Second Stage: Mispricing1	Second Stage: Mispricing2
IDR$_{2SLS}$		−0.008 *	−0.048 ***
		(−1.76)	(−5.16)
SIZE	0.056 ***	−0.120 ***	−0.105 ***
	(6.05)	(−33.79)	(−13.97)
LEV	−0.010 **	0.075 ***	0.042 ***
	(−2.21)	(36.72)	(9.65)
ln(Trading)	−0.095 *	0.018	0.056
	(−1.92)	(0.85)	(1.23)
ln(Inshd)	0.279 *	0.256 ***	1.507 ***
	(1.75)	(3.78)	(10.52)
ln(1 + Analyst)	0.024 ***	0.107 ***	0.062 ***
	(2.83)	(28.88)	(7.96)
ln(Liquidity)	−3.517	−16.966 ***	−17.544 ***
	(−0.62)	(−6.90)	(−3.37)
SDS	0.000	0.002 ***	0.002 ***
	(0.39)	(7.42)	(2.84)
SLS	0.000	0.003 ***	0.007 ***
	(0.20)	(6.74)	(8.09)
TSV	−0.001	−0.001 ***	−0.001
	(−1.57)	(−5.22)	(−1.26)
Year FE	YES	YES	YES
Industry FE	YES	YES	YES
Adj R^2	0.63	0.42	0.17
N	9071	9071	9071

Note: The table reports the two-stage least squares (2SLS) regression analysis results for examining whether information ranking explains mispricing. All models are based on Equation (6). The definitions of the variables are shown in detail in Table 1 and Section 3. The t-statistics are based on standard errors clustered by industry and year and reported in the parenthesis. *, **, *** denote statistical significance at 10%, 5%, and 1%, respectively.

5. Conclusions

After Enron acquired a substantial debt risk, WorldCom, Tyco, and Merck were also involved in accounting scandals that not only caused an increase in the stock market margin but also reduced investor confidence. This study uses the IDR indicators established by the SFI to divide the IDR score into seven points. During the sample period of 2005 to 2014, we obtain the data of 10,686 listed companies. This study reveals that the information disclosure work evaluation system promoted by the SFI and IDR significantly affects the quality and amount of information disclosed by the evaluated enterprises. Moreover, the empirical results of this study reveal that the transparency indicator of information disclosure helps to reduce the degree of mispricing. Considering the disadvantages of low liquidity and high capital costs that may accompany low information transparency, companies focusing on information disclosure will eventually reduce their degree of mispricing.

From the perspective of the external environment, the size and transparency of the monopolistic industry will help reduce the mispricing of enterprise value. Additionally, this study provides further evidence that industry product market competition is separated into three groups. Negative relationships between IDR and mispricing are only observed in competitive industries because of their relatively high financial risk and default probability, which prompts investors to consider information transparency. If a firm increases their information transparency, investors will have more interest and confidence in investing in the firm, leading to reduced mispricing. This evidence supports the notion that IDRs effectively reduce mispricing in competitive industries. Policies related to the promotion of information disclosure outside of the SFI can also be affirmed using our results. Moreover, information disclosure ranking firms are found to be more ethical, trustworthy, and honest, and managers are encouraged to undertake actions that boost long-term sustainable development, thus resulting in less mispricing.

Author Contributions: Writing: B.W. and H.-Y.H.; Providing idea and data: K.-C.H. and I-M.J.; Revising and editing: S.X.

Acknowledgments: This manuscript was edited by Wallace Academic Editing.

References

1.   Jensen, M.C.; Meckling, W.H. Theory of the firm: Managerial behavior, agency costs and ownership structure. *J. Financ. Econ.* **1976**, *3*, 305–360. [CrossRef]
2.   Fama, E.F. Agency problems and the theory of the firm. *J. Political Econ.* **1980**, *88*, 288–307. [CrossRef]
3.   Fama, E.F.; Jensen, M.C. Separation of ownership and control. *J. Law Econ.* **1983**, *26*, 301–325. [CrossRef]
4.   Bushman, R.M.; Smith, A.J. Financial Accounting Information and Corporate Governance. *J. Account. Econ.* **2001**, *32*, 237–333. [CrossRef]
5.   Healy, P.M.; Palepu, K.G. Information asymmetry, corporate disclosure, and the capital markets: A review of the empirical disclosure literature. *J. Account. Econ.* **2001**, *31*, 405–440. [CrossRef]
6.   Glosten, L.R.; Milgrom, P.R. Bid, ask, and transaction prices in a specialist market with heterogeneously informed traders. *J. Financ. Econ.* **1985**, *14*, 71–100. [CrossRef]
7.   Diamond, D.W.; Verrecchia, R.E. Disclosure, liquidity, and the cost of capital. *J. Financ.* **1991**, *46*, 1325–1359. [CrossRef]
8.   Botosan, C.A. Disclosure level and the cost of equity capital. *Account. Rev.* **1997**, *72*, 323–349.
9.   Healy, P.M.; Hutton, A.P.; Palepu, K.G. Stock performance and intermediation changes surrounding sustained increases in disclosure. *Contemp. Account. Res.* **1999**, *16*, 485–520. [CrossRef]
10.   Francis, J.; Nanda, D.; Olsson, P. Voluntary disclosure, earnings quality, and cost of capital. *J. Account. Res.* **2008**, *46*, 53–99. [CrossRef]
11.   Gao, P. Disclosure quality, cost of capital, and investor welfare. *Account. Rev.* **2010**, *85*, 1–29. [CrossRef]
12.   Hughes, J.S.; Liu, J.; Liu, J. Information asymmetry, diversification, and cost of capital. *Account. Rev.* **2007**, *82*, 705–729. [CrossRef]
13.   Lambert, R.; Leuz, C.; Verrecchia, R.E. Accounting information, disclosure, and the cost of capital. *J. Account. Res.* **2007**, *45*, 385–420. [CrossRef]
14.   Chung, H.; Judge, W.Q.; Li, Y.H. Voluntary disclosure, excess executive compensation, and firm value. *J. Corp. Financ.* **2015**, *32*, 64–91. [CrossRef]
15.   Merton, R.C. A simple model of capital market equilibrium with incomplete information. *J. Financ.* **1987**, *42*, 483–510. [CrossRef]
16.   Welker, M. Disclosure policy, information asymmetry, and liquidity in equity markets. *Contemp. Account. Res.* **1995**, *11*, 801–827. [CrossRef]
17.   Leuz, C.; Verrecchia, R.E. The economic consequences of increased disclosure. *J. Account. Res.* **2000**, *38*, 91–124. [CrossRef]
18.   Heflin, F.; Subramanyam, K.R.; Zhang, Y. Regulation FD and the financial information environment: Early evidence. *Account. Rev.* **2003**, *78*, 1–38. [CrossRef]
19.   Klapper, L.F.; Love, I. Corporate governance, investor protection, and performance in emerging markets. *J. Corp. Financ.* **2004**, *10*, 703–728. [CrossRef]
20.   Bai, C.E.; Liu, Q.; Lu, J.; Song, F.M.; Zhang, J. Corporate governance and market valuation in China. *J. Comp. Econ.* **2004**, *32*, 599–616. [CrossRef]
21.   Black, B.S.; Inessa, L.; Rachinsky, A. Corporate governance indices and firms' market values: Time series evidence from Russia. *Emerg. Mark. Rev.* **2006**, *7*, 361–379. [CrossRef]
22.   Braga-Alves, M.V.; Shastri, K. Corporate governance, valuation, and performance: Evidence from a voluntary market reform in Brazil. *Financ. Manag.* **2011**, *40*, 139–157. [CrossRef]
23.   Ho, K.C.; Pan, L.H.; Lin, C.T.; Lee, S.C. Information disclosure, product market competition, and firm value: Evidence from Taiwan. *Soc. Sci. Electron. Publ.* **2016**. [CrossRef]
24.   Elliott, R.K.; Jacobson, P.D. Costs and benefits of business information disclosure. *Account. Horiz.* **1994**, *8*,

80–96.

25. Bloomfield, R.; Fischer, P.E. Disagreement and the cost of capital. *J. Account. Res.* **2011**, *49*, 41–68. [CrossRef]

26. Baker, M.; Stein, J.; Wurgler, J. When does the market matter? Stock prices and investment of equity-dependent firms. *Q. J. Econ.* **2003**, *118*, 969–1005. [CrossRef]

27. Stambaugh, R.F.; Yuan, Y. Mispricing factors. *Rev. Financ. Stud.* **2017**, *30*, 1270–1315. [CrossRef]

28. Sloan, R.G. Do stock prices fully reflect information in accruals and cash flows about future earnings? *Account. Rev.* **1996**, *71*, 289–315.

29. Ma, J.Z.; Deng, X.; Ho, K.C.; Tsai, S.B. Regime-switching determinants for spreads of emerging markets sovereign credit default swaps. *Sustainability* **2018**, *10*, 2730. [CrossRef]

30. Beretta, S.; Bozzolan, S. A framework for the analysis of firm risk communication. *Int. J. Account.* **2004**, *39*, 265–288. [CrossRef]

31. Beretta, S.; Bozzolan, S. Quality versus Quantity: The case of forward-looking disclosure. *J. Account. Audit. Financ.* **2008**, *23*, 333–375. [CrossRef]

32. Gelb, D.S.; Strawser, J.A. Corporate social responsibility and financial disclosure: An alternative explanation for increased disclosure. *J. Bus. Ethics* **2001**, *33*, 1–13. [CrossRef]

33. Chih, H.L.; Shen, C.H.; Kang, F.C. Corporate social responsibility, investor protection, and earnings management: Some international evidence. *J. Bus. Ethics* **2007**, *79*, 179–198. [CrossRef]

34. Choi, T.H.; Pae, J. Business ethics and financial reporting quality: Evidence from Korea. *J. Bus. Ethics* **2011**, *103*, 403–427. [CrossRef]

35. Murata, K. Analyzing environmental continuous improvement for sustainable supply chain management: Focusing on its performance and information disclosure. *Sustainability* **2016**, *8*, 1256. [CrossRef]

36. Manes-Rossi, F.; Tiron-Tudor, A.; Nicolò, G.; Zanellato, G. Ensuring more sustainable reporting in Europe using non-financial disclosure—De Facto and De Jure evidence. *Sustainability* **2018**, *10*, 1162. [CrossRef]

37. Li, M.; Tian, A.; Li, S.; Qi, X. Evaluating the quality of enterprise environmental accounting information disclosure. *Sustainability* **2018**, *10*, 2136. [CrossRef]

38. Bae, S.M.; Masud, A.K.; Kim, J.D. A cross-country investigation of corporate governance and corporate sustainability disclosure: A signaling theory perspective. *Sustainability* **2018**, *10*, 2611. [CrossRef]

39. Tang, Y.; Miao, X.; Zang, H.; Gao, Y. Information disclosure on hazards from industrial water pollution incidents: Latent resistance and countermeasures in China. *Sustainability* **2018**, *10*, 1475. [CrossRef]

40. Chu, C.C.; Ho, K.C.; Jiang, I.M.; Lo, C.C.; Karathanasopoulos, A. Information disclosure and transparency ranking system and firms' value deviation: Evidence from Taiwan. *Rev. Quant. Financ. Account.* **2018**, 1–27. [CrossRef]

41. Hail, L. The impact of voluntary corporate disclosure on the ex-ante cost of capital for Swiss firms. *Eur. Account. Rev.* **2002**, *11*, 741–773. [CrossRef]

42. Drake, M.S.; Myers, J.N.; Myers, L.A. Disclosure quality and the mispricing of accruals and cash flow. *J. Account. Audit. Financ.* **2009**, *24*, 357–384. [CrossRef]

43. Jiao, Y. Corporate disclosure, market valuation, and firm performance. *Financ. Manag.* **2011**, *40*, 647–676. [CrossRef]

44. Kobayashi, T.; Iwanaga, Y.; Kudoh, H. Japanese patent index and stock performance. *J. Financ. Perspect.* **2014**, *2*, 151–162.

45. Lee, H.L.; Lee, H. Effect of information disclosure and transparency ranking system on mispricing of accruals of Taiwanese firms. *Rev. Quant. Financ. Account.* **2015**, *44*, 445–471. [CrossRef]

46. Pan, L.H.; Lin, C.T.; Lee, S.C.; Ho, K.C. Information ratings and capital structure. *J. Corp. Financ.* **2015**, *31*, 17–32. [CrossRef]

47. Bens, D. The determinants of the amount of information disclosed about corporate restructurings. *J. Account. Res.* **2002**, *40*, 1–20. [CrossRef]

48. Healy, P.; Palepu, K.G. The effect of firms' financial disclosure strategies on stock prices. *Account. Horiz.* **1993**, *7*, 1.

49. Giroud, X.; Mueller, H.M. Does corporate governance matter in competitive industries? *J. Financ. Econ.* **2010**, *95*, 312–331. [CrossRef]

50. Giroud, X.; Mueller, H.M. Corporate governance, product market competition, and equity prices. *J. Financ.* **2011**, *66*, 563–600. [CrossRef]

51. Hou, K.; Robinson, D.T. Industry concentration and average stock returns. *J. Financ.* **2006**, *61*, 1927–1956. [CrossRef]
52. Gong, Y.; Ho, K.C. Does corporate social responsibility matter for corporate stability? Evidence from China. *Qual. Quant.* **2018**, *52*, 2291–2319. [CrossRef]
53. Rhodes-Kropf, M.; Robinson, D.T.; Viswanathan, S. Valuation waves and merger activity: The empirical evidence. *J. Financ. Econ.* **2005**, *77*, 561–603. [CrossRef]
54. Berger, P.G.; Ofek, E. Diversification's effect on firm value. *J. Financ. Econ.* **1995**, *37*, 39–65. [CrossRef]
55. Brick, I.E.; Palmon, O.; Wald, J.K. CEO compensation, director compensation, and firm performance: Evidence of cronyism. *J. Corp. Financ.* **2006**, *12*, 403–423. [CrossRef]
56. Dittmar, A.; Mahrt-Smith, J. Corporate governance and the value of cash holdings. *J. Financ. Econ.* **2007**, *83*, 599–634. [CrossRef]
57. Beedles, W.L. A micro-econometric investigation of multi-objective firms. *J. Financ.* **1977**, *32*, 1217–1233. [CrossRef]
58. Hauner, D.; Prati, A.; Bircan, C. The interest group theory of financial development: Evidence from regulation. *J. Bank. Financ.* **2013**, *37*, 895–906. [CrossRef]
59. Boone, A.; White, J.T. The effect of institutional ownership on firm transparency and information production. *J. Financ. Econ.* **2015**, *117*, 508–533. [CrossRef]
60. Cui, J.; Jo, H.; Na, H. Does corporate social responsibility affect information asymmetry? *J. Bus. Ethics* **2018**, *3*, 549–575. [CrossRef]
61. Gong, Y.; Ho, K.C. Corporate social responsibility and managerial short-termism. *Asia-Pac. J. Account. Econ.* **2018**, *25*, 1–27. [CrossRef]
62. Larcker, D.F.; Rusticus, T.O. On the use of instrumental variables in accounting research. *J. Account. Econ.* **2010**, *49*, 186–205. [CrossRef]

14

Size, Internationalization and University Rankings: Evaluating and Predicting Times Higher Education (THE) Data for Japan

Michael McAleer [1,2,3,4,5,*], **Tamotsu Nakamura** [6] **and Clinton Watkins** [6]

[1] Department of Finance, Asia University, Taichung 41354, Taiwan
[2] Discipline of Business Analytics, University of Sydney Business School, Sydney 2006, Australia
[3] Econometric Institute, Erasmus School of Economics, Erasmus University Rotterdam, 3000 Rotterdam, The Netherlands
[4] Department of Economic Analysis and ICAE, Complutense University of Madrid, 28040 Madrid, Spain
[5] Institute of Advanced Sciences, Yokohama National University, Yokohama 240-8501, Japan
[6] Graduate School of Economics, Kobe University, Kobe 657-8501, Japan; nakamura@econ.kobe-u.ac.jp (T.N.); watkins@econ.kobe-u.ac.jp (C.W.)
* Correspondence: michael.mcaleer@gmail.com

Abstract: International and domestic rankings of academics, academic departments, faculties, schools and colleges, institutions of higher learning, states, regions, and countries are of academic and practical interest and importance to students, parents, academics, and private and public institutions. International and domestic rankings are typically based on arbitrary methodologies and criteria. Evaluating how the rankings might be sensitive to different factors, as well as forecasting how they might change over time, requires a statistical analysis of the factors that affect the rankings. Accurate data on rankings and the associated factors are essential for a valid statistical analysis. In this respect, the Times Higher Education (THE) World University Rankings represent one of the three leading and most influential annual sources of international university rankings. Using recently released data for a single country, namely Japan, the paper evaluates the effects of size (specifically, the number of full-time-equivalent (FTE) students, or FTE (Size)) and internationalization (specifically, the percentage of international students, or IntStud) on academic rankings using THE data for 2017 and 2018 on 258 national, public (that is, prefectural or city), and private universities. The results show that both size and internationalization are statistically significant in explaining rankings for all universities, as well as separately for private and non-private (that is, national and public) universities, in Japan for 2017 and 2018.

Keywords: international and domestic rankings; size; internationalization; national; public and private universities; changes over time

JEL Classification: C18; C81; I23; Y1

1. Introduction

It is well known that a broad range of higher-education rankings of academics, academic departments, faculties/schools/colleges, institutions of higher learning, states, regions, and countries are of academic and practical interest and importance to students, parents, academics, and private and public institutions. The international and domestic rankings are typically based on a variety of arbitrary methodologies and criteria, which means they are not optimal from a statistical perspective. Moreover, evaluating how the rankings might be sensitive to different factors, as well as forecasting how they might change over time, requires a statistical analysis of the wide variety of factors that affect the rankings.

The primary purpose of this paper was to evaluate and predict the relationships over time among rankings and two crucial factors. The three leading and most influential annual sources of international and domestic university rankings are as follows:

(1)   Shanghai Ranking Consultancy Academic Ranking of World Universities (ARWU) (originally compiled and issued by Shanghai Jiao Tong University), founded in 2003;

(2)   Times Higher Education (THE) World University Rankings, founded in 2010 (*THE–QS World University Ranking*, in partnership with QS, 2004–2009);

(3)   Quacquarelli Symonds (QS) World University Rankings, founded in 2010 (*THE–QS World University Ranking*, in partnership with THE, 2004–2009).

ARWU was the first agency to rank world universities, and was followed closely by THE–QS, which used a different methodology. Since 2010, ARWU, THE, and QS used different methodologies, with each having their supporters and critics.

As stated succinctly by THE (2018) [1]:

"The Times Higher Education World University Rankings, founded in 2004, provide the definitive list of the world's best universities, evaluated across teaching, research, international outlook, reputation, and more. THE's data are trusted by governments and universities and are a vital resource for students, helping them choose where to study."

THE (2018) [1] recently provided the Young Universities Rankings, World Reputation Rankings, Emerging Economy Rankings, Japan University Rankings, Asia University Rankings, World University Rankings, United States (US) College Rankings, and, most recently, Latin America Rankings and Europe Teaching Rankings. These separate rankings provide a rich source of data for two countries, namely the USA and Japan (see THE (2018) [2] and THE (2018) [3], respectively, for further details), and alternative groupings of countries and regions (for Asia, see THE (2018) [4]) (https://www.timeshighereducation.com/world-university-rankings/2018/regional-ranking#!/page/0/length/25/sort_by/rank/sort_order/asc/cols/stats).

Institutions of higher learning in the US were analyzed extensively and comprehensively over an extended period. However, this was not the case in Japan, as data on a wide range of national, public, and private universities were not readily available. Recently, THE (2018) [5] provided data for Japan on numerical rankings for 258 national, public (that is, prefectural or city), and private universities.

THE (2018) [5] gives the following explanation of the dataset:

"The Times Higher Education Japan University Rankings 2018, based on 13 individual performance metrics, are designed to answer the questions that matter most to students and their families when making one of the most important decisions of their lives—who to trust with their education.

This year's methodology includes the same 11 indicators as last year, as well as two additional internationalization measures: the number of students in international exchange programs, and the number of courses taught in a language other than Japanese.

The rankings include the top-ranked 150 universities by overall score, as well as any other university that is in the top 150 for any of the four performance pillars (resources, engagement, outcomes, and environment). Scores in each pillar are provided when the university is in the top 150, while a dash ("–") indicates that the institution is not ranked in the top 150 for that pillar.

Institutions outside the top 150 are shown with a banded rank ("151+") and a banded score ("9.4–38.2": these two numbers represent the lowest and highest scores of all universities ranked outside the top 150), and are displayed in alphabetical order."

The dataset includes a number of factors that are used in defining the ranking, but they cannot be used to predict the rankings. For purposes of predicting rankings in advance of obtaining the data that are used to construct them, two factors that should have a significant effect on rankings will be used to evaluate and predict the effects of **size** (specifically, the number of full-time-equivalent (FTE) students, or **FTE (Size)**) and **internationalization** (specifically, the percentage of international students, or **IntStud**) on academic rankings of the private and non-private (that is, national and public) universities in Japan. Sources of whether universities are national, public, or private are given at the following websites, as well as on the respective university websites:

National:

http://www.mext.go.jp/en/about/relatedsites/title01/detail01/sdetail01/1375122.htm;

Public:

http://www.mext.go.jp/en/about/relatedsites/title01/detail01/sdetail01/1375124.htm;

Private:

http://www.mext.go.jp/en/about/relatedsites/title01/detail01/sdetail01/sdetail01/1375152.htm.

The analysis of the data on these three key variables will enable a statistical analysis of, and response to the following issues relating size and internationalization of non-private and private universities to their respective rankings over time:

(i). Are private or non-private universities more highly ranked?

(ii). Are private or non-private universities larger in terms of size?

(iii). Do private or non-private universities have a higher degree of internationalization?

(iv). Do the size, internationalization, and rankings of private and non-private universities change over time?

(v). Are there differences in the effects of size and internationalization on the rankings of private universities?

(vi). Are there differences in the effects of size and internationalization on the rankings of non-private universities?

(vii). Do the effects of size and internationalization change over time for private and non-private universities?

There is extensive literature on university rankings and, more generally, on methodologies used to generate such rankings. There are numerous studies relative to a number of industries that compared results from different methods, and approaches that emphasize the differences and similarities related to rankings, as highlighted below.

Carrico et al. (1997) [6] considered data envelope analysis and university selection. Hu et al. (2017) [7] analyzed a hybrid fuzzy DEA/AHP methodology for ranking units in a fuzzy environment. Dale and Krueger (2002) [8] estimated the payoff to attending a more selective college through an application of selection on observables and unobservables. Eccles (2002) [9] evaluated the use of university rankings in the United Kingdom. Federkeil (2002) [10] examined some aspects of ranking methodology of German universities. Kallio (1995) [11] considered the factors influencing the college choice decisions of graduate students. Liu et al. (2005) [12] commented on the "fatal attraction" of academic ranking of world universities using scientometrics. lo Storto (2016) [13] analyzed the ecological efficiency-based ranking of cities based on a combined DEA cross-efficiency and Shannon's entropy method. McDonough et al. (1998) [14] evaluated college rankings based on democratized college knowledge. Meredith (2004) [15] analyzed why universities compete in the ratings game with an empirical analysis of the effects of the US News and World Report College Rankings. Merisotis (2002) [16] examined the ranking of higher-education institutions. Pavan et al. (2006) [17] evaluated data mining by total ranking methods based on a case study on optimization of the "pulp and bleaching" process in the paper industry. Lastly, van Raan (2005) [18] examined the fatal attraction ranking of universities by bibliometric methods.

Additional research papers that examined international and domestic university rankings can be found in a wide range of international journals. Some recent papers based on scientific publishing, country-specific and industrial linkage factors, and the associated policy implications include Tijssen et al. (2016) [19], Piro and Sivertsen (2016) [20], Shehatta and Mahmood (2016) [21], Moed (2017) [22], Kivinen et al. (2017) [23], Pietrucha (2018) [24], and Johnes (2018) [25].

The remainder of the paper is organized as follows: Section 2 discusses the data and descriptive statistics, while the empirical analysis is presented in Section 3, and some concluding remarks are given in Section 4.

2. Data and Descriptive Statistics

As discussed in Section 1, in the dataset released in THE (2018d), cardinal rankings are given for the leading 100 and 101 universities in 2017 and 2018, respectively, with 50 universities listed in intervals from 101–110, 111–120, 121–130, 131–140, and 141–150. The remaining 108 universities are listed equally as 151+.

Table 1a,b show the universities that have more than 20% internationalization, where IntStud denotes the percentage of international students, in 2017 and 2018, respectively. The universities are essentially all private, with seven of seven and six of seven in Table 1a,b, respectively. The sole exception is Akita International University (AIU), a public (specifically, prefectural) university, in Table 1b. Ritsumeikan Asia Pacific University has the highest IntStud scores in both years, with 46.5% and 53.4%, in 2017 and 2018, respectively, as well as being ranked 24th and 21st in Japan in these two years. At 12, AIU has the highest ranking of the universities in the two tables, with all the other private universities being ranked in the range 151+.

Table 1. (a) More than 20% IntStud 2017. **(b)** More than 20% IntStud 2018.

University	Rank	Type	Prefecture	IntStud
(a)				
Ritsumeikan Asia Pacific University (APU)	24	Private	Oita	46.50
Digital Hollywood University	151+	Private	Tokyo	35.10
Kobe International University	151+	Private	Hyogo	31.00
Tokyo Fuji University	151+	Private	Tokyo	30.60
Okayama Shoka University	151+	Private	Okayama	22.90
Tokuyama University	151+	Private	Yamaguchi	21.00
Hokuriku University	151+	Private	Ishikawa	20.40
(b)				
Ritsumeikan Asia Pacific University (APU)	21	Private	Oita	53.40
Osaka University of Tourism	151+	Private	Osaka	38.90
Kobe International University	151+	Private	Hyogo	24.10
Hokuriku University	151+	Private	Ishikawa	20.90
Kanagawa Dental University	151+	Private	Kanagawa	20.50
Akita International University	12	Public	Akita	20.40
Osaka University of Economics and Law	151+	Private	Osaka	20.10

Note: IntStud denotes the percentage of international students.

Of the seven universities in Table 1a, four universities do not appear in Table 1b. In fact, apart from Digital Hollywood University, which drops from 35.1% in Table 1a to 5.7% in Table 3b, Tokyo Fuji University, Okayama Shoka University, and Tokuyama University seem to have disappeared altogether in terms of IntStud after 2017. Of the seven universities in Table 1b, Osaka University of Tourism, Kanagawa Dental University, AIU, and Osaka University of Economics and Law are new entrants, although, as discussed previously, only AIU has a cardinal ranking, with the others being ranked above 151.

Table 2a,b show the universities with IntStud scores in the range of 10–20% for 2017 and 2018, respectively, with 14 of 16 and 14 of 21 being private universities in the two years. However, the two national universities, Tokyo Institute of Technology and Nagaoka University of Technology, are ranked at fourth and 17th, and fourth and 21st in Table 2a,b, respectively, while the remaining 14 universities are ranked outside the top 100. The seven national universities are ranked in the top 21 in Table 2b, with only Waseda University, Sophia University, and International Christian University, all of which are located in Tokyo, as the only private universities in the top 100. It is clear that the national universities dominate the rankings in the IntStud range 10–20%.

Table 2. (a) 10–20% IntStud 2017. **(b)** 10–20% IntStud 2018.

University	Rank	Type	Prefecture	IntStud
(a)				
Osaka University of Economics and Law	151+	Private	Osaka	16.70
Hagoromo University of International Studies	151+	Private	Osaka	15.50
Meikai University	141–150	Private	Chiba	14.90
Sanyo Gakuen University	151+	Private	Okayama	14.80
Nagoya Keizai University	151+	Private	Aichi	14.40
Takaoka University of Law	151+	Private	Toyama	12.70
Osaka Sangyo University	151+	Private	Osaka	12.50
Kanto Gakuen University	151+	Private	Gunma	11.70
Nagaoka University of Technology	17	National	Niigata	11.50
Ashikaga Institute of Technology	151+	Private	Tochigi	11.10
Seigakuin University	151+	Private	Saitama	11.00
Kibi International University	151+	Private	Okayama	10.70
Tokyo Institute of Technology	4	National	Tokyo	10.70
Tokyo International University	141–150	Private	Saitama	10.40
Nagasaki International University	151+	Private	Nagasaki	10.30
Reitaku University	101–110	Private	Chiba	10.30
(b)				
Nagoya Keizai University	151+	Private	Aichi	18.50
Josai International University	151+	Private	Chiba	17.40
Meikai University	151+	Private	Chiba	16.40
Tokyo International University	151+	Private	Saitama	16.00
Nagoya University of Commerce & Business	111–120	Private	Aichi	15.90
Hagoromo University of International Studies	151+	Private	Osaka	15.60
Shizuoka Eiwa Gakuin University	151+	Private	Shizuoka	15.60
Seigakuin University	151+	Private	Saitama	14.10
Osaka Sangyo University	151+	Private	Osaka	13.30
The University of Tokyo	1	National	Tokyo	12.40
Reitaku University	121–130	Private	Chiba	12.20
Tohoku University	3	National	Miyagi	11.60
Hitotsubashi University	14	National	Tokyo	11.50
Nagaoka University of Technology	21	National	Niigata	11.50
University of Tsukuba	9	National	Ibaraki	11.50
Tokyo Institute of Technology	4	National	Tokyo	10.90
Kyushu University	5	National	Fukuoka	10.60
Waseda University	11	Private	Tokyo	10.60
Nagasaki International University	151+	Private	Nagasaki	10.40
Sophia University	15	Private	Tokyo	10.40
International Christian University	16	Private	Tokyo	10.00

Note: IntStud denotes the percentage of international students.

Universities with IntStud scores in the range 5–10% for 2017 and 2018 are shown in Table 3a,b, respectively. Of the 35 universities in Table 3a, 18 are private, while 11 of 29 universities in Table 3b are private. These are much higher percentages than those in Tables 1 and 2. However, in Table 3a, 11 of the 17 non-private universities are ranked in the top 20, while only three private universities, namely Waseda University, International Christian University, and Sophia University, with rankings of 10th, 15th, and 18th, respectively, are listed in the top 100 universities.

Table 3. (**a**) 5–10% IntStud 2017. (**b**) 5–10% IntStud 2018.

University	Rank	Type	Prefecture	IntStud
(a)				
Hitotsubashi University	14	National	Tokyo	9.80
Nagoya University	4	National	Aichi	9.80
University of Tsukuba	9	National	Ibaraki	9.50
Sophia University	18	Private	Tokyo	9.40
Takushoku University	151+	Private	Tokyo	9.40
The University of Tokyo	1	National	Tokyo	9.20
Osaka University	6	National	Osaka	8.40
Tokyo University of Foreign Studies	27	National	Tokyo	8.00
Kyushu University	7	National	Fukuoka	7.90
Fukuoka Women's University	48	Public	Fukuoka	7.80
Tohoku University	2	National	Miyagi	7.50
Kyoto Gakuen University	151+	Private	Kyoto	7.40
Tokyo Medical and Dental University (TMDU)	38	National	Tokyo	7.20
Toyohashi University of Technology (TUT)	37	National	Aichi	7.20
Tokyo University and Graduate School of Social Welfare	151+	Private	Gunma	7.10
Waseda University	10	Private	Tokyo	7.10
Ashiya University	151+	Private	Hyogo	6.80
Hokkaido University	8	National	Hokkaido	6.70
Yamanashi Gakuin University	151+	Private	Yamanashi	6.70
Kyoto University	3	National	Kyoto	6.60
Utsunomiya Kyowa University	151+	Private	Tochigi	6.60
Tokyo University of Marine Science and Technology	36	National	Tokyo	6.50
Yokohama National University	33	National	Kanagawa	6.50
Toyama University of International Studies	151+	Private	Toyama	6.40
Baiko Gakuin University	151+	Private	Yamaguchi	6.10
Gifu Keizai University	151+	Private	Gifu	6.10
Hiroshima University	12	National	Hiroshima	5.80
International Christian University	15	Private	Tokyo	5.70
Musashino University	151+	Private	Tokyo	5.60
Musashino Art University	151+	Private	Tokyo	5.50
Ryutsu Keizai University	141–150	Private	Ibaraki	5.50
Kobe University	13	National	Hyogo	5.40
Tokyo Polytechnic University	151+	Private	Kanagawa	5.30
Sapporo University Women's Junior College	151+	Private	Hokkaido	5.20
Kyushu Sangyo University	121–130	Private	Fukuoka	5.10
(b)				
Fukuoka Women's University	62	Public	Fukuoka	9.00
Nagoya University	7	National	Aichi	8.70
Tokyo University of Foreign Studies	17	National	Tokyo	8.50
Tokyo Medical and Dental University (TMDU)	39	National	Tokyo	8.40
Yokohama College of Commerce	151+	Private	Kanagawa	8.20
Kyoto University	1	National	Kyoto	8.00
Yokohama National University	25	National	Kanagawa	7.80
Tokyo University of Marine Science and Technology	41	National	Tokyo	7.60
Hokkaido University	6	National	Hokkaido	7.50
Keio University	10	Private	Tokyo	7.30
Osaka University	8	National	Osaka	6.70
Hiroshima University	13	National	Hiroshima	6.60
Toyohashi University of Technology (TUT)	38	National	Aichi	6.60
Baiko Gakuin University	151+	Private	Yamaguchi	6.40
Musashino Art University	151+	Private	Tokyo	6.40
Tama Art University	151+	Private	Tokyo	6.30

Table 3. *Cont.*

University	Rank	Type	Prefecture	IntStud
Musashino University	151+	Private	Tokyo	6.20
Yamanashi Gakuin University	151+	Private	Yamanashi	6.10
The University of Electro-Communications	55	National	Tokyo	6.00
Kanazawa University	20	National	Ishikawa	5.90
Ritsumeikan University	23	Private	Kyoto	5.90
Kobe University	18	National	Hyogo	5.80
Digital Hollywood University	151+	Private	Tokyo	5.70
Kyoto University of Foreign Studies	92	Private	Kyoto	5.70
Tokyo University of the Arts	151+	National	Tokyo	5.60
Asia University	151+	Private	Tokyo	5.30
Saitama University	70	National	Saitama	5.20
Kyoto Institute of Technology	42	National	Kyoto	5.10
Ochanomizu University	32	National	Tokyo	5.10

Note: IntStud denotes the percentage of international students.

In Table 3b, eight of the 18 non-private universities are in the top 20, while 17 of 18 are in the top 100; the sole exception is Tokyo University of the Arts, having a ranking in the 151+ group. On the contrary, only three private universities of 11, namely Keio University, Ritsumeikan University, and Kyoto University of Foreign Studies, with rankings of 10th, 23rd, and 92nd, respectively, are listed in the top 100 in Table 3. As in Tables 1 and 2, national universities tend to dominate the rankings in terms of IntStud scores.

The plots between Rank and IntStud, and between Rank and FTE (Size), are shown in Figure 1a,b and Figure 2a,b, for 2017 and 2018, respectively. It is clear that there are positive linear relationships for Rank with IntStud and FTE (Size) in both years, especially if a single outlier was deleted in 2017 in Figure 1a, and two outliers were deleted in Figure 1b.

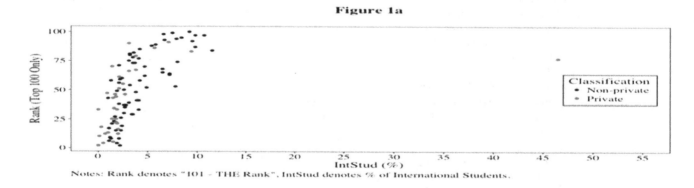

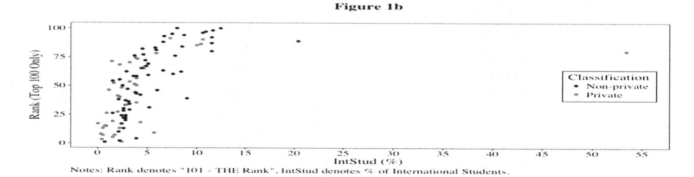

Figure 1. (**a**) Rank and Intstud, 2017; (**b**) Rank and Intstud, 2018.

Figure 2a

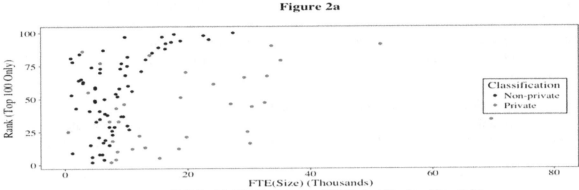

Notes: Rank denotes "101 - THE Rank". FTE(Size) denotes FTE Student Numbers (thousands).

Figure 2b

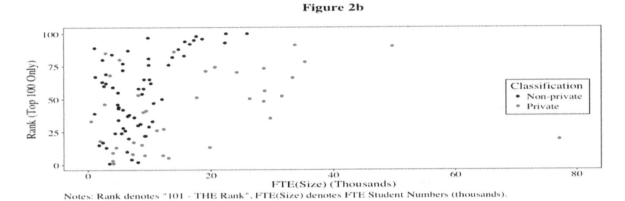

Notes: Rank denotes "101 - THE Rank". FTE(Size) denotes FTE Student Numbers (thousands).

Figure 2. (**a**) Rank and FTE (Size), 2017; (**b**) Rank and FTE (Size), 2018.

The pairwise linear relationship between Rank and IntStud was steeper for private than for non-private universities in both 2017 and 2018, but there seems to be little difference from one year to the next. Unlike Figure 1a,b, the pairwise linear relationship between Rank and FTE (Size) was steeper for non-private than for private universities in Figure 2a,b in 2017 and 2018, respectively, with little apparent difference in the relationship between the two variables from one year to the next.

3. Empirical Analysis

As mentioned in Section 2, there are only 100 universities that are given cardinal rankings for 2017 and 2018. For this reason, only the first 100 leading universities in Japan were used for estimating and testing the effects of size and internationalization on the rankings of non-private (that is, national and public) and private universities.

The linear regression models to be estimated were variations of the following:

$$Rank = intercept + a* IntStud + b* FTE (size) + error,$$

where Rank denotes "101—THE rank", IntStud denotes "% of international students", FTE (size) denotes "FTE student numbers (Thousands)", and the random error is presumed to satisfy the classical assumptions, which can be tested using the Breausch–Pagan test of homoskedasticity, the RESET test of no functional form misspecification, and the Jarque–Bera test of normality.

The estimates of the linear regression models, with the rankings being explained by IntStud and FTE (size), are based on 100 and 101 universities in 2017 and 2018, respectively, with 33 and 38 private universities, respectively, and 67 and 63 non-private universities, respectively, in 2017 and 2018. As the numbers of observations across the three tables, as well as for the two years, are different, the R-squared values cannot be compared.

The estimates of the linear regression models of Rank on IntStud and FTE (size) for all (that is, private and non-private) universities, private universities, and non-private universities in the top 100 universities, are given in Table 4a,c, respectively. The results for both years are presented in each table. "Rank" is defined as "101—THE rank", such that universities with a higher ranking are given a lower cardinal number.

Table 4. (**a**) Regressions of Rank on IntStud and number of full-time-equivalent students (FTE (size)) for the top 100 universities. (**b**) Regressions of Rank on IntStud and FTE (size) for private universities (from top 100). (**c**) Regressions of Rank on IntStud and FTE (size) for non-private universities (from top 100).

	2017	2018
	(a)	
Intercept	32.62 ***	30.08 ***
	(4.78)	(5.07)
IntStud	2.732 ***	2.479 ***
	(0.493)	(0.319)
FTE (size)	0.584 **	0.650 *
	(0.250)	(0.357)
Breusch–Pagan	48.23 ***	42.55 ***
Jarque–Bera	3.92	7.27 **
RESET	43.72 ***	45.44 ***
Wald Test	16.82 ***	33.49 ***
Observations	100	101
Adjusted R^2	0.254	0.301
Residual Standard Error	24.98 (df = 97)	24.43 (df = 98)
	(b)	
Intercept	24.43 ***	25.35 ***
	(6.70)	(7.86)
IntStud	1.509 ***	1.454 ***
	(0.138)	(0.214)
FTE (size)	0.623 *	0.623
	(0.309)	(0.383)
Breusch–Pagan	0.83	5.00 *
Jarque–Bera	1.80	1.13
RESET	14.02 ***	14.41 ***
Wald Test	60.62 ***	23.97 ***
Observations	33	38
Adjusted R^2	0.223	0.247
Residual Standard Error	24.42 (df = 30)	25.00 (df = 35)
	(c)	
Intercept	13.21 **	11.00 **
	(5.57)	(4.76)
IntStud	6.560 ***	5.067 ***
	(0.568)	(0.437)
FTE (size)	1.646 ***	1.985 ***
	(0.414)	(0.311)
Breusch–Pagan	9.05 **	1.09
Jarque–Bera	1.95	1.43
RESET	3.24 **	7.11 ***
Wald Test	68.49 ***	92.47 ***
Observations	67	63
Adjusted R^2	0.615	0.659
Residual Standard Error	17.84 (df = 64)	16.79 (df = 60)

Dependent Variable: Rank. Notes: Rank denotes "101—THE rank", IntStud denotes "% of international students", FTE (size) denotes "FTE student numbers (thousands)"; * $p < 0.1$, ** $p < 0.05$, *** $p < 0.01$.

When the data for private and non-private universities from the top 100 universities were combined in Table 4a, both IntStud and FTE (size) were positive and statistically significant in both years. This is consistent with the pairwise findings in Figure 1a,b and Figure 2a,b that were discussed above. The estimated coefficients of IntStud and FTE (size) were separately similar for each of the two years.

The Lagrange multiplier tests for heteroscedasticity (Breusch–Pagan) were significant, but did not affect the validity of statistical inference as the standard errors were based on the Newey–West HAC consistent covariance matrix estimator. The Lagrange multiplier tests for non-normality (Jarque–Bera) were significant, which means that the errors were not normally distributed. Ramsey's RESET test for functional form suggests there may be some model misspecification, especially regarding the non-linearity of the relationship among Rank, IntStud, and FTE (size).

The regression estimates for private universities selected from the top 100 universities are given for the two years in Table 4b. Overall, the results are quantitatively similar to those in Table 4a, with the estimates being positive and statistically significant. In particular, the estimated coefficients of IntStud and FTE (size) were separately similar, not only for each of the two years, but also with the estimates for all universities in Table 4a, especially the estimated effects of FTE (size).

The Lagrange multiplier test for heteroscedasticity (Breusch–Pagan) was significant, but did not affect the validity of statistical inferences as the standard errors were based on the Newey–West HAC consistent covariance matrix estimator. The Lagrange multiplier test for non-normality (Jarque–Bera) was significant, which means that the errors were not normally distributed, Ramsey's RESET test for functional form suggests there may be some model misspecification, especially regarding the non-linearity of the relationship among Rank, IntStud, and FTE (size). The Lagrange multiplier tests for heteroscedasticity were either insignificant or marginally significant, while the Lagrange multiplier tests for non-normality were insignificant. The RESET functional form tests suggest there may be a non-linear relationship among Rank, IntStud, and FTE (size).

Table 4c presents the regression estimates for non-private universities selected from the top 100 universities for the two years. As compared with the estimates shown in Table 4a,b, the results are quantitatively dissimilar. Although the estimated coefficients of IntStud and FTE (size) were separately similar for each of the two years, with the estimates being positive and statistically significant in all cases, the estimates of the coefficients for both IntStud and FTE (size) were considerably larger than their counterparts in Table 4a,c for both 2017 and 2018.

The Lagrange multiplier test for heteroscedasticity (Breusch–Pagan) was significant for 2017 but not for 2018, while the Lagrange multiplier tests for non-normality (Jarque–Bera) were insignificant, which means that the errors were normally distributed for each of the two years. As in the case of Table 4a,b, Ramsey's RESET test for functional form suggests there may be some model misspecification, especially regarding the non-linearity of the relationship among Rank, IntStud, and FTE (size).

Overall, there seemed to be strong positive and statistically significant effects of both IntStud and FTE (size) on Rank in 2017 and 2018, regardless of whether the data for the top 100 private and non-private universities were combined, as in Table 4a, or examined separately, as in Table 4b,c.

4. Concluding Remarks

As international and domestic rankings are typically based on arbitrary methodologies and criteria, evaluating how the rankings might be sensitive to different factors, as well as forecasting how they might change over time, requires a statistical analysis of the factors that affect the rankings. The Times Higher Education (THE) World University Rankings represent a leading and influential annual source of international university rankings.

Using recently released data for Japan, the paper evaluated the effects of size (specifically, the number of full-time-equivalent (FTE) students, or FTE (size)) and internationalization (specifically, the percentage of international students, or IntStud) on academic rankings using THE data for 2017 and 2018 on national, public (that is, prefectural or city), and private universities. The results showed that both FTE (size) and IntStud were statistically significant in explaining rankings for all universities, as well as separately for private and non-private (that is, national and public) universities, in Japan for 2017 and 2018.

As discussed in Section 1, the purpose of the paper was to answer the following questions (the answers are given in **bold**):

(i).   Are private or non-private universities more highly ranked? (**Non-private**)

(ii).   Are private or non-private universities larger in terms of size? (**Private**)

(iii). Do private or non-private universities have a higher degree of internationalization? (**In general, private**)

(iv).   Do the size, internationalization, and rankings of private and non-private universities change over time? (**Slightly**)

(v).   Are there differences in the effects of size and internationalization on the rankings of private universities? (**Yes**)

(vi).   Are there differences in the effects of size and internationalization on the rankings of non-private universities? (**Yes**)

(vii). Do the effects of size and internationalization change over time for private and non-private universities? (**Not between 2017 and 2018**)

Further empirical analysis could be undertaken for private and non-private universities in Japan, as well as for the US, Europe, Asia, and Latin America; however, the distinction between private and non-private universities is prevalent primarily for the US.

A deeper analysis of the issue requires much richer data, which might be forthcoming in the foreseeable future. Limitations of the analysis include the late arrival of some data series, which can make the prediction of rankings problematic.

The paper is intended for the Special Issue of the journal on "Sustainability of the Theories Developed by Mathematical Finance and Mathematical Economics with Applications". In this sense, the paper is an application of applied econometrics to evaluate and predict university rankings using size and internationalization from the Times Higher Education (THE) data for Japan.

Author Contributions: Data curation, M.M. and C.W.; conceptualization, M.M.; funding acquisition, M.M. and T.N.; methodology, M.M.; project administration, M.M. and T.N.; software, C.W.; validation, M.M. and C.W.; formal analysis, M.M.; investigation, M.M. and C.W.; resources, M.M. and T.N.; writing—original draft preparation, M.M.; writing—review and editing, M.M.; visualization, T.N.

Acknowledgments: The authors are most grateful to three reviewers for very helpful comments and suggestions. For financial support, the first author wishes to acknowledge the Ministry of Science and Technology (MOST), Taiwan, and the Australian Research Council.

References

1.   Times Higher Education. World University Rankings. 2018. Available online: https://www.timeshighereducation.com/world-university-rankings (accessed on 26 September 2018).

2.   Times Higher Education. Best universities in the United States 2019. 2018. Available online: https://www.timeshighereducation.com/student/best-universities/best-universities-united-states (accessed on 26 September 2018).

3.   Times Higher Education. Best universities in Japan. 2018. Available online: https://www.timeshighereducation.com/student/best-universities/best-universities-japan (accessed on 26 September 2018).

4.   Times Higher Education. Asia University Rankings 2018. 2018. Available online: https://www.timeshighereducation.com/world-university-rankings/2018/regional-ranking#!/page/0/length/25/sort_by/rank/sort_order/asc/cols/stats (accessed on 26 September 2018).

5. Times Higher Education. Japan University Rankings 2018. 2018. Available online: https: //www.timeshighereducation.com/rankings/japan-university/2018#!/page/0/length/25/sort_ by/rank/sort_order/asc/cols/stats (accessed on 26 September 2018).

6. Carrico, C.S.; Hogan, S.M.; Dyson, R.G.; Athanassopoulos, A.D. Data envelope analysis and university selection. *J. Oper. Res. Soc.* **1997**, *48*, 1163–1177. [CrossRef]

7. Hu, C.-K.; Liu, F.-B.; Hu, C.-F. A hybrid fuzzy DEA/AHP methodology for ranking units in a fuzzy environment. *Symmetry* **2017**, *9*, 273. [CrossRef]

8. Dale, S.; Krueger, A. Estimating the payoff to attending a more selective college: An application of selection on observables and unobservables. *Q. J. Econ.* **2002**, *117*, 1491–1527. [CrossRef]

9. Eccles, C. The use of university rankings in the United Kingdom. *High. Educ. Eur.* **2002**, *27*, 423–432. [CrossRef]

10. Federkeil, G. Some aspects of ranking methodology—The CHE ranking of German universities. *High. Educ. Eur.* **2002**, *27*, 389–397. [CrossRef]

11. Kallio, R.E. Factors Influencing the College Choice Decisions of Graduate Students. *Res. High. Educ.* **1995**, *36*, 109–124. [CrossRef]

12. Liu, N.C.; Cheng, Y.; Liu, L. Academic ranking of world universities using Scientometrics: A comment on the "Fatal Attraction". *Scientometrics* **2005**, *64*, 101. [CrossRef]

13. Lo Storto, C. Ecological efficiency based ranking of cities: A combined DEA cross-efficiency and Shannon's entropy method. *Sustainability* **2016**, *8*, 124. [CrossRef]

14. McDonough, P.; Antonio, A.L.; Walpole, M.; Perez, L.X. College rankings: Democratized college knowledge for whom? *Res. High. Educ.* **1998**, *39*, 513–537. [CrossRef]

15. Meredith, M. Why do universities compete in the ratings game? An empirical analysis of the effects of the U.S. News & World Report College Rankings. *Res. High. Educ.* **2004**, *45*, 443–461.

16. Merisotis, J.P. On the ranking of higher education institutions. *High. Educ. Eur.* **2002**, *27*, 361. [CrossRef]

17. Pavan, M.; Todeschini, R.; Orlandi, M. Data mining by total ranking methods: A case study on optimisation of the "pulp and bleaching" process in the paper industry. *Ann. Chim.* **2006**, *96*, 13–27. [CrossRef] [PubMed]

18. Van Raan, A.F.J. Fatal attraction: Ranking of universities by bibliometric methods. *Scientometrics* **2005**, *62*, 133. [CrossRef]

19. Tijssen, R.J.W.; Yegros-Yegros, A.; Winnink, J.J. University-industry R&D linkage metrics: Validity and applicability in world university rankings. *Scientometrics* **2016**, *109*, 677–696. [PubMed]

20. Piro, F.N.; Sivertsen, G. How can differences in international university rankings be explained? *Scientometrics* **2016**, *109*, 2263–2278. [CrossRef]

21. Shehatta, I.; Mahmood, K. Corrrelation among top 100 universities in the major six global rankings: Policy implications. *Scientometrics* **2016**, *109*, 1231–1254. [CrossRef]

22. Moed, H.F. A critical comparative analysis of five world university rankings. *Scientometrics* **2017**, *110*, 967–990. [CrossRef]

23. Kivinen, O.; Hedman, J.; Artukka, K. Scientific publishing and global university rankings: How well are top publishing universities recognized? *Scientometrics* **2017**, *112*, 679–695. [CrossRef]

24. Pietrucha, J. Country-specific determinants of world university rankings. *Scientometrics* **2018**, *114*, 1129–1139. [CrossRef] [PubMed]

25. Johnes, J. University rankings: What do they really show? *Scientometrics* **2018**, *115*, 585–606. [CrossRef]

15

The Three Musketeers Relationships between Hong Kong, Shanghai and Shenzhen before and after Shanghai–Hong Kong Stock Connect

Andy Wui-Wing Cheng [1], Nikolai Sheung-Chi Chow [2,*], David Kam-Hung Chui [1] and Wing-Keung Wong [1,3,4]

[1] Department of Economics and Finance, The Hang Seng University of Hong Kong, Hong Kong
[2] Research School of Economics, Australian National University, Canberra 0200, Australia
[3] Department of Finance, Fintech Center, and Big Data Research Center, Asia University, Taichung 41354, Taiwan
[4] Department of Medical Research, China Medical University Hospital, Taichung 41354, Taiwan
[*] Correspondence: nikolaichow0809@gmail.com

Abstract: This study examines the sustainability of financial integration between China (represented by Shenzhen and Shanghai) stock markets and Hong Kong stock market over the period of pre and post launch of the Stock Connect Scheme. This paper aims to fill the gap in the financial literature by providing empirical research on the dynamics of the financial integration process, and examining the sustainability of financial integration among the three Chinese stock markets. We apply cointegration and both linear and nonlinear causalities to investigate whether the Shanghai–Hong Kong Stock Connect has any impact on both market capitalizations and market indices of Hong Kong, Shanghai, and Shenzhen markets. Through cointegration tests and linear Granger causality techniques, it was found that the stock markets from mainland China are increasingly influencing the Hong Kong stock market after the introduction of the Stock Connect Scheme; however, when using nonlinear Granger causality analysis for confirming China market dominance, the result shows an reverse relationship whereby the Hong Kong stock market is still relevant to understand and predict China stock market after the introduction of the Stock Connect Scheme. Overall, our findings support the view that the Shanghai–Hong Kong Stock Connect has a significant impact on both market capitalizations and market indices of the Hong Kong, Shanghai, and Shenzhen markets, but Hong Kong stock market is still relevant to understand and predict China stock market after the introduction of the Stock Connect Scheme. The change in share premium difference between mainland China's domestic A-share markets and Hong Kong's H-share market could change investors' appetites or sentiments. Further research includes examining whether there is any functional relationship including nonlinear relationship and studying the dynamic drivers of the relationships.

Keywords: financial integration; cointegration; error correction; linear and nonlinear causality

1. Introduction

Stock market integration is an area of considerable interest and debate among academics and market practitioners. With regard to mainland China, where there has been continuous financial reform in terms of market deregulation and an aggressive pro-growth strategy, integration with neighboring markets has intensified, and whether integration can sustain better, in particular with Hong Kong. Given their economic similarities, the financial integration of mainland China's stock markets, Shanghai and Shenzhen, and that of Hong Kong has made remarkable progress over the past 10 years. In 2002 and 2006, the China Securities Regulatory Commission (CSRC) took to the airwaves, preempting the global financial media, to announce the Qualified Foreign Institutional Investor (QFII) and Qualified Domestic Institutional Investor (QDII) schemes respectively. The QFII scheme, under the existing restricted flow of capital accounts in China, allows qualified investors to invest in certain security products in China. In May 2007, the QDII scheme, which initially permitted Chinese institutions and residents to invest in fixed-income and money-market products overseas, was widened to include equity products in designated stock markets. These two arrangements have further increased the integration of mainland China and Hong Kong. The latter, the stock market of which is ranked as the seventh largest in the world and the third largest in Asia in terms of market capitalization (The World Federation of Exchanges and Bloomberg, June 2017), is a Special Administrative Region of China and a major financial center. Moreover, Hong Kong is committed to strengthening financial integration among the stock markets in China and make the integration sustains better. Financial theory suggests that an integrated regional market performs more efficiently than segmented individual market. Member markets can enhance the efficient allocation of capital in regions where the funding requirement is greatest. The attraction of cross-border fund flows is that they can improve the markets' liquidity and lower the cost of capital for firms [1]. The study on presence of herd formation in Chinese markets supports rational asset pricing models and market efficiency [2]. The general cointegration relationship between the prices of H-shares and A-shares, which are cross-listed Chinese stocks in both markets, across January 1999 to March 2009. It is found that significant improvements in the long-run expectation of H-share discounts compared with A-shares, the level of short-run co-movements in prices, and the magnitude of error corrections [3]. By applying stock market capitalization as a measure to identify countries that are taking the lead in establishing an integrated stock market in the Asia–Pacific region, the authors conclude that China and Hong Kong are the potential market leaders among other advanced equity markets (Japan, Australia, Singapore, and New Zealand). The reason is that China and Hong Kong exhibit unidirectional causality toward the other markets [4]. There is an increase in market integration among the different stock markets in the Greater China region, (China, Hong Kong, and Taiwan) from July 1993 to June 2013. Further, less volatile and sensitive responsiveness indicate improved stock market efficiency among the markets due to improved regulatory frameworks and better macroprudential policies, thereby enabling the more efficient absorption of market information [5].

The economies of Shanghai, Shenzhen, and Hong Kong constitute one of the most dynamic economic zones in the region. With closer trade and financial interaction, such as the QFII, QDII, RQFII, and RQDII (the Renminbi QFII and the Renminbi QDII respectively), the Shanghai–Hong Kong Stock Connect in 2014, and the Shenzhen–Hong Kong Stock Connect arrangement in 2016, the interaction of the Chinese stock markets has become a topic of global interest. However, there is a need for additional analysis regarding the nature and strength of these financial linkages. Although considerable researches have been conducted to investigate financial integration among East Asian countries and the effects on other world markets, little work has been conducted on the important aspect of financial linkages within China and the sustainability of financial integration within China. Further, given the geographic and economic closeness between the two regions of mainland China and Hong Kong, each of which could have significant influence over the other through increasing interaction [6,7], the current study fills the gap in the financial literature by providing empirical research on the dynamics of the financial integration process and examine the sustainability of financial integration among the three Chinese stock markets. In addition, this study enables us to discover the market leader within the country. The identification of the potential market leader can help policymakers to ensure policy coordination, enhance market development, and maintain market stability in the event of financial turmoil among the three stock markets. Given the decreasing benefit of diversification among these markets, this study is also of interest to investment practitioners when they allocate assets. The 'Stock Connect' Scheme appeared to provide a turning point in China's financial market development. It represents a remarkable move to the quality and sustainability of the growth for China's stock markets. The long-term objective of the scheme is to reorient growth to make it more balanced and more sustainable from different perspectives, such as market structure, connections with international practices and investors. It is a promising sign of push for reform to increase foreign investors' access to China's capital markets. Each of these moves had broader significance for ensuring a continue development and sustainable growth through policy reforms.

In this study, we use cointegration, linear and nonlinear causalities to investigate whether the Shanghai–Hong Kong Stock Connect has any impact on the market capitalizations and market indices of the Hong Kong, Shanghai, and Shenzhen markets. Our study deviates from the time series of the literature, which primarily examine nonlinear causal relationships using nonlinear causality tests. The nonlinear causality test can detect a nonlinear deterministic process that originally "looks" random. The nonlinear causality test used in the current study could be considered a complementary test for the linear causality test because the latter cannot detect a nonlinear type of causal relationship. The nonparametric approach adopted in this study can capture the nonlinear nature of the relationship between stock markets. The approach would not be mis-specified if the two variables, *market capitalization* and *market index*, are related nonlinearly or if regime changes (structural breaks) occur due to a crisis. We will discuss this issue further in the methodology section.

The remaining of the paper is structured as follows. Section 2 provides background information on the Shanghai–Hong Kong Stock Connect scheme. In Section 3, we present a review of the relevant literature regarding financial integration. The limitations of these studies are also noted. Section 4 describes the data and the methodology. The empirical results regarding both linear and nonlinear causality among various stock markets are discussed in Section 5. Section 6 concludes the paper.

2. Characteristics of the Shanghai–Hong Kong Stock Connect

The year 2015 marked a breakthrough in the Chinese and Hong Kong stock markets. The implementation of the Shanghai–Hong Kong Stock Connect allowed international investors direct access to the Shanghai stock market through the Hong Kong Stock Exchange. This initiative enables northbound and southbound trading within aggregate quotas of RMB300 billion and RMB250 billion, respectively. The quotas are calculated on a netting basis at the end of each trading day. Under the scheme, the daily quotas set a limit for daily net buy value of cross-boundary trades. The northbound daily quota is around RMB13 billion, while the southbound daily quota is around RMB10.5 billion. Under the scheme, except B-shares and shares included on the Risk Alert Board, investors can trade certain stocks listed on the Shanghai Stock Exchange that are not included as constituent stocks of the relevant indices but have corresponding H-shares listed in Hong Kong. The scheme also indicates that only mainland institutional investors and individual investors who have RMB500,000 in their accounts are allowed to trade stocks of the Hang Seng Composite Large Cap Index and Hang Seng Composite MidCap Index together with all H-shares that are not stocks of the relevant indices but have corresponding A-shares listed in Shanghai, except for those not traded in Hong Kong dollars and H-shares that are not listed in Shanghai. The Shanghai–Hong Kong Stock Connect helps to create a "single" stock market that ranks as the second and third largest worldwide in terms of market capitalization and turnover value respectively.

3. Literature Review

The first study in this area date back to the late 1980s and early 1990s, which apply the cointegration model to study the relationship between two stock markets [4,8–10]. Following this research, a substantial number of studies have focused on the degree of integration among different markets within geographic regions and the connections between international markets. The study on international stock-price linkages and co-movements of fundamentals within a multivariate cointegration framework finds that a common stochastic trend in the US, Canada, Germany, Japan, and the UK [11]. While studying the stock market linkages of a group of Pacific-Basin countries with US and Japan by estimating the multivariate cointegration model, it is suggested that the relaxation of the restrictions might have strengthened international market interrelations [12]. Furthermore, the four markets in Latin America (Argentina, Brazil, Chile, and Mexico), together with the US stock market, have significant permanent components that cause cointegration in the long run [13]. In other direction, the transmission of shocks between the U.S. and foreign markets to delineate interdependence from contagion of the US financial crisis by constructing shock models for partially overlapping and non-overlapping markets is examined [14]. The center of gravity within stock market integration studies has also moved from the markets in the Western hemisphere to the market linkages in Asian emerging markets, particularly for the periods before and after the 1997–98 Asian financial crisis. For example, the dynamic linkages of Asian stock markets before and after the crisis are examined. It is revealed that the relationships among East Asian stock markets are time-varying; for instance, Hong Kong and Singapore responded significantly sooner to the financial turmoil that was occurring in most Asian markets. More importantly, the empirical findings about the degree of stock market integration vary [15–18]. The linkages among the Southeast Asian stock markets are examined too and it is found that no evidence of a long-term relationship among the stock markets from 1988 to 1997; however, the degree of integration increases when the author conducts a correlation analysis. The results show that the returns of Indonesia, the Philippines, and Thailand were closely affected by the Singaporean market [19]. The long-term equilibrium relationships and short-term causality effects among stock markets in the US, Japan are investigated, and 10 other Asian economies, including Hong Kong, from January 1995 to May 2001. It is found that cointegration relationships both before and after the Asian financial crisis. Further, it is concluded that the degree of integration within the region increased after the crisis [20]. The degree of financial integration among selected East Asian countries from 1988 to 2006 by applying the panel unit root and cointegration approach is investigated too. The results show that high-income countries have better financial integration than middle-income countries and the sustainability of financial integration is better for high-income countries than middle-income countries [21]. The stock market integration in Asia is examined and it is found that the degrees of integration between mature and emerging equity markets differ. It is also shown that individual stock markets in Asia are more sensitive to regional events compared with global events. The difference in mature and emerging equity markets is mainly due to political, economic, and institutional issues [22]. As we can see, the above studies have a common characteristic: the comparisons are focused on different nations from a cross-country border perspective. Moreover, few studies have investigated different economies within China. The current study focuses on this less-visited field and fills the gap in the literature.

Nevertheless, there are a few related studies. The causal linkages among the Shanghai, Shenzhen, and Hong Kong stock markets are examined and it is found that the stock index series is non-stationary and that cointegrating vectors and error correction models do not exist for the index series. It is concluded that Granger causality shows a positive feedback mechanism from Shenzhen to Shanghai, while Hong Kong causes volatility in Shanghai but not vice versa [23]. By employing the daily values of the stock-price indices for the Shanghai, Shenzhen, and Hong Kong markets from 1992 to 2002, potential gains of intermarket timing for Hong Kong investors are found [24]. The financial integration in the Greater China region (China, Taiwan, and Hong Kong) is examined, it is indicated that a trend of increasing financial interaction in the region [25]. The China's A-share market and Hong Kong's stock market are closely integrated; however, there is little evidence to link them to the world market [26–28]. A similar study shows that at the time of their research, there was a spillover effect between the markets in the region and that the Chinese market was affected by its neighbors [7].

The impact of the Shanghai–Hong Kong Stock Connect is examined by using a pairwise linear causality test to check linear causal relationships between the closing prices of the SSE Composite Index and the Hong Kong Hang Seng Index (HSI). The authors find that the SSE takes a leading role after the implementation of Stock Connect Scheme [29]. The A- and H-share premium puzzle is investigated from the perspective of the effect of the Shanghai–Hong Kong Stock Connect policy. It is shown that the Shanghai–Hong Kong Stock Connect policy is effective at reducing the A- and H-share price gap [30]. A model of trading costs to consider the effect of the introduction of the Shanghai–Hong Kong Stock Connect is applied. It is found that the SSE, which may have had lower trading costs than those of the

Hong Kong Stock Exchange, seems to have developed higher trading costs in the period leading to the Stock Connect's introduction [31]. The variations in dependence and risk spillover between Chinese and London stock markets before and after Shanghai–Hong Kong Stock Connect and Shenzhen–Hong Kong Stock Connect are investigated, it is found that Shanghai–Hong Kong Stock Connect program enhances the dependence between Chinese and London stock markets, while the overall dependence decreases slightly after the Shenzhen–Hong Kong Stock Connect program [32].

4. Data and Methodology

4.1. Data Description

We use the daily stock market capitalizations and market indices of Hong Kong, Shanghai, and Shenzhen from January 2005 to December 2016, a total of 2817 observations. The data employed in the analysis is obtained from Bloomberg Financial Services. The data is divided into the following two data sets: 1) the "before" period from January 2005 to November 2014, which is the period before the Shanghai–Hong Kong Stock Connect, and 2) the "after" period from November 2014 to December 2016, which is the period after the Shanghai–Hong Kong Stock Connect. The starting point in 2005 marked an important milestone for Chinese stock market reform because it was then that China started changing its state-owned securities into tradable shares.

Table 1 shows the descriptive statistics for the three markets before and after the introduction of the Shanghai–Hong Kong Stock Connect. Hong Kong has the largest market capitalization and market index in both periods. The Shanghai stock market has the largest standard deviation for market capitalization and Hong Kong has the largest standard deviation for market index. In addition, market capitalization and market index are skewed in both periods. Excess kurtosis is deemed to be kurtosis greater than 3 for both of the variables and all markets, except for the variables of Hong Kong and Shenzhen in the "before" period and Hong Kong's market index in the "after period." We use the Jarque–Bera (JB) test to examine whether the data are normally distributed. Both market capitalization and market index are rejected to be normally distributed in both of the periods and all markets.

Table 1. Descriptive Statistics for Stock Market Capitalizations and Market Indices.

	Market Capitalization			Market Index		
	Hong Kong	**Shanghai**	**Shenzhen**	**Hong Kong**	**Shanghai**	**Shenzhen**
Before						
Mean	2149.56	1999.64	485.12	2603.88	364.12	133.30
Maximum	3424.25	3891.59	864.10	4082.25	810.67	223.21
Minimum	818.13	254.36	99.97	1420.72	122.21	28.66
Std. Dev.	694.35	915.89	196.73	464.31	131.82	53.71
Skewness	−0.40 ***	−0.85 ***	−0.82 ***	−0.30 ***	0.44 ***	−0.70 ***
Kurtosis	2.03 ***	−7.06 ***	2.41 ***	2.69 ***	3.93 ***	2.21 ***
Jarque–Bera	153.81 ***	306.93 ***	292.79 ***	43.184 ***	156.95 ***	247.58 ***
After						
Mean	3249.04	4274.35	1065.69	2954.59	518.35	306.35
Maximum	4069.50	6623.38	1684.08	3669.84	832.07	505.82
Minimum	2665.16	3002.20	752.91	2373.58	400.53	215.68
Std. Dev.	300.25	679.62	163.69	292.65	94.27	53.67
Skewness	0.91 ***	1.32 ***	1.46 ***	0.49 ***	1.40 ***	1.33 ***
Kurtosis	3.70 ***	4.58 ***	5.79 ***	2.81	4.37 ***	5.53 ***
Jarque–Bera	80.22 ***	197.98 ***	341.85 ***	21.04 ***	204.03 ***	282.46 ***

Notes: The figures for market capitalizations and market indices are in US billion dollars. *, **, and *** denote significance at the 10%, 5%, and 1% levels, respectively.

The normalized time series for market capitalizations and market indices in the three markets for both periods are plotted in Figure 1. The figure shows that the variables are moving closer after the introduction of the Shanghai–Hong Kong Stock Connect in November 2014.

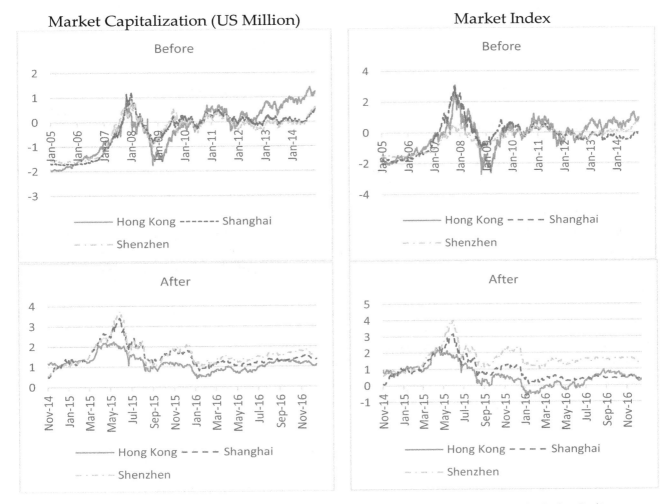

Figure 1. Shanghai, Shenzhen, and Hong Kong Stock Market Capitalizations and Market Indices.

4.2. Methodology

4.2.1. Cointegration

We conduct bivariate and multivariate cointegration for our variables. In order to estimate the long-run relationship between x_t and y_t, we first employ the following simple cointegration:

$$y_t = \beta_0 + \beta_1 x_t + e_t, \tag{1}$$

where y_t represents either the Hong Kong stock index or its market capitalization, x_t represents either the stock index or its market capitalization in Shanghai or the Shenzhen stock markets, and e_t is the residual for $t = 1, \ldots, T$. The test examines the residuals in regression (1) of I (1) variables. If x_t and y_t are I (1) and cointegrated, e_t is I (0). This finding means that the error term is stationary. Integration implies that a long-term linear relationship exists between series x_t and y_t.

In order to establish whether there is any cointegration relationship between the two vectors of the time series, we use three variables: $x_t = (x_{1,t}, x_{2,t})'$ and $y_t = (y_t)'$, where y_t represents either the Hong Kong stock index or its market capitalization, $x_{1,t}$ represents either the Shanghai stock index or its market capitalization, and $x_{2,t}$ represents either the Shenzhen stock index or its market capitalization. If all the variables $(x_{1,t}, x_{2,t}, y_t)$ are integrated in degree one, academics and practitioners will be interested to examine whether any cointegration relationship exists among them. In order to analyze this issue, we employ the Johansen cointegration test to estimate the cointegrating vectors [33–35]. According to Johansen's procedure, the p-dimensional unrestricted vector autoregression (VAR) model should be first specified with k lags as follows:

$$Z_t = \sum_1^k A_i Z_{t-i} + \Psi D_t + U_t,$$ (2)

where $Z_t = [x_{1,t}, x_{2,t}, y_t]'$ is a 3×1 vector of stochastic variables, D_t is a vector of dummies, and A_i is an $n \times n$ matrix. If U_t is found to be a vector of $I(0)$ residuals, a vector error correction model (VECM) could be constructed as follows:

$$\Delta Z_t = \sum_1^{k-1} \Phi_i \Delta Z_{t-1} + \Pi Z_{t-1} + \Psi D_t + U_t.$$ (3)

The hypothesis of cointegration is formulated as a reduced rank of the Π matrix. If the rank of Π (r) is less than or equal to 2, such that $\Pi = \alpha\beta'$ and $\Pi Z_{t-1} \sim I(0)$, r cointegrating vectors exist in β and the last $(3-r)$ columns of the speed adjustment coefficients or loadings in α are zero [10]. Therefore, the matrix $\beta' Z_t$ constitutes r cointegrating equations and $\beta' Z_{t-1}$ represents r disequilibrium error terms.

In order to conduct the cointegration test, we employ the likelihood ratio (LR) reduced rank test for the null hypothesis of, at most, r cointegrating vectors, which is given by the trace statistic, λ_{trace}. Moreover, the null hypothesis of r against the alternative of r–1 cointegrating vectors is known as the maximal eigenvalue statistic, λ_{max}, as shown in the following:

$$\lambda_{trace} = -T \sum_{i=r+1}^n \ln(1 - \lambda_i), \ \lambda_{max} = -T \ln(1 - \lambda_i),$$ (4)

where $\lambda_i > \ldots > \lambda_3$ denotes three eigenvalues of the corresponding eigenvectors.

4.2.2. Linear Granger Causality

If two $I(1)$ vectors, x_t and y_t, are cointegrated, the following error-correction mechanism (ECM) should be used to test Granger causality between the variables of interest:

$$\begin{pmatrix} \Delta x_t \\ \Delta y_t \end{pmatrix} = \begin{pmatrix} A_{x[2\times1]} \\ A_{y[1\times1]} \end{pmatrix} + \begin{pmatrix} A_{xx}(L)_{[2\times2]} & A_{xy}(L)_{[2\times1]} \\ A_{yx}(L)_{[1\times2]} & A_{yy}(L)_{[1\times1]} \end{pmatrix} \begin{pmatrix} \Delta x_{t-1} \\ \Delta y_{t-1} \end{pmatrix} + \begin{pmatrix} \alpha_{x[2\times1]} \\ \alpha_{y[1\times1]} \end{pmatrix} \cdot ecm_{t-1} + \begin{pmatrix} e_{x,t} \\ e_{y,t} \end{pmatrix},$$ (5)

where ecm_{t-1} is lag 1 of the error correction term, $\alpha_{x[2\times1]}$ and $\alpha_{y[1\times1]}$ are the coefficient vectors for the error correction term ecm_{t-1}, and $\Delta x_t = (\Delta x_{1,t}, \Delta x_{2,t})'$ and $\Delta y_t = (\Delta y_t)'$ are the corresponding stationary differencing series. There are now two sources of causation of $y_t(x_t)$ by $x_t(y_t)$, either through the lagged dynamic terms, $\Delta x_{t-1}(\Delta y_{t-1})$, or through the error correction term, ecm_{t-1}. Thereafter, the null hypothesis, $H_0 : A_{xy}(L) = 0 (H_0 : A_{yx}(L) = 0)$ and/or $H_0 : \alpha_x = 0 (H_0 : \alpha_y = 0)$, can be tested to identify the Granger causality relationship using the LR test. We will discuss testing the null hypotheses, $H_0^1 : A_{xy}(L) = 0$ and $H_0^2 : A_{yx}(L) = 0$, when two $I(1)$ vectors, x_t and y_t, are not cointegrated.

However, if two $I(1)$ vectors, x_t and y_t, are not cointegrated, the following VAR model should be used to test Granger causality between the variables of interest:

$$\begin{pmatrix} \Delta x_t \\ \Delta y_t \end{pmatrix} = \begin{pmatrix} A_{x[2\times1]} \\ A_{y[1\times1]} \end{pmatrix} + \begin{pmatrix} A_{xx}(L)_{[2\times2]} & A_{xy}(L)_{[2\times1]} \\ A_{yx}(L)_{[1\times2]} & A_{yy}(L)_{[1\times1]} \end{pmatrix} \begin{pmatrix} \Delta x_{t-1} \\ \Delta y_{t-1} \end{pmatrix} + \begin{pmatrix} e_{x,t} \\ e_{y,t} \end{pmatrix},$$ (6)

where all the terms are defined in Equation (1). Testing the linear causality relationship between x_t and y_t is equivalent to testing the following null hypotheses: $H_0^1 : A_{xy}(L) = 0$ and $H_0^2 : A_{yx}(L) = 0$. There are four different situations for the causality relationships between x_t and y_t in (4): (a) rejecting H_0^1 but not rejecting H_0^2 implies a unidirectional causality from y_t to x_t, (b) rejecting H_0^2 but not rejecting H_0^1 implies a unidirectional causality from x_t to y_t, (c) rejecting both H_0^1 and H_0^2 implies the existence of feedback relations, and (d) not rejecting both H_0^1 and H_0^2 implies that x_t and y_t are not rejected as independent [36–38].

4.2.3. Nonlinear Granger Causality

The linear Granger causality test discussed in Section 4.2.2 is based on the assumption that the relationship between the variables is linear. In order to further investigate whether any nonlinear relationship exists between vectors x_t and y_t, we conduct a nonlinear causality test [36,37]. Evidence of nonlinear relationships between stock markets is found in various studies. For example, The evidence of significant nonlinear dependence in stock markets is found [39,40]. It is explained that the complex and chaotic dynamics are likely to emerge in different parts of an economic system [40]. Further, the pattern between different objectives may appear random following many statistical tests; however, a more effective result may be achieved by using tests that consider the possibility of a nonlinear pattern. Therefore, some nonlinear models have been developed in studies relating to economics and finance. For example, it is noticed that the nonlinear structure in stock-price movements is motivated by asset behavior that follows nonlinear models [41]. A nonparametric test is developed to detect the nonlinear causal relationship between two variables [42]. The nonlinear causality test to the multivariate setting is extended [36,37], and the test is further extended to panel data [38]. Nonlinear Granger causality are also applied by some other scholars [43,44].

In order to identify any nonlinear Granger causality relationship from any two vector series, $x_t = (x_{1,t}, x_{2,t})'$ and $y_t = (y_t)'$, we first use the linear model for $\{x_t\}$ and $\{y_t\}$ to identify their linear causal relationships and obtain the corresponding residuals, $\{\hat{\varepsilon}_{1t}\}$ and $\{\hat{\varepsilon}_{2t}\}$. Thereafter, we apply a nonlinear Granger causality test to the residual series, $\{\hat{\varepsilon}_{1t}\}$ and $\{\hat{\varepsilon}_{2t}\}$, of the two examined variables to identify the remaining nonlinear causal relationships between their residuals. We denote $X_t = (X_{1,t}, \ldots, X_{n1,t})'$ and $Y_t = (Y_{1,t}, \ldots, Y_{n2,t})'$ to be the corresponding residuals of any two vectors of the examined variables.

We first define the lead vector and lag vector of a time series, say $X_{i,t}$, as follows: for $X_{i,t}$, $i = 1, \ldots, n_1$, the m_{x_i}-length lead vector and the L_{x_i}-length lag vector of $X_{i,t}$ are
$$X_{i,t}^{m_{x_i}} \equiv \left(X_{i,t}, X_{i,t+1}, \ldots, X_{i,t+m_{x_i}-1}\right), m_{x_i} = 1, 2, \ldots, t = 1, 2, \ldots, \text{ and}$$
$$X_{i,t-L_{x_i}}^{L_{x_i}} \equiv \left(X_{i,t-L_{x_i}}, X_{i,t-L_{x_i}+1}, \ldots, X_{i,t-1}\right), L_{x_i} = 1, 2, \ldots, t = L_{x_i} + 1, L_{x_i} + 2, \ldots,$$
respectively. We denote $M_x = \left(m_{x1}, \ldots, m_{x_{n_1}}\right)$, $L_x = \left(L_{x1}, \ldots, L_{x_{n_1}}\right)$, $m_x = \max(m_{x1}, \ldots, m_{n_1})$, and $l_x = \max\left(L_{x1}, \ldots, L_{x_{n_1}}\right)$.

The m_{y_i}-length lead vector, $Y_{i,t}^{m_{y_i}}$, the L_{y_i}-length lag vector, $Y_{i,t-L_{y_i}}^{L_{y_i}}$, of $Y_{i,t}$, and M_y, L_y, m_y, and l_y can be defined similarly.

Using this modeling approach, we extend [36,37,42,45] to derive the following statistic,

$$H = \sqrt{n}\left(\frac{C_1\left(M_x + L_x, L_y, e, n\right)}{C_2\left(L_x, L_y, e, n\right)} - \frac{C_3(M_x + L_x, e, n)}{C_4(L_x, e, n)}\right), \tag{7}$$

to test the null hypothesis, H_0, that $Y_t = (Y_{1,t}, \ldots, Y_{n2,t})'$ does not strictly Granger cause $X_t = (X_{1,t}, \ldots, X_{n1,t})'$. [37,38] have more information on the test statistic.

5. Empirical Results and Discussion

5.1. Unit Root Test

We employ the classical unit root augmented Dickey–Fuller (ADF) test to examine whether there is any unit root in the market capitalizations and the market indices for the "before" and "after periods" and for all markets by taking into consideration the following conditions: "without a constant and trend", "a constant", and "both a constant and trend". The results of the ADF tests are presented in Table 2. From the table, the null hypothesis that the series is non-stationary cannot be rejected for market capitalizations, market indices, and for all markets in both periods. However, the hypothesis that the first differences of market capitalizations and market indices are non-stationary is rejected in all markets and in both periods, regardless of allowing for a constant, both a constant and trend, or none of these. This suggests that market capitalizations and market indices are $I(1)$ for all markets in both periods.

Table 2. ADF Unit Root Tests—Level and First Difference of Variables.

Variable/Market	Level			First Difference		
	Without a Constant and Trend	With a Constant	With a Constant and Trend	Without a Constant and Trend	With a Constant	With a Constant and Trend
Market Capitalization—Before						
Hong Kong	1.682711	−1.919425	−2.205666	−52.60101 ***	−52.65588 ***	−52.66070 ***
Shanghai	2.353194	−2.180448	−1.120584	−48.22354 ***	−48.34105 ***	−48.40782 ***
Shenzhen	1.694196	−1.698022	−1.354723	−45.59289 ***	−45.64103 ***	−45.65093 ***
Market Capitalization—After						
Hong Kong	−0.086144	−1.584134	−1.763568	−20.45296 ***	−20.43241 ***	−20.41225 ***
Shanghai	0.612571	−2.410414	−2.848671	−16.90724 ***	−16.91163 ***	−16.98909 ***
Shenzhen	0.627730	−2.566980	−2.583824	−20.38275 ***	−20.37833 ***	−20.41032 ***
Market Index—Before						
Hong Kong	0.626803	−2.371107	−2.637028	−49.52579 ***	−49.52618 ***	−49.51887 ***
Shanghai	1.066231	−1.934023	−1.517596	−47.77306 ***	−47.79211 ***	−47.81669 ***
Shenzhen	1.563084	−1.661637	−1.471991	−45.09358 ***	−45.14931 ***	−45.15690 ***
Market Index—After						
Hong Kong	−0.334852	−1.494780	−1.686786	−21.77970 ***	−21.76091 ***	−21.73916 ***
Shanghai	0.167181	−1.673607	−2.844149	−16.82485 ***	−16.81046 ***	−16.88770 ***
Shenzhen	0.456605	−2.337842	−2.277986	−20.02130 ***	−20.01022 ***	−20.04949 ***

Notes: The critical ADF values are based on one-sided p-value. *, **, and *** denote significance at the 10%, 5%, and 1% levels, respectively.

5.2. Cointegration

Table 3 presents the results of the cointegration test for the market capitalizations and the major market indices of the Hong Kong, Shanghai, and Shenzhen markets in both periods, "before" and "after". In the Johansen cointegration test, different numbers of lags and different informational criteria could suggest different lag lengths for the explanatory variable; moreover, the different criteria could cause conflicting results. In order to circumvent this limitation, we use Lag 1 to Lag 4 when applying the Johansen cointegration test for each variable. With regard to market capitalization, the Hong Kong, Shanghai, and Shenzhen markets are cointegrated at the 10% significance level at least in the "before" and "after" periods. With regard to market indices, the Hong Kong, Shanghai, and Shenzhen markets are cointegrated at the 10% significance level at least in the "after" period and are not cointegrated in the "before" period. This finding infers that the Shanghai–Hong Kong Stock Connect has a significant impact on the market indices, but not on the market capitalizations, of the Hong Kong, Shanghai, and Shenzhen markets in the sense that the market indices of these markets become cointegrated after the introduction of the Shanghai–Hong Kong Stock Connect but are not cointegrated before its introduction. Nonetheless, the market capitalizations of the Hong Kong, Shanghai, and Shenzhen markets are cointegrated before and after the introduction of the Shanghai–Hong Kong Stock Connect. Alternatively, we can say that the introduction of the Shanghai–Hong Kong Stock Connect has no effect on the cointegration of the market capitalizations in the Hong Kong, Shanghai, and Shenzhen markets.

Table 3. The Johansen Cointegration Test.

	Trace statistic				Maximal Eigenvalue Statistic			
Lags	1	2	3	4	1	2	3	4
Market Capitalization—Before								
	50.41438 ***	49.85247 ***	50.27316 ***	48.99552 **	26.82384 **	26.53612 **	27.53781 **	28.16635 **
Market Capitalization—After								
	40.62609 *	41.72919 *	43.53722 **	43.44726 **	23.51745 *	25.62289 *	25.46559 *	24.03629 *
Market Index—Before								
	31.64630	30.98641	30.39318	28.58406	15.41028	15.02911	14.67202	13.22303
Market Index—After								
	41.76066 *	43.02648 **	46.48707 **	47.99164 **	28.48594 **	29.83725 **	32.73789 ***	34.94959 ***

Notes: *, **, and *** denote significance at the 10%, 5%, and 1% levels, respectively.

We conduct the Engle–Granger two-step cointegration test as a complementary analysis to the Johansen cointegration test. Table 4 presents the results for each of the variables and for different pairs of markets for the "before" and "after" periods. The results suggest that a cointegration relationship exists between Hong Kong and Shanghai and between Hong Kong and Shenzhen for the market capitalizations and market indices in the "after" period but not in the "before" period. These results are consistent with those in Table 3 and provide more information. First, the results of Tables 3 and 4 are the same for the market indices such that the Shanghai–Hong Kong Stock Connect has a significant impact on the market indices of the Hong Kong, Shanghai, and Shenzhen markets in the sense that the market indices of these markets become cointegrated after the introduction of the Shanghai–Hong Kong Stock Connect but are not cointegrated before its introduction.

Table 4. Cointegrations between Shanghai, Shenzhen, and Hong Kong.

Dependent Variable	Independent Variable	Tau-Statistic for ADF Test	
		Before	After
Market Capitalization			
Hong Kong	Shanghai	−1.807367	−3.702708 ***
Shanghai	Hong Kong	−1.812675	−3.697735 ***
Hong Kong	Shenzhen	−2.366831	−3.428527 ***
Shenzhen	Hong Kong	−2.375368	−3.422214 ***
Market Index			
Hong Kong	Shanghai	−1.909637	−2.507151 *
Shanghai	Hong Kong	−1.871656	−2.499474 *
Hong Kong	Shenzhen	−1.765747	−2.694529 *
Shenzhen	Hong Kong	−1.630341	−2.676564 *

Notes: *, **, and *** denote significance at the 10%, 5%, and 1% levels, respectively.

However, Table 3 shows that the market capitalizations of the Hong Kong, Shanghai, and Shenzhen markets are cointegrated before and after the introduction of the Shanghai–Hong Kong Stock Connect, while Table 4 shows that the market capitalizations between the Hong Kong and Shanghai markets and between the Hong Kong and Shenzhen markets are cointegrated after, but not before, the introduction of the Shanghai–Hong Kong Stock Connect. Readers may regard these results as contradictory because Table 4 shows that the market capitalizations between the Hong Kong and Shanghai markets and between the Hong Kong and Shenzhen markets are not cointegrated before the introduction of the

Shanghai–Hong Kong Stock Connect, while Table 3 shows that the market capitalizations of the Hong Kong, Shanghai, and Shenzhen markets are cointegrated in the "before" period. Nonetheless, we note that the results are still consistent. For example, the market capitalization between Hong Kong and Shanghai is not cointegrated in the "before" period; however, after including Shenzhen, the market capitalizations of the Hong Kong, Shanghai, and Shenzhen markets are cointegrated in the "before" period. There is no contradiction. Overall, the results from Tables 3 and 4 conclude that the Shanghai–Hong Kong Stock Connect has a significant impact on the market indices and market capitalizations of the Hong Kong, Shanghai, and Shenzhen markets in the sense that in the pairings of Hong Kong–Shanghai and Hong Kong–Shenzhen, both variables are not cointegrated before the introduction of the Shanghai–Hong Kong Stock Connect but are cointegrated after its introduction. Nonetheless, the Shanghai–Hong Kong Stock Connect has a greater impact on the market indices of the Hong Kong, Shanghai, and Shenzhen markets in the sense that these market indices are not cointegrated before the introduction of the Shanghai–Hong Kong Stock Connect but are cointegrated after its introduction.

5.3. Linear Causality

Given the cointegration test results in Tables 3 and 4, we employ VECM and VAR for the multivariate linear Granger causality test for the corresponding return data. Namely, we use the VECM for market capitalizations in the "before" and "after" periods and for market indices in the "after" period. Further, we apply VAR for the market indices in the "before" period. Because linear Granger causality test results are sensitive to the chosen number of lags [1,46,47], we perform the test by applying Lag 1 to Lag 4 to ensure the persistence of the causality effect. Table 5 presents the results.

The results in Table 5 suggest that for market capitalizations, Shanghai and Shenzhen together strongly linear cause Hong Kong only in the "after" period; however, Hong Kong does not linear cause Shanghai and Shenzhen in the "before" and "after" periods. With regard to the market indices, Table 5 also indicates that Shanghai and Shenzhen together strongly linear cause Hong Kong in the "before" and "after" periods and that Hong Kong also strongly linear causes Shanghai and Shenzhen in the "before" period. In the "after" period, Hong Kong only weakly linear causes Shanghai and Shenzhen.

Table 5. Multivariate Linear Causality Test.

Lags	1	2	3	4
Market Capitalization—Before				
Shanghai, Shenzhen do not linear cause Hong Kong	7.38371	9.375204	10.72305	13.5075
Hong Kong does not linear cause Shanghai, Shenzhen	10.91606	11.3073	12.10023	15.50066
Market Capitalization—After				
Shanghai, Shenzhen do not linear cause Hong Kong	24.53035 ***	25.04021 ***	25.89332 **	27.30361 **
Hong Kong does not linear cause Shanghai, Shenzhen	7.541288	10.57955	10.38692	12.52102
Market Index—Before				
Shanghai, Shenzhen do not linear cause Hong Kong	29.53564 ***	32.25287 ***	41.44762 ***	45.33166 ***
Hong Kong does not linear cause Shanghai, Shenzhen	26.19195 ***	35.55226 ***	40.05167 ***	50.15208 ***
Market Index—After				
Shanghai, Shenzhen do not linear cause Hong Kong	16.33123 **	18.64942 **	21.32368 **	23.37843 *
Hong Kong does not linear cause Shanghai, Shenzhen	8.691268	15.81915 *	19.27024 *	22.04703

Notes: *, **, and *** denote significance at the 10%, 5%, and 1% levels, respectively.

Again, and as a complementary analysis to the multivariate linear causality tests for both variables, Tables 6 and 7 exhibit the results of the individual linear causality tests for each variable of different stock exchange pairs. The results in Table 6 suggest that for market capitalizations in the "before" period, Shenzhen strongly linear causes Hong Kong, while Hong Kong strongly linear causes Shanghai and weakly linear causes Shenzhen. In the "after" period, Table 6 suggests that Shanghai strongly linear causes Hong Kong, while Hong Kong strongly linear causes Shanghai and weakly linear causes Shenzhen.

Table 6. Pairwise Linear Granger Causality Test—Market Capitalizations.

Null Hypothesis (Before)	Lag 1	Lag 2	Lag 3	Lag 4
Shanghai does not linear cause Hong Kong	0.978580	2.012203	2.192758	2.387463
Hong Kong does not linear cause Shanghai	8.537985 ***	8.480986 **	9.559701 **	10.36996 **
Shenzhen does not linear cause Hong Kong	5.348578 **	6.381996 **	6.677565 *	8.543683 *
Hong Kong does not linear cause Shenzhen	5.051887 **	4.996726 *	4.784889	5.999298
Null Hypothesis (After)				
Shanghai does not linear cause Hong Kong	3.879897 **	5.268828 *	7.771181 *	11.00691 **
Hong Kong does not linear cause Shanghai	2.926277 *	4.441486	6.289897 *	8.776270 *
Shenzhen does not linear cause Hong Kong	0.012944	1.287811	1.721678	4.355685
Hong Kong does not linear cause Shenzhen	3.585345 *	4.261239	5.759532	10.40691 **

Notes: *, **, and *** denote significance at the 10%, 5%, and 1% levels, respectively.

The results in Table 7 suggest that for the market indices, both Shanghai and Shenzhen strongly linear cause Hong Kong separately, but Hong Kong does not linear cause either Shanghai or Shenzhen in the "before" period. In the "after" period, both Shanghai and Shenzhen do not linear cause Hong Kong separately and Hong Kong does not linear cause Shanghai or Shenzhen.

Table 7. Pairwise Linear Granger Causality Test—Market Indices.

Null Hypothesis (Before)	Lag 1	Lag 2	Lag 3	Lag 4
Shanghai does not linear cause Hong Kong	8.893183 ***	9.610947 ***	10.01526 ***	9.858900 **
Hong Kong does not linear cause Shanghai	1.427837	1.441529	1.406733	2.249378
Shenzhen does not linear cause Hong Kong	16.52512 ***	16.90540 ***	17.56947 ***	17.47762 ***
Hong Kong does not linear cause Shenzhen	0.191262	1.128381	1.054686	1.968744
Null Hypothesis (After)				
Shanghai does not linear cause Hong Kong	1.650946	3.070147	4.425512	6.041571
Hong Kong does not linear cause Shanghai	1.099184	3.331752	4.805973	5.678313
Shenzhen does not linear cause Hong Kong	0.309486	0.787259	0.978551	2.257896
Hong Kong does not linear cause Shenzhen	0.426839	0.524547	1.352728	2.567101

Notes: *, **, and *** denote significance at the 10%, 5%, and 1% levels, respectively.

Table 4 shows the results of the pairwise cointegrations. However, for those pairs of variables that are cointegrated, we have to include the speeds of the adjustments in the ECM linear Granger causality model in Equation (3). The estimates of the speeds of adjustments are given in Tables 8 and 9 for market capitalizations and market indices respectively. With regard to market capitalizations, the averages of the estimated speeds of adjustments in any market are smaller than 0.049 (in absolute value), implying that in general any movement away from the long-term equilibrium between the various market pairs is slow to correct. An estimate of 0.049, at the upper limit of the means, implies a 4.9% adjustment back to equilibrium in a given trading day. Similarly, for the market indices, the averages of the estimated speeds of adjustments in any market are smaller than 0.032 (in absolute value), implying that in general any movement away from the long-term equilibrium between the various market pairs is slow to correct. An estimate of 0.032, at the upper limit of the means, implies a 3.2% adjustment back to equilibrium in a given trading day.

Table 8. Speeds of Adjustments in the Linear Granger Causality Test—Market Capitalizations.

Null Hypothesis (Before)	Lag 1	Lag 2	Lag 3	Lag 4
Shanghai does not linear cause Hong Kong	n/a	n/a	n/a	n/a
Hong Kong does not linear cause Shanghai	n/a	n/a	n/a	n/a
Shenzhen does not linear cause Hong Kong	n/a	n/a	n/a	n/a
Hong Kong does not linear cause Shenzhen	n/a	n/a	n/a	n/a
Null Hypothesis (After)				
Shanghai does not linear cause Hong Kong	−0.004669	−0.005398	−0.006306	−0.006973
Hong Kong does not linear cause Shanghai	−0.044791 ***	−0.046493 ***	−0.048387 ***	−0.048581 ***
Shenzhen does not linear cause Hong Kong	−0.007094	−0.007855	−0.009215	−0.010231
Hong Kong does not linear cause Shenzhen	−0.039959 ***	−0.040460 ***	−0.042351 ***	−0.043781 ***

Notes: *, **, and *** denote significance at the 10%, 5%, and 1% levels, respectively.

Table 9. Speeds of Adjustments in the Linear Granger Causality Test—Market Indices.

Null Hypothesis (Before)	Lag 1	Lag 2	Lag 3	Lag 4
Shanghai does not linear cause Hong Kong	n/a	n/a	n/a	n/a
Hong Kong does not linear cause Shanghai	n/a	n/a	n/a	n/a
Shenzhen does not linear cause Hong Kong	n/a	n/a	n/a	n/a
Hong Kong does not linear cause Shenzhen	n/a	n/a	n/a	n/a
Null Hypothesis (After)				
Shanghai does not linear cause Hong Kong	−0.000644	−0.001230	−0.001977	−0.003281
Hong Kong does not linear cause Shanghai	−0.028955 ***	−0.029045 ***	−0.030224 ***	−0.031811 ***
Shenzhen does not linear cause Hong Kong	−0.003705	−0.004845	−0.006024	−0.007039
Hong Kong does not linear cause Shenzhen	−0.020618 ***	−0.021161 ***	−0.021848 ***	−0.023016 ***

Notes: *, **, and *** denote significance at the 10%, 5%, and 1% levels, respectively.

5.4. Nonlinear Causality

We suggest that linear and nonlinear causality relationships could be independent in the sense that the existence of a linear causality relationship does not infer the existence of a nonlinear causality relationship and vice versa. Therefore, we propose investigating whether there is any change in nonlinear causality relationships after the introduction of the Shanghai–Hong Kong Stock Connect. Consequently, we report in Table 10 the results of the multivariate nonlinear Granger causality tests of different markets' market capitalizations and stock indices. We find that for market capitalizations and market indices, Shanghai and Shenzhen strongly nonlinearly cause Hong Kong in the "before" and "after" periods, while Hong Kong strongly nonlinearly causes Shanghai and Shenzhen in the "before" period and only weakly nonlinearly causes Shanghai and Shenzhen in the "after" period.

The Three Musketeers Relationships between Hong Kong, Shanghai and Shenzhen...

235

Table 10. Multivariate Nonlinear Causality Test.

Lags	1	2	3	4
Market Capitalization—Before				
Shanghai, Shenzhen do not nonlinearly cause Hong Kong	4.210291 ***	4.920050 ***	5.380364 ***	4.844110 ***
Hong Kong does not nonlinearly cause Shanghai, Shenzhen	4.687631 ***	5.005889 ***	5.065219 ***	4.561966 ***
Market Capitalization—After				
Shanghai, Shenzhen do not nonlinearly cause Hong Kong	2.116468 **	2.820839 ***	2.350409 ***	1.308816 *
Hong Kong does not nonlinearly cause Shanghai, Shenzhen	0.653933	1.520695 *	0.199958	0.971179
Market Index—Before				
Shanghai, Shenzhen do not nonlinearly cause Hong Kong	4.542631 ***	4.828466 ***	4.973165 ***	4.293640 ***
Hong Kong does not nonlinearly cause Shanghai, Shenzhen	5.358980 ***	5.774119 ***	4.827240 ***	5.010060 ***
Market Index—After				
Shanghai, Shenzhen do not nonlinearly cause Hong Kong	2.037944 **	2.242687 **	1.624614 *	1.186182
Hong Kong does not nonlinearly cause Shanghai, Shenzhen	−0.221909	0.426697	−0.855035	0.523144

Notes: *, **, and *** denote significance at the 10%, 5%, and 1% levels, respectively.

Again, and as a complementary analysis to the nonlinear Granger causality tests for all three stock exchanges, Tables 11 and 12 present the results of the individual nonlinear Granger causality tests for market capitalizations and the market indices respectively for each stock exchange pair. Table 11 suggests that for market capitalizations, Shanghai–Hong Kong and Shenzhen–Hong Kong are two interactive pairwise markets in which strong bi-directional nonlinear Granger causalities are found in the "before" period. In the "after" period, Table 11 suggests that Shanghai and Shenzhen strongly nonlinearly cause Hong Kong individually, while Hong Kong only weakly nonlinearly causes Shanghai and Shenzhen individually.

Table 11. Pairwise Nonlinear Causality Test—Market Capitalizations.

Null Hypothesis (Before)	Lag 1	Lag 2	Lag 3	Lag 4
Shanghai does not nonlinearly cause Hong Kong	3.795365 ***	4.551167 ***	5.164434 ***	4.694305 ***
Hong Kong does not nonlinearly cause Shanghai	4.619768 ***	5.187093 ***	5.304950 ***	4.865725 ***
Shenzhen does not nonlinearly cause Hong Kong	3.804926 ***	4.500830 ***	5.043632 ***	4.707949 ***
Hong Kong does not nonlinearly cause Shenzhen	4.225535 ***	5.039040 ***	5.194823 ***	4.742640 ***
Null Hypothesis (After)				
Shanghai does not nonlinearly cause Hong Kong	1.468207 *	2.749260 ***	2.277180 **	1.434418 *
Hong Kong does not nonlinearly cause Shanghai	0.800458	1.572935 *	0.540221	1.133238
Shenzhen does not nonlinearly cause Hong Kong	2.458619 ***	2.952265 ***	2.404669 ***	1.366114 *
Hong Kong does not nonlinearly cause Shenzhen	1.977940 **	2.261325 **	0.900703	1.065920

Notes: The *, **, and *** denote the significance at 10%, 5% and 1% levels, respectively.

With regard to the market indices, Table 12 suggests that Shanghai–Hong Kong and Shenzhen–Hong Kong are two interactive pairwise markets in which strong bi-directional nonlinear Granger causalities are found in the "before" period. In a similar way to market capitalizations (see Table 11), Table 12 indicates that Shanghai and Shenzhen strongly nonlinearly cause Hong Kong individually, while Hong Kong only weakly nonlinearly causes Shanghai and Shenzhen individually.

Table 12. Pairwise Nonlinear Causality Test—Market Indices.

Null Hypothesis (Before)	Lag 1	Lag 2	Lag 3	Lag 4
Shanghai does not nonlinearly cause Hong Kong	4.337560 ***	4.680782 ***	4.778670 ***	3.847159 ***
Hong Kong does not nonlinearly cause Shanghai	5.296137 ***	5.917483 ***	5.496391 ***	5.363044 ***
Shenzhen does not nonlinearly cause Hong Kong	3.972803 ***	4.353763 ***	4.490202 ***	4.149760 ***
Hong Kong does not nonlinearly cause Shenzhen	4.303810 ***	5.414131 ***	5.009831 ***	4.677395 ***
Null Hypothesis (After)				
Shanghai does not nonlinearly cause Hong Kong	1.565120 *	2.511137 ***	1.870381 **	1.411452 *
Hong Kong does not nonlinearly cause Shanghai	−0.117091	0.654299	−0.268652	0.819147
Shenzhen does not nonlinearly cause Hong Kong	2.348446 ***	2.349964 ***	1.817364 **	1.465420 *
Hong Kong does not nonlinearly cause Shenzhen	1.401143 *	1.890706 **	0.670792	0.896187

Notes: *, **, and *** denote significance at the 10%, 5%, and 1% levels, respectively.

6. Conclusions

We summarize all our empirical results in Tables 13 and 14. Table 13 shows that for market capitalization, Shanghai and Shenzhen exist a high degree of cointegration with Hong Kong before and after the implementation of the Stock Connect Scheme. As for causality, the strong effect found before the rollout of the Scheme under the nonlinear analysis from Shanghai and Shenzhen to Hong Kong ($SH, SZ \Rightarrow HK$) remains unchanged during the post implementation period. However, the nonlinear causality effect from Hong Kong to Shanghai and Shenzhen ($HK \Rightarrow SH, SZ$) decreased after the implementation of the Stock Connect Scheme.

Table 13. Summary of Multivariate Test Results.

Variables	Cointegration	Causality	$SH, SZ \Rightarrow HK$	$HK \Rightarrow SH, SZ$
Market Capitalization (Before)	Strongly	Linear	x	x
		Nonlinear	strongly	strongly
Market Capitalization (After)	Strongly	Linear	strongly	x
		Nonlinear	strongly	weakly
Market Index (Before)	X	Linear	strongly	strongly
		Nonlinear	strongly	strongly
Market Index (After)	Strongly	Linear	strongly	weakly
		Nonlinear	strongly	x

Table 14. Summary of Pairwise Test Results.

Variables	Cointegration SH with HK	Cointegration SZ with HK	Causality	$SH \Rightarrow HK$	$SZ \Rightarrow HK$	$HK \Rightarrow SH$	$HK \Rightarrow SZ$
Market Capitalization (Before)	x	x	Linear	x	strongly	strongly	strongly
			Nonlinear	strongly	strongly	strongly	strongly
Market Capitalization (After)	✓	✓	Linear	strongly	x	strongly	strongly
			Nonlinear	strongly	strongly	weakly	strongly
Market Index (Before)	x	x	Linear	strongly	strongly	x	x
			Nonlinear	strongly	strongly	strongly	strongly
Market Index (After)	✓	✓	Linear	x	x	x	x
			Nonlinear	strongly	strongly	x	strongly

With regard to the market indices, no cointegration is found before the Stock Connect Scheme. However, Shanghai and Shenzhen exhibit a high degree of cointegration with Hong Kong after the rollout of the scheme. Regarding causality effect, a bi-directional causality relationship between Shanghai/Shenzhen and Hong Kong *(SH, SZ Δ HK)* is found before the rollout of the Stock Connect Scheme, despite whether it is obtained from linear or nonlinear analysis. However, such causality relationship is changed where a uni-directional causality from Shanghai and Shenzhen to Hong Kong *(SH, SZ ⇒ HK)* dominates after the implementation of the Stock Connect Scheme. Therefore, the causality effect from Hong Kong to Shanghai and Shenzhen *(HK ⇒ SH, SZ)* diminished after the rollout of the Scheme.

Table 14 shows the pairwise test results. From both market capitalization and market index perspectives, neither the Shanghai nor the Shenzhen market is cointegrated with Hong Kong market before the implementation of Stock Connect Scheme. However, on a pairwise base, cointegration relationships for Shanghai/Hong Kong and Shenzhen/Hong Kong are found after the rollout of the scheme. The findings from pairwise test support the view that the Stock Connect Scheme has a significant impact on both market capitalizations and market indices of the Hong Kong, Shanghai, and Shenzhen markets. The Hong Kong stock market is still relevant to understand and predict China stock market after the implementation of the Stock Connect Scheme.

This principal contribution of this study lies in the development of a model that makes it possible to capture the degree of integration between the Chinese and Hong Kong stock markets following the implementation of the Shanghai–Hong Kong Stock Connect. Our results suggest that market integration has evolved progressively. Over the past three decades, Hong Kong has gradually become a means for international investors to access Chinese assets. The Stock Connect Scheme is an innovative move with significant impacts to both Hong Kong and mainland stock markets. Policy makers lay out a broad strategy of market-oriented reform but in a manner that is controllable and expandable for cross-border Renminbi (RMB) flow by connecting Mainland market to international investors. It paves the way and is a natural consequence of steps that China is taking to open-up its capital account and facilitate the move towards RMB internationalization, which is critical both to the political and economic developments of China. The design of the Stock Connect Scheme provides a sustainable and scalable model for further expansion to world's major stock markets. Therefore, it is unsurprising to see the correlation of market capitalization occurring before the introduction of the Stock Connect Scheme as a positive development resulting from a wider investor base. It is also perhaps not that surprising to see the non-stationary observation of market index performance before the introduction of the scheme. This situation is reflected in the gradual growth of H-shares in the leading index constituents.

Further, as time has passed, the restrictions on accessing mainland markets have eased; thus, overseas investors can now access China's A-share market via a qualified quota known as QFII. Likewise, the introduction of RQFII in 2011 has allowed an investment outflow to international markets. In addition, higher levels of such co-movements are expected. Figures 2 and 3 show the growth of the QFII and RQFII quotas, respectively.

One of the obvious observations is that the weakening of the investment outflow from Hong Kong to China after the introduction of the Stock Connect Scheme also weakens Hong Kong's influence on China. While this study's tests generally agree on the evidence of linear causality for market capitalizations and the market indices before and after the introduction of the Stock Connect Scheme from China to Hong Kong, it is interesting to find nonlinear cases from 2015 onward that suggest a bilateral and possibly nonlinear degree of causal influence on each market. Heuristically, the speed of capital flow from one market to another and the difference in the H-share and A-share premium (see Figure 4) could drive the direction of funds. On the one hand, it is not difficult to see how Hong Kong has provided cheaper asset-buying opportunities in the past decade; on the other, the change in share premium difference between mainland China's domestic A-share markets and Hong Kong's H-share market could direct investors' appetites or sentiments. It is suggested here that these are aspects for further research in order to establish the type of nonlinear functional relationship and the dynamic drivers of such relationships.

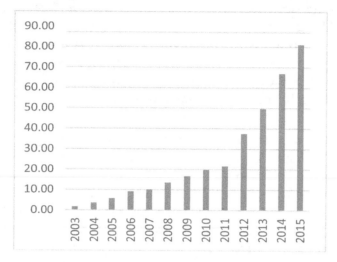

Figure 2. QFII Quota (**A**pprovals since 2003 (US$bn), Data source: SSE).

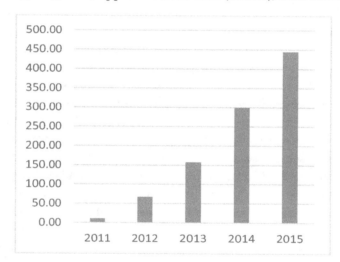

Figure 3. RQFII Quota (Approvals since 2011 (RMBbn), Data source: SSE).

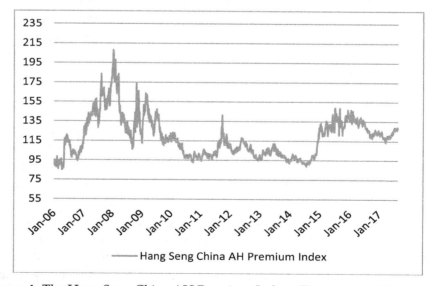

Figure 4. The Hang Seng China AH Premium Index. (Data source. Bloomberg.)

This paper studies sustainability of financial integration among Shenzhen, Shanghai, and Hong Kong stock markets. An extension of our paper could study sustainability of other aspects of financial markets, for example, sustainability in warrant markets [48], sustainability in REITs [49], sustainability in equity return dispersion and stock market volatility [50], sustainability in herding behaviour [51], sustainability in portfolio selection [52], and sustainability in credit risk [53].

Author Contributions: Conceptualization, A.W.-W.C. and D.K.-H.C.; methodology, N.S.-C.C. and W.-K.W.; software, N.S.-C.C.; validation, A.W.-W.C. and D.K.-H.C.; formal analysis, N.S.-C.C. and W.-K.W.; investigation, N.S.-C.C. and W.K.W.; resources, A.W.-W.C. and D.K.-H.C.; data curation, A.W.-W.C. and D.K.-H.C.; writing—original draft preparation, N.S.-C.C. and W.-K.W.; writing—review and editing, N.S.-C.C. and W.-K.W.; visualization, N.S.-C.C. and W.-K.W.; supervision, A.W.-W.C. and W.-K.W.; project administration, A.W.-W.C. and D.K.-H.C.; funding acquisition, A.W.-W.C. and D.K.-H.C.

Acknowledgments: The fourth author would also like to thank Robert B. Miller and Howard E. Thompson for their continuous guidance and encouragement.

References

1. Click, R.W.; Plummer, M.G. Stock market integration in ASEAN after the Asian financial crisis. *J. Asian Econ.* **2005**, *16*, 5–28. [CrossRef]

2. Demirer, R.; Kutan, A.M. Does herding behavior exist in Chinese stock markets? *J. Int. Finac. Mark. Inst. Money* **2006**, *16*, 123–142. [CrossRef]

3. Cai, C.X.; McGuinness, P.B.; Zhang, Q. The pricing dynamics of cross-listed securities: The case of Chinese A-and H-shares. *J. Bank. Finace* **2011**, *35*, 2123–2136. [CrossRef]

4. Taylor, M.P.; Tonks, I. The internationalisation of stock markets and the abolition of UK exchange control. *Rev. Econ. Stat.* **1989**, *71*, 332–336. [CrossRef]

5. Jin, X. Volatility transmission and volatility impulse response functions among the Greater China stock markets. *J. Asian Econ.* **2015**, *39*, 43–58. [CrossRef]

6. Janakiramanan, S.; Lamba, A.S. An empirical examination of linkages between Pacific-Basin stock markets. *J. Int. Finac. Mark. Inst. Money* **1998**, *8*, 155–173. [CrossRef]

7. Johansson, A.C.; Ljungwall, C. Spillover effects among the Greater China stock markets. *World Dev.* **2009**, *37*, 839–851. [CrossRef]

8. Chan, K.C.; Gup, B.E.; Pan, M.S. An empirical analysis of stock prices in major Asian markets and the United States. *Financ. Rev.* **1992**, *27*, 289–307. [CrossRef]

9. Arshanapalli, B.; Doukas, J. International stock market linkages: Evidence from the pre-and post-October 1987 period. *J. Bank. Finace* **1993**, *17*, 193–208. [CrossRef]

10. Engle, R.F.; Granger, C.W. Co-integration and error correction: Representation, estimation, and testing. *Econometrica* **1987**, *55*, 251–276. [CrossRef]

11. Kasa, K. Common stochastic trends in international stock markets. *J. Monet. Econ.* **1992**, *29*, 95–124. [CrossRef]

12. Phylaktis, K.; Ravazzolo, F. Stock market linkages in emerging markets: Implications for international portfolio diversification. *J. Int. Finac. Mark. Inst. Money* **2005**, *15*, 91–106. [CrossRef]

13. Diamandis, P.F. International stock market linkages: Evidence from Latin America. *Glob. Finance J.* **2009**, *20*, 13–30. [CrossRef]

14. Tan, H.B.; Cheah, E.T.; Johnson, J.E.; Sung, M.C.; Chuah, C.H. Stock market capitalization and financial integration in the Asia Pacific region. *Appl. Econ.* **2012**, *44*, 1951–1961. [CrossRef]

15. Baharumshah, A.Z.; Sarmidi, T.; Tan, H.B. Dynamic linkages of Asian stock markets. *J. Asia Pac. Econ.* **2003**, *8*, 180–209. [CrossRef]

16. Daly, K.J. Southeast Asian stock market linkages: Evidence from pre-and post-October 1997. *ASEAN Econ. Bull.* **2003**, *20*, 73–85. [CrossRef]

17. Cavoli, T.; Rajan, R.; Siregar, R. *A Survey of Financial Integration in East Asia: How Far? How Much Further to Go?* Centre for International Economic Studies, University of Adelaide: Adelaide, Australia, 2004.

18. Huyghebaert, N.; Wang, L. The co-movement of stock markets in East Asia: Did the 1997–1998 Asian financial crisis really strengthen stock market integration? *China Econ. Rev.* **2010**, *21*, 98–112. [CrossRef]

19. Ng, H.T. Stock Market Linkages in South–East Asia. *Asian Econ. J.* **2002**, *16*, 353–377. [CrossRef]

20. Yang, J.; Kolari, J.W.; Min, I. Stock market integration and financial crises: The case of Asia. *Appl. Financ. Econ.* **2003**, *13*, 477–486. [CrossRef]

21. Guillaumin, C. Financial integration in East Asia: Evidence from panel unit root and panel cointegration tests. *J. Asian Econ.* **2009**, *20*, 314–326. [CrossRef]

22. Yu, I.W.; Fung, K.P.; Tam, C.S. Assessing financial market integration in Asia–equity markets. *J. Bank. Finace* **2010**, *34*, 2874–2885. [CrossRef]

23. Zhu, H.; Lu, Z.; Wang, S.; Soofi, A.S. Causal linkages among Shanghai, Shenzhen, and Hong Kong stock markets. *Int. J. Theor. Appl. Finance* **2004**, *7*, 135–149. [CrossRef]

24. Tourani-Rad, A.; Yi, Y. A Tale of Three Stock Markets: Timing between Hong Kong, Shanghai and Shenzhen. *Manag. Finance* **2004**, *30*, 60–77. [CrossRef]

25. Cheung, Y.W.; Chinn, M.D.; Fujii, E. China, Hong Kong, and Taiwan: A quantitative assessment of real and financial integration. *China Econ. Rev.* **2003**, *14*, 281–303. [CrossRef]

26. Wang, Y.; Di Iorio, A. Are the China-related stock markets segmented with both world and regional stock markets? *J. Int. Finac. Mark. Inst. Money* **2007**, *17*, 277–290. [CrossRef]

27. Wang, Y.; Di Iorio, A. The cross section of expected stock returns in the Chinese A-share market. *Glob. Finance J.* **2007**, *17*, 335–349. [CrossRef]

28. Wang, Y.; Di Iorio, A. The cross-sectional relationship between stock returns and domestic and global factors in the Chinese A-share market. *Rev. Quant. Finance Account.* **2007**, *29*, 181–203. [CrossRef]

29. Huo, R.; Ahmed, A.D. Return and volatility spillovers effects: Evaluating the impact of Shanghai-Hong Kong Stock Connect. *Econ. Model.* **2017**, *61*, 260–272. [CrossRef]

30. Fan, Q.; Wang, T. The impact of Shanghai–Hong Kong Stock Connect policy on AH share price premium. *Finance Res. Lett.* **2017**, *21*, 222–227. [CrossRef]

31. Kashyap, R. Hong Kong–Shanghai Connect/Hong Kong–Beijing Disconnect? Scaling the Great Wall of Chinese Securities Trading Costs. *J. Trading* **2016**, *11*, 81–134. [CrossRef]

32. Yang, K.; Wei, Y.; He, J.; Li, S. Dependence and risk spillovers between mainland China and London stock markets before and after the Stock Connect programs. *Phys. A Stat. Mech. Its Appl.* **2019**, *526*, 120883. [CrossRef]

33. Johansen, S. Statistical analysis of cointegration vectors. *J. Econ. Dyn. Control* **1988**, *12*, 231–254. [CrossRef]

34. Johansen, S.; Juselius, K. Maximum likelihood estimation and inference on cointegration—With applications to the demand for money. *Oxf. Bull. Econ. Stat.* **1990**, *52*, 169–210. [CrossRef]

35. Johansen, S. Estimation and hypothesis testing of cointegration vectors in Gaussian vector autoregressive models. *Econometrica* **1991**, *59*, 1551–1580. [CrossRef]

36. Bai, Z.D.; Wong, W.K.; Zhang, B.Z. Multivariate linear and non-linear causality tests. *Math. Comput. Simul.* **2010**, *81*, 5–17. [CrossRef]

37. Bai, Z.D.; Li, H.; Wong, W.K.; Zhang, B.Z. Multivariate causality tests with simulation and application. *Stat. Probab. Lett.* **2011**, *81*, 1063–1071. [CrossRef]

38. Chow, S.C.; Cunado, J.; Gupta, R.; Wong, W.K. Causal Relationships between Economic Policy Uncertainty and Housing Market Returns in China and India: Evidence from Linear and Nonlinear Panel and Time Series Models. *Stud. Nonlinear Dyn. Econom.* **2018**, *22*. [CrossRef]

39. Scheinkman, J.A.; LeBaron, B. Nonlinear dynamics and stock returns. *J. Bus.* **1989**, *62*, 311–337. [CrossRef]

40. Brock, W.A.; Hsieh, D.A.; LeBaron, B.D. *Nonlinear Dynamics, Chaos, and Instability: Statistical Theory and Economic Evidence*; MIT Press: Cambridge, MA, USA, 1991.

41. Hsieh, D.A. Chaos and nonlinear dynamics: Application to financial markets. *J. Finance* **1991**, *46*, 1839–1877. [CrossRef]

42. Baek, E.; Brock, W. *A General Test for Nonlinear Granger Causality: Bivariate Model*; Iowa State University and University of Wisconsin at Madison Working Paper; Iowa State University and University of Wisconsin: Madison, WI, USA, 1992.

43. Chow, S.C.; Gupta, R.; Suleman, T.; Wong, W.K. Long-Run Movement and Predictability of Bond Spread for BRICS and PIIGS: The Role of Economic, Financial and Political Risks. *J. Rev. Glob. Econ.* **2019**, *8*, 239–257. [CrossRef]

44. Chow, S.C.; Vieito, J.P.; Wong, W.K. Do both demand-following and supply-leading theories hold true in developing countries? *Phys. A Stat. Mech. Appl.* **2019**, *513*, 536–554. [CrossRef]

45. Hiemstra, C.; Jones, J.D. Testing for linear and nonlinear Granger causality in the stock price-volume relation. *J. Finance* **1994**, *49*, 1639–1664.

46. Brocato, J.; Smith, K.L. Velocity and the Variability of Money Growth: Evidence from Granger-Causality Tests: Comment. *J. Money Credit Bank.* **1989**, *21*, 258–261. [CrossRef]

47. Chung, P.J.; Liu, D.J. Common stochastic trends in Pacific Rim stock markets. *Q. Rev. Econ. Finance* **1994**, *34*, 241–259. [CrossRef]

48. Wong, W.K.; Lean, H.H.; McAleer, M.; Tsai, F.-T. Why are Warrant Markets Sustained in Taiwan but not in China? *Sustainability* **2018**, *10*, 3748. [CrossRef]

49. Gupta, R.; Lv, Z.H.; Wong, W.K. Macroeconomic Shocks and Changing Dynamics of the U.S. REITs Sector. *Sustainability* **2019**, *11*, 2776. [CrossRef]

50. Demirer, R.; Gupta, R.; Lv, Z.H.; Wong, W.K. Equity Return Dispersion and Stock Market Volatility: Evidence from Multivariate Linear and Nonlinear Causality Tests. *Sustainability* **2019**, *11*, 351. [CrossRef]

51. Batmunkh, M.-U.; McAleer, M.; Moslehpour, M.; Wong, W.K. Confucius and Herding Behaviour in the China and Taiwan Stock Markets. *Sustainability* **2018**, *10*, 4413. [CrossRef]

52. Li, Z.; Li, X.; Hui, Y.C.; Wong, W.K. Maslow Portfolio Selection for Individuals with Low Financial Sustainability. *Sustainability* **2018**, *10*, 1128. [CrossRef]

53. Mou, W.M.; Wong, W.K.; McAleer, M. Financial Credit Risk Evaluation Based on Core Enterprise Supply Chains. *Sustainability* **2018**, *10*, 3699. [CrossRef]

Permissions

All chapters in this book were first published in MDPI; hereby published with permission under the Creative Commons Attribution License or equivalent. Every chapter published in this book has been scrutinized by our experts. Their significance has been extensively debated. The topics covered herein carry significant findings which will fuel the growth of the discipline. They may even be implemented as practical applications or may be referred to as a beginning point for another development.

The contributors of this book come from diverse backgrounds, making this book a truly international effort. This book will bring forth new frontiers with its revolutionizing research information and detailed analysis of the nascent developments around the world.

We would like to thank all the contributing authors for lending their expertise to make the book truly unique. They have played a crucial role in the development of this book. Without their invaluable contributions this book wouldn't have been possible. They have made vital efforts to compile up to date information on the varied aspects of this subject to make this book a valuable addition to the collection of many professionals and students.

This book was conceptualized with the vision of imparting up-to-date information and advanced data in this field. To ensure the same, a matchless editorial board was set up. Every individual on the board went through rigorous rounds of assessment to prove their worth. After which they invested a large part of their time researching and compiling the most relevant data for our readers.

The editorial board has been involved in producing this book since its inception. They have spent rigorous hours researching and exploring the diverse topics which have resulted in the successful publishing of this book. They have passed on their knowledge of decades through this book. To expedite this challenging task, the publisher supported the team at every step. A small team of assistant editors was also appointed to further simplify the editing procedure and attain best results for the readers.

Apart from the editorial board, the designing team has also invested a significant amount of their time in understanding the subject and creating the most relevant covers. They scrutinized every image to scout for the most suitable representation of the subject and create an appropriate cover for the book.

The publishing team has been an ardent support to the editorial, designing and production team. Their endless efforts to recruit the best for this project, has resulted in the accomplishment of this book. They are a veteran in the field of academics and their pool of knowledge is as vast as their experience in printing. Their expertise and guidance has proved useful at every step. Their uncompromising quality standards have made this book an exceptional effort. Their encouragement from time to time has been an inspiration for everyone.

The publisher and the editorial board hope that this book will prove to be a valuable piece of knowledge for researchers, students, practitioners and scholars across the globe.

List of Contributors

Vasily E. Tarasov
Skobeltsyn Institute of Nuclear Physics, Lomonosov
Moscow State University, Moscow 119991, Russia
Faculty of Information Technologies and Applied
Mathematics, Moscow Aviation Institute (National
Research University), Moscow 125993, Russia

Antonio Díaz
Department of Economics and Finance, University of
Castilla-La Mancha, 02071 Albacete, Spain

Marta Tolentino
Department of Economics and Finance, University of
Castilla-La Mancha, 13003 Ciudad Real, Spain

Junkee Jeon
Department of Applied Mathematics & Institute of
Natural Science, Kyung Hee University, Seoul 01811,
Korea

Geonwoo Kim
School of Liberal Arts, Seoul National University of
Science and Technology, Seoul 01811, Korea

Yuri S. Popkov
Federal Research Center "Computer Science and
Control" of Russian Academy of Sciences, 119333
Moscow, Russia
Institute of Control Sciences of Russian Academy of
Sciences, 117997 Moscow, Russia
Department of Software Engineering, ORT Braude
College, 216100 Karmiel, Israel

Yanlin Yang and Chenyu Fu
Center for Economic Development Research and Center
of Population, Resource & Environmental Economics
Research, School of Economics and Management,
Wuhan University, Wuhan 430072, China

Yijuan Liang
Agricultural Education and Development Research
Center, Southwest University, Chongqing 400715, China
School of Economics and Management, Southwest
University, Chonging 400715, China

Xiuchuan Xu
School of Economics and Management, Southwest
University, Chonging 400715, China

Alan T.Wang and Yu-Hong Liu
Institute of Finance, National Cheng Kung University,
Tainan City 70101, Taiwan

Yu-Chen Chang
JP Morgan, 8F No. 108, Sec. 5, Xinyi Road., Xinyi Dist.,
Taipei City 11047, Taiwan

WeiMing Mou
College of Economics and Management, Changzhou
Institute of Technology, Changzhou 213022, China

Wing-Keung Wong
Department of Finance, Fintech Center Big Data Research
Center, Asia University, Taichung 41354, Taiwan

Michael McAleer
Department of Finance, Asia University, Taichung
41354, Taiwan
Econometric Institute, Erasmus School of Economics,
Erasmus University Rotterdam, 3000 Rotterdam,
The Netherlands
Department of Economic Analysis and ICAE,
Complutense University of Madrid, 28040 Madrid, Spain
Institute of Advanced Sciences, Yokohama National
University, Yokohama 240-8501, Japan

David E. Allen
Department of Finance, School of Mathematics and
Statistics, University of Sydney, Sydney, NSW 2006,
Australia
Department of Finance, College of Management, Asia
University, Wufeng 41354, Taiwan
School of Business and Law, Edith Cowan University,
Joondalup, WA 6027, Australia

Michael McAleer
Department of Finance, College of Management, Asia
University, Wufeng 41354, Taiwan
Discipline of Business Analytics, University of Sydney
Business School, NSW 2006, Australia
Econometric Institute, Erasmus School of Economics,
Erasmus University, 3062 Rotterdam, The Netherlands
Department of Economic Analysis and ICAE,
Complutense University of Madrid, 28040 Madrid, Spain
Department of Mathematics and Statistics, University
of Canterbury, Christchurch 8041, New Zealand
Institute of Advanced Sciences, Yokohama National
University, Yokohama, Kanagawa 240-8501, Japan

Riza Demirer
Department of Economics & Finance, Southern
Illinois University Edwardsville, School of Business,
Edwardsville, IL 62026-1102, USA

Rangan Gupta
Department of Economics, University of Pretoria, Pretoria 0002, South Africa

Zhihui Lv
KLASMOE & School of Mathematics and Statistics, Northeast Normal University, Changchun 130024, China

Wing-Keung Wong
Department of Finance, Fintech Center, and Big Data Research Center, Asia University, Taichung 41354, Taiwan
Department of Medical Research, China Medical University Hospital, Taichung 40402, Taiwan
Department of Economics and Finance, Hang Seng University of Hong Kong, Shatin, Hong Kong 999077, China

Jamiu Adetola Odugbesan
Department of Business Administration, Faculty of Economics and Administrative Sciences, Cyprus International University, Haspolat, Mersin 10, Turkey

Husam Rjoub
Department of Accounting and Finance, Faculty of Economics and Administrative Sciences, Cyprus International University, Haspolat, Mersin 10, Turkey

Batmunkh John Munkh-Ulzii
Department of International Relations, National University of Mongolia, Ulaanbaatar 14200, Mongolia

Michael McAleer
Department of Finance, Asia University, Taichung 41354, Taiwan
Discipline of Business Analytics, University of Sydney Business School, Sydney, NSW 2006, Australia
Econometric Institute, Erasmus School of Economics, Erasmus University Rotterdam, 3000 Rotterdam, The Netherlands
Department of Economic Analysis and ICAE, Complutense University of Madrid, 28040 Madrid, Spain
Institute of Advanced Sciences, Yokohama National University, Yokohama 240-8501, Japan

Massoud Moslehpour
Department of Business Administration, Asia University, Taichung 41354, Taiwan

Wing-Keung Wong
Department of Finance, Asia University, Taichung 41354, Taiwan

Bing Wang
School of Accounting, Fujian Jiangxia University, Fuzhou 350108, China

Si Xu
School of Economics & Management, South China Normal University, Guangzhou 510006, China

Kung-Cheng Ho
School of Finance, Collaborative Innovation Center of Industrial Upgrading and Regional Finance (Hubei), Zhongnan University of Economics and Law, Wuhan 430073, China

I-Ming Jiang
Faculty of Digital Finance, College of Management, Yuan Ze University, Taoyuan 32003, Taiwan

Hung-Yi Huang
Department of Business Administration, Soochow University, Taipei 10048, Taiwan

Michael McAleer
Department of Finance, Asia University, Taichung 41354, Taiwan
Discipline of Business Analytics, University of Sydney Business School, Sydney 2006, Australia
Econometric Institute, Erasmus School of Economics, Erasmus University Rotterdam, 3000 Rotterdam, The Netherlands
Department of Economic Analysis and ICAE, Complutense University of Madrid, 28040 Madrid, Spain
Institute of Advanced Sciences, Yokohama National University, Yokohama 240-8501, Japan

Tamotsu Nakamura and Clinton Watkins
Graduate School of Economics, Kobe University, Kobe 657-8501, Japan

Andy Wui-Wing Cheng and David Kam-Hung Chui
Department of Economics and Finance, The Hang Seng University of Hong Kong, Hong Kong

Nikolai Sheung-Chi Chow
Research School of Economics, Australian National University, Canberra 0200, Australia

Wing-Keung Wong
Department of Economics and Finance, The Hang Seng University of Hong Kong, Hong Kong
Department of Finance, Fintech Center, and Big Data Research Center, Asia University, Taichung 41354, Taiwan
Department of Medical Research, China Medical University Hospital, Taichung 41354, Taiwan

Index

Printed in the USA
CPSIA information can be obtained
at www.ICGtesting.com
JSHW060156191223
53955JS00006B/172